Lecture Notes in Computer Science   11032

Commenced Publication in 1973
Founding and Former Series Editors:
Gerhard Goos, Juris Hartmanis, and Jan van Leeuwen

More information about this series at http://www.springer.com/series/7409

Andrea Kő · Enrico Francesconi (Eds.)

Electronic Government and the Information Systems Perspective

7th International Conference, EGOVIS 2018
Regensburg, Germany, September 3–5, 2018
Proceedings

 Springer

Editors
Andrea Kő (iD)
Corvinus University of Budapest
Budapest
Hungary

Enrico Francesconi
Institute of Legal Information Theory
and Techniques
Florence
Italy

·

ISSN 0302-9743   ISSN 1611-3349 (electronic)
Lecture Notes in Computer Science
ISBN 978-3-319-98348-6   ISBN 978-3-319-98349-3 (eBook)
https://doi.org/10.1007/978-3-319-98349-3

Library of Congress Control Number: 2018950464

LNCS Sublibrary: SL3 – Information Systems and Applications, incl. Internet/Web, and HCI

This Springer imprint is published by the registered company Springer Nature Switzerland AG
The registered company address is: Gewerbestrasse 11, 6330 Cham, Switzerland

Preface

The 7th International Conference on Electronic Government and the Information Systems Perspective, EGOVIS 2018, took place in Regensburg, Germany, during September 3–6. The conference belongs to the 29th DEXA Conference Series.

The international conference cycle EGOVIS focuses on information systems and ICT aspects of e-government. Information systems are a core enabler for e-government/governance in all its dimensions: e-administration, e-democracy, e-participation, and e-voting. EGOVIS brought together experts from academia, public administrations, and industry to discuss e-government and e-democracy from different perspectives and disciplines, i.e., technology, policy and/or governance, and public administration.

The Program Committee accepted 19 papers from recent research fields such as open data, digitalization, identity management and e-government architectures, innovation, open government, intelligent systems, and semantic technologies. Beyond theoretical contributions, papers cover e-government experiences from all over the world; cases are presented from Europe and South America.

This proceedings volume is organized into six sections according to the conference sessions.

We were honored that the EGOVIS 2018 keynote speech was given by Prof. Roland Traunmüller: He is one of the pioneers in e-government studies and has contributed for many years to identifying limits and opportunities in the field. Prof. Traunmüller's speech discussed digitalization as challenge for e-government.

The chairs of the Program Committee wish to thank all the reviewers for their valuable work; the reviews raised several research questions to discuss at the conference. We would like to thank Gabriela Wagner for the administrative support and assisting us in proper scheduling.

We wish pleasant and beneficial learning experiences for the readers. We hope that the discussion will continue after the conference between the researchers and contribute to building a global community in the field of e-government.

July 2018

Enrico Francesconi
Andrea Kő

Organization

General Chair

Roland Traunmüller   University of Linz, Austria

Program Committee Co-chairs

Enrico Francesconi   Italian National Research Council, Italy
Andrea Kő   Corvinus University Budapest

Honorary Chairs

Wichian Chutimaskul   King Mongkut's University of Technology, Thailand
Fernando Galindo   University of Zaragoza, Spain

Program Committee

Luis Álvarez Sabucedo	Universidade de Vigo, Spain
Jaro Berce	University of Ljubljana, Slovenia
Francesco Buccafurri	Università degli Studi Mediterranea di Reggio Calabria, Italy
Alejandra Cechich	Universidad Nacional del Comahue, Argentina
Wojciech Cellary	Poznan University of Economics, Poland
Wichian Chutimaskul	King Mongkut's University of Technology, Thailand
Flavio Corradini	University of Camerino, Italy
Vytautas Cyras	Vilnius University, Lithuania
Joan Francesc Fondevila Gascón	Universitat Pompeu Fabra, Spain
Enrico Francesconi	Italian National Research Council, Italy
Ivan Futo	National Tax and Customs Administration, Hungary
András Gábor	Corvinus University of Budapest, Hungary
Fernando Galindo	University of Zaragoza, Spain
Francisco Javier García Marco	University of Zaragoza, Spain
Stefanos Gritzalis	University of the Aegean, Greece
Henning Sten Hansen	Aalborg University, Denmark
Christos Kalloniatis	University of the Aegean, Greece
Nikos Karacapilidis	University of Patras, Greece
Evangelia Kavakli	University of the Aegean, Greece
Bozidar Klicek	University of Zagreb, Croatia
Hun-yeong Kwon	Korea University, South Korea
Andrea Kő	Corvinus University Budapest, Hungary

Herbert Leitold	E-Government Innovation Center EGIZ, Austria
Marian Mach	Technical University of Kosice, Slovakia
Peter Mambrey	University of Duisburg-Essen, Germany
Bálint Molnár	Eötvös Loránd University, Hungary
Mara Nikolaidou	Harokopio University of Athens, Greece
Javier Nogueras	University of Zaragoza, Spain
Monica Palmirani	University of Bologna, Italy
Aljosa Pasic	Atos, Spain
Andrea Polini	UNICAM, Italy
Reinhard Posch	Technical University Graz, Austria
Aires J. Rover	Federal University of Santa Catarina, Brazil
Erich Schweighofer	University of Vienna, Austria
Zoltán Szabó	Corvinus University of Budapest, Hungary
Ella Taylor-Smith	Edinburgh Napier University, UK
Costas Vassilakis	University of the Peloponnese, Greece
Gianluigi Viscusi	EPFL - CDM -CSI, Switzerland
Robert Woitsch	BOC Asset Management, Austria
Chien-Chih Yu	National ChengChi University, China (Taiwan Province)

External Reviewer

Barbara Re	University of Camerino, Italy

Contents

Semantic Technologies and the Legal Aspects

Open Data and Open Innovation

E-government Cases - Data and Knowledge Management

Digitalization and Transparency

Co-production of Digital Services: Definitions, Frameworks, Cases and Evaluation Initiatives - Findings from a Systematic Literature Review

Gustavo Almeida[1]([✉]) [ID], Claudia Cappelli[2] [ID], Cristiano Maciel[3] [ID], and Yamile Mahecha[4] [ID]

[1] Federal Fluminense University – UFF, Niterói, Brazil
`goalmeida@gmail.com`
[2] Federal University of Rio de Janeiro State – UNIRIO, Rio de Janeiro, Brazil
`claudia.cappelli@uniriotec.br`
[3] Federal University of Mato Grosso – UFMT, Cuiabá, Brazil
`crismac@gmail.com`
[4] Federal Rural University of Rio de Janeiro – UFRRJ, Seropédica, Brazil
`lined.ramos@gmail.com`

Abstract. Customers are no longer passive consumer of products and services and engaged in a more active role in which they influence the organizations, develop and improve products and change the consuming experience [1]. This new role and collaborative trend is often defined as co-production. The present article had as it main objective to survey the models, frameworks, methods, recommendations, evaluations, definitions, concepts, challenges, required conditions, difficulties and learned lessons related to co-production of digital services. We performed a systematic review to identify the literature produced dealing with these questions from 1998 to 2016. Our systematic review followed the protocol recommended by [12]. After the definition of six research questions, we defined the scope of the survey and the related keywords. The search query produced 94 references. Two thematic axis emerged from the data: models and definitions of co-production (57%) and cases, challenges and implementation details (43%). Most articles were published in conferences (26), followed by journals (17). The selected articles were read and the main findings presented. Findings are presented along implications. Suggestions for future research agenda are presented.

Keywords: Systematic literature review · Co-production · Digital services

1 Introduction

Public and private organizations are better equipped to reach their customers than ever, due to the evolution of information and communication technologies based on Internet and new interactive and collaborative tools. In that context, customers have changed their role from a passive consumer of products and services to a more active role in

© Springer Nature Switzerland AG 2018
A. Kő and E. Francesconi (Eds.): EGOVIS 2018, LNCS 11032, pp. 3–19, 2018.
https://doi.org/10.1007/978-3-319-98349-3_1

which they influence the organizations, developing new products, improving the products and consuming experience [1]. This new role and collaborative trend is known as co-creation. According to Rasool and Pathania [1] co-creation describes how social and technological changes allow interaction of individuals, organizations and groups in order to collaborate and solve problems by a joint creation of value. Although the concept co-creation is experimenting a growing interest in both academia and industry, the concept has deeper roots. According to Szkuta, Pizzicanella and Osimo [2], the co-production concept emerged in the 70s to define services delivered with a high degree of user involvement, and has reemerged in research agenda with the advent of digital services. Leading Cities Reports shows that the modern concept of co-creation had its origins in the business world, as early as in the 1990's regarding a new form of engagement with customers [3].

In the process of co-creation of value, the experience and the results depends vastly on consumers, since each person participating in the process affects the co-creation process, giving his/her personal touch to the final product or service. In that context, the clients would participate in the production of the products that they consume, and in this process would create value, therefore customers are considered the main source of innovative ideas for firms [4]. The same concept is often applied to the government-citizen relationship, where traditionally, the government would provide services without participation of citizens in any part of public policies, so applying co-production in public sector would mean creating solutions involving people, not just creating solutions having the citizens as recipients [5].

Co-production comprehends all cooperation forms between producers and consumers, citing the collaboration with public and government bodies in the service delivery in areas of education, maintenance of clean environments and local security [6]. Prahalad and Ramaswamy [7] have identified that an unprecedented number of contact points between organizations and final consumers have emerged due to technological changes brought by the web, digital contents, fast digital connections and new connected devices. The impact of the shifting role of the consumers, and stated that companies can no longer design products, develop processes and deliver marketing communications without the participation of their consumers [4]. Now, customers have new tools to co-create value and use the interaction as the basis for co-creation. The same is true regarding the relationship between citizens and governments.

An increasing demand for greater participation, transparence and voice in public endeavors is being observed in most countries. The co-creation process changes the balance of power, since government traditionally occupied a role of inviting the public in for comments on pre-determined programs, starts to function in a more iterative decision making process, and for this process to occur there is requirement for higher degrees of trust and transparency between citizens and government officials [3]. According to Hartley [8] co-production is a "a complex and iterative process through which problems are defined; new ideas are developed and combined; prototypes and pilots are designed, tested and redesigned; and new solutions are implemented, diffused and problematized. Although the theme is of growing importance, researchers agree that there is a general lack of models to understand and define co-production, and the initiatives that could serve as starting point for a successful implementation [9].

Thus, the present research aims to identify and summarize the current definitions dimensions and models of co-production of digital services and highlight the best practices, research approaches, pioneer projects, challenges and evaluation initiative, by conducting a systematic review. A systemic literature review is "means to identify, evaluate and interpret all available research relevant to an issue, area, or phenomenon of interest in a particular research." [10]. Systematic reviews are based on a defined research strategy, which intends to detect as much relevant literature as possible, guiding the research process and places the researcher before the different areas and approaches of the issue in focus, making possible to evaluate the relevance of the efforts undertaken previously while preventing the overlap of efforts.

This research report has five sections. This Sect. 1 just presented is an introduction to the issue of co-production and the need to systematize the knowledge produced. The Sect. 2 presents the methodology; the Sect. 3 presents the execution of systematic review. The Sect. 4 describes results of the two set of articles, while the Sect. 5 presents conclusions and directions for future research.

2 Methodology

The present article had as it main objective to survey the models, frameworks, methods, recommendations, evaluations, definitions, concepts, challenges, required conditions, difficulties and learned lessons related to the participative production (co-production) of digital services. Thus, for systemic literature review proposed in this paper were applied the ten steps defined by Brereton et al. for a systematic review [11]. The ten steps into three main phases: planning, execution and reviewing of documentation. Figure 1 illustrates the process of systematic review of the literature applied in this study.

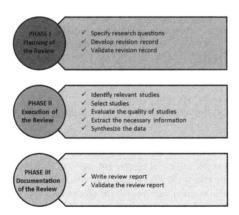

Fig. 1. The process of systematic literature review Adapted from: Brereton et al. [11]

To meet the objectives specified above, we developed six questions that were translated into keywords. The definition of keywords is an essential part of the literature review process, as the correct definition of keywords is essential to define appropriate search strings, as the strings determine search results [12]. The questions that originated the keywords were: (Q1) "What models of participatory production (co-production) of digital services have been proposed?" (Q2) "What methods of evaluating participatory production (co-production) of digital services have been proposed?" (Q3) "What has been defined as the participatory production (coproduction) of digital services?" (Q4) "What are the necessary conditions for the participatory production (coproduction) of digital services?" (Q5) "What are the ongoing initiatives for participatory production (coproduction) of digital services? (Q6) "How have participatory (coproducing) digital service initiatives been implemented, including tools, target audiences, timeframes?"

We selected Web of Science database maintained by Thomson Reuters Scientific, due to its features and wide coverage in computer science, and social sciences. The database is a multidisciplinary database that indexes the most cited journals in their respective fields, capturing more than 65 million citations annually. The query[1] available in Table 1 is divided in three parts, as recommended for a systematic review: (a) **population** – group or phenomena studied (digital services) (b) **intervention** – what is to be observed in the context (coproduction, participative production, co-design) and (c) **results** – resulting data from the studies (models, evaluation, definitions, concepts, initiatives, details, according to the question) [10–12]:

Table 1. Keywords for population, intervention and results for each question

Q	Population	Intervention	Results
Q1	(digital NEAR[a]/3 service*) OR (e $gov* NEAR/3 service*) OR (e-gov* NEAR/3 service*) OR (-e$servic*) OR (-e-servic*) OR (electron* NEAR/3 servi*) OR (on$lin* NEAR/3 servi*) OR (on-lin* NEAR/3 servi*) OR (one-stop) OR (one$stop))	(co-production) OR (co$production) OR (participat* NEAR/2 production) OR (participat* NEAR/2 plan*) OR (participat* NEAR/2 design*) OR (participat* NEAR/2 creat*) OR (co-design OR co$design) OR (co-operativ* OR co$operativ* OR colaborativ* OR co-author* OR co $author*) NEAR/1 (design* OR method*) OR ("open innovation") OR ("open service* innovation"))	(model* OR framework* OR method* OR propos* OR guidance* OR guidelin*)
	Results (Population and Intervention are the same as Q1)		
Q2	(evaluat* OR assess* OR aprais* OR ratin* OR valuat*)		
Q3	(definition* OR define* OR "field of study" OR concept* OR construc* OR ((-e$democra*) OR (-e-democra*)))		
Q4	((challenge*) OR (condit*) OR (requirement*) OR (requis*) OR (issue*) OR ("citizen* evaluation*") OR (factor*) OR (succes*) OR (fail*) OR (learn* NEAR/1 lesson*))		
Q5	((initiativ* OR implementat* OR adopt* OR deploy* OR case* OR platfor* OR portal* OR citizen participat* OR tool OR government OR city OR state OR municipal*)		
Q6	(("implementation process") OR (participat* process) OR (implementation) OR ("platform implementation") OR scope OR (participat* implementation) OR (detail*) OR (implementation NEAR/3 process**) OR (tool detail*) OR ("year*") OR ("month*") OR specific* OR program*)		

[a]The operator NEAR/x is used to find records where the terms joined by the operator are within a specified number of words of each other. See https://images.webofknowledge.com/images/help/WOS/hs_search_operators.html for more information.

---

[1] Query parts: (a) population (b) intervention and (c) results were joined by AND operator.

3   Execution of the Query

The strings were inserted in the Web of Science platform to return articles published until December of 2016, returning results for all the questions (Q1 returned 63 articles; Q2 = 25; Q3 = 33; Q4 = 45; Q5 = 71; Q6 = 63). We aggregated the questions into a single query that returned 94 results. In the first step of the analysis, we selected articles or references using the inclusion and exclusion criteria displayed in Table 2:

Table 2. Inclusion and exclusion criteria for the selection of articles

Inclusion criteria	Exclusion criteria
CI1- Publications that describe models of coproduction of digital services	**CE1-** Publications in which the keywords do not show in the title, abstract or full text
CI2- Publications that present evaluation methods of participation of digital services	**CE2-** Publications in which the context of the keywords is not related to the questions
CI3- Publications that define co-production of digital services	**CE3-** Publications that only cite possibilities of participative production of digital services, but do not explain or describe it
CI4- Publications that describe or discuss conditions for co-production of digital services	**CE4-** Publications that contain the keywords but do not describe possibilities for collaborative production of digital services
CI5- Publications that describe ongoing initiatives for co-production of digital services	**CE5-** Publications that cite but do not describe co-production process or initiatives
CI6- Publications that describe initiatives manners or methods by which co-production of digital services have been implemented	**CE6-** Similar publications that have been published (same author and theme) with only minor adjustments

We applied the set of criteria in the 94 articles returned by the query. After the application of inclusion and exclusion criteria, we retained 20 articles related to questions Q1 to Q3 and 15 for Q4 through Q6. The characterization of articles in relation to the year of publication is present in Fig. 2:

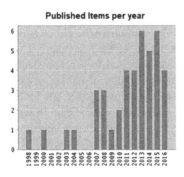

Fig. 2. Published items per year – Web of Science

With regard to the origin of the authors of published articles, the country with the highest number of articles published is Sweden with 14 articles (33%) followed by Italy with five articles, then England, Finland and Scotland present approximately 10% of articles (4 articles each). In terms of research area: the area with more articles was Computer Science with a total of 23 articles (representing 54.76%), then the areas of Business Economics and Information Science Library Science presented 7 articles each, representing 16.67%, then we have articles classified in the Engineering area with 5 articles corresponding to 11.90% of references. Regarding outlets for publication, most of articles were found in conferences (26 articles), followed by journals (17).

From the analysis of the articles, we identified two thematic axes. The first one being represented by the set of articles dealing with dimensions, models, definitions and evaluation proposals related to the coproduction of digital services, corresponding 57% of references, while the second axis includes references that present challenges, conditions, difficulties, initiatives and projects, including detailed on the implementation of these initiatives, with approximately 43% of the references.

Next, the list of articles selected in each research question will be presented. The classification of these articles was performed after a critical analysis that categorized each article according to the question that more related to the work in question.

4   Results

4.1   Results from Questions 1 to 3

In this section, we present research that address and discuss issues related to the dimensions, models, definitions and evaluation proposals related to the coproduction of digital services. We found 20 articles, described in sequence.

Forsgren [13] authored the first article. He developed a framework for the proposition of co-design digital platforms, defined as the joining of organizational tools and technology involving a complex blend of stakeholders participating in the design of new solutions, more specifically, e-services. The framework proposed is based on committees with open hearing process that that control four elicited key areas, including its implementation in new projects as a model for evaluation existing projects.

Anthopoulos, Panagiotis and Tsoukalas [14] state that several surveys found that users evaluate digital public services and tend to use traditional methods rather than using digital channels when interacting with the public administration, and they usually do not recommend the use of digital services to others. They present collaborative and participatory tools and methods designed to use knowledge and experience of public servants to improve design and execution of public services. Authors defend this is a viable solution for the development of one-stop shops for e-Government, and the same time encouraging citizens and citizens to participate in the delivery of e-gov services.

Olphert and Damodaran [15] build upon Enid Mumford's ideas - an ethical, sociotechnical, and participatory approach to the design of ICT systems, using his ideas about the benefits and process of participation, using citizen engagement initiatives, and then comparing e-gov with the proposed values, finding that the prevalent approach is techno-centric with minimal citizens' engagement. The benefits that governments could achieve from adoption of a sociotechnical, participatory approach to e-government development are discussed, highlighting the role of capacity building.

Löfstedt [16] supports the user participation and involvement in the process of designing and developing public e-Services. They performed an analysis of Social Systems Design in the context of local public e-Services to identify possibilities to improve user participation and involvement. They found that ideas of Social Systems Design could be used for the development of user-centered e-Services, and as a foundation for the development of methods that depend on user participation and involvement.

Antikainen and Nakki [17] article presents Owela, an online platform for service co-design. Still active, the platform collects user feedback, experiences and ideas from different physical and online sources and offers a place for co-design, providing users with tools for creating their own products and services together with other users. They found that tools and methods used for in offline settings could not be directly migrated to the digital platform, implicating that the design process should be completely redesigned to function well and logically when in an online process.

Tung and Yuan [18] proposed a service design framework for value co-production, engaging a mutualism perspective employing an intelligent service design using design science, and implementing e-services by simulation. The Service Design Framework is composed of two dimensions continuity of co-production and mutual adaptability, that is, the exchange of service/benefit and relationship involved in a service production and consumption. The model also indicate how the interactions and service/benefit exchange occurs between the service provider and the consumer, while building a partnership by the service participants due to mutual adaptability by each participant.

Ruland, Borosund and Varsi [19] present a case in health care. They proposed a service to be integrated into routine clinical practice allowing patients to stay connected with expert nurses and other health care providers to post questions and receive advice online. User requirements, factors for successful adoption, implementation and maintenance of services and usability were collected with focus groups, workshops, heuristic evaluations and usability testing. The insights from the participatory design process are shared as a support for other researchers willing to implement similar projects.

Holgersson et al. [20] highlight the prominence of e-services, and the key role of user participation. In that regard, the main contribution of the paper is their review of a series of approaches to user participation, and its suitability to e-government service development. Four main challenges were identified: (a) identification the user target segment, (b) identification of individual users within each segment, (c) user participation, and (d) lack of adequate skills required for participation, being the roadmap for a successful participation of users in e-gov. services development.

Bonacin, Melo, Simoni et al. [21] is the first and only paper dealing with accessibility and interoperability issues while co-producing digital services. Their contribution was an outline for a process model aimed to allow the identification and specification of accessible e-government services with the participation of the interested parties, using a socially shared perspective. Their model employed practice in the domain, while using organizational semiotics artifacts with the objective to motivate participation and discussion. Christiansson [22] presents the case of model developed in co-production between a University and a Municipality in the Smart Cities Project. They used action research paradigm to support the municipality in the method of thinking, describing and improving business process, in a way that should be uniform, focused and reflective. The co-production process depended on close relationships, openness and disposition to learn and share in several informal meetings, workshops. Structured and unstructured interviews were conducted, and involved personnel worked together to produce analysis and define and produce the outcomes of the project. Findings were presented in a Common Process Model, with a methodology comprised of set of values, concepts, a modelling structure, roles, directives, guidelines and templates to support the identification, measurement and the improvement of business processes and eservices.

Wigand [23] discuss the impact of Gov 2.0, and the use of collaborative web technologies to engage citizens, foster co-production, and encourage transparency in government. He employs theories of Diffusion of Innovation, Social Influence, and Collective Intelligence to understand how Gov 2.0 applications and technologies enable transformations in delivery of e-services. Wigand analyzes US Federal initiatives using social media and find that interactions are creating communities to transform the way traditional communication work and how new organizational boundaries are formed.

Fogli [24] present a case study in a municipality to improve the process of creation of e-services, using an approach based on meta-design and the development conducted by the end-user, to allow the civil servants to design and develop e-government applications to general citizens and administrative employees. The approach dealt specially with the visual interaction of the tools to support experts and the creation of mechanisms to generate user interfaces, application logic and databases in an automatically.

Karlsson et al. [25] present a comparison between three approaches to user participation, namely: participatory design, user-centered design, and user innovation, regarding their adequacy with the strategic e-service goals of the European Union and US. Three challenges that guide the consideration for the approach to be selected were identified: (a) unclear user target segments can hinder the attainment of usability and relevance goals; (b) the type of participation can obstruct the reach of democracy goals, and (c) lack of adequate skills can inhibit the reach of efficiency goals.

Bridge [26] discuss the Australian Department of Human Services case as a valid experience of co-design of e-services with citizens' involvement in the design and delivery of services, using online and social media services to implement in DHS a more citizen centric service delivery. The case is a journey with three distinct regarding public intervention: – informing, consulting, and co-designing. DHS developed a 'maturity model' for co-design capability to help guide development and implementation involving the phases of: engage to understand, engage to develop and engage to deploy.

Gugliotta, Niglia and Schina [27] evaluated e-government services that have a user centric approach in Europe. Among the 450 cases available in the ePractice Portal, they selected 74 experiences having at least two out of three user-centricity criteria measuring the user involvement: 1. Co-design; 2. Development and Implementation;

3. Deployment and Running. The final cohort discussed the best 40 cases. A model was developed to evaluate services using customizes metrics, divided into user-centric and replicability metrics. The user-centric metric had three levels: low, medium and high, with four factors in two categories. First category was User Centered Approach with "share ideas and co-create content (P1)" and "provide information to improve the service (P2)", the second category was "Best Practice Evaluation" with the factors "user evaluation (P3)" and "participation in decisions (P4)". Other metric employed was the replicability, which is the measurement of the potential of a service to be provided in other contexts. Findings indicate diverse methods and tools could attain citizen engagement, not only ICT-based, due to low level of ICT proficiency in some communities.

Vicini, Bellini and Sanna [28] present the case of San Raffaele Scientific Institute's City of the Future Living Lab (CFLL), which is a small-scale city prototype. The co-creation process has four concurrent phases: Co-Design, Implementation, Experimentation, and Evaluation. Co-design has three sub-phases: scoping, ideation and elicitation, starting with an analysis of the selected scenario, in which users' needs, preference and behaviors are examined using methods such as observation, shadowing and interviewing, with detailed research into market segmentations and tendencies.

Conruyt [29] defines the "e-co-innovation" a new form of electronic and collaborative innovation, which respects the ecology, the ecosystems, the education and the ethics. He proposes a Living Lab in an educational setting to implement an e-co-innovation process, placing the user as the center of the process, employing an approach based on Semiotic Web, using the Creativity or Co-design platform to build e-services with pilot users. It includes a multimedia platform similar to those on TV studios with physical and virtual spaces to discuss ideas or projects, create models and mock-ups, and experiment them in either synchronous way (focus group) or asynchronous (video forum on the Internet). The platform is a co-working, co-learning and communication environment to researchers and developers, entrepreneurs and users to define cooperatively the characteristics of e-services that are best suited to needs (attitudes) and to effective uses (behaviors) of users. In the educational case, the objective is to find agreement (coherence, consensus) between the participants, through mediation between diverse persons: teachers on one side, and the learners on the other side, for a mutual understanding.

Nusir and Bell [30] tested the suitability of the use of the Repertory Grid technique to understand cognitive elements in the design process. They found that the technique allows research participants to express their interpretation about a particular topic, when used with representative participants, being a suitable research technique for gathering and analyzing qualitative and quantitative data. They employed the method to guide interviews with 19 participants from three groups - government staff (service providers), citizens workers (government entities/service), and citizens (users). They built a list of thirty-nine user requirement with quantitative and qualitative techniques in five categories: service initiating and scoping, service planning and analyzing, service development and deployment, service evaluation and updating, and service usability.

Kauppinen [31] article is a position paper that presents and supports an approach toward a more open model involving diverse actors in civil society into the process of innovation and production of public e-services. He claims that the once dominating government-centric definition and development of public e-services is slowly shifting to a more open user-centric approach, where citizens able to participate and collaborate in various public innovation processes and e-platforms, resulting in services more widely used, with better quality and cost effectiveness.

Harrison and Waite [32] present the Service-Dominant logic, which places consumers of services as naturally involved in service co-production. More important, the logic shifts the definition of value as a characteristic in service to value in the empowerment of the customer to customize. The research had a qualitative stage with focus groups, discovering four e-empowerment aspects: information access, improved understanding, autonomous decision-making and behavior change. The research suggest that consumers need to experience cognitive, affective and conative empowerment collectively to perceive the value co-creation in its fullest; the authors identified this stage as holistic e-empowerment. In addition, citizens that participated in service co-production perceived the most value from e-empowerment in all dimensions, while ones that had less participation in service co-production perceived a partial sense of empowerment.

4.2   Results from Questions 4 to 6

In this section, we present the results related to questions 4 to 6, with papers that address and discuss issues related to challenges, conditions, difficulties, initiatives and projects, including detailed information on the implementation of these initiatives. We found 15 articles. Eriksén, Dittrich, Fiedler and Aurell [33] authored the first article in the second set of questions. The paper describes TANGO (Thematic Arenas Nourish Growth Opportunities) an e-government arena, based in Sweden, which has as its objective to establish concrete, a problem-based and development-oriented cooperation between the public sector, private enterprise and university-based research to design public e-services. The paper is a short, positional paper that calls for a better understanding of questions leading to co-production of digital services, and how to engage multiple actors.

Blazevic and Lievens [34] recognize the increase in customer involvement in service provision and innovation, and users or citizens coproducing knowledge in the specific case of e-services. The article is case study with qualitative methods with customers to understand their role in the knowledge coproduction process, and their influence on innovations initiatives from the service provider perspective. Data originated from three e-service channels: (a) Self-service technology (b) Proactive feedback provision and (c) Customer virtual community. Data collection process lasted more than a year and included interviews, observations of online meetings, corporate and customer documentation, involving managers, engineers, and customers. Among the study findings, three customers' roles were found: passive user, active informer, and bidirectional creator, varying in terms of the degree of active knowledge coproduction. The specifics of the roles and its implications are discussed in detail.

Gilbert and Zachry [35] describe the case of a peer-supported design process undertaken in the creation of the Haystack Exchange, a novel online knowledge sharing application. The process engaged students as co-designers, in various phases of the development of the prototype, such as benchmarking, discussing online communities' issues in the literature and redesigning the system, according to different deployment scenarios. In the mentioned study, the student engagement was a key factor, caused by their perception of a meaningful involvement, such as improving a real system, and by being able to interact and connect with other fellow students in new forms.

Lundberg and associates [36] present the case of the Swedish project "My Care Pathways" created to allow citizens to track their health, providing online access to their historic, current and potential upcoming events. The paper identifies several challenges and proposed suggestions in a variety of issues in different domains: (a) business models; (b) legal; (c) interoperability; (d) user interface; (e) organizational.

Juell-Skielse, Hjalmarsson, Johannesson and Rudmark [37] describe a case from Travelhack, a public transportation company of Stockholm. The study aimed to investigate the motivation for individuals engage in innovation on open data. The survey indicated that the top three factors triggering the participation in collaborative production of digital services were intrinsic motivational factors: "fun and enjoyment", "intellectual challenge" and "status and reputation". They found a lack of support from the public organizations for subsequent phases of the design, execution and monitoring of the software, and no mechanisms to support the service development life cycle, focusing on actions to promote the completion and continuity of the developed prototypes.

Szkuta, Pizzicannella, Osimo [2] performed a scoping study with six cases to obtain a detailed assessment of the collaborative production, divided in two dimensions: data source and service provider. The "data source" dimensions: government or the citizen and the "service provider" dimensions three possibilities: government, civil society and private sector. Enabling conditions for collaborative e-government services were found: low cost of setup, low cost of failure and fast failure, under the concept of fail small, fast and forward and the lack of need for permissions to use data. They found a relationship between the quality of the service and quantity of users. The incentives were different for the stakeholders involved (innovators, citizens and government).

Holgersson and Karlsson [38] aimed to understand conditions for citizen's participation in production of e-services in Sweden. Citizens were interviewed to explore their willingness and ability to participate in public e-service development according to three user participation schools: User-Centered Design (UCD), Participatory Design (PD) and User Innovation (UI). Nine propositions were presented to explain citizens' willingness and ability to participate. The model suggests that for public e-services aimed to inexperienced users, UCD approach is best suited than PD and UI. They also found that ability for participation is high when UCD and PD are used.

Alm, Janecek and Forsgren [39] describes the case of Scandinavian Arlines (SAS) adoption of co-design research using 'Eva', an avatar that interacts with customers in questions related to airline's demands. The research method had four main co-design phases: a) co-design of the problem situation and ideal scenarios b) co-design of one or a few specified useful views with implementation integrated solutions and related measure of performance systems c) co-Implementation of selected integrated solution d) co-evaluation and feedback based on key stakeholder views. After the implementation of the features, a survey was created to evaluate the impact of the redevelopment.

Gidlund [40] presents a review of the concept of participation in the design of public e-services by studying the concept in six central policy documents. The analysis revealed a need for understanding how the participation process occurs and how it can be improved. The process had several steps, starting with meetings to define the issues, and capture ideas, then a second meeting to create the stories that were to be digitalized. Participants were asked to define local points and mark the points in a map, regarding a series of criteria, such as most interesting, dangerous, calm, and suitable for tourists and children, most memorable place in town and so on. This process led to contributions, expression of opinions and an atmosphere that encouraged discussions.

Conruyt et al. [41] discuss the concept of sign management, and present the sign-based methodology as a condition for opening the era of Semiotic Web (Web of Signs) over Semantic Web (Web of Things). The first step in the process is to generate ideas in the Living Lab. The second step was to co-design mock-ups and prototypes, and experiment them in a physical meeting place called the Creativity Platform, which is the co-working, co-learning and communication space for researchers and developers, businesses and users, to jointly define characteristics of e-services to diminish gap between expectations and use. Third step formalizes a solution that fits user needs. Evaluation of e-services created consider users of the project: end-users have their own identities, activities, tasks and give meaning to the obtained results. Researchers found that living labs proved attractive as a manner to democratize innovation with people. The success of the e-service was not only related to technical success, instead it depended more on the quality of human-computer interaction mediated by the technology.

French and Teal [42] present experience laboratories in the Digital Health and Care Institute in The Glasgow School of Art –Scotland. The project managed to explore and develop a prototype of a 'Directory App', to support ambulance clinicians in ensuring the most appropriate patient care through providing a directory of information about alternative services and points of care.

The project used the concept of an Experience Lab (EL), which lasted for two days. First day was used to gather requirements for the Directory App. Participants investigated current and likely future information needs of ambulance clinicians, and explored ideas for the use and functionality. A mapping session produced a physical map of the services, allowing the participants to suggest future services. Role-playing was used to provide realistic scenarios from the user perspective. Second day involved co-design of directory, testing the existing directories and comparing with ideal co-created directory in day one, using the cognitive walkthrough method, furnishing key requirements related to information, navigation, interface design, functionality and infrastructure. In addition, participants discussed and identified the required information, the data sources and procedures for maintenance and updates.

Vassilakopoulou, Grisot and Aanestad [43] use the service design approach to analyze two cases in Norway to design patient oriented e-services for appointments with healthcare providers. Both cases were analyzed from data from several sources, such as interviews (28 in first case and 15 for second), observation data from 49 weekly meetings, design workshops and thematic meetings, document analysis. The first case was of a national service for booking appointments with General Practitioners (GPs) in Norway, while the second case is the design and development of a hospital based service for appointments with different clinics. Both designs were the result of a collective construction of understanding. The views of designers and the users were challenged and negotiated during the design process. They found that the medical bookings require more co-production than initially assumed. The co-production process indicated that the activities were not limited to the digital touchpoints, since it required placing attention on the interactive relationships between the actors, expanding the design scope from a purely technical approach to broader understanding of the scope.

Kauppinen, Luojus and Lahthi [44] present a method to involve citizens in open innovation, by detailing the case of WeLive, a design game built to help participants in co-design workshops to innovate and develop more concrete and detailed digital service concepts that utilize open data. Design games are methods that stage participation, with rules and tangible game pieces that guide the design process, and additionally, but rarely compete over a "single winner". In the co-design process, games create common language, promote a creative and attitude more positive towards exploration and facilitate the envisioning and enacting possibilities. "Persona cards" and "needs cards" were created to give information about the citizens what would use the services and what services would need to be provided, respectively. In addition, "information cards" designed to list the open data resources available for citizens. These cards are part of the board game, which has a space for the description of the new digital service. The game was evaluated in eight workshops. Each game lasted for about two hours and half. They found many benefits in terms of: a) gamified elements b) rules of the game c) benefits for WeLive projects d) benefits for participants e) benefits for cities and public sector.

Agbakoba et al. [9] analyzed Living it Up program and detailed the factors that affect the deployment on digital health and well-being technologies case. The program was structured in four phases: (i) solution exploration, (ii) prototyping, (iii) development of products and services and (iv) large scale roll out. The implementation and deployment process is detailed and analyzed with data from five participant observation sessions, three meetings with stakeholders and six semi-structured interviews. Findings were concentrated in six themes and the respective issues: (a) cultural shifts in mindsets and work practices (b) establishing roles, responsibilities and setting collective aims (c) person centered vs service centered design (d) user engagement, participation and enrolment versus sustainability; (e) resource allocation, funding and infrastructure; (f) measuring effectiveness and benefits realization. Researchers found that broad stakeholder engagement, such as co-design activities might lead to an increased adoption of services from users in the long term, while a great number of users might generate different implementing priorities, which may hinder or delay the deployment of services.

5 Conclusions

The systematic review and the associated queries proved successful as we found various implementations details associated with success cases, and challenges encountered. Diverse forms of conceptualizing the co-production concept were identified, the use of the concept in digital services production and planning. We found that co-production still has a long way until it is more widely employed. Even the use of digital services still needs to be better established, since some users still prefer services provided in brick and mortar settings. In this regard, good part of the articles were devoted to increase user participation, and define what would be the best strategy to engage citizen in the co-production of services.

The long time to develop and produce solutions may be an issue, since citizens may lose contact and disengage. We did not find a universally accepted model of co-production, indicating that the area is still defining its boundaries and key references. Although some design frameworks were found, they are still in design phase. Most initiatives employed a model that is divided into (a) identify issues, (b) proposal of candidate solutions and (c) citizen involvement in the choice of the decision to be implemented (d) collaborative construction and evaluation of the solution, with slight variations between proposals. Other finding is that co-production is not only about digitalizing the existing methods, it involves new methods to allow participation, which may or not be digital.

Articles related to challenges, conditions, difficulties, initiatives and projects, including detailed information on the implementation of these initiatives, proved very interesting, presenting a view of the current state of practice. Among the main challenges, we highlight a tendency of using mostly developers and neglecting other important contributions from general population, and lack of continuity of participation by the different actors involved, mainly citizens. The lack of digital literacy also is frequently mentioned although some projects managed to introduce the concepts to the citizens, and then improve their interest. Citizen participation was key in this process, and managing it seem to be the central factor of success in all the implementations.

From the articles, it seems clear that users need to be involved, supported and convinced of their power to change the proposed situation. Among the techniques employed, gamification seemed promising, even if conducted on non-digital platforms. That is, to develop digital services, the strategy does not need to be high tech.

Most of the initiatives, employed focus groups, local workshops, games, and personal interaction. The human interaction in the process seems more important than the technical aspects of the digital platforms. Future research should build in these questions, better structure and test models in other settings and populations, and try to better understand how to properly not only co-develop digital services, but also guarantee their adoption by citizens.

References

1. Rasool, G., Pathania, A.: Revisiting marketing mix study of evidences for investigating innovative role of technology in co-creation. J. Gen. Manag. Res. **1**(1), 37–50 (2014)
2. Szkuta, K., Pizzicannella, R., Osimo, D.: Collaborative approaches to public sector innovation: a scoping study. Telecommun. Policy **38**(5–6), 558–567 (2014)
3. Agusti, C., et al.: Co-Creating Cities. Defining Co-Creation as a Means of Citizen Engagement (2014, unpublished)
4. Prahalad, C.K., Ramaswamy, V.: Co-creation experiences: the next practice in value creation. J. Interact. Mark. **18**(3), 5–14 (2004)
5. Alves, H.: Co-creation and innovation in public services. Serv. Ind. J. **33**(7–8), 671–682 (2013)
6. Etgar, M.: A descriptive model of the consumer co-production process. J. Acad. Mark. Sci. **36**(1), 97–108 (2008)
7. Prahalad, C.K., Ramaswamy, V.: Co-opting customer competence. Harvard Bus. Rev. **78**(1), 79–90 (2000)
8. Hartley, J., Sørensen, E., Torfing, J.: Collaborative innovation: a viable alternative to market competition and organizational entrepreneurship. Public Adm. Rev. **73**(6), 821–830 (2013)
9. Agbakoba, R., Mcgee-Lennon, M., Bouamrane, M., Watson, N., Mair, F.: Implementation factors affecting the large-scale deployment of digital health and well-being technologies: a qualitative study of the initial phases of the 'Living-It-Up' programme. Health Inform. J. **22**(4), 867–877 (2016)
10. Kitchenham, B.A.: Procedures for performing systematic reviews. Keele University (2004)
11. Brereton, P., Kitchenham, B.A., Budgen, D., Turner, M., Khalil, M.: Lessons from applying the systematic literature review process within the software engineering domain. J. Syst. Softw. **80**(4), 571–583 (2007)
12. Biolchini, J., Mian, P.G., Natali, A.C.C., Travassos, G.H.: Systematic review in software engineering. Tech. Rep. ES **679**(5), 45 (2005)
13. Forsgreen, O.: eService co-design platforms. In: Eadoption and the Knowledge Economy: Issues, Applications, Case Studies, vol. 1. IOS Press (2004)
14. Anthopoulos, L.G., Siozos, P., Tsoukalas, I.A.: Applying participatory design and collaboration in digital public services for discovering and re-designing e-government services. Gov. Inf. Q. **24**(2), 353–376 (2007)
15. Olphert, W., Damodaran, L.: Citizen participation and engagement in the design of e-government services: the missing link in effective ICT design and delivery. J. Assoc. Inf. Syst. **8**(9), 491 (2007)
16. Löfstedt, U.: Social systems design as a vehicle towards local public e-services for and by citizens. Syst. Pract. Action Res. **20**(6), 467–476 (2007)
17. Antikainen, M., Näkki, P.: Connecting customers and designers at Owela œ Online platform for service co-design. In: VTT Symposium on Service Science, Technology and Business (2007)
18. Tung, W.F., Yuan, S.T.: A service design framework for value co-production: insight from mutualism perspective. Kybernetes **37**(2), 226–240 (2008)
19. Ruland, C.M., Borosund, E., Varsi, C.: User requirements for a practice-integrated nurse-administered online communication service for cancer patients. In: Nursing Informatics, pp. 221–225, June 2009
20. Holgersson, J., Söderström, E., Karlsson, F., Hedström, K.: Towards a roadmap for user involvement in e-government service development. In: Wimmer, M.A., Chappelet, J.-L., Janssen, M., Scholl, H.J. (eds.) EGOV 2010. LNCS, vol. 6228, pp. 251–262. Springer, Heidelberg (2010). https://doi.org/10.1007/978-3-642-14799-9_22

21. Bonacin, R., Melo, A.M., Simoni, C.A., Baranauskas, M.C.C.: Accessibility and interoperability in e-government systems: outlining an inclusive development process. Univ. Access Inf. Soc. **9**(1), 17–33 (2010)
22. Christiansson, M.T.: A common process model to improve eService solutions-the municipality case. In: 11th European Conference on eGoverment-ECEG 2011, 16–17 June 2011, Ljubliana Slovenia (2011)
23. Lux Wigand, F.D.: Gov 2.0 and beyond: using social media for transparency, participation and collaboration. In: Fong, S. (ed.) NDT 2011. CCIS, vol. 136, pp. 307–318. Springer, Heidelberg (2011). https://doi.org/10.1007/978-3-642-22185-9_26
24. Fogli, D.: Designing visual interactive systems in the e-government domain. In: Proceedings of the International Working Conference on Advanced Visual Interfaces, May 2012
25. Karlsson, F., Holgersson, J., Söderström, E., Hedström, K.: Exploring user participation approaches in public e-service development. Gov. Inf. Q. **29**(2), 158–168 (2012)
26. Bridge, C.: Citizen centric service in the Australian department of human services: the department's experience in engaging the community in co-design of government service delivery and developments in e-government services. Aust. J. Public Adm. **71**(2), 167–177 (2012)
27. Gugliotta, A., Niglia, F., Schina, L.: An user-centric check of the available e-government services in Europe. In: 13th European Conference on eGovernment ECEG 2013, Como, Italy, June 2013
28. Vicini, S., Bellini, S., Sanna, A.: User-driven service innovation in a smarter city Living Lab. In: 2013 International Conference on Service Sciences (ICSS), April 2013
29. Conruyt, N.: E-co-innovation for making e-services living labs as a human-centered digital ecosystem for education with ICT. In: 2013 7th IEEE International Conference on Digital Ecosystems and Technologies (DEST), July 2013
30. Nusir, M., Bell, D.: The development of government to citizens e-service design process: feature identification using repertory grid. In: Proceedings of the 13th European Conference on Research Methodology for Business and Management Studies, ECRM 2014, June 2014
31. Kauppinen, S.: Enhancing public e-service development with citizens' self-organized collaboration. In: 2015 SSR International Conference on Social Sciences and Information, Tokio, Japan (2015)
32. Harrison, T., Waite, K.: Impact of co-production on consumer perception of empowerment. Serv. Ind. J. **35**(10), 502–520 (2015)
33. Eriksén, S., Dittrich, Y., Fiedler, M., Aurell, M.: It takes more than two... developing a TANGO arena for regional cooperation around e-government. In: Traunmüller, R. (ed.) EGOV 2003. LNCS, vol. 2739, pp. 472–475. Springer, Heidelberg (2003). https://doi.org/10.1007/10929179_87
34. Blazevic, V., Lievens, A.: Managing innovation through customer coproduced knowledge in electronic services: an exploratory study. J. Acad. Mark. Sci. **1**(138–151), 36 (2008)
35. Gilbert, M.D., Mark, Z.: Sharing time: engaging students as co-designers in the creation of an online knowledge sharing application. In: Proceedings of the 30th ACM International Conference on Design of Communication, October 2012
36. Lundberg, N., et al.: My care pathways-creating open innovation in healthcare. In: MedInfo, pp. 687–691 (2013)
37. Juell-Skielse, G., Hjalmarsson, A., Johannesson, P., Rudmark, D.: Is the public motivated to engage in open data innovation? In: Janssen, M., Scholl, H.J., Wimmer, M.A., Bannister, F. (eds.) EGOV 2014. LNCS, vol. 8653, pp. 277–288. Springer, Heidelberg (2014). https://doi.org/10.1007/978-3-662-44426-9_23
38. Holgersson, J., Karlsson, F.: Public e-service development: understanding citizens' conditions for participation. Gov. Inf. Q. **31**(3), 396–410 (2014)

39. Alm, H., Janecek, P., Forsgren, O.: Co-design research and business development: case of Scandinavian Airlines (SAS). Syst. Pract. Action Res. **27**(5), 465–483 (2014)
40. Gidlund, K.L.: Makers and shapers or users and choosers participatory practices in digitalization of public sector. In: Tambouris, E., et al. (eds.) EGOV 2015. LNCS, vol. 9248, pp. 222–232. Springer, Cham (2015). https://doi.org/10.1007/978-3-319-22479-4_17
41. Conruyt, N., Sébastien, V., Sébastien, O., Sébastien, D., Grosser, D.: Sign management for the future of e-education: examples of collaborative e-services in a living lab (Invited paper). In: Mercier-Laurent, E., Owoc, M.L., Boulanger, D. (eds.) AI4KM 2014. IAICT, vol. 469, pp. 1–20. Springer, Cham (2015). https://doi.org/10.1007/978-3-319-28868-0_1
42. French, T., Teal, G.: Co-designing a digital directory of services. Procedia Comput. Sci. **63**, 445–450 (2015)
43. Vassilakopoulou, P., Grisot, M., Aanestad, M.: Co-creation of patient-oriented services: design of electronic booking for Norwegian healthcare. In: Oinas-Kukkonen, H., Iivari, N., Kuutti, K., Öörni, A., Rajanen, M. (eds.) SCIS 2015. LNBIP, vol. 223, pp. 193–207. Springer, Cham (2015). https://doi.org/10.1007/978-3-319-21783-3_14
44. Kauppinen, S., Luojus, S., Lahti, J.: Involving citizens in open innovation process by means of gamification: the case of WeLive. In: Proceedings of the 9th Nordic Conference on Human-Computer Interaction, Gothenburg, Sweden, October 2016

The Effects of Co-creation on Citizens' Intentions to Accept Virtual Civil Servants

Yuting Lin[1] and Her-Sen Doong[2(✉)]

[1] Department of Management, Imperial College Business School,
Imperial College London, South Kensington, London SW7 2AZ, UK
y.linl4@imperial.ac.uk
[2] Department of Management Information Systems, National Chiayi University,
Chiayi 60054, Taiwan
hsdoong@mail.ncyu.edu.tw

Abstract. Many governments have implemented software agents – virtual civil servants (VCSs) – in order to offer citizens better experiences when they choose the service they require. However, VCSs have not created as many benefits as was originally expected of them, leaving citizens frustrated and dissatisfied. Consequently, effective VCS design has become a critical issue. Grounded on previous research into co-creation, we suggest that citizens would perceive VCSs to be more effective if the agents were to engage them in the co-creation process by interacting directly with them; this would also enable the VCSs to provide services that are more closely aligned with citizens' preferences. Hence, this study will contribute to e-Government literature by explaining how a co-creation policy regarding VCSs' might impact on both citizens' behavior and on their subsequent acceptance of what they have to offer. A key practical implication of our findings, therefore, is that governments may benefit substantially from collating citizens' preferences, while citizens would receive the required services more effectively, thereby engendering a sense of satisfaction toward their governments.

Keywords: Accept · Electronic government service · Co-creation

1 Introduction

Information technology is used in e-governance by using an infrastructure designed to enhance the accessibility and deliverance of government services to citizens [1]. E-Government has become one of the most common service platforms for citizens; however, citizens may find it difficult to discover services that satisfy their needs due to their limited capacity to comprehend the vast amount of information on government websites. Virtual civil servants (VCSs), therefore, carry out such tasks by directing citizens to the precise information they require; consequently, they have been adopted by several countries.

According to the theory of "Computers as Social Actors (CASAs)", when interacting with e-media, individuals subconsciously attribute human characteristics, such as social rules and expectations, to technology [2]. Such a phenomenon is more

© Springer Nature Switzerland AG 2018
A. Kő and E. Francesconi (Eds.): EGOVIS 2018, LNCS 11032, pp. 20–28, 2018.
https://doi.org/10.1007/978-3-319-98349-3_2

apparent when technological artifacts are perceived to possess human-like features [3]. The Taiwanese government, for example, developed a Government-to-Citizen VCS called 'e-Housekeeper' in order to bridge the gap between online and offline citizens, which was implemented on its e-Government portal (https://msg.nat.gov.tw/) for the purposes of, (i) providing services and recommendations based on citizens' preferences, location and profiles, (ii) filtering unnecessary information in order to reduce cognitive loads, (iii) minimizing complex searches, (iv) enhancing decision quality, and (v) increasing citizens' satisfaction with governments. Due to the success of e-Housekeeper, the Taiwanese government has announced a Government-to-Business VCS named e-Helper.

Although a VCS, such as e-Housekeeper, plays a rather good role as a 'government employee/agency', some problems may exist. For example, (i) because there is not an effective software agent design rule, it might provoke negative responses [4] and (ii) users could expend a lot of effort filtering criteria, causing an agent's suggestion precision to be lower than it should be [5]. Such design problems also impact on social affiliation. Even if VCSs may satisfy citizens' needs, the question of how to incorporate the capacity to facilitate social interactions, thereby influencing citizens' loyalty towards e-Government services is still unknown. Moreover, previous research on the consequence of individuals' intentions to accept software agents has predominantly investigated their utilitarian value, since the agent's aim is to both reduce effort and provide decision assistance. Given these challenges, we argue that VCSs development should require an investment, to some degree, of citizens' co-creational effort.

In summary, this research examines the role of co-creation in influencing the acceptance of services and suggestions offered by VCSs on a e-Government platform. We argue that citizens would be more willing to participate in co-creation processes, despite their concerns about saving energy – i.e. the IKEA effect. Therefore, we shall propose traditional VCSs and engaged VCSs in order to validate our arguments regarding citizens' intentions to accept e-Government services.

2 Design of Engaged Intelligent Agents of e-Government

This research paper, which is grounded in co-creation theory [7, 9–11], aims to explore how varying degrees of engagement will affect citizens' decisions to accept VCSs. Consequently, we have defined "co-creation of e-Government services" as a "process through which governments initiate collaborative developments with citizens in an attempt to jointly foster personalized e-Government services". Two types of VCSs – (i) traditional and (ii) engaged, were established. The traditional VCSs are those mainly used on some current e-Government websites to assist in minimizing searching time and efforts, thereby provide services in accordance with the participant's specific preferences, browsing history, or similar profiles, while filtering unnecessary information, thereby reducing the participant's cognitive effort and enhance their satisfaction.

In this paper, we adopt the four challenges of co-creation as proposed by Prahalad and Ramaswamy [6] in order to design distinct engaged VCSs. However, one of the challenges of mobilizing citizen communities is not considered in this research owing to the suitability in the building process together with a reluctance on the part of citizens to disclose private information on social networks. Specifically, the major functions that correspond to the challenges are, (i) numerous interactive conversations between citizens and VCSs regarding encouraging active dialogue, (ii) diverse choice options, such as managing citizen diversity, and (iii) processing experience based on citizens' own profiles, such as gender or personal information – i.e. co-creating personalized experiences. We propose that engaged VCSs should be additionally based on the abovementioned three major functions. The Table 1 below summarizes the detailed functions among the distinct levels of engagement of VCSs.

Table 1. Functional design of virtual civil servants (VCSs)

Functions	Types of VCSs	
	Traditional VCSs	Engaged VCSs
Preferences collection	V	V
Suggestions and services provision	V	V
Interactive conversations		V
Diverse choice options		V
Personalized experiences		V

3 Research Propositions

This research attempts to design different levels of engagement of VCSs in order to enlarge citizen participation in the creation of e-Government services. By doing so, the more citizens' preferences are collected by VCSs, the more suitable will be the services offered. In return, citizens may well become more willing to use and transfer their loyalty to VCSs. It is important to note that although the model shown below simply demonstrates the outcome variable, which is an intention to accept VCSs, we define such acceptance as both adopting VCSs and considering the services that are recommended by VCSs. For the sake of readability, the intention to accept VCSs will be used thereafter. Our research model and its corresponding propositions are as follows (Fig. 1):

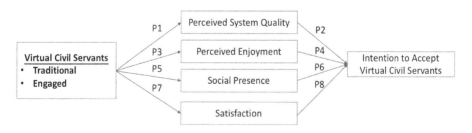

Fig. 1. Research model

The perceived system quality of online decision aids is defined as the extent to which citizens consider how tools perform assigned tasks [12]. Wang and Benbasat demonstrated that what information individuals are willing to provide to intelligent agents would affect the quality of advices [13]. When citizens' preferences are exact and clearly collected, VCSs could generate more suitable services to match their needs, in which as the quality of VCSs will be perceived as high. Consequently, engaged VCSs that possess interaction, diversity and personalization functions will elicit preferences as individual inputs more than traditional VCSs do. Citizens may recognize the recommended services fitting their needs and then perceive a high quality of VCSs. Thus, the perceived system quality of engaged VCSs is greater than that of traditional VCSs. Taken together, we posit that:

- P1: Engaged VCSs result in higher perceived system quality than traditional VCSs.

"Perceived usefulness", which refers to users' subjective benefits resulting from utilizing information systems in the context of job performance, has been confirmed to influence users' intentions to accept technological artifacts [14]. When citizens have a higher level of perceived usefulness, their willingness to adopt VCSs is boosted. On the basis of the research for this paper, "perceived usefulness" is regarded as a similar concept to "perceived system quality". Therefore, we argue that VCSs built by the co-creation process are perceived as having a high level of system quality, thus increasing the likelihood of users adopting VCSs together with the recommended services. Taken together, we posit that:

- P2: Perceived system quality positively influences citizens' intention to accept VCSs.

"Perceived enjoyment" is a term used for describing users' emotions while interacting with information systems. Besides the utilitarian value of the agent, such enjoyment refers to the extent to which users enjoy their activities with agents. It has been shown to influence users' intentions to accept technological artifacts in a wide range of contexts, such as instant communication tools, e-learning media, and online shopping [15, 16]. Moreover, perceived enjoyment is one of the indicators used to understand citizens' utilitarian motivations behind their shopping behavior [17]. In the traditional retail environment, when consumers experience pleasant emotions, they become satisfied with the relationship between sellers and buyers, thereby increasing the opportunities for placing orders [18]. This holds true in the e-commerce environment. Such hedonic and immersive feelings during the purchasing process are key drivers to predict consumers' attitudes [19].

Applied to the context of e-Government, citizens would rely on e-Government platforms to build the VCSs collaboratively. During back-and-forth interactions between themselves and VCSs, additional functions, such as personalized experiences and diverse choice options, might result in more enjoyment. Hence, engaged VCSs that possess co-creation processes are more likely to lead to more enjoyment than traditional VCSs do. It is inevitable that interactive dynamism may create a certain amount of effort [5, 11]. That said, engaged VCSs provide citizens with personalized experiences and diverse choice options to offset one's desire to save effort, leading to a higher degree of satisfaction. Thus, perceived enjoyment from engaging with VCSs is greater than it is from traditional VCSs. Yüksel [20] has demonstrated the direct effect of perceived enjoyment on individuals' intentions to accept technological artifacts. Similarly, we argue that citizens are more likely to feel enjoyment during the interactions with VCSs, which may influence their decisions to adopt VCSs and also to consider following their recommendations. Taken together, we posit that both:

- P3: Engaged VCSs will result in higher perceived enjoyment than traditional VCSs, and that
- P4: Perceived enjoyment positively influences citizens' intention to accept VCSs.

"Social presence" refers to the feelings of being with others, which is used to measure how users perceive the existence of other individuals who are physically far from them [21]. Later on, in the domain of artificial intelligence, this notion has been applied to anthropomorphized virtual agents, computers, robots and so on [22]. The importance of social presence has also stimulated academic interest in examining the sense of connection between a website and its visitors [23], which leads to greater trust in online vendors [23, 24], higher willingness to purchase [25], and much more consumer loyalty [26, 27].

On the basis of the previous lines of reasoning, engaged VCSs, with features such as interaction, diverse choices and personalization, would provide a citizen with the actual feeling of being with a civil servant. Thus, engaged VCSs could elicit a greater perception of social presence than traditional VCSs could. Moreover, engaged VCSs have extra functions, such as diverse choice options and personalized experiences than traditional VCSs do, which generate a higher level of social presence. In addition, according to CASA theory [2] and similarity-attraction theory [28], users will perceive technology to have social characteristics when such technological artifacts possess similar attributes to human actions. Once these characteristics seem to resemble their users, the users might feel enjoyment and be comfortable when interacting with technology, resulting in a greater willingness to accept the system. We support the notion that citizens feel as if they are in a physical office when they are communicating with engaged VCSs, particularly when they are receiving self-relevant services suggested by our designed VCSs. As such, citizens will perceive a social presence that will increase the likelihood that they will accept the idea of VCSs. Taken together, we posit that:

- P5: Engaged VCSs will result in more social presence than traditional VCSs, and that
- P6: A social presence positively influences citizens' intention to accept VCSs.

Information and communication technologies (ICT) have brought about many possibilities for consumers to participate in business innovations [29]. In particular, the emergence of the Internet provides companies with unique and creative opportunities to utilize individuals' visionary inventions or knowledge. The most common method is to develop products jointly through such collaborations as generating and evaluating creative ideas, establishing and proving product concepts and prototype constructions. Prahalad and Ramaswamy [30] believed that unique co-creation experiences should be dependent on purposeful interactions between individuals and businesses by means of the Internet and also by way of social communities and that, moreover, experiential environments should also be constructed to empower individuals to create their own experiences.

The disconfirmation model explains the gap between perceived and expected levels of goods/services resulting in satisfaction [31]. Whether or not consumers are satisfied with companies' products or services, this concern is regarded as a significant surrogate measure for businesses to succeed and to maintain their long-term competitiveness [32]. Over recent decades, researchers in the domains of marketing and consumer behavior considered satisfaction to have been a pivotal issue in both theoretical and managerial foundations [33]. In general, satisfaction has been described as the extent to which users perceive that their needs, goals, and desires have been fully met, therefore, this evaluation will positively influence behavioral intentions [34].

Conventionally, satisfaction was considered to be a cognitive state that is influenced by cognitive antecedents. However, in recent research, satisfaction has been connected with cognitive and affective perspectives [35]. Both these aspects are indispensable for the creation of satisfaction, and, in turn, to positively affect behavioral intentions [36]. In the context of e-Government, owing to the co-creation experience, citizens should expect the services provided by VCSs to meet, or surpass, their expectations, thereby increasing their wish to continue using the system and accept the services recommended by the system. Taken together, we posit that:

- P7: Engaged VCSs will result in higher satisfaction than traditional VCSs, and that
- P8: Satisfaction positively influences individual's intention to accept VCSs.

4   General Discussion and Managerial Implications

The borders between online and offline services today have become blurred owing to the emergence of digital consumption. Such a trend has led some businesses to fade away, while others have developed various products to fulfill a wide range of individual needs. In the context of e-Government, citizens are finding it difficult to choose from such an extensive array of services that are all equipped with numerous features and functions. Given these complex choice sets, in order to offer their citizens a better experience, some governments are implementing VCSs, hence they are designing VCSs that can generate personalized services that are as favorable as possible and that do not result in negative feelings for their citizens.

From the perspective of governments, the cost of implementing innovative online services, such as VCSs, is relatively high since, should they fail to create as many benefits as expected, they will face serious losses. Such a negative effect may also hold true for citizens, who if they feel frustrated with VCSs that do not provide the service they require, will criticize their government for wasting money. Consequently, the design principle of VCSs is hugely important to consider how it is likely to impacts, either negatively or positively, on citizens' behavioral intentions.

This research has been based on previous literature and researches; in order to make best use of it, we propose an investigation into the co-creation effects of VCSs on citizens' acceptance intentions. We suggest that citizens would perceive VCSs to have a high level of quality when agents not only engage citizens in co-creation processes through numerous interactive dialogues, but also provide services that fit their preferences. Furthermore, we would argue that co-creation experiences will enhance citizens' perceived system quality, perceived enjoyment, social presence perception and satisfaction, thereby affecting their intention to adopt VCSs.

While previous studies have shown there to be influential determinants of software agent acceptance, little is known about whether they have demonstrated beneficial or detrimental aspects of co-creation vis-a-vis traditional VCSs as opposed to engaged VCSs regarding their effect on user behavioral intentions. On one hand the greater co-production intensity might negatively impact user satisfaction with the coproduction process [37], however, on the other hand, the IKEA effect might lead to increases in valuation of self-assembly products [38]. In light of the research gaps, mentioned above, under current e-Government conditions, we contend that citizens would be willing to contribute a certain amount of effort in terms of participation in co-creation processes in order to reinforce their sense of ownership of a personalized VCSs. Such collaboration would also be likely to help them to include their preferences into the building process, thereby identifying more closely with the process [8]. Therefore, engaged VCSs that include interactive functions such as diverse choice options and personalized experience, could increase the likelihood of engaged VCSs becoming acceptable.

Overall, we believe that this study will contribute to e-Government literature by unpacking the impact of co-creation on citizens' behavioral intentions towards the acceptance of VCSs. Also, by harnessing a co-creation approach in the process of such development, governments will collect more citizen preferences and obtain more feedback. This is a win-win situation where citizens are able in return to become engaged in creating their own VCSs step by step. Such a mutually beneficial cycle through interactive processes will enable them to express their preferences in greater detail. Thus, citizens would not only receive much more relevant e-Government services, but also they would gain co-creational experience which would further enhance their satisfaction with their government.

References

1. Das, A., Singh, H., Joseph, D.: A longitudinal study of e-government maturity. Inf. Manag. **54**, 415–426 (2017)
2. Reeves, B., Nass, C.I.: The Media Equation: How People Treat Computers, Television, and New Media Like Real People and Places. Cambridge University Press, Cambridge (1996)
3. Nass, C., Moon, Y.: Machines and mindlessness: social responses to computers. J. Soc. Issues **56**, 81–103 (2000)
4. Westbrook, R.A., Black, W.C.: A motivation-based shopper typology. J. Retail. **61**(1), 78–103 (1985)
5. Lee, Y.E., Benbasat, I.: Research note—the influence of trade-off difficulty caused by preference elicitation methods on user acceptance of recommendation agents across loss and gain conditions. Inf. Syst. Res. **22**, 867–884 (2011)
6. Prahalad, C.K., Ramaswamy, V.: Co-opting customer competence. Harv. Bus. Rev. **78**, 79–90 (2000)

7. Ramaswamy, V.: Co-creation of value—towards an expanded paradigm of value creation. Mark. Rev. St. Gallen **26**, 11–17 (2009)
8. Ramaswamy, V., Ozcan, K.: What is co-creation? An interactional creation framework and its implications for value creation. J. Bus. Res. **84**, 196–205 (2018)
9. Prahalad, C.K., Ramaswamy, V.: Co-creation experiences: the next practice in value creation. J. Interact. Mark. **18**, 5–14 (2004)
10. Kohler, T., Fueller, J., Matzler, K., Stieger, D., Füller, J.: Co-creation in virtual worlds: the design of the user experience. MIS Quart. **35**(3), 773–788 (2011)
11. Gebauer, J., Füller, J., Pezzei, R.: The dark and the bright side of co-creation: triggers of member behavior in online innovation communities. J. Bus. Res. **66**, 1516–1527 (2013)
12. McKnight, D.H., Choudhury, V., Kacmar, C.: Developing and validating trust measures for e-commerce: an integrative typology. Inf. Syst. Res. **13**, 334–359 (2002)
13. Wang, W., Benbasat, I.: Interactive decision aids for consumer decision making in e-commerce: the influence of perceived strategy restrictiveness. MIS Q. **33**(2), 293–320 (2009)
14. Davis, F.D.: Perceived usefulness, perceived ease of use, and user acceptance of information technology. MIS Q. **13**(3), 319–340 (1989)
15. Koufaris, M.: Applying the technology acceptance model and flow theory to online consumer behavior. Inf. Syst. Res. **13**, 205–223 (2002)
16. Van der Heijden, H.: User acceptance of hedonic information systems. MIS Q. **28**(4), 695–704 (2004)
17. Babin, B.J., Darden, W.R., Griffin, M.: Work and/or fun: measuring hedonic and utilitarian shopping value. J. Consum. Res. **20**, 644–656 (1994)
18. Reynolds, K.E., Beatty, S.E.: Customer benefits and company consequences of customer-salesperson relationships in retailing. J. Retail. **75**, 11–32 (1999)
19. Childers, T.L., Carr, C.L., Peck, J., Carson, S.: Hedonic and utilitarian motivations for online retail shopping behavior. J. Retail. **77**, 511–535 (2001)
20. Yüksel, A.: Tourist shopping habitat: effects on emotions, shopping value and behaviours. Tour. Manag. **28**, 58–69 (2007)
21. Short, J., Williams, E., Christie, B.: The Social Psychology of Telecommunications. Wiley, Hoboken (1976)
22. Biocca, F.: The Cyborg's dilemma: progressive embodiment in virtual environments. J. Comput. Mediat. Commun. **3**, JCMC324 (1997)
23. Hassanein, K., Head, M.: The impact of infusing social presence in the web interface: an investigation across product types. Int. J. Electron. Commer. **10**, 31–55 (2005)
24. Gefen, D., Straub, D.W.: Managing user trust in B2C e-services. E-Service J. **2**, 7–24 (2003)
25. Simon, S.J.: The impact of culture and gender on web sites: an empirical study. ACM SIGMIS Database: Database Adv. Inf. Syst. **32**, 18–37 (2000)
26. Cyr, D., Hassanein, K., Head, M., Ivanov, A.: The role of social presence in establishing loyalty in e-service environments. Interact. Comput. **19**, 43–56 (2007)
27. Kumar, N., Benbasat, I.: Research note: the influence of recommendations and consumer reviews on evaluations of websites. Inf. Syst. Res. **17**, 425–439 (2006)
28. Bryne, D., Clore Jr., G., Worchel, P.: The effect of economic similarity-dissimilarity as determinants of attraction. J. Pers. Soc. Psychol. **4**, 220–224 (1966)
29. Di Gangi, P.M., Wasko, M.: Open innovation through online communities. In: King, W. (ed.) Knowledge Management and Organizational Learning. Annals of Information Systems, vol. 4, pp. 199–213. Springer, Heidelberg (2009). https://doi.org/10.1007/978-1-4419-0011-1_13
30. Prahalad, C.K., Ramaswamy, V.: The new frontier of experience innovation. MIT Sloan Manag. Rev. **44**, 12–18 (2003)

31. Martin, D., O'Neill, M., Hubbard, S., Palmer, A.: The role of emotion in explaining consumer satisfaction and future behavioural intention. J. Serv. Mark. **22**, 224–236 (2008)
32. Law, A.K., Hui, Y., Zhao, X.: Modeling repurchase frequency and customer satisfaction for fast food outlets. Int. J. Qual. Reliab. Manag. **21**, 545–563 (2004)
33. Martín-Consuegra, D., Molina, A., Esteban, Á.: An integrated model of price, satisfaction and loyalty: an empirical analysis in the service sector. J. Prod. Brand Manag. **16**, 459–468 (2007)
34. Mohammadi, H.: Investigating users' perspectives on e-learning: an integration of TAM and IS success model. Comput. Hum. Behav. **45**, 359–374 (2015)
35. Bigné, J.E., Andreu, L., Gnoth, J.: The theme park experience: an analysis of pleasure, arousal and satisfaction. Tour. Manag. **26**, 833–844 (2005)
36. Burton, S., Sheather, S., Roberts, J.: Reality or perception? The effect of actual and perceived performance on satisfaction and behavioral intention. J. Serv. Res. **5**, 292–302 (2003)
37. Haumann, T., Güntürkün, P., Schons, L.M., Wieseke, J.: Engaging customers in coproduction processes: how value-enhancing and intensity-reducing communication strategies mitigate the negative effects of coproduction intensity. J. Mark. **79**, 17–33 (2015)
38. Norton, M.I., Mochon, D., Ariely, D.: The IKEA effect: when labor leads to love. J. Consum. Psychol. **22**, 453–460 (2012)

Critical Factors that Impact Process Management Implementation Strategies: A Case Study of a Government Agency

Renato Neder[1(✉)] ⓘ, Paulo Augusto Ramalho de Souza[1(✉)] ⓘ,
Olivan da Silva Rabêlo[1] ⓘ, Elisandra Marisa Zambra[1(✉)] ⓘ,
Cristiano Maciel[1,2(✉)] ⓘ, Rodrigo Mello[3(✉)] ⓘ,
Samara Vaz da Cunha Trejan[2(✉)] ⓘ,
and Alexandre M. dos Anjos[1(✉)] ⓘ

[1] Universidade Federal de Mato Grosso, Cuiabá, MT, Brazil
renatoneder@gmail.com, olivanrabelo@gmail.com,
elisandrazambra@gmail.com, crismac@gmail.com,
dinteralexandre@gmail.com, pauloramalho@ufmt.br
[2] Fundação de Apoio da Universidade Federal de Mato Grosso - Uniselva,
Cuiabá, MT, Brazil
trejan@uniselva.tce.mt.gov.br
[3] Tribunal de Contas do Estado do Mato Grosso, Cuiabá, MT, Brazil
rodrigo.ares@gmail.com

Abstract. Process management used as a managerial strategy can allow organizations to improve performance. Hence the need to understand the factors that may cause interference when adopting this strategy in an organization. Based on academic literature, a research tool was developed contemplating six critical factors that potentially impact the implementation of Process Management strategies. The research was divided into two phases: the first phase confirmed the conceptual model by means of 141 observations obtained from the State Audit Court of the state of Mato Grosso (Tribunal de Contas do Mato Grosso - TCE-MT); the second phase conducted an analysis of structural equations using the partial least squares regression method. The results reveal that Governance, Performance and People factors positively impact the process-oriented organizational culture of the TCE-MT.

Keywords: Process management · Governance · Performance
Information technology · People · Organizational culture

1 Introduction

Process Management (PM) probably originated from Total Quality Management (TQM). TQM is a management effort whose roots lie in the Japanese administration model developed in post-World War II period, with the aim of improving the quality of products and processes underlying production. Prior to the emergence of this tool, flaws were only detected during the later stages of production, usually with finished products.

© Springer Nature Switzerland AG 2018
A. Kő and E. Francesconi (Eds.): EGOVIS 2018, LNCS 11032, pp. 29–42, 2018.
https://doi.org/10.1007/978-3-319-98349-3_3

TQM began to allow quality control in various stages of the production process, leading to reduced loss and waste while optimizing the use of resources, thus creating the basis for the development of the Process Management (PM) model. This, in turn, constitutes an administrative paradigm that suggests a shift in the management organization models from the vertical focus on the business functions for horizontal models focused on processes, tasks and activities.

In vertical management models, the organization is conceived by means of its business functions, thus emphasizing specialization, where each functional area is responsible for a determined set of tasks. Despite its hegemony, this management paradigm presents a few shortcomings, the biggest of which, it is believed, is the lack of understanding of the organization from a systemic perspective. This has a strong impact on governance, since the systemic vision is required for optimal computerization of processes. On the other hand, PM enjoys the main advantage of integrating business functions, emphasizing an integrated view of the organization. Thus, organizational bureaucracy can be improved, since integration can promote improvement in organizational efficiency.

In light of this, it is notable that organizational technologies and the innovation of management models such as, for instance, process management, are able to boost the organization, since they permit the mapping and subsequent reorganization of processes in order to improve the quality of products and services focused on the client. Process Management can also facilitate internal communication and provide the development of manuals that allow clients and employees to understand the organization's many functions, thus improving organizational learning and laying the foundations for a knowledge management model. Another advantage of PM is its focus on the organization's client, which allows it to establish administrative resources to better meet its needs. The PM perspective is regarded as a strategy for change which has the potential to maximize organizational performance. Therefore, the present study aims to develop a research tool to measure critical factors that impact the implementation strategy of process management, given a theoretical assumption that relates Implementation Strategy of PM directly with Organizational Culture. It must be highlighted that approaches to management challenges in the public sector are adopted in other countries, such as in the Swedish case study that discussed challenges for BPM in townhouses [32]. This assumption arises from the interpretation of the research conducted by Bandara, Alibabaei and Aghdasi [2], which proposes the existence of various cultural factors that positively or negatively impact PM actions in an organization. This set of cultural factors will be called, in the scope of this article, Process-Oriented Organizational Culture, considered a proxy for the performance of PM implementation strategy.

In light of this goal, a research tool was developed based on academic literature, which contemplates six critical factors that potentially impact the implementation of Process Management strategies. The research was divided into two phases: the first phase confirmed the conceptual model by means of 141 observations obtained from the State Audit Court of the state of Mato Grosso (Tribunal de Contas do Mato Grosso - TCE-MT) [13, 33]; the second phase conducted an analysis of structural equations using the partial least squares regression method. The results reveal that Governance,

Performance and People factors positively impact the process-oriented organizational culture of the TCE-MT.

2 Critical Factors for Process Management (PM)

Table 1 summarizes the literature review conducted for this research in order to define critical success factors in a multidimensional perspective regarding the pre-implementation of Process Management in organizations.

The preliminary bibliographic analysis presented several factors that impact Process-Oriented Organizational Culture. This research delimited the use of only the factors that appeared in at least four different publications from the chosen set of publications, considering the 10 most referenced papers in the Web of Science database. This strategy made it possible to isolate six factors, namely: Information Technology; Organizational Culture; Governance; Performance; Strategic Alignment; and People. See Table 1 containing the authors and their respective factors. The label "Not applicable" was used when no references to the term were found.

Table 1. Theorists and factors.

[24]	[22]	[25]	[29]	[27]	[5]
Roseman and De Bruin (2005)	Ravesteyn and Versendaal (2010)	Rosemann and Vom Brocke (2010)	Trkman (2010)	Škrinjar and Trkman (2013)	Buh; Kovačič and Štemberger (2015)
Organizational culture	Organizational culture	Organizational culture	Not applicable	Not applicable	Organizational culture
Information technology	Information technology	Information technology	Information technology	Information technology	Information Technology
Governance	Governance	Governance	Not applicable	Not applicable	Governance
Performance	Performance	Not applicable	Performance	Performance	Performance
Not applicable	Strategic alignment	Strategic alignment	Strategic alignment	Strategic alignment	Strategic alignment
Not applicable	People	People	People	People	People

These factors will be discussed in this section. Before, however, some assumptions about process-oriented Organizational Culture will be addressed.

Hajo and Reijers [12] introduce the concept of process orientation along with a set of factors that hold the potential to improve management practices of an organization. Furthermore, the author points out that process orientation can lead to successful strategic Process Management actions. The following terms are synonymous with Process Orientation, according to Hajo and Reijers [12]: Horizontal Organizations; Process-centered organizations and process-focused organizations.

Practices related to Process Management are very much reflected in the organizational culture. For Bandara, Alibabaei and Aghdasi [2], organizational culture provides guidelines for understanding that some cultural characteristics in organizations offer adequate conditions for a successful PM project. These cultural characteristics form a dimension of the culture that shall be called, in the scope of this article, Process-Oriented Organizational Culture. Thus, it is assumed that organizations that have experienced greater maturity in this cultural trait find it easier to develop PM strategies.

The authors add that culture is composed of a few dimensions that can be characterized as a means to achieve success in PM deployment strategies, such as: increasing process formalization and business planning; greater acceptance and readiness towards organizational change; and reduced authority, decentralization and a greater tendency to collaborate [2].

2.1 Organizational Culture

Culture introduces relevant characteristics in the context of organizations. According to Rosemann and Vom Brocke [25], culture incorporates the collective values and beliefs of a group of people aimed at shaping attitudes and behavior related to the process of improving organization performance, which in turn may influence the implementation of Process Management in a given organization.

Schein [26], in his work Organizational Culture and Leadership, states that culture is a multidimensional and multifaceted phenomenon that cannot be easily reduced to a few large dimensions. Culture reflects the group's effort to work and learn. Culture, therefore, not only plays the role of providing stability, meaning and predictability in the present, it is also the result of functionally effective decisions from the past.

Due to this dimensional multiplicity, the culture of an organization impacts, in a greater or lesser way, any organizational effort in which social relations are at stake. In implementing PM strategies, this impact is direct since it requires considerable socio-cultural commitment in order to achieve success.

2.2 Information Technology

Investments in information technology are able to leverage business tasks and several types of managerial efforts, including PM. In this sense, Groznik and Maslaric [9] propose that process reengineering is based on the efficient use of Information Technology, therefore companies must invest in IT. In contrast, business process investments are also identified as an opportunity to promote better integration between IT and the organization's business areas.

Rahimi, Møller and Hvamc [20] point out that IT presents a wide range of business opportunities. Among these opportunities, the development of PM can be highlighted, which can be understood as a managerial effort aiming to promote improvement and organizational change and thus relies heavily on IT efforts.

The concept of IT governance, according to Rahimi, Møller and Hvam [22], can be seen as a key factor for PM efforts. This is probably because IT governance seeks to standardize procedures and activities related to information technology. Additionally, engaging in a comparative analysis, the authors demonstrate that both the PM and the IT fields are co-responsible for aligning the business with their strategies. In addition, the development of information systems finds a strong ally in PM, since, in order to develop software, programmers and data analyst teams usually adopt business procedures as a starting point.

2.3 Governance

For Rohloff [23], governance is a relevant factor in organizations because it elucidates transparency in business processes. Governance relays to employees the perspective of a deeper comprehension regarding goals, roles, content, and responsibilities of PM, as well as understanding how its implementation progresses.

Thus, internal communication within the organization, based on transparency associated with governance, leads to increased awareness concerning the need for managerial processes, increasing the chances of embracing PM initiatives [23].

Rahimi, Møller and Hvam [20] suggest the term Business Process Governance in reference to accountability and the strategic decision-making process in PM. In this sense, PM can be thought of as an administrative act of governance.

For Thompson et al. [28], PM promotes accountability, decision-making processes and systems of reward, providing relevant and transparent guidelines for individual actions. This way, an organization that enjoys a certain maturity level in terms of governance will possibly find it easier to manage its business processes.

2.4 Performance

Tracking the performance of processes allows the organization to verify that they are working as planned. Therefore, performance analysis methodologies are understood as an important starting point for the adoption of an efficient PM strategy.

A recurring feature observed during the process of deploying new management models in organizations relates to the lack of consistent and effective ways of documenting and controlling the impacts and the extent of organizational changes arising from this deployment [17].

It should be emphasized that the implementation of PM should be followed by the assessment of the results of "new processes" that should be measured in comparison with the processes they replaced, especially related to time, cost, productivity, quality and capital [10].

For Lee and Dale [16], PM requires that all key processes be followed by performance measures and analyzes in order to address critical steps in the process, meet client requirements, avoid mistakes, reduce inconsistency, minimize cycle duration, and increase productivity.

It should be noted that performance measurement is a key factor for achieving success in PM strategies. Therefore, an organization whose performance measurement policies are already taking place enjoys advantages when implementing these strategies.

2.5   Strategic Alignment

Strategic alignment aims continuing analysis of organizational priorities and business processes. The lack of harmony and alignment between strategy and process orientation can be one of the main flaws when implementing a PM project [1].

According to Škrinjar and Trkman [27], the goals of a process should be aligned with the strategic goals of an organization. Furthermore, it is important to build general consensus regarding the PM strategy and it is crucial for senior management to be actively involved in the PM strategy.

According to Hung [14], in order to achieve long-term success and improve performance, a PM project must be associated with a relevant organizational strategy in order to maximize the improvement value of the process.

The most significant predictor of PM success may be its alignment with the organization's strategy. Likewise, the lack of connectivity between organizational strategies and process strategies is one of the main reasons for failures in Process Management projects [3]. An organization that presents clear and defined strategies is more likely to change its course in the face of the uncertainties that the business environment imposes upon organizations.

2.6   People

The main objective of business process management is to improve organizational processes. Considering that a process can be described as a set of tasks performed by humans or machines, understanding the role that people play in PM efforts can determine their implementation and maintenance efforts.

According to Bandara, Alibabaei and Aghdasi [2], the term 'people', in the context of Business Process Management (BPM), refers to individuals and groups within the organization who will be influenced by the PM effort. People are one of the most important elements in maintaining, improving, and changing business processes, as well as being responsible for establishing organizational strategies.

For Trkman [29], an important variable of the People dimension refers to the use of both specialized and unspecialized employees to carry out activities in each process. Therefore employee specialization is directly linked to BPM efforts, since processes, as well each person's responsibilities, must be well established. Furthermore, another important factor that should be taken into account is the openness of individuals towards the changes that will be implemented in their work processes, since an effective and certain PM requires an organizational and individual commitment to change.

3   Methodological Procedures

Methodology is understood as the path chosen by researchers to reach their goals. The present research study can be characterized as quantitative and exploratory, seeking the development and subsequent validation of a tool that assesses the factors that are critical for a successful implementation of Process Management strategies. As a case study, the tool was applied in a state-level government agency in Brazil, the State Audit Court of the state of Mato Grosso (Tribunal de Contas do Mato Grosso - TCE-MT) [13].

3.1   Research Model Development and Application

A research tool was proposed with the aim of measuring the possibility of success in the implementation of process management strategies in the target organization. Its development was based on literature review that pointed to several critical success factors for the implementation of PM strategies, as presented in Table 1.

The assertions were developed based on a standard of Likert-type responses containing 07 points [11], which were created through theoretical-conceptual variables raised in the literature. These factors and assertions are shown in Table 2.

The technical and semantic validation of the assertions was carried out by building a theoretical framework of the tool, with the purpose of assessing the interviewees' understanding of the data collection tool. It was noted that a group of four employees of the organization assisted in this stage of tool consolidation.

3.2   Theoretical Assumptions

Based on the research and the tool created for this research, some hypotheses were outlined for the research, namely:

H1: The factor Strategic Alignment is positively related to Process-Oriented Culture.

H2: The Governance factor is positively related to Process-Oriented Culture.

H3: The Performance factor is positively related to Process-Oriented Culture.

H4: The People factor is positively related to Process-Oriented Culture.

H5: The Information Technology factor is positively related to Process-Oriented Culture.

3.3   Data Collection and Analysis

Data collection was carried out with employees of the government accountability office of the state of Mato Grosso (Tribunal de Contas de Mato Grosso - TCE-MT) [13], through the application of online surveys.

The analyses were conducted using Confirmatory Factor Analysis (CFA) techniques and Structural Equations. The CFA was used to measure the validity and reliability of the research tool, while the Structural Equations were employed in testing the theoretical model that structured the research and the aforementioned hypotheses.

4   Case Study

This research was based on a case study of the government accountability office located in the state of Mato Grosso (TCE/MT). This is an organization designed to provide governance and accountability of public fund management of the state of Mato Grosso, in Brazil [13]. The organization employs approximately 550 people in permanent positions.

4.1   Research Subjects

The data were collected in a non-probabilistic way and included all the employees of the government agency. This was accomplished by sending an e-mail containing a web link of the survey to all the permanent employees of the TCE-MT. The application process lasted 30 days and 141 answered were received.

By the end of the survey evaluation, 118 responses were considered to be valid. The average age of the survey respondents was 40 years old, and 55% of respondents reported to own a higher education degree and some type of post-graduate degree.

Table 2. Factors/theorists/assertions.

Factors and theorists	Assertions
Process-oriented organizational culture: [2, 12, 25, 26, 30, 31]	QC02 - Employees strive to constantly improve institutional processes
	QC03 - Leaders regularly invite employees to think of ideas for improving institutional processes
	QC13 - Sector leaders are open to radical changes for improving the performance of institutional processes
	QC14 - Managers regularly encourage interdepartmental meetings to discuss improvements in institutional processes
Information technology: [7, 20, 21]	QTI02 - Do you know if process management tools are used in the organization?
	QTI03 - Do you effectively use any process management tool in your work in the organization?
Governance: [8, 19, 20, 27, 29]	QG01 - Institutional Processes are clearly defined in the organization
	QG02 - Clear definition of which employees are responsible for the organization's institutional processes
	QG03 - Decisions regarding the organization's institutional processes are transparent
Performance: [2, 21, 27]	QD02 - Performance indicators are regularly reported within the organization
	QD04 - Organizational performance indicators are measurable
	QD0 - Organizational performance indicators are used as an tool for constant improvement
	QD06 - The organization regularly invests in improving the quality of its institutional processes
Strategic Alignment: [1, 3, 14, 28]	QAE01 - Senior management is actively involved in efforts to improve processes
	QAE02 - The goals of the organization's institutional processes originate from and are associated with the organization's strategy

(continued)

Table 2. (*continued*)

Factors and theorists	Assertions
	QAE04 - Improvements in the organization's institutional processes are collectively discussed
People: [2, 29]	QP02 - Changes in the organization's processes are satisfactorily communicated to employees
	QP03 - Employees regularly attend training in process management
	QP05 - Employees discuss ways of improving processes they are involved in with their colleagues and leaders

Table 3. Group of CFA indicators.

	Strategic alignment	Culture	Governance	Performance	People	Information technology
Strategic alignment	**0.904**					
Culture	0.808	**0.825**				
Governance	0.852	0.803	**0.888**			
Performance	0.843	0.797	0.807	**0.863**		
People	0.765	0.787	0.755	0.726	**0.830**	
Information technology	0.542	0.540	0.622	0.619	0.611	**0.882**
Cronbach's alpha	0.888	0.842	0.866	0.886	0.774	0.736
Composite reliability	0.931	0.895	0.918	0.921	0.869	0.875
Average variance extracted	0.818	0.681	0.789	0.745	0.688	0.778

4.2   Analyses

This section presents the results of applying the Confirmatory Factor Analysis (CFA) and Structural Equations.

Confirmatory Factor Analysis. For this analysis, the latent variables were modeled reflexively and, for this reason, before evaluating the structural coefficients, the authors assessed: convergent validity, discriminant validity and construct reliability [11, 15].

The software used was Smart-PLS version 3.2.7, following the recommendation of Brown [4]. For each latent variable that was identified, indicators were assigned. Among the factors, structural arrows were included so that all dimensions could be interconnected.

Adjustments to the model and analysis of results followed the recommendations of Hair et al. [11], which determines that the factor loads are higher than 0.70. The CFA was used to evaluate which items possessed construct validity and reliability, those which presented low factor loads (lack of convergent validity and reliability) were excluded from the scale. Indicators that presented high cross-loading were also excluded because, according to Hair et al. [11], they may indicate lack of discriminant validity. Table 3 summarizes the indicators of the adjusted tool.

The results reveal that all indicators were satisfactory and that the tool presented convergent and discriminant validity. For Marôco et al. [18] discriminant validity is an important indicator of the quality of the model adjustment, since it determines if there is multicollinearity between variables. In order to test the tool, latent variables were modeled in the reflexive mode [11, 15]. The software used was SmartPLS version 3.2.7, following the recommendation of Ringle, Wende and Becker.

The model adjustment and subsequent result analysis followed the recommendations of [11], who suggest that the factor loads of the variables should be higher than 0.70. It is also observed that the Average Variance Extracted should present indexes that are greater than 0.50.

Analysis of Structural Equations. After the tool was debugged and validated, an Analysis of Structural Equations was developed. The structural model was created based on theory and is represented in Fig. 1. This model allowed the authors to test the hypotheses.

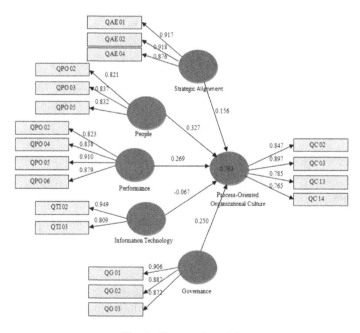

Fig. 1. Structural model.

The structural coefficients were estimated by bootstrap, considering a sample of 118 observations and 3,000 resamples, in order to obtain the distribution test t [6].

Table 4. Structural model metrics.

	Coefficients	standard error	Test T	Hypothesis test
Strategic alignment	0.156	0.127	1.229	Rejected H1
Governance	0.250	0.112	2.231	Confirmed H2
Performance	0.269	0.129	2.094	Confirmed H3
People	0.327	0.090	3.642	Confirmed H4
Information technology	−0.067	0.075	0.883	Rejected H5

Therefore, it can be inferred that the Governance, Performance and People factors directly impact Process-Oriented Organizational Culture, considering the outlook of the TCE-MT employees who participated in the research.

Hypotheses H2, H3 and H4 were confirmed, considering $p < 0.05$ for Process-Oriented Culture. In this way it can be inferred that the Governance, Performance and People factors directly impact the Process-Oriented Organizational Culture, considering the vision of the TCE-MT collaborators who participated in the research.

5   Conclusions

There is a shortage in the supply of tools that evaluate the critical factors that are able to influence Process Management strategies. Therefore, this study sought to develop a tool that would be able to assess the relationship between the following dimensions: Process-Oriented Organizational Culture; Information Technology; Governance; Performance; Strategic Alignment; and People.

After consecutive stages of tool assessments deploying Confirmatory Factor Analysis, a 7-point Likert scale with 19 assertions was validated, as can be seen in Table 2. The end tool demonstrated reliability, convergent validity and discriminant validity, as evidenced through the analysis of the indicators presented in Table 4.

The test of the theoretical-structural model of the research revealed that the Governance, Performance and People constructs display a direct relationship with the Process-Oriented Organizational Culture construct. The indicators presented in Table 4 confirm the research hypotheses H2, H3 and H5 and refute the hypotheses H1 and H5.

Considering the data, it is assumed that organizations that have acquired a greater level of maturity in the Governance, Performance and People factors are more likely to successfully implement Process Management policies. On the other hand, it can be inferred that the factors Strategic Alignment and Information Technology have not directly impacted Process-Oriented Organizational Culture, according to employees' view.

In terms of scientific research, this study suffers certain limitations. The first is the use of only six factors that were more substantiated in the literature for the implementation of process management strategies in organizations. Another limitation is the lack of analysis of the degree of involvement of the researched subjects with the organization's processes.

Yet another limitation of the research is analyzing a single case, which limits the amplitude of the study. A suggestion for future research is to expand the scope of researched institutions.

As a practical contribution, the application of this research tool is a way of reflecting about the potential implementation of a process-oriented management model, while seeking ways to improve its management.

Finally, it is worth mentioning the methodological contribution of this research with the development of a research tool that makes it possible to measure critical factors that potentially impact the implementation of a Process Management strategy. Moreover, the use of the Process-Oriented Organizational Culture factor as a proxy for executing a Process Management strategy may allow a pre-implementation diagnosis.

In Memoriam. We would like to dedicate this paper to José Carlos Marques – our co-author, our colleague, our friend – who fatally passed away and could not seeits final version accepted and published.

Acknowledgements. We would like to thank the UFMT, TCE-MT and Uniselva Foundation for all the support to develop and publish this research.

References

1. Bai, C., Sarkis, J.: Grey-based DEMATEL model for evaluating business process management critical success factors. Int. J. Prod. Econ. **146**(1), 281–292 (2013)
2. Bandara, W., Alibabaei, A., Aghdasi, M.: Means of achieving business process management success factors. In: 4th Australasian Conference on Information Systems (ACIS 2009) [Electronic Resource], on Proceedings, pp. 1–17. Athens University of Economics and Business, Athens (2009)
3. Bandara, W., Gable, G.G., Rosemann, M.: Critical success factors of business process modeling. In: Working Paper, pp. 1–32 (2007). https://eprints.qut.edu.au/8755/. Accessed 10 Nov 2017
4. Brown, T.A.: Confirmatory Factor Analysis for Applied Research. The Guilford Press, New York (2006)
5. Buh, B., Kovačič, A., Indihar Štemberger, M.: Critical success factors for different stages of business process management adoption–a case study. Econ. Res. - Ekonomska istraživanja **28**(1), 243–57 (2015)
6. Cruz, A.P.C., Frezatti, F., Bido, D.S.: Estilo de liderança, controle gerencial e inovação: Papel das alavancas de controle. RAC-Revista de Administração Contemporânea **19**(6), 772–794 (2015)
7. De Haes, S., Van Grembergen, W.: An exploratory study into IT governance implementations and its impact on business/IT alignment. Inf. Syst. Manag. **26**(2), 123–137 (2009)
8. Goeke, R.J., Antonucci, Y.L.: Differences in business process management leadership and deployment: is there a connection to industry affiliation? Inf. Resourc. Manag. J. (IRMJ) **26** (2), 43–63 (2013)
9. Groznik, A., Maslaric, M.: Investigating the impact of information sharing in a two-level supply chain using business process modeling and simulations: a case study. In: Proceedings of 23rd European Conference on Modelling and Simulation ECMS, pp. 39–45 (2009)

10. Guha, S., Kettinger, W.J., Teng, J.T.: Business process reengineering: building a comprehensive methodology. Inf. Syst. Manag. **10**(3), 13–22 (1993)
11. Hair, J.F., Babin, B., Money, A., Samouel, P.: Fundamentos de métodos de pesquisa em administração. Bookman, Porto Alegre (2005)
12. Hajo, A.R.: Implementing BPM systems: the role of process orientation. Bus. Process Manag. J. **12**(4), 389–409 (2006)
13. Girata, N.N.H, Maciel, C.: eGov website evolution study within strategic planning. In: 15th Annual International Conference on Proceedings of the 15th Annual International Conference on Digital Government Research - dg.o 2014, pp. 69–78. ACM Press, Aguascalientes (2014)
14. Hung, R.Y.Y.: Business process management as competitive advantage: a review and empirical study. Total Qual. Manag. Bus. Excell. **17**(1), 21–40 (2006)
15. Jarvis, C.B., Mackenzie, S.B., Podsakoff, P.M.: A critical review of construct indicators and measurement model misspecification in marketing and consumer research. J. Consum. Res. **30**(2), 199–218 (2003)
16. Lee, R.G., Dale, B.G.: Business process management: a review and evaluation. Bus. Process Manag. J. **4**(3), 214–225 (1998)
17. Lee, S., Ahn, H.: Assessment of process improvement from organizational change. Inf. Manag. **45**(5), 270–280 (2008)
18. Marôco, J.: Análise de equações estruturais: Fundamentos teóricos, software & aplicações. 2nd edn. ReportNumber, Pêro Pinheiro (2014)
19. Niehaves, B., Plattfaut, R., Becker, J.: Business process management capabilities in local governments: a multi-method study. Gov. Inf. Q. **30**(3), 217–225 (2013)
20. Rahimi, F., Møller, C., Hvam, L.: Business process management and IT management: the missing integration. Int. J. Inf. Manag. **36**(1), 142–154 (2016)
21. Ravesteyn, P., Batenburg, R.: Surveying the critical success factors of BPM-systems implementation. Bus. Process Manag. J. **16**(3), 492–507 (2010)
22. Ravesteyn, P., Versendaal, J.: Success factors of business process management systems implementation. In: 18th Australasian Conference on Information Systems (ACIS 2007) [Electronic Resource], on Proceedings, pp. 396–405. University of Southern Queensland, Toowoomba (2007)
23. Rohloff, M.: Case study and maturity model for business process management implementation. In: Dayal, U., Eder, J., Koehler, J., Reijers, H.A. (eds.) BPM 2009. LNCS, vol. 5701, pp. 128–142. Springer, Heidelberg (2009). https://doi.org/10.1007/978-3-642-03848-8_10
24. Rosemann, M.; De Bruin, T.: Application of a holistic model for determining BPM maturity. BP Trends, pp. 1–21 (2005). https://www.bptrends.com/publicationfiles/. Accessed 10 Nov 2017
25. Rosemann, M., Vom Brocke, J.: The six core elements of business process management. In: Vom Brocke, J., Rosemann, M. (eds.) Handbook on business Process Management, pp. 105–122. Springer, Heidelberg (2010). https://doi.org/10.1007/978-3-642-00416-2_5
26. Schein, E.H.: Organizational Culture and Leadership, 3rd edn. Wiley, San Francisco (2004)
27. Škrinjar, R., Trkman, P.: Increasing process orientation with business process management: Critical practices. Int. J. Inf. Manag. **33**(1), 48–60 (2013)
28. Thompson, G., Seymour, L.F., O'Donovan, B.: Towards a BPM success model: an analysis in South African financial services organisations. In: Halpin, T., et al. (eds.) BPMDS/EMMSAD -2009. LNBIP, vol. 29, pp. 1–13. Springer, Heidelberg (2009). https://doi.org/10.1007/978-3-642-01862-6_1
29. Trkman, P.: The critical success factors of business process management. Int. J. Inf. Manag. **30**(2), 125–134 (2010)

30. Vom Brocke, J., Sinnl, T.: Culture in business process management: a literature review. Bus. Process Manag. J. **17**(2), 357–378 (2011)
31. Willaert, P., Van den Bergh, J., Willems, J., Deschoolmeester, D.: The process-oriented organisation: a holistic view developing a framework for business process orientation maturity. In: Alonso, G., Dadam, P., Rosemann, M. (eds.) BPM 2007. LNCS, vol. 4714, pp. 1–15. Springer, Heidelberg (2007). https://doi.org/10.1007/978-3-540-75183-0_1
32. Lönn, C.-M., Uppström, E.: Process management challenges in swedish public sector: a bottom up initiative. In: Wimmer, M.A., Janssen, M., Scholl, H.J. (eds.) EGOV 2013. LNCS, vol. 8074, pp. 212–223. Springer, Heidelberg (2013). https://doi.org/10.1007/978-3-642-40358-3_18
33. de Oliveira, L.K.B., Maciel, C.: Transparency and social control via the citizen's portal: a case study with the use of triangulation. In: Kő, A., Leitner, C., Leitold, H., Prosser, A. (eds.) EGOVIS/EDEM 2013. LNCS, vol. 8061, pp. 112–124. Springer, Heidelberg (2013). https://doi.org/10.1007/978-3-642-40160-2_10

Challenges in e-Government Technology and e-voting

Improving Opinion Analysis Through Statistical Disclosure Control in eVoting Scenarios

Pol Blasco[1], José Moreira[2,3], Jordi Puiggalí[4], Jordi Cucurull[4(✉)],
and David Rebollo-Monedero[2]

[1] Marfeel Solutions S.L., Barcelona, Spain
pol.blasco@marfeel.com
[2] Universitat Politècnica de Catalunya, Barcelona, Spain
{jose.moreira,david.rebollo}@entel.upc.edu
[3] University of Birmingham, Birmingham, UK
j.moreira-sanchez@cs.bham.ac.uk
[4] Scytl Secure Electronic Voting S.A., Barcelona, Spain
{jordi.puiggali,jordi.cucurull}@scytl.com

Abstract. This work addresses the problem of Statistical Disclosure Control (SDC) on an electronic voting scenario. Electoral datasets containing voting choices linked to voters demographic profile information, can be used to perform fine-grained analysis of citizen opinion. However, it is strongly required to protect voters' privacy. Traditional SDC techniques study methods to met some predefined privacy criteria, assuming a trustworthy owner that knows the values of the confidential attributes. Unfortunately, this assumption cannot be made in our scenario, since its dataset contains secret voting choices, which are unknown until they are properly anonymized and decrypted. We propose a protocol and a system architecture to perform SDC in datasets with encrypted attributes, while minimizing the amount of information an attacker can learn about the secret data. The protocol enables the release of electoral datasets, which allow governments and third parties to gain more insight into citizen opinion, and improve decision making processes and public services.

Keywords: Statistical disclosure control · Electronic voting
Open data

1 Introduction

Governments are improving their decision making processes by gathering citizen opinion with participative processes such as surveys, referendums or consultations. Privacy concerns in these processes are similar to those in elections. Therefore, citizen privacy has to be preserved and their opinion kept secret until the end of the process. However, the participative processes objective is to gather citizen opinion, not to select a representative. For this reason, the fine analysis of the results is of paramount importance in order to gain information that

© Springer Nature Switzerland AG 2018
A. Kő and E. Francesconi (Eds.): EGOVIS 2018, LNCS 11032, pp. 45–59, 2018.
https://doi.org/10.1007/978-3-319-98349-3_4

goes beyond the aggregated opinions. For instance, it is interesting to identify population subsets, e.g., young people, that do not share the population's majority preference. This allows governments to consider minority groups in order to achieve maximums consensus in the policy and decision making.

In order to keep the link between the participation and voters' opinion datasets secret [11], statistical analysis in traditional opinion gathering processes is done over anonymous votes. Therefore, it is not possible to analyze the results based on voter profiles, such as gender, age or social status. Such analysis can only be based on participation information (e.g., percentage of young voters that participated) or on geolocation (e.g., opinion of citizens from a specific region). In electronic voting, voter privacy is usually guaranteed by cryptographic mechanisms, e.g. by encrypting the vote before being cast.

Statistical disclosure control (SDC) techniques protect the privacy of datasets records once they are released [6,10], i.e. preventing, to some degree, matching an individual with his confidential information. Current techniques [12,13,17, 19] assume the dataset owner has access to its whole content, and that the records' privacy has to be protected only before releasing the dataset. However, in electronic voting scenarios [2,11] voter privacy is very important and must be protected even from election authorities and managers, who may have access to electoral datasets and/or the election private key. This presents new challenges, since SDC techniques have to be applied before vote contents are known.

In this paper, we analyze how SDC techniques can enable a detailed opinion analysis based on voter profiles, while protecting voter privacy. We propose an electronic counting SDC (EC-SDC) protocol that links voters profile information to their voting option, while protecting their privacy. EC-SDC processes the voters' information dataset, containing encrypted attributes, and outputs a dataset that fulfills the electronic voting voter privacy [11] and a predefined SDC privacy criterion [19]. As a result, the EC-SDC protocol can help improve data analysis and decision making processes in electronic voting scenarios.

2   Preliminaries

In this section we briefly review some concepts about electronic voting and SDC that are used in the rest of the paper. For a more complete discussion on these topics, we refer the reader, e.g., to [2,11] and [6,10], respectively.

2.1   Privacy in Electronic Voting

The following is a simplified description of a voting system (see Fig. 3):

- *Voting Client.* This is the software that executes the voting protocol at the voter's side. It prepares the encrypted, signed ballot with the voter's choice.
- *Voting Server.* This is the communication endpoint for the Voting Client. It performs voter authentication and ballot validation.

- *Bulletin Board.* It helps ensure election verifiability. Usually, a limited number of entities are allowed to write in it, e.g., the Voting Server, the Ballot Anonymization Module, and the Decryption Module.
- *Ballot Anonymization Module.* It helps ensure voter privacy by performing votes mixing or homomorphic aggregation. It can be cryptographically verifiable, it is independent from the election credentials and it can be safely delegated to external, untrusted service providers.
- *Decryption Module.* Performs the distributed decryption of the mixed ballots using the election private key provided by the Election Authorities.

An overview of the voting process for n voters is as follows:

1. Voter i authenticates to the Voting Server.
2. The Voting Client prepares a ballot y_i, as the encrypted chosen option v_i, and signs it with the voter's private key.
3. If the Voting Server concludes that the received ballot y_i is valid, it publishes the tuple (i, y_i) on the Bulletin Board.
4. Once the voting phase is closed, no more ballots are accepted.
5. The encrypted ballots $y_1, \ldots, y_n$, without voters' identities, are sent to the Ballot Anonymization Module and its output posted to the Bulletin Board.
6. The previous output is decrypted by the Election Authorities, usually with a distributed threshold decryption cryptosystem to prevent electoral fraud, and posted to the Bulletin Board. Finally, the election result is computed.

Voter privacy in electronic voting can be achieved by encrypting the vote and implementing an anonymization mechanism that prevents correlation between voters and decrypted votes. Voter anonymization mechanisms are implemented either during the voting process [8] or during vote decryption and counting [3,4,14]. The main assumption of the first mechanisms is that the encrypted votes received by the voting system cannot be correlated to the identity of the voter (e.g., two agency protocols), while the latter assume that this could be possible but not necessary (e.g., homomorphic tally and mixnet-based systems). Since we are interested in having access to voter's profile information, we focus our proposal on the second set of anonymization mechanisms, executed during decryption and counting. This is equivalent to the situation of postal votes, where the outer envelopes can be linked to the voter identity until the vote is put in the ballot box for counting. The strict privacy and verifiability requirements of traditional electronic voting schemes [1,5,11] make impossible to conduct detailed statistical analysis using the released information (participation and opinion datasets). Our proposal addresses this situation, so that third parties can gain more utility, while accepting some admissible, arbitrarily small increase in the privacy risk.

2.2   SDC and Microaggregation

There are two obvious extreme cases in the privacy-utility balance of a released dataset. On one hand, the maximum utility –and minimum privacy– is attained if the owner releases the whole unprocessed dataset. At the other end, the maximum privacy –and minimum utility– is reached when the owner does not make accessible the sensible information on the released dataset.

SDC is about the processing (distorting) of datasets containing sensitive information, and how to balance data privacy and data utility between the two extreme cases above [6,10]. Each record in the dataset contains a set of attributes that are classified as *identifiers, key attributes* and *confidential attributes*. Key attributes contain demographic information, such as age and gender, which may be used to link an individual to a record in the dataset. On the other hand, confidential attributes contain sensitive, private information, such as religion or political preferences. The protection of the records in the released dataset is measured under a predefined *privacy criterion*, and the aim is to satisfy this criterion while minimizing the *distortion* introduced on the data.

An important, well-known privacy criterion is that of *k-anonymity* [18]. A dataset is *k*-anonymous if each combination of key attributes is shared by at least *k* records. A set of records that share the same key attributes is called a *cluster*. Hence, *k*-anonymity requires that each record in the dataset belongs to a cluster of size at least *k*. However, while *k*-anonymity protects the exact identification of a record in the dataset, it does not prevent the disclosure of confidential attributes. For example, consider a cluster whose records have the same values for the confidential attributes. The shortcomings of *k*-anonymity motivated the design of more elaborated privacy criteria that take into account the confidential attributes [12,13,17,19]. In this work we focus on the *p-sensitive k-anonymity* criterion [19], which requires that the dataset is *k*-anonymous, and that each cluster has at least *p* different values of each confidential attribute.

On the other hand, the dataset distortion is defined as some distance measure between the key attributes of the original and the perturbed datasets. More formally, consider an input and an output (perturbed) datasets

$$D_{\text{in}} = \{(i, x_i, v_i)\}_{i=1}^n, \qquad D_{\text{out}} = \{(\hat{x}_i, v_i)\}_{i=1}^n,$$

respectively, where for the *i*th entry, x_i is the array of key attributes, v_i is the array of confidential attributes, and $\hat{x}_i$ is the array of perturbed key attributes. For the particular case of ℓ numerical key attributes, each x_i and $\hat{x}_i$ can be viewed as vectors in the ℓ-dimensional Euclidean space. The distortion is measured as:

$$\frac{1}{\ell n} \sum_{i=1}^n d^2(x_i, \hat{x}_i), \tag{1}$$

where d is the usual Euclidean distance between vectors. For the case of categorical or mixed categorical and numerical key attributes, one should consider appropriate definitions for distance and distortion [7,18].

With the privacy and distortion measures defined, the problem is to transform the dataset into a new dataset that meets the privacy criterion and minimizes the distortion. This problem has been shown to be NP-hard [15]. Therefore, *microaggregation algorithms* provide heuristic methods to obtain an approximate solution, e.g., [7,17]. These algorithms operate in two steps: first grouping the records into clusters, and then perturbing the key attributes within each cluster.

In the clustering step, microaggregation algorithms group similar records, in terms of the distance measure, into N disjoint clusters $S_1, \ldots, S_N$, which satisfy the privacy criterion. For convenience, we identify a cluster S_j by the subset of record indexes that it contains, i.e., $S_j \subseteq \{1, \ldots, n\}$. In the perturbation step the algorithms compute the *centroid* of each cluster, which is defined, for numerical arrays of key attributes, as the average of the arrays within each cluster

$$\hat{x}(j) = \frac{1}{|S_j|} \sum_{i \in S_j} x_i, \qquad \text{for } j = 1, \ldots, N. \tag{2}$$

In the released dataset the array of key attributes of each record i is replaced by its cluster centroid. That is, records in cluster S_j are assigned the array of key attributes $\hat{x}(j)$. Formally, $\hat{x}_i = \hat{x}(j)$ such that $i \in S_j$. Hence, the records within a cluster become indistinguishable from each other.

One of the most commonly used microaggregation algorithms to achieve k-anonymity is the maximum distance to average vector (MDAV) [7], which executes the clustering step iteratively. Most of the existing microaggregation algorithms execute the clustering phase using not only key attributes, but also confidential attributes [12,13,17,19]. However, in our scenario, the confidential attributes, i.e., the voting options, are also *secret* (encrypted), and its content cannot be accessed by the algorithm. A recent related result [16] deals with the problem of achieving k-anonymity on electoral datasets, where the presence of each participant is uncertain, through the execution of a pre-election microaggregation process. In contrast, the goal of our proposal is to define a post-election microaggregation process that achieves p-sensitive k-anonymity without uncertain presence, but with secret attributes.

3 Problem Formulation

We assume that a total of n voters have cast a valid and correct vote. Moreover, we also assume the existence of a Statistical Data Provider (SDP) which enables public access to voters' identities and key attributes, $\{(i, x_i)\}_{i=1}^n$, e.g., census data. Additionally, the SDP also supplies a probability mass function (pmf) of the voters' voting preferences, which could be obtained from exit polls or electoral surveys.

Hence, the Election Authorities posses an input dataset of n records $D_{\text{in}} = \{(i, x_i, y_i)\}_{i=1}^n$, each composed of the voter identity i, a vector of key attributes x_i and a secret attribute y_i, which is the encryption of the voting option v_i. Our goal is to transform this dataset into another that is p-sensitive k-anonymous, while minimizing the distortion introduced.

The verifiability constraints of the underlying voting protocol requires that we output two collections: a collection of N clusters of voters' identities, $\mathcal{S} = \{S_1, \ldots, S_N\}$, and a collection of multisets of decrypted votes, $\mathcal{V} = \{V_1, \ldots V_N\}$.

Input dataset D_{in} (Identifiers: Name; Key Attributes (x_i): Age, Gender, Hourly Wage; Secret Attribute (y_i): Encrypted Vote)

Name	Age	Gender	Hourly Wage	Encrypted Vote
Charlie	26	M	\$30	Enc[A]
Ava	35	F	\$28	Enc[B]
Hugo	47	M	\$45	Enc[A]
Emma	21	F	\$18	Enc[C]
Grace	40	F	\$48	Enc[B]
Benjamin	34	M	\$40	Enc[A]
Daniel	42	M	\$45	Enc[B]
Finn	30	M	\$25	Enc[A]
Isabella	28	F	\$27	Enc[B]

Output dataset D_{out} (Identifiers: Name; Key Attributes (x_i): Age, Gender, Hourly Wage; Confidential Attribute (v_i): Vote)

	Name	Age	Gender	Hourly Wage	Vote	
S_1	Emma	21	F	\$18	A B C	V_1
	Charlie	26	M	\$30		
	Isabella	28	F	\$27		
S_2	Finn	30	M	\$25	B A A	V_2
	Benjamin	34	M	\$40		
	Ava	35	F	\$28		
S_3	Grace	40	F	\$48	A B B	V_3
	Daniel	42	M	\$45		
	Hugo	47	M	\$45		

Fig. 1. Example of input and output datasets. The input dataset contains secret attributes, whereas the output dataset contains the decrypted confidential attributes grouped in multisets.

(Suppressed Identifiers: Name; Perturbed Key Attributes ($\hat{x}_i$): Age, Gender, Hourly Wage; Confidential Attribute (v_i): Vote)

Name	Age	Gender	Hourly Wage	Vote	
---	25	F	\$25	A	V_1
---	25	F	\$25	B	
---	25	F	\$25	C	
---	33	M	\$31	A	V_2
---	33	M	\$31	A	
---	33	M	\$31	B	
---	43	M	\$46	A	V_3
---	43	M	\$46	B	
---	43	M	\$46	B	

Fig. 2. Example of output dataset without identifiers and with centroid substitution. The dataset is 2-sensitive 3-anonymous.

The votes in V_j correspond to the voting preferences cast by the voters in S_j. The implied dataset, D_{out}, can be constructed by combining $\mathcal{V}$ and $\mathcal{S}$ with the content of the SDP, and it is expected to meet the privacy criterion. An example of input and output datasets is depicted in Fig. 1.

A clarification is probably in order at this point. Since D_{out} discloses the exact identifiers and key attributes of the voters, one might raise privacy concerns about releasing it. Such an specific output is provided for the verifiability and auditability of the underlying electronic voting protocol, and to the public availability of the SDP. Nonetheless, D_{out} is in conformity with the customary worst-case assumption in the SDC literature. Such assumption states that an attacker (with background information or access to the SDP) is able to re-identify the individuals within a cluster. As long as the exact relationship with the records and their confidential attributes remains uncertain, the privacy is not compromised. Hence, D_{out} does not provide extra information on the key attributes other than what the attacker already knows. In practically relevant cases, where the SDP is not public and the attacker does not has full access to it, the Election Authorities could simply release the perturbed version of D_{out}, as shown in Fig. 2. However, for a worst case threat assessment we should consider the original version of D_{out}.

Therefore, we would like to find the optimal number of clusters N and the optimal partition of the voters' set S, such that the distortion of D_{out} is minimized. These optimal values of N and S depends on the voters' voting preferences, on the values of k and p, and on the distortion measure.

Also, during the protocol execution, and to fulfill the voter privacy requirement, the Election Authorities must not have access to the confidential attribute v_i freely. That is, even though D_{out} has to adhere to a reasonable privacy criterion, the Election Authorities must not gain significantly more information about any particular voter than what could be gained from observing D_{out}.

Combining these requirements (i.e., satisfying the privacy measure while not having access to the plain confidential attributes) poses new challenges that links the fields of electronic voting and SDC.

3.1   Threat Model

Since we assume the voting phase is closed, we exclude from our analysis the threat model associated to the underlying electronic voting protocol.

Conventional attacks in SDC scenarios include: homogeneity (or similarity), skewness, and background-knowledge attacks [7,17]. It is assumed that, in a worst-case scenario, attackers know all the publicly available information from the SDP and the released dataset D_{out}. In particular, they know the correspondence between voters' identifiers and clusters. Nonetheless, they cannot link a confidential attribute with the associated identifier within a cluster.

In an EC-SDC scenario, we can classify the attackers into three categories:

- *External attackers.* Any kind of attacker that does not participate in the execution of the protocol, and is willing to break voter's privacy, e.g., identify how a voter voted. He will use only the publicly available information.
- *Malicious collaborative entities.* Entities which execute delegated, computationally demanding tasks (such as vote mixing), but they do not possess decryption key shares. Besides any public available data, they can also have access to some intermediate, not publicly available computations.
- *Malicious authorities.* Election Authorities with the decryption key shares, with access to the output of the Decryption Module, even if this output is not published in the Bulletin Board, and to the data the other attackers can access. Our trust model assumes that any additional information that these entities could gain will only be used privately, and not made public.

The goal of our protocol is that the information it generates does not enable external attackers nor malicious collaborative entities to gain more information than the one gained in a traditional SDC process. Unfortunately, this goal cannot be fully achieved for the case of malicious authorities. In this case, we will strive to minimize the amount of additional information that they can gain.

4 Architecture Design and Workflow

In this section we describe how the EC-SDC protocol is integrated into a suitable voting scheme, as described in Sect. 2.1. Again, the aim is to release a p-sensitive k-anonymous dataset D_{out}, such that the distortion compared to the input dataset D_{in} is small, while minimizing the amount of information that the EC-SDC entities can gain with respect the information released.

An overview of the EC-SDC protocol is as follows. The process starts once the voting phase is closed. Based on data available from the voting process, and from public census data, a cluster size is estimated. Next, a microaggregation algorithm is executed using this cluster size, and the voters are grouped into k-anonymous clusters. The output of this process is made public. Then, each cluster is independently anonymized and its ballots decrypted. In a first iteration, this decryption is not made public, since the privacy criterion is not guaranteed to be satisfied for all the records. Using this information, the original clusters are modified in order to satisfy the p-sensitive k-anonymous requirement. These new clusters are, again, anonymized, and finally decrypted and made public.

4.1 Entities Involved

The entities involved are, on one hand, those described in Sect. 2.1. However, two of them require minor changes in order to cope with the requirements of the EC-SDC protocol. The Ballot Anonymization Module must be able to execute clustered anonymization. And the Decryption Module must group the decrypted votes into multisets $V_1, \ldots, V_N$ of prescribed voters, and it has to execute two decryption processes instead of a single one. Additionally, the following new entities take part in the EC-SDC protocol:

- *Statistical Data Provider.* It publicly distributes census and statistical data, relating voter identities with their corresponding key attributes, $\{(i, x_i)\}_{i=1}^n$.
- *SDC Cluster Size Estimation Module.* It is controlled by the Election Authorities, who specify the p-sensitive k-anonymity criterion. It executes the SDC_KEst algorithm below to obtain an estimated cluster size $k_{\text{est}} \geq k$.
- *SDC Microaggregation Module.* It executes the SDC_Microaggregation algorithm, making public its output, i.e., the partition of the voters into clusters.
- *SDC Privacy Enforcement Module.* It works close to the Decryption Module. It executes the SDC_PrivacyEnforce algorithm, which modifies the collection of clusters computed by the SDC Microaggregation Module $\mathcal{S}$ to meet the privacy criterion. The new partition of the voter set $\mathcal{S}'$ is also made public.

4.2 Algorithms

The set of algorithms introduced by the EC-SDC protocol are:

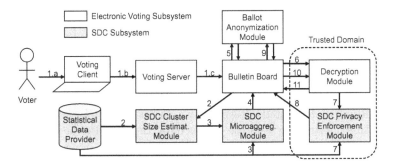

Fig. 3. Workflow of the EC-SDC protocol.

SDC_KEst(π, p, k) $\rightarrow k_{est}$: Using a pmf of voting preferences π, and the privacy parameters p, k, it estimates a minimum cluster size $k_{est} \geq k$ so that, with high probability, there is a small number of non p-sensitive k-anonymous clusters. The details of this algorithm can be found in the Appendix.

SDC_Microaggregate(D_{in}, k_{est}) $\rightarrow \mathcal{S}'$: It executes the MDAV microaggregation algorithm from [7], which uses only the key attributes from the dataset provided by the Statistical Data Provider D_{in}. Its output is a preliminary partition $\mathcal{S}' = \{S'_1, \ldots, S'_{N'}\}$ of the set of voters into N' clusters that are k_{est}-anonymous. It heuristically strives to minimize the distortion introduced.

ClusteredAnonymize($\mathcal{S}, (y_1, \ldots, y_n)$) $\rightarrow (Y_1, \ldots, Y_N)$: It receives a collection of N clusters $\mathcal{S}$, and the array of cast ballots $(y_1, \ldots, y_n)$, and executes an independent anonymization process for each cluster $S_j \in \mathcal{S}$. It outputs the corresponding anonymized ballot tokens Y_j, and any required cryptographic proof. Each Y_j is the output of, e.g. an homomorphic aggregation or a mixing.

SDC_PrivacyEnforce($D_{in}, p, k, \mathcal{S}', \mathcal{V}$) $\rightarrow \mathcal{S}$: It receives the preliminary partition $\mathcal{S}'$ of N' clusters, and the corresponding collection of decrypted votes multisets $\mathcal{V}$. Then it identifies any cluster $S'_j \in \mathcal{S}'$ that fails to satisfy the p-sensitive k-anonymity requirement. Next, it merges each such cluster with the closest p-sensitive k-anonymous cluster, in terms of centroid distance, and assigns a new centroid to the cluster. The output is a (possibly) modified set of $N \leq N'$ clusters $\mathcal{S} = \{S_1, \ldots, S_N\}$ satisfying the privacy criterion.

4.3   Overall Workflow

The workflow of the EC-SDC protocol, depicted in Fig. 3, is as follows:

1. Voter i, Voting Client and Voting Server follow the electronic voting protocol. The tuple voter identifier-ballot (i, y_i) is posted in the Bulletin Board.
2. The SDC Cluster Size Estimation Module reads the information from the Bulletin Board and the Statistical Data Provider, and executes SDC_KEst.
3. Using the cluster size estimation from the previous step, and the input dataset $D_{in} = \{(i, x_i, y_i)\}_{i=1}^{n}$, the SDC Microaggregation Module executes the algorithm SDC_Microsaggregate.

4. The output of the previous step, i.e. a preliminary partition of the voter identities into clusters $\mathcal{S}' = \{S'_1, \ldots, S'_{N'}\}$, is published in the Bulletin Board.
5. The Ballot Anonymization Module reads the Bulletin Board, and executes ClusteredAnonymize. It publishes the clustered anonymized ballot tokens back in the Bulletin Board, along with any required proof.
6. The Decryption module reads the output of the previous step, and obtains the multiset of decrypted votes for each cluster $\mathcal{V}' = \{V'_1, \ldots, V'_{N'}\}$.
7. Using this information, and the census data, the SDC Privacy Enforcement Module executes the SDC_PrivacyEnforce algorithm.
8. The (possibly new) partition of the voters' identities into clusters from the previous step $\mathcal{S} = \{S_1, \ldots, S_N\}$, is published in the Bulletin Board.
9. The Ballot Anonymization Module reads again the Bulletin Board, and executes ClusteredAnonymize for the new set of clusters. It also publishes the results in the Bulletin Board.
10. The Decryption Module reads again the information from the Bulletin Board, and decrypts the anonymized ballots produced in the last iteration.
11. Finally, the Decryption Module publishes the collections of clusters $\mathcal{S} = \{S_1, \ldots, S_N\}$, and multisets of decrypted votes $\mathcal{V} = \{V_1, \ldots, V_N\}$, with the proofs of correct decryption.

The output dataset D_{out} is therefore implied by grouping the records in D_{in} according to the clustered identifiers from $\mathcal{S}$, and associating the corresponding confidential attributes from $\mathcal{V}$.

4.4   Threat Assessment

In this section we show how the EC-SDC protocol mitigates the threats identified in Sect. 3.1. First note that the protocol does not run a conventional microaggregation process using the confidential attributes $v_1, \ldots, v_n$, since it only has access to the secret attributes $y_1, \ldots, y_n$. Hence, the best it can do is to estimate in Step 2 a cluster size so that, with high probability, almost all the clusters computed in Step 3 are p-sensitive k-anonymous. Once the corresponding votes are anonymized, the Election Authorities proceed to decrypt them using the distributed decryption algorithm.

The Election Authorities have access to the decrypted, but unpublished, preliminary multisets V'_j in Step 6. At this step, it might be the case that some of the clusters fail to be p-sensitive. For this reason, the cluster size is estimated so that this event occurs with an arbitrarily small probability (see the Appendix at the end of this document). Moreover, this event occurs randomly, and a malicious authority cannot choose arbitrarily the identity the voters whose privacy is at risk. Although this events have a small probability of occurring, we require the trust assumption that even if they happen, they are not going to be published by the Election Authorities, and hence their consideration as a Trusted Domain.

The potential break on the privacy criterion in Step 6 justifies that the decryption cannot be published at a first stage. Since the system possesses the decrypted votes of each cluster, these can be merged to satisfy the privacy criterion. The new clusters are anonymized again to break the correlation for any external observer. Thus, an external observer has access only to the voters belonging to a cluster S_j and the corresponding multiset of votes V_j, but the exact correspondence within a cluster is unknown to him. Hence, the privacy criterion is fulfilled. This is also true for a malicious collaborative entity from the Ballot Anonymization Module, which has no access to the preliminary decryption.

5   Numerical Results

In order to show the potential applications and trade-offs of the EC-SDC protocol, we study numerically a synthetic dataset. Note that due to the strong protections of voters' privacy, there are no public datasets containing individual-level demographic data linked to the individual voting option.

The input dataset D_{in} has a total of $n = 50.000$ records, and each record is identified by $\ell = 10$ key attributes and a single secret attribute, which corresponds to the voting option. We have considered a total of 3 numerical key attributes: age, annual income, and commuting time; and 7 categorical key attributes: gender, education, employment status, health status, marital status, region of residence, and district of residence type. Each categorical key attribute has a limited number of possible values (e.g., marital status is either single, married, or divorced), while numerical key attributes are continuous values constrained to a range. We consider a total of $m = 9$ candidates (Candidate A to Candidate I), and that there are no null or blank votes.

To generate the population, we associate a pmf to each key attribute and voting option. The dataset is built by generating n records whose key attributes and vote options are sampled independently according to the pmf's. In order to account for the fact that voters with similar key attributes have similar voting preferences, we generate 13 voter profiles, each with its own key attributes and voting option pmf's, and merge the resulting populations into a single dataset.

We compare the anonymized dataset D_{out} with the original dataset D_{in} considering that, in this experimental scenario, we can access to the individual decrypted votes v_i to assess the trade-offs introduced by the EC-SDC protocol. As is customary for SDC applications [7], we use the Euclidean and Hamming distances for the numerical and categorical attributes, respectively. We compute the total distance between two records as the weighted sum of the Euclidean distance, weighted by 4, and the Hamming distances of each categorical attribute, weighted by 1. While the numerical attributes of the centroids are computed using the average attribute (2), categorical attributes of the centroids are computed with the mode. The distortion is measured as the average square distance between records in D_{in} and centroids in D_{out}.

In Fig. 4 we present a case of use of the EC-SDC protocol. We compare the result of two queries executed both on the original dataset D_{in} and on the perturbed dataset D_{out}. In Fig. 4a we query about voting preferences for voters that live in Region 1, have employment status "retired" and health status

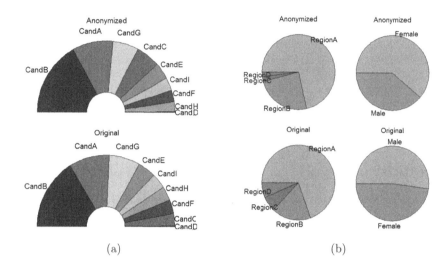

(a)   (b)

Fig. 4. Execution of different queries on the original and anonymized datasets: (a) voters' voting preferences, and (b) region of residence and gender.

"bad." Although the results in both datasets are quite similar, there are some differences, due to the distortion incurred in the anonymization process. For example, Candidates D and G are under-represented in the anonymized dataset. In Fig. 4b we query about the region and gender of the voters that support candidate A, between 50 and 60 years old, with an annual income between 25,000 and 35,000 EUR, whose commuting time is less than 30 min.

In Fig. 5a we study the proportion of clusters that are not p-sensitive versus the cluster size k. The value of k_{est}, as computed by the SDC_KEst algorithm, is shown with a marker symbol. In average, the proportion of such bad clusters is a decreasing function of k, and an increasing function of the privacy parameter p. Hence, it is important to remark that an adequate choice of k_{est} is of paramount importance to achieve low distortion and few privacy leak risks.

The utility-privacy trade-off is studied in Fig. 5b. The utility is shown for fixed values of k, i.e., $k = \{10, 50, 100\}$, and the estimated k_{est}. In general, the distortion increases (i.e., the utility decreases) as p grows up. The utility value of k_{est} is similar to that of $k = 10$ and $k = \{50, 100\}$ for small and large values of p, respectively; however, the utility value of k_{est} is higher for all other values of p. Hence, we conclude that the SDC_KEst algorithm estimates proper values for k_{est} and its utility is superior to other alternatives that use fixed values of k.

Finally, in Fig. 6, we consider that the voting preference pmf for the ith candidate is proportional to $\frac{1}{i^\gamma}$, i.e., it follows the Zipf's law with parameter γ. In particular, for $\gamma = 0$, the voting preference pmf is uniform, and becomes more skewed as γ increases. The figure shows the influence of the skewness parameter γ in the computation of k_{est} for several values of p. We note that the value of k_{est} increases with that of γ and with p. These results are as expected, since with a uniform distribution ($\gamma = 0$) requires a smaller cluster size to satisfy the p-sensitive property than a very skewed distribution.

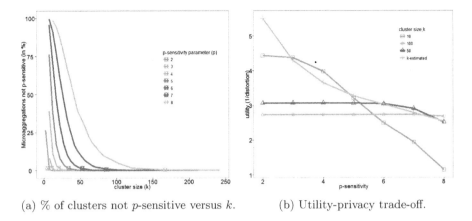

(a) % of clusters not p-sensitive versus k.   (b) Utility-privacy trade-off.

Fig. 5. Internal attacker privacy-leak risk and utility-privacy trade-off.

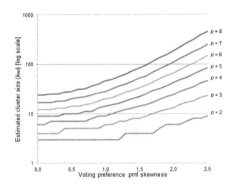

Fig. 6. k_{est} for different voting preference pmf and p-sensitive privacy criterion.

6   Conclusion

It is undeniable that detailed data analysis on large datasets can help governments and decision makers to take better decisions and offer better services. Citizen participative processes provide a largely underexploited, important source of information. Nonetheless, such information cannot be freely released. The main challenge that this scenario poses is that the citizen privacy has to be guaranteed from both a voting and a SDC perspective.

In this paper we have presented a method to perform detailed opinion analysis in electronic voting scenarios, based on voters' demographic profiles. Therefore, the protocol that we propose enables third parties to drill down into the opinion of specific collectives, while keeping a low voter privacy risk.

The protocol is designed to execute a SDC process on datasets with encrypted data. It strives to optimize some parameters in order to minimize the privacy leak risk. Under some assumptions regarding the voter profile the protocol is shown to satisfy the required privacy criteria.

Acknowledgments. The authors would like to thank Xavier Alsina and Alexey Akimov for their collaboration and helpful comments. This work has been partly supported by the Spanish Ministry of Industry, Energy and Tourism (MINETUR) through the "Acción Estratégica Economía y Sociedad Digital (AEESD)" funding plan, through Project ref. TSI-100202-2013-23 "Data-Distortion Framework (DDF)."

Appendix: Estimation of the Cluster Size

In order to execute the microaggregation algorithm in Step 3, an appropriate value of the cluster size must be estimated using the SDC_KEst algorithm.

Our procedure assumes that the votes are cast under a common voting profile $\pi = (\pi_1, \ldots, \pi_m)$. That is, each voter chooses option i with probability π_i. This information can be provided, e.g., by the Statistical Data Provider in the form of surveys or exit polls. We acknowledge that this is a quite strong assumption, but it is a necessary first step toward the problem nonetheless.

Let X_k be the m-ary vector r.v. that counts the number of votes cast for each of the m voting options in a cluster of size k. Therefore, X_k follows a multinomial distribution with parameters k and π. Additionally, let $W_k = \mathrm{wt}(X_k)$ denote the hamming weight of X_k, i.e., the number of nonzero positions in X_k. Then, a cluster fails to satisfy the p-sensitive privacy property whenever $W_k < p$. This event occurs with probability

$$\rho(k) = 1 - \Pr\{W_k \geq p\} = 1 - \sum_{x:\mathrm{wt}(x) \geq p} \frac{k!}{x_1! \cdots x_m!} \pi_1^{x_1} \ldots \pi_m^{x_m},$$

where the sum runs over all the m-ary vectors x of nonnegative integers whose components sum k. It is easy to see that $\Pr\{W_k \geq p\} \geq \Pr\{W_{k-1} \geq p\}$, which signifies that $\rho(k)$ is a decreasing function of k, as the intuition suggests.

Our aim is to estimate a cluster size k_{est} so that, with probability at least $1 - \epsilon$, a proportion of $\geq 1 - \delta$ clusters satisfy the p-sensitive k-anonymity privacy criterion, for sufficiently small values of ϵ and $\delta > \rho(k)$. For a total of $N = n/k$ clusters, let N^* be the number of clusters satisfying the privacy criterion. Hence, using the Chernoff bound [9], we see that

$$\Pr\{N^* \geq N(1 - \delta)\} \geq 1 - e^{-N \, \mathrm{D}(\delta \| \rho(k))}, \tag{3}$$

where $\mathrm{D}(\delta \| \rho(k))$ denotes the Kullback-Leibler divergence between two Bernoulli distributed r.v.'s with parameters δ and $\rho(k)$, respectively. Therefore, the SDC_KEst algorithm obtain an estimation of the cluster size as

$$k_{\mathrm{est}} = \max\{k, \min\{k' : e^{-\frac{n}{k} \mathrm{D}(\delta \| \rho(k'))} \leq \epsilon\}\}.$$

References

1. Bernhard, D., Cortier, V., Galindo, D., Pereira, O., Warinschi, B.: SoK: a comprehensive analysis of game-based ballot privacy definitions. In: Proceedings of the IEEE Symposium on Security and Privacy (S&P), San Jose, CA, pp. 499–516, May 2015

2. Bernhard, D., Warinschi, B.: Cryptographic voting — a gentle introduction. In: Aldini, A., Lopez, J., Martinelli, F. (eds.) FOSAD 2012-2013. LNCS, vol. 8604, pp. 167–211. Springer, Cham (2014). https://doi.org/10.1007/978-3-319-10082-1_7

3. Chaum, D.: Untraceable electronic mail, return addresses, and digital pseudonyms. Commun. ACM **24**(2), 84–88 (1981)

4. Cramer, R., Gennaro, R., Schoenmakers, B.: A secure and optimally efficient multi-authority election scheme. In: Fumy, W. (ed.) EUROCRYPT 1997. LNCS, vol. 1233, pp. 103–118. Springer, Heidelberg (1997). https://doi.org/10.1007/3-540-69053-0_9

5. Delaune, S., Kremer, S., Ryan, M.D.: Verifying privacy-type properties of electronic voting protocols. J. Comput. Secur. **17**(4), 435–487 (2009)

6. Domingo-Ferrer, J., Mateo-Sanz, J.M.: Practical data-oriented microaggregation for statistical disclosure control. IEEE Trans. Knowl. Data Eng. **14**(1), 189–201 (2002)

7. Domingo-Ferrer, J., Torra, V.: Ordinal, continuous and heterogeneous k-anonymity through microaggregation. Data Min. Knowl. Discov. **11**(2), 195–212 (2005)

8. Fujioka, A., Okamoto, T., Ohta, K.: A practical secret voting scheme for large scale elections. In: Seberry, J., Zheng, Y. (eds.) AUSCRYPT 1992. LNCS, vol. 718, pp. 244–251. Springer, Heidelberg (1993). https://doi.org/10.1007/3-540-57220-1_66

9. Hoeffding, W.: Probability inequalities for sums of bounded random variables. J. Am. Stat. Assoc. **58**(301), 13–30 (1963)

10. Hundepool, A., et al.: Statistical Disclosure Control. Surv. Method. Wiley, Chichester (2012)

11. Jonker, H., Mauw, S., Pang, J.: Privacy and verifiability in voting systems: methods, developments and trends. Comput. Sci. Rev. **10**, 1–30 (2013)

12. Li, N., Li, T., Venkatasubramanian, S.: t-closeness: privacy beyond k-anonymity and l-diversity. In: Proceedings of the IEEE International Conference on Data Engineering (ICDE), Istanbul, Turkey, pp. 106–115, April 2007

13. Machanavajjhala, A., Gehrke, J., Kifer, D., Venkitasubramaniam, M.: l-diversity: privacy beyond k-anonymity. In: Proceedings of the IEEE International Conference on Data Engineering (ICDE), p. 24, Apr 2006

14. Neff, C.A.: A verifiable secret shuffle and its application to E-voting. In: Proceedings of the ACM Conference on Computer and Communications Security (CCS), Philadelphia, PA, USA, pp. 116–125 (2001)

15. Oganian, A., Domingo-Ferrer, J.: On the complexity of optimal microaggregation for statistical disclosure control. UNECE Stat. J. **18**(4), 345–354 (2001)

16. Rebollo-Monedero, D., Forné, J., Soriano, M.: p-probabilistic k-anonymous microaggregation for the anonymization of surveys with uncertain participation (2016, submitted)

17. Rebollo-Monedero, D., Forné, J., Soriano, M., Puiggalí-Allepuz, J.: k-anonymous microaggregation with preservation of statistical dependence. Inf. Sci. **342**(1), 1–23 (2016)

18. Samarati, P., Sweeney, L.: Protecting privacy when disclosing information: k-anonymity and its enforcement through generalization and suppression. Technical report, Computer Science Laboratory, SRI International (1998)

19. Truta, T.M., Vinay, B.: Privacy protection: p-sensitive k-anonymity property. In: Proceedings of the International Workshop on Privacy Data Management (PDM), p. 94. IEEE Computer Society (2006)

Key Factors in Coping with Large-Scale Security Vulnerabilities in the eID Field

Silvia Lips[1], Ingrid Pappel[2], Valentyna Tsap[2], and Dirk Draheim[2(✉)]

[1] Politsei, Pärnu mnt. 139, 15060 Tallinn, Estonia
silvia.lips@politsei.ee
[2] Large-Scale Systems Group, Tallinn University of Technology,
Akadeemia tee 15a, 12618 Tallinn, Estonia
{ingrid.pappel,valentyna.tsap,dirk.draheim}@ttu.ee

Abstract. In 2017, the encryption vulnerability of a widespread chip led to major, nation-wide eID card incidents in several EU countries. In this paper, we investigate the Estonian case. We start with an analysis of the Estonian eID field in terms of stakeholders and their responsibilities. Then, we describe the incident management from the inside perspective of the crisis management team, covering the whole incident timeline (including issues in response, continuity and recovery). From this, we are able to derive key factors in coping with large-scale security vulnerabilities in the eID field (public-private partnership, technical factors, crisis management, documentation), which encourages further research and systematization.

Keywords: e-identity · e-governance · e-services · IT security
Crisis management · Business continuity management

1 Introduction

Since the 1990s, Estonia was one of those republics that rapidly developed a priority on ICT. Since then, year by year, the country has shown a remarkable progress in building up elements and components of today's digital society. In particular, this regards the area of eID (electronic identity) management, which is a crucial enabler for the digital society. First eID cards were issued as early as in 2002, becoming mandatory documents. A full replacement with the new standard ID card has finished in 2006, and simultaneously, the state set up the required infrastructure for the entire e-services system. In these endeavors, public-private partnership turned out to be a winning model that ensured further smooth implementation, rollout and up-take of eID. Throughout all the time, based on continuous improvement of its public services and their delivery, Estonia has gained its citizens' trust. The matter of security (and trust) has always been and remains one of the top requirements in this area.

In 2017, Estonia encountered a nation-wide, urgent e-identity security issue: a potential encryption vulnerability of the chips used in current eID cards has

© Springer Nature Switzerland AG 2018
A. Kő and E. Francesconi (Eds.): EGOVIS 2018, LNCS 11032, pp. 60–70, 2018.
https://doi.org/10.1007/978-3-319-98349-3_5

been encountered and reported by Check and Slovak researchers. This paper provides in-depth description of the incident and the steps taken by the government authorities towards solving this crisis.

In Sect. 2 we will describe the Estonian eID ecosystem components. In Sect. 3, we will delve into the scope of the discovered security vulnerability, including its technical aspect and Estonia's approach of dealing with the occurred situation. In Sect. 4, we will identify the key factors in coping with the security crisis. We will finish the paper with a conclusion in Sect. 5.

2   The Estonian eID Ecosystem

Electronic ID and electronic signature are crucial building blocks in any serious e-government initiative, compare, e.g., with [1,2]. In this section, we will describe the Estonian eID ecosystem. Before we can analyze the factors in coping with large-scale security vulnerabilities, it is important to understand how the entire system works; who the main stakeholders are; what kind of eID tokens are used; and what role and influence the eID field has in the context of Estonian e-governance and electronic services.

2.1   Estonian eID Scheme Stakeholders

The Estonian eID ecosystem [3,4] is a unique and well-operating network consisting of different players and roles. Main authorities in the scheme (Fig. 1) are the Estonian Police and Border Guard Board (PBGB) and the Information System Authority (RIA).

- RIA operates in the governing area of the Ministry of Economic Affairs and Communications[1]. It coordinates the development and administration of the state's information system, organizes activities related to information security, coordinates the functioning of the public key infrastructure and handles security incidents that occur in Estonian computer networks[2]. In general, it can be said that RIA is the eID technical competence center.
- PBGB operates in the governing area of the Ministry of the Interior and is responsible for the identity management and the issuance of identity documents. This authority holds, manages and procures contracts necessary for keeping up the eID scheme (eID carriers, personalization service, certification service etc.). Current partner regarding the ID-1 format documents is a French security company Gemalto AG[3].
- Gemalto AG (via the associated company Trüb Baltic AS) manufactures and personalizes the eID cards and provides certification service (trust service) using SK ID Solutions AS as a sub-contractor.

---

[1] https://www.mkm.ee/en.

[2] https://www.ria.ee/en/.

[3] https://www.gemalto.com/.

Fig. 1. Estonian eID main stakeholders

- The ICT and development center (SMIT)[4] offers different ICT services (management and development of information systems, technical support etc.) in the whole internal security area under the Ministry of Interior.

In addition to the above-mentioned organizations, the Ministry of Foreign Affairs[5] issues identity documents and is responsible for diplomatic documents. The Technical Regulatory Authority (TJA)[6] has a supervisory role over the trust service providers [5]. Banks are e-service providers in the eID environment. Furthermore, some banks offer PIN-replacement services for eID cards.

2.2   Estonian eID Tokens

The ID-card is a mandatory identity document for citizens of Estonia enabling electronic authentication and qualified electronic signature [6] according to the eIDAS regulation [7]. The same type of card is issued to the European Union citizens residing in Estonia [8]. In addition to the ID-card there are many different eID tokens with the same electronic functionalities available:

1. Residence permit cards – issued to the third country nationals and persons with undetermined citizenship [9].
2. Digital identity cards (including e-residency cards) – voluntary secondary document for digital use only.

---

[4] https://www.smit.ee/.
[5] http://vm.ee/en.
[6] https://www.tja.ee/en.

3. Diplomatic identity cards – cards with full eID functionality issued by Estonian Ministry of Foreign Affair for diplomatic purposes.

As a convenient alternative to the card format, mobile IDs can be used. All of the available eID tokens enable electronic authentication and qualified electronic signature according to the eIDAS regulation.

With this wide variety of eID tokens the state has ensured access to e-services on equal basis to all interest groups. In addition to the authentication and signing solutions that are provided by the state, there are several other options available provided by private sector entities (e.g. bank links, smart-IDs, pin calculators etc.).

2.3   The Role of eID in e-Governance and e-Services

The usage of eID in Estonia is relatively high. 98% of Estonians have ID-cards and about 2/3 of the holders use their card regularly[7]. This means that the usage of e-services is remarkably high and the role of e-governance in the country is crucial.

According to [10], 99% of bank transfers in Estonia are made electronically, 98% of tax returns are made via the e-Tax board, 95% of prescribed medications are bought using digital prescriptions, etc. From the government perspective the state portal eesti.ee acts as single point of contact to the e-services offered by the state – ranging from health and medical related services to services in the area of business and entrepreneurship[8]. The total number of e-services in the country offered by public and private sector is around 2000.

The state portal eesti.ee is a gate to the Estonian e-state. The eID serves as a key that enables a secure access to all public and private e-services. This explains the vital role and importance of the eID in Estonia.

3   About Security Vulnerability

On the 30th of August 2017 RIA was informed about a potential security vulnerability in the Estonian eID card chips. The vulnerability was discovered by Slovak and Czech scientist during their research regarding RSA key generation and reported in [11]. At that time, it was not clear what number of cards is actually affected. This section gives an overview about the nature and scope of the security vulnerability and how it was handled.

3.1   Technical Description and Scope of the Security Vulnerability

In [11, 12] it has been reported that a wide range of cryptographic chips produced by Infineon Technologies AG are vulnerable with respect to RSA (Rivest-Shamir-Adleman) key pair generation. One of those chips is implemented in Estonian

---

[7] https://e-estonia.com/solutions/e-identity/id-card/.
[8] https://www.eesti.ee/en/.

eID cards starting from October 2014. As a result of the chip's vulnerability, it became possible to calculate the RSA private key of an eID card holder with the knowledge of the corresponding RSA public key with critically less computational complexity than should be expected from properly implemented RSA system. As a consequence, all Estonian eID cards issued after 16.10.2014 were potentially vulnerable – in total about 750.000 issued cards with full eID functionality. This was about 2/3 of all issued cards (ID cards, residence permit cards, digital identity cards including e-residency cards). The mobile ID solution used by about 70.000 users was not affected due to its different technical solution.

Based on these numbers and the users' high dependence of the eID-based services, it can be said that the state had to deal with a very sensitive and large-scale security issue. Hence, a solution had to be implemented rapidly and at the same time, all possible risks and consequences had to be acknowledged by the parties that were involved into the crisis handling.

3.2   Process of Handling the Security Vulnerability in Estonia

After receiving the information about the vulnerability, RIA convened a roundtable of experts to prepare preliminary directions for a solution and communication. Technical and communication working groups worked in parallel. Results of the both working groups were presented to the government.

It was the first time that the state faced such a large-scale security topic in the eID field and the government decided to take an open approach and discuss the issue veraciously. The main reason for this was to retain trust towards e-solutions and e-governance. The crisis management was delegated to RIA and PBGB (Fig. 2).

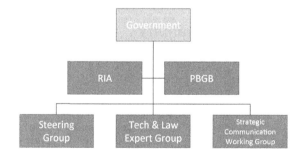

Fig. 2. Delegation of crisis management during the 2017 Estonian eID card incident.

In both organizations (RIA and PBGB), crisis managers were entitled. Under the management of RIA, a steering group of managers of involved authorities met regularly. At least two times a week working group of technical and law experts met to present latest findings and improvements and negotiate technical nuances.

As the vulnerability concerned the majority of the eID users, communication played a decisive role in the whole process. The main challenge was to explain the technically complex topic in a simple and understandable way in order to avoid general panic and to give clear guidelines. Therefore, in parallel to seeking for a technical solution, a group of communication experts from the different authorities dealt with strategical communication matters.

As a preventive measure, access to the LDAP (Lightweight Directory Access Protocol) catalogue service for certificate status requests has been limited. The access to the service has been limited to authorized entities to prevent uncontrolled downloads from the eID card users public key database. (after the successful recovery from the incident, the service was opened again on 20.11.2017).

The technical working group concluded that the best way to solve the security issue is to implement elliptic curve cryptography (ECC) in eID documents. This decision led to three types of development works:

1. With respect to new cards: adjustments of the eID card production capacities to implement ECC and to ensure readiness to personalize new cards;
2. 1. With respect to 750.000 already issued cards: update of already existing software enabling a certificate renewal procedure
   (a) in PBGB service points (the document holder can come to a PBGB service point and an official will renew certificates on site).
   (b) in document holder's personal computer (the document holder can renew his/her certificates remotely on his/her PC).

The renewal process started in the end of October 2017, after adjustments to the eID cards production had been implemented. In the beginning of November, all certificates were suspended in order to avoid possible damage. Therefore, it became impossible to use them in the e-environment unless renewed. With renewed certificates, eID cards could be used as usual. Starting from April 2018, the suspended certificates will be revoked and renewal will not be possible anymore, and therefore, those eID holders who did not renew it by that time will have to apply for a new document in case they want to use it in the e-environment.

3.3 Positive and Negative Effects of the Vulnerability

When it comes to occurrence of similar incidents, negative and positive aspects can be identified and used for further consideration and analysis of problem solving. At this moment, the aspects presented below are identified.

At the negative side:

- Debate regarding accountability – accountability is usually a matter that needs to be clarified during the process; but very often it is not the easiest part. These legal ongoing debates are tiring and expensive.
- Media pressure and noise – the number of people working in eID field in Estonia is rather limited. In some cases, the media pressure was quite intensive and started even to disturb experts' work.

- Some crucial functionality was temporarily lost - to resolve the security issue quickly, this had to be accepted. The Estonian eID card has an encryption functionality that was not possible to develop as fast as needed. As a consequence, in the new secure eID cards with ECC the encryption function was temporarily missing. This influenced majorly those users who used this functionality for secure document transmission (including many public sector authorities).
- Other ongoing activities were set on a hold – eID experts worked about 5 months to solve the security issue and various important projects were set on a hold until the end of the crisis.

At the positive side:

- Raised eID awareness – the eID field was in media from different angles almost every day during the active crisis period from September to December 2017. The case was published and analyzed publicly in detail. The awareness about eID functionality and use cases was definitely raised.
- Raised security awareness – in addition to eID awareness, the security awareness improved. The real case in the security field encouraged different security related debates in society.
- Stronger public and private cooperation – when the vulnerability was discovered all public and private authorities started to offer their help to the mainly involved authorities. The private sector was ready to contribute in any way to solve the issue as fast as possible. After this experience, it was clear that in complex situations the cooperation between public and private sector is very advantageous.
- Improved crisis management readiness – after dealing with concrete crisis and analyzing the results it was possible to make general conclusions and improve the existing crisis management system where needed.

3.4   How Other Affected States Coped with the Vulnerability

In addition to Estonia, Slovakia, Austria and Spain faced the same security vulnerability. Austria was the first country who reworked all its eID certificates on 09.06.2017 and informed other EU member states about it. CERT Estonia, which is a unit under the RIA responsible for the security incident management in the country, received this information on 20.06.2017. As the number of the certificates revoked by Austria was only few thousand, it did not have large scale impact in the country.

On 23.10.2017, the Ministry of Interior of Slovakia officially informed about suspension of the qualified electronic signature certificates on Slovak eID cards [13]. Both countries, Slovakia and Estonia suspended their certificates at about the same time. According to the information received from RIA, in the Slovakian case about 300.000 eID cards were affected.

The Spain case may seem to be the most interesting one. In the middle of November 2017, it was still not clear how Spain is going to handle the security vulnerability and no communication was made [14]. There is around 60 million eID cards on the market but according to RIA information, not all of them were affected. All certificates of the potentially vulnerable eID cards were finally suspended (more than 10 million) [15]. Despite of a huge number of suspended certificates, the overall effect in the country was not remarkable as the usage of eID in Spain is very low.

4   Key Factors in Coping with the Estonian eID Crisis

This section is oriented towards the main factors that played a key role while solving the Estonian eID crisis and towards the lessons learned from positive and negative perspectives on it. In each crisis situation, there is a vast amount of different aspects and probably, no single correct recipe or way to solve it. However, some key factors that help to cope with the situation more easily or to prevent even bigger damage can be identified. In the Estonian case we found that public-private partnership, technical solutions in use, crisis management, and communication are crucial factors.

4.1   Public-Private Partnership

In case of large-scale security vulnerabilities, there is no certain way of handling it and necessary competences range from ICT developers and security experts to communication specialist. Therefore, it might not be reasonable for a country to employ these competences permanently. More preferable is to have a good and supportive expert network that can be engaged if needed.

In the Estonian case, the PPP (public-private partnership) [16] performed very well and all public and private sector stakeholders and interested parties made their contribution. A specific expertise and resources were made available for public use. The small size of Estonia may play a role here, yet professional communities in the eID field are usually quite small everywhere. Therefore, the Estonian case might be considered as a good example of how PPP works effectively.

4.2   Technical Success Factors

From a technical point of view, the existence of an alternative eID token was crucial. Mobile ID was the only token that was not affected by the security vulnerability. People who already had it did not have to worry about their eID card status and further use of e-services. People who did not yet have mobile ID could apply for it easily and keep using e-services.

The other key factor was the *availability of an alternative renewal solution* after enabling a modified certification renewal process. It was possible to renew certificates in the PBGB service points as well as remotely on a user's PC. The renewal solution helped to save already issued eID cards and people had alternatives to choose from. Furthermore, the remote update solution helped to prevent an overloading of the PBGB service points.

4.3   Crisis Management

It was highly beneficial that a single authority (RIA) was responsible for the overall coordination from start to end. RIA acted as a single point of contact and the entire flow of important information needed for making strategic decisions was managed centrally. Using special expert level working groups simplified the work and enabled the discussion and weighting of various alternative solutions before the selection of the final one.

The *project-based management* used in the Estonian case can be considered as a success story. Different alternative project plans were put together taking into account instable and changing circumstances. Depending on the situation, plans were easy to exchangeable and to use. The public sector is usually considered more conservative and rather slowly changing. The Estonia eID crisis showed that it is possible to implement new approaches very fast. The state made a step closer to the users and opened extra temporary service points for renewal in hospitals, bigger shopping centers etc., which not only provided more options to citizens but also allowed to avoid overloading of PBGB service points.

4.4   Documentation and Verification

In a crisis situation, a need for juridical interpretation of state and European Union legal acts and contract clauses has occurred often. Therefore, *having lawyers and legal advisors in the technical working group* already in the early stage of the crisis was essential. Even if the timeframes were strict, a new *technical solution* has yet to be verified, audited, or reviewed before going live in order to prevent further mistakes or creating new security weaknesses. The adjustment of Estonian eID cards production capacities was verified and, changes in software were reviewed by independent third parties. After the crisis RIA ordered an *overall study* on how the eID crisis was managed inside the country, what were the main lessons learned and what can be improved. The study will be based on qualitative interviews with managers, experts and specialist who participated in the crisis settlement. On the basis of this, we suggest to turn the experience gathered during this incident into a rigorous, formal continuity management process [17–20].

5   Conclusion

The discovered RSA key vulnerability can be seen as one of those numerous risks that should be expected when it comes to technologies that a state's functionality so strongly relies on. Estonian experience with encountering a security issue that is a potential threat to country's now fundamental components demonstrates a rather strong and vigorous approach. The government has promptly reacted once the issue was announced convening all engaged stakeholders and experts allowing for solving the problem as fast as possible, taking into account carefully the associated risks and scenarios notwithstanding the urgency.

It is important to bear in mind here that regardless of how reliable and complex a technical solution can be, its reliability remains relative [21]. Every system, hardware or software is vulnerable to unknown attacks and there is no way of keeping this so-called status quo when we define a solution to be secure. A plausible conjecture that can be put here, based on what was said above, is for those in charge to take into account the risks of occurrence of similar threats and invest sufficient resources into retaining possible suitable auxiliaries for problem-solving if such events take place. The lessons learned that we outlined in this paper are generalized conclusions which derive from studying and analyzing this incident that happened recently, therefore we are aiming to extend them further once a more detailed and in-depth research will be conducted after collecting additional data and insights from stakeholders.

Hence, we are convinced that the Estonian practice of handling the e-identity security issue crisis is a decent example and a result of an effective and agile management, which relied heavily on public-private partnership, openness, technological advances of the country and continuous reviews and analysis of performance.

References

1. Marsalek, A., Zefferer, T., Reimair, F., Karabat, Ç., Soykan, E.U.: Leveraging the adoption of electronic identities and electronic-signature solutions in Europe. In: Proceedings of the Symposium on Applied Computing, SAC 2017, pp. 69–71. ACM, New York (2017)
2. Luna-Reyes, L.F., Sandoval-Almazan, R., Puron-Cid, G., Picazo-Vela, S., Luna, D.E., Gil-Garcia, J.R.: Understanding public value creation in the delivery of electronic services. In: Janssen, M., et al. (eds.) EGOV 2017. LNCS, vol. 10428, pp. 378–385. Springer, Cham (2017). https://doi.org/10.1007/978-3-319-64677-0_31
3. Muldme, A., Pappel, I., Lauk, M., Draheim, D.: A survey on customer satisfaction in national electronic ID user support. In: 2018 International Conference on eDemocracy eGovernment (ICEDEG), pp. 31–37, April 2018
4. Tsap, V., Pappel, I., Draheim, D.: Key success factors in introducing national e-identification systems. In: Dang, T.K., Wagner, R., Küng, J., Thoai, N., Takizawa, M., Neuhold, E.J. (eds.) FDSE 2017. LNCS, vol. 10646, pp. 455–471. Springer, Cham (2017). https://doi.org/10.1007/978-3-319-70004-5_33
5. Republic of Estonia: Electronic identification and trust services for electronic transactions act. https://www.riigiteataja.ee/en/eli/527102016001/
6. Pappel, I., Pappel, I., Tepandi, J., Draheim, D.: Systematic digital signing in estonian e-government processes. In: Hameurlain, A., Küng, J., Wagner, R., Dang, T.K., Thoai, N. (eds.) Transactions on Large-Scale Data- and Knowledge-Centered Systems XXXVI. LNCS, vol. 10720, pp. 31–51. Springer, Heidelberg (2017). https://doi.org/10.1007/978-3-662-56266-6_2
7. European Union: Regulation (EU) no. 910/2014 of the European Parliament and of the council of 23 july 2014 on electronic identification and trust services for electronic transactions in the internal market and repealing directive 1999/93/EC (2014)
8. Republic of Estonia: Identity documents act. https://www.riigiteataja.ee/en/eli/521062017003/

9. Republic of Estonia: Aliens act. https://www.riigiteataja.ee/en/eli/501112017003/
10. E-Governance Adacemy: e-Estonia - e-governance in practice. eGA, Tallinn (2016). https://goo.gl/JfpwNN
11. Nemec, M., Sys, M., Svenda, P., Klinec, D., Matyas, V.: The return of coppersmith's attack: practical factorization of widely used RSA moduli. In: Proceedings of the 2017 ACM SIGSAC Conference on Computer and Communications Security, CCS 2017, pp. 1631–1648. ACM, New York (2017)
12. Svenda, P., et al.: The million-key question - investigating the origins of RSA public keys. In: 25th USENIX Security Symposium, pp. 893–910. USENIX Association (2017)
13. První certifikační autorita: Safety of starcos cards. I.CA News Feed, November 2017. http://www.ica.cz/News?IdNews=363
14. Meyer, D.: ID card security - Spain is facing chaos over chip crypto flaws. ZDNet, November 2017. https://goo.gl/8xWizW
15. Leyden, J.: Confusion reigns over crypto vuln in Spanish electronic ID smartcards - certs revoked, but where are the updates? The register, November 2017
16. Paide, K., Pappel, I., Vainsalu, H., Draheim, D.: On the systematic exploitation of the Estonian data exchange layer X-road for strengthening public private partnerships. In: 11th International Conference on Theory and Practice of Electronic Governance, ICEGOV 2018. ACM (2018)
17. British Standards Institution: Business continuity management - part 1: code of practice, British Standard BS 259991:2006. BSI Group, London (2006)
18. British Standards Institution: Societal security - business continuity management systems - requirements. BSI Group, London (2014)
19. Draheim, D.: Smart business process management. In: 2011 BPM and Workflow Handbook, Digital Edition. Future Strategies, Workflow Management Coalition, pp. 207–223 (2012)
20. Draheim, D., Pirinen, R.: Towards exploiting social software for business continuity management. In: Workshops on Database and Expert Systems Applications (DEXA), pp. 279–283. IEEE Press, September 2011
21. Buldas, A., Saarepera, M.: Are the current system engineering practices sufficient to meet cyber crime? In: Tryfonas, T. (ed.) HAS 2017. LNCS, vol. 10292, pp. 451–463. Springer, Cham (2017). https://doi.org/10.1007/978-3-319-58460-7_31

Discovering and Analyzing Alignment Problems in a Public Organization

Dóra Őri$^{(\boxtimes)}$ and Zoltán Szabó

Department of Information Systems, Corvinus University of Budapest,
Budapest, Hungary
{DOri, Szabo}@informatika.uni-corvinus.hu

Abstract. Strategic alignment is a key challenge in many organizations, even in the public sector. This paper concentrates on the formal aspects of alignment (organisational design), the method is based on a strategic alignment perspective-driven approach, by integrating alignment concepts to enterprise architecture management models. Misalignment symptoms were translated into architecture models providing testable rules for analysis. The empirical investigation focuses on a road management authority, and rule testing approaches were used to identify formally described misalignment symptoms in the EA models. Several misalignment symptoms were discovered and assessed with the framework. The proposed approach can be an efficient method to analyse alignment problems and facilitate strategic harmonization in public sector organizations.

Keywords: Strategic alignment · Misalignment
Enterprise architecture management

1 Introduction

IT induced redesign of organizations is a frequently discussed topic [14, 16], and the problem of strategic alignment is a central issue as there is no evidence of how to reach fit between structure and new technology, that is a crucial issue in the current era of digital transformation. By the possibilities of IT, organisations have growing abilities to change the nature of their activities, to modify their relationships and to expand their capabilities. Strategic alignment was originally defined as concerning the inherently dynamic fit between external and internal domains, such as the product/market, strategy, administrative structures, business processes and IT [6]. Economic performance is argued to be enhanced by finding the right fit between external positioning and internal arrangements. The Strategic Alignment Model developed by Henderson and Venkatraman [6] includes at least four basic elements: business strategy, organisational infrastructure and operations, IT strategy and IT infrastructure. Alignment is a key issue for management according to many surveys, but we still miss an appropriate methodology that facilitate business and IT synchronization. In this paper we would like to summarize an enterprise architecture (EA) based method to explore and analyse alignment problems, based on a case study of a public organization. We will focus on the public sector specific issues and discuss the applicability of the proposed analysing approach.

© Springer Nature Switzerland AG 2018
A. Kő and E. Francesconi (Eds.): EGOVIS 2018, LNCS 11032, pp. 71–85, 2018.
https://doi.org/10.1007/978-3-319-98349-3_6

The rest of the paper is organised as follows: Sect. 2 presents the organisational context. Section 3 introduces the typical alignment problems in the public sector. In Sect. 4 a rule-based methodology for misalignment assessment is summarised. Section 5 analyses the case organisation according to the proposed framework. Section 6 evaluates the framework and proposes interpretation for symptom detection results. At the end of the paper conclusions are drawn.

2 Organisational Context

The empirical investigation focuses on a road management authority. The organization is a non-profit government corporation that handles matters relating to road safety, road traffic management and transportation for around 32000 km national public road network. The scope of activities spans from road operation and road maintenance over professional services to providing road information. Road-related activities consist of road condition checking, pavement maintenance and reparation, roadside maintenance, off-pavement landscape maintenance, snow removal and deicing of roads and the installation, reparation, and replacement of traffic engineering devices. Professional services consist of the management of road operator licenses, road network protection, quality control and maintaining the national road register. In its actual form the authority was set up in 2006 as a successor of a previous road management government authority. The head quarter and three sites are located in Budapest, and the authority has approx. 170 branches around Hungary. In 2016 the authority employed around 8200 employees.

Road control initiative is a pilot project for setting up the Enterprise Architecture Management (EAM) [19] practice in the authority. The initiative is part of an integrated road network development project which aims to transform the internal operation as well as to optimise processes in order (1) to increase operational efficiency and transparency within the road management authority, (2) to achieve cost-efficient public task execution, (3) to provide a nation-wide integrated management system, (4) to increase access to management information, (5) to create the premises for standardised services, (6) to increase traffic safety. As part of the above introduced integrated road network development project, the road control project is concerned with the implementation of a traveling warrant system.

The goal of the project was manifold: to achieve real-time road control information forwarding, to deliver up-to-date information and control specifications onboard, to provide exact information retrieval about past activities and coordinates by place and by date, to provide electronic administration about road control, to provide an expandable and integral solution for road control support, to decrease paper administration related to road control tasks. The project was set up to eliminate the following problems related to the previous road control solution: (1) administration overload, (2) too many isolated information systems, (3) slow escalation of road control-related information, (4) non-automated read-in of road control-related data, (5) non-electronic retrieval of previous road control routes and coordinates.

The drivers of the project arose from the problems related to the previous implementation, namely: to avoid redundant data recording, to get an up-to-date master data register, to achieve lower maintenance and development costs, to achieve lower exposure to suppliers, to increase profitable duty time, to provide fast, route-based information retrieval, to decrease administration overload, to provide the opportunity for online intervention. These challenging goals can be achieved through tactical and strategic IT initiatives, providing perfect subject for the analysis of alignment problems.

3 Alignment Problems in the Public Sector

Public sector organizations can be defined and modelled using the classic building blocks of any organizations, but they have specific features and many specialties. Value generation can be less direct in the public sector (not measurable in money), the number and influence of stakeholders creates a very complex socio-economic environment, where much less guidance is available than in the market sector. The structure, infrastructure and process (hard factors) and the knowledge, culture, beliefs, skills (soft factors) are very inflexible, these organizations are less agile. Maximization of value creation from IT investments is a general expectation in public sector, but differently from private companies, goals are anchored to the socio-economic requirements than measurable financial benefits. Strategic alignment is a key challenge for organizations of the public sector, where the complexity of harmonization between strategic planning and IT planning, dynamic adjustments of services to the changing needs generates growing demands for organization engineering and IT management.

Alignment concept has several potential approaches. The model proposed by Henderson and Venkatraman [6] is focusing on the dynamic fit between business and IT domains, covering the classic formal organization science dimensions like strategy, IT systems, organisational structure, processes, skills, etc., that are close to the concepts of enterprise architecture management. A more human, leadership and culture-oriented approach described by Luftman et al. [7] emphasizing managerial behaviours that promote harmonization to maximize the value adding potential of IT. In public sector strategic alignment concept can be defined as the direct linkage of IT goals to the organisational goals, and the level of organisational commitment [18]. Rusu and Jonathan [12] investigated the issue of IT alignment in public organizations, using categorization based on the dimensions of Strategic Alignment Maturity model.

Henderson and Venkatraman [6, 16] argue that the inability to realize value from IT investments is, in part, due to the lack of alignment between the business and IT strategies of organisations. They view strategy as involving both formulation and implementation, and their concept of strategic alignment is based on two fundamental assumptions. (1) Economic performance is directly related to the ability of management to create a strategic fit between the position of an organisation in the competitive product-market arena and the design of an appropriate administrative structure to support its execution. This assumption is consistent with the generally accepted axiom that strategic choices in the external and internal domains should be consistent. (2) Strategic fit is inherently dynamic. Thus, strategic alignment is not an event but a process of continuous adaptation and change.

Our focus in this research is based on the assumption that better alignment is a dynamic activity resulted in higher performance and value. Although leadership and managerial aspects of the alignment problem is a crucial success factor, we will concentrate on the formal aspects of alignment (organisational design), building our approach to the Venkatraman model, by integrating it to the concepts of EAM. The overall goal is to harmonize IT and organisational strategy, implement and maintain an appropriate organisational and IT infrastructure and the related management processes. Improved organisational design (including the business and IT domains) will ensure higher performance and less misalignment related issues.

While organisations address alignment achievement, they are continually suffering from misalignments. These difficulties (the misalignments) encumber the achievement of alignment. Misalignment analysis (detecting, correcting and preventing misalignment) is an important step in achieving alignment since it helps to understand the nature and the barriers of alignment. Several approaches have been proposed as misalignment assessment frameworks [2, 11, 15]. Our conceptual analysis relates to the concept of strategic alignment and aims to approach strategic alignment from the perspective of misalignment. The problem of revealing the typical symptoms of misalignment will be addressed in order to assess the state of alignment in an organisation. Misalignment in the above mentioned formal dimensions of public sector organisations are also prevalent issues, so detecting, assessing and correcting them will ensure better performance and value-adding potential.

4   Methodology for Alignment Assessment

As the result of organisational and IT complexity, the discovery of alignment problems is not a trivial task, that has strategic, cultural dimensions (surveys and interviews are appropriate tools for analysis), but there are also hard (evidence based) aspects, that can be formally analysed. Our approach is intended to provide an EAM based method appropriate for the purpose. Enterprise architecture is the construction of an organisation, described by its composing entities and their relationships. EA is an organising logic for business processes and IT infrastructure in order to review, maintain and control the whole operation of an organization [19]. Enterprise architecture management – as a management philosophy concerned with organisational change – provides several advantages by improving IT efficiency (decreasing redundancy, ensuring homogeneity, integration, consistency and reusability); by enabling IT effectiveness (ensuring goals, strategy, conformity, results orientation and schedule orientation); by improving IT reliability (reducing risk) [8]. EAM can be a major facilitator of strategic alignment by detecting, analysing and preventing misalignment problems and achieving competitiveness [17]. A few EAM-based misalignment assessment frameworks (e.g. [3, 4, 13, 20]) have already been proposed in recent literature.

In a former approach [9, 10] an XML-based analysis tool was created, which detected the symptoms of misalignment in EA models with rule assessment techniques. The applied research methodology used a strategic alignment perspective-driven approach. In the first step, traditional alignment perspectives were connected to typical misalignment symptoms. In the second step, relevant artefacts were provided with the misalignment symptoms, i.e. the EA models which may contain the symptom in question. In the third step, suitable EA analysis types were suggested to the misalignment symptoms. These investigations were able to detect the symptoms in the recommended containing artefacts. Misalignment symptoms, containing artifacts and recommended EA analysis types came from catalogs that were based on recent literature.

To assess the state of misalignment with the above introduced methodology, we need the following concepts from an EA model base: (1) Alignment perspectives: This list contains the corresponding alignment perspective for symptom detection. (2) Misalignment symptom catalog: This list comprises the perceived misalignment symptoms. (3) Artifact catalog: This list encompasses the possible containing EA models. (4) EA analysis catalog: This list includes the possible EA analysis types to recommend. (5) Presence in the artifact: This concept describes the sign of the symptom in the EA models. (6) Occurrence on model entity level: This concept defines how the symptom is manifested on model entity level. (7) Occurrence in XML model export: This item describes how the symptom is manifested in the XML export of the EA model. (8) XML-based query: This query describes how the corresponding symptom can be examined in the XML exports of the EA models.

In terms of rule construction, misalignment symptom queries were written by using the XPath language and the Schematron language. XPath language were used both in context setting (where the node under analysis is determined) and testing (where the logical expression of detecting the symptom is defined). Schematron language were used for making assertions about patterns (i.e. misalignment symptoms) found in the XML exports of the EA models. Schematron-based queries with embedded XPath expressions were written and validated in an XML validation tool.

Based on the rule construction phase, rule testing approaches were used to identify formally described misalignment symptoms in the EA models. On the basis of the rule testing phase, results were interpreted in terms of the alignment-misalignment continuum. First, processed and tested rules were converted back into misalignment symptoms. This step was vital for the proper interpretation of the detected symptoms. Secondly, the location of the identified symptoms was analysed. This step provided information about the location of badly-working routines both from physical and logical perspectives. Finally, re-alignment activities were recommended according to the nature and location of the detected misalignment symptoms.

According to the proposed method, misalignment assessment can result in three categories of misalignment symptoms: (1) Symptoms that can be handled and revealed in EA scope. (2) Symptoms that can be handled in EA scope in a reduced extent, i.e. analytical potential only for simplified, incomplete symptom detection. The symptom loses from its original content, i.e. an in-depth analysis is not performed. However, it is applicable for a preparatory test. (3) Symptoms that cannot be handled and detected solely in EA scope, other information sources are needed for symptom detection.

Symptoms that can be handled in EA scope (1) include the following examples: Undefined or multiple hierarchy or lines of reporting. Undefined business process goals, business process owners. Out of date technological infrastructure. Incompatible platforms or technologies. Lack of data ownership. The fact that not all entities attributes are read at least by one process. For symptoms that can be handled in EA scope in a reduced extend (2) the following examples can be presented: Lack of applications interfaces. The data management should be automatic among the application systems. Finally, symptoms that cannot be handled solely in EA scope (3) include the following examples: No formal architectural integration at functional organisation level. Application functionality does not support at least one business process activity. Sporadically existing or Technical Service Level Agreements. Users managed differently in different applications.

5 Case Study

The empirical investigation focuses on the road management authority. The study was carried out in a fragment of the road management authority's EA model structure. It describes a road control initiative, showing the relevant EA models and artifacts to be modified during the progression of the project. The road control project was set off to outline the process of road control with EA methods over 2 set of changes. The as-is state presents the actual state of road control activities. To-be No. 1.0 and To-be No. 2.0 phases deal with the changes in process execution, supportive applications and underlying technological infrastructure.

5.1 Preliminary Review

Before commencing misalignment symptom detection at the case organisation, preliminary reviews were organised in order to get acquainted with the conditions in the organisational state. Preliminary reviews were conducted by interviewing stakeholders of the initiative. Interviews served as an initial consultation about influential areas to review and the perceived problems concerning business-IT alignment. The most important organisational areas that have been comprehended at the road management authority before proceeding business-IT assessments included: (1) Business Strategy, (2) Business Functions, (3) Business Roles, (4) Business Process Map and Business Process Models, (5) IT Strategy, (6) IT Process Map and IT Process Models, (7) Application Portfolio and Application Interfaces, (8) IT Service Portfolio and Service Catalogue, (9) available EA Models, (10) Architecture Repository, (11) Architecture Maturity and EA Model Reliability, (12) Business/IT Ideas, Propositions and Innovation, (13) Investment Planning. The previously introduced business-IT areas under review and precursory interviews on malfunctioning structures have revealed several problematic business-IT areas and therefore provided us with preliminary assumptions on alignment problems and possible organisational areas for misalignment investigations.

5.2 Application of the Analysis Framework

Preliminary reviews on the case organisation provided us with a list of influential areas to review and an analysis of assumed malfunctioning areas. *Table 1* lists the perceived misalignment symptoms. The coding of the symptoms stems from the extensive misalignment symptom list presented in Őri [10]. Symptoms S.01, S.10, S.12, S.13, S.15 were significantly present in the project under review. In contrast, symptoms S.14 and S.20 were barely noticeable. Symptoms S.07 and S.17 were perceived in the whole organisation, rather than the project under review.

Table 1. Perceived misalignment symptoms in the case organisation

Code	Misalignment symptom
S.01	Undefined organisational mission, strategy, and goals
S.02	Undefined business process goals, business process owners
S.05	Undefined or multiple hierarchy or lines of reporting
S.06	Application functionality does not support at least one business process activity
S.07	Business process task supported by more than one application
S.10	Insufficient IT resources
S.12	Lack of skills to develop or innovate certain types of products
S.13	Poor IT planning and portfolio management
S.14	Under capacity infrastructure
S.15	Lack or poor systems performance monitoring
S.16	Out of date technological infrastructure
S.17	Technological heterogeneity
S.18	Incompatible platforms or technologies
S.20	Information consistency or integrity problems
S.24	Sporadically existing or Technical Service Level Agreements
S.27	No formal architectural integration at functional organisation level
S.32	Lack of data ownership
S.38	Users managed differently in different applications
S.39	Lack of application interfaces
S.52	Not all data entity attributes are read at least by one process
S.57	The data management should be automatic among the application systems

The entire symptom list was then analysed according to the affected EA layer. *Business Architecture* layer analysis was necessary in detecting the following symptoms: Undefined organisational mission, strategy, and goals, Undefined business process goals, business process owners, Undefined or multiple hierarchy or lines of reporting, Application functionality does not support at least one business process activity, Business process task supported by more than one application, Lack of skills to develop or innovate certain types of products, Poor IT planning and portfolio management, No formal architectural integration at functional organisation level.

The analysis of *Data Architecture* was required to detect the following symptoms: Information consistency or integrity problems, No formal architectural integration at functional organisation level, Lack of data ownership, The data management should be automatic among the application systems.

The framework required the analysis of *Application Architecture* in case of the following symptoms: Application functionality does not support at least one business process activity, Business process task supported by more than one application, Poor IT planning and portfolio management, No formal architectural integration at functional organisation level, Users managed differently in different applications, Lack of application interfaces, Not all data entity attributes are read at least by one process, The data management should be automatic among the application systems.

Finally, *Technology Architecture* layer analysis was required to assess the following symptoms: Insufficient IT resources, Under capacity infrastructure, Lack or poor systems performance monitoring, Out of date technological infrastructure, Technological heterogeneity, Incompatible platforms or technologies, Sporadically existing or Technical Service Level Agreements, No formal architectural integration at functional organisation level.

The analysis was followed by the exclusion of non-analysable symptoms. In summary, S.06, S.10–15, S.20, S.24, S.27, S.38, S.57 symptoms were excluded from further analysis. Justifications for excluding these symptoms were presented in detail. S.06 Application functionality does not support at least one business process activity was excluded on the basis that the model base of the case organisation did not contain a specified catalogue about application functionalities for each application in use. For this reason, the symptom could be validated against the model base of the case organisation. S.10 Insufficient IT resources symptom was excluded because of the fact that the modeling of Technology Architecture did not provide the adequate depth of analysis for these kinds of malfunctions. S.12 Lack of skills to develop or innovate certain types of products symptom was excluded because there was no sign of competency and skill catalogue on EA modeling level. The catalogue of skills in product innovation is not followed up in the modeling environment. S.13 Poor IT planning and portfolio management symptom was excluded by reason of the lack of instance about the performance and quality of the corresponding processes on EA modeling level. S.14 Under capacity infrastructure symptom was excluded because based on the fundamental nature of EAM, EA modeling is not capable of tracking capacity levels and violations. There are other dedicated processes to manage these types of malfunctions. S.15 Lack or poor systems performance monitoring symptom was excluded on the basis that there was no instance of the corresponding process and its performance on EA modeling level. S.20 Information consistency or integrity problems symptom was excluded because EA modeling is by nature not capable of tracking malfunctions of information integrity. There are other dedicated processes to manage these types of malfunctions. S.24 Sporadically existing or missing Technical Service Level Agreements symptom was excluded because there was a dedicated process to manage these types of malfunctions. EA modeling is by nature not capable of tracking malfunctions in the service level management process. S.27 No formal architectural integration at functional organisation level symptom was excluded because the available fragment of EA models did not provide the necessary analytical depth for this type of symptom. S.38 Users managed differently in different applications symptom was excluded on the basis that the available fragment of EA models did not provide the necessary analytical depth for this type of symptom. Finally, S.57 The data management should be automatic among the application systems symptom was excluded by the reason that EA modeling is by nature not capable of tracking malfunctions in application architecture-wide data management. There are other dedicated processes to manage these types of malfunctions.

Analysable misalignment symptoms were assessed with the framework. The occurrences in EA model, on model entity level and in XML-based EA model export organised the rule construction and testing. The following summary presents the building blocks for detecting these misalignment symptoms.

S.02 Undefined business process goals, business process owners. Lack of model presence for (1) business process goals, (2) business process owners presents the occurrence in EA model. Missing elements and connections for business process goal and business process owner representation must be looked for on model entity level. In the XML export the presence or absence of process goals or responsible person at business process tasks must be analysed.

S.05 Undefined or multiple hierarchy or lines of reporting. Either undefined or multiple hierarchy or lines of reporting reveals the occurrence in EA model. Missing or multiple connections between business roles for reporting line representation must be looked for on model entity level. In the XML export multiple relations between Node type: Business collaboration and Node type: Business collaboration in terms of lines of reporting must be assessed.

S.07 Business process task supported by more than one application. Sum of supportive application functions exceeds 1 per business process tasks means the occurrence in EA model. On model entity level more than 1 application functions must be looked for connected to business process tasks. In the XML export relations between Node type: Business process task and Node type: Application function must be analysed.

S.16 Out of date technological infrastructure. There is a catalogue on up to date technological elements. EA models may contain out of date technological infrastructure elements. On model entity level, those technological infrastructure elements must be looked for, which are not listed in the up to date technological element catalogue. In the XML export the infrastructure usage model and technological element catalogue must be compared in terms of technological element versions.

S.18 Incompatible platforms or technologies. There is a list of compatible hardware elements. EA models may contain incompatible hardware elements compared to the list. On model entity level, those hardware elements must be scanned, which are not listed in the compatible hardware element catalogue. In the XML export the infrastructure usage model and technological element catalogue must be compared in terms of hardware elements.

S.32 Lack of data ownership. The EA model presents the occurrence by the lack of responsible data owner in data entity models. On model entity level, the lack of responsible person attribute in data entity models must be analysed. In the XML export the presence or absence of responsible person at data entities must be assessed.

S.52 Not all data entity attributes are read at least by one process. By scanning data usage in business process models, there are data entities that are not used by any business process tasks. This is how the EA model presents the symptom. On model entity level, there are data entities from the data entity catalogue that are not present on any business process model. In the XML export business process models and data entity catalogue must be compared in terms of data entities.

After summarizing the analysed misalignment symptoms, one selected symptom will be further investigated, illustrating the technical details of the framework. Detection of misalignment symptom S.05 Undefined or multiple hierarchy or lines of reporting consisted of the following technical steps: Containing EA models included an organization decomposition diagram, in which multiple connections were assessed between business collaboration entities for reporting line representation. The occurrence on model entity level included the number of relations where relation attribute type: has superior between Node type: Business collaboration and Node type: Business collaboration. The scheme of the XML-based query consisted of the following points: For every node where node type = business collaboration: (1) Check whether the element (node type = business collaboration) has a valid subordinated element (node type = business collaboration) (S.05/A) (2) Check whether node relation reference to superior where relation attribute type = has superior equals with another node relation reference to superior where node type = has superior (S.05/B) (3) Report business collaboration nodes with valid subordinated business collaboration node (S.05/A) (4) Alert business collaboration nodes where the same node relation reference is given to superior (S.05/B). To cover the above mentioned aspects, the Schematron query was written in the following format:

```
<pattern name="S.05/A Undefined or multiple hierarchy or lines of re-
porting">
<rule context="ObjectDefinition[@Node Type='{business collaboration}']">
<report test="@ObjectDefinition.ID=following-sibling::[@NodeType=
'{business collaboration}']/ConnectionDefinition[@Connection Defini-
tion.Type='{has superior}']/@ToObjectDefinition.IdRef or @ObjectDefini-
tion.ID=preceding-sibling::ObjectDefinition[@TypeNum='{business collabo-
ration}']/ConnectionDefinition[@Connection Definition.Type='{has supe-
rior}']/@ToObjectDefinition.IdRef">
Alert: S.05/A Undefined or multiple hierarchy or lines of reporting
</report>   </rule>    </pattern>
<pattern name="S.05/B Undefined or multiple hierarchy or lines of re-
porting">
<rule context="ObjectDefinition[@NodeType='{business collaboration}']">
<report test="ConnectionDefinition[@ToObjectDefinition.IdRef= par-
ent::ObjectDefinition/following-sibling::ObjectDefinition[@Node
Type='{business collaboration}']/ConnectionDefinition[@ConnectionDefini-
tion.Type='{has superior}']/@ToObjectDefinition.IdRef] or ConnectionDef-
inition[@ToObjectDefinition.IdRef= parent::ObjectDefinition/predecing-
sibling::ObjectDefinition[@NodeType='{business collaboration}']/Connec-
tionDefinition[@ConnectionDefinition.Type='{has superior} ']/@ToOb-
jectDefinition.IdRef]">
Alert: S.05/B Undefined or multiple hierarchy or lines of reporting
</report>    </rule>    </pattern>
```

6   Discussion of the Framework Based on the Case

The case study provided considerable insight into the applicability of the proposed research framework. In addition, it has demonstrated the utility and usability of the proposed framework as well. The detection results confirmed the usefulness of the proposed research framework as a misalignment assessment framework.

Misalignment symptom analysis and detection provided insights about query types. Evidence from the case study suggested that there are distinct types of misalignment symptoms that can be detected by the proposed analysing framework. The case study demonstrated that the method is applicable for detecting the following types of misalignment symptoms: (1) Symptoms in which the presence or lack of the certain types of attributes has to be investigated. (2) Symptoms in which the cardinality of certain connection types has to be analysed. (3) Symptoms in which more models have to be compared. (4) Symptoms in which more model variants have to be analysed and compared during the progression of the project.

The paper provided a complex framework for detecting misalignment symptoms in complex EA model structure, showing that the framework has highlighted significant analytical potential. In addition, the study provided support for transforming misalignment symptoms into misalignment queries via rule generation and rule testing techniques.

6.1   Interpretation of Symptoms

Misalignment symptom S.02 was validated against the EA models of Road Control Process 1.0 and Road Control Process 2.0 looking for the lack of business process owners. There were no business processes without business process owners either in 1.0 or in 2.0 version. As for constraints, the query validated only the lack of business process owners. The lack of business process goals was not investigated in the case study because there was no modeling instance for business process models with business process goals. A possible extension is that the query also examines the presence or lack of business process goals on an appropriate EA model in the road control initiative. Another constraint was that the query did not examine whether or not a business process needs an owner. There must be cases where business processes do not need a business process owner, e.g. if a business process is atomic with only one business process task. This examination is not included in the query, therefore another possible extension is to alter the query to investigate this stipulation as well. As for results validation in practice, the follow-up interviews revealed that the case context sets that business processes (business process tasks which are represented as business processes in the EA models of the case organisation) with superior business processes do not need a business process owner. In this sense, the query reveals the general state of business processes in terms of business process owners, but further examination is needed to narrow the query with the previously introduced stipulation. However, in this state of the EA models, there is no instance on attribute level that would indicate the superior or subordinated manner of a business process task.

Misalignment symptom S.05 was validated against the EA model of Road Control Roles and Reporting Lines looking for multiple lines of reporting. This statement narrows the scope of the query, i.e. undefined lines of reporting were not examined by the query. The query contained 2 parts: S.05/A was concerned with a structural examination, i.e. whether the business collaboration element has a valid subordinated element. The query for S.05/A indicated three business collaboration elements which have a valid subordinated element. S.05/B examined whether a subordinated element has the same superior element with another subordinated element. The query for S.05/B indicated one superior element has two subordinated elements. A possible extension of the query is to examine the undefined lines of reporting as well. Follow-up interviews revealed that the query explores a real misalignment problem in the road control initiative. The service under review works 0–24 throughout the year. However, the particular subordinated service depends on winter/summer shifts and working hours. E. g. in the final minutes of duty time there might be two parallel reporting lines at the same time due to poor regulation compliance or geographical distance.

Misalignment symptom S.07 was validated against the EA models of Road Control System 1.0 with Services and Road Control System 2.0 with Services. Misalignment symptom S.07 was not detected in EA model Road Control System 1.0 with Services. In terms of setting constraints to the query, note that the distinction between applications and application functions is necessary. In the EA models under review application functions were connected to business process tasks instead of applications. Business process tasks with more than one supportive application function do not imply the presence of the misalignment symptom in question. Misalignment problems arise if more than one supportive application is connected to a business process task. In this sense, the query was not able to detect the symptom precisely due to the depth of modeling. There was no modeling instance for supportive applications only for supportive application functions per business process tasks. Therefore, the query could not measure the cardinality of supportive applications, but only the cardinality of supportive application components to business process tasks. A possible extension of the symptom detection is to repeat the investigation after having the necessary modeling instances. Follow-up interviews to validate the symptom revealed that the EA models under review contained application functions instead of applications. In this sense, the above-introduced extension is needed to detect the cardinality of applications.

Misalignment symptom S.16 was validated against the EA models of Road Control System 1.0 Infrastructure Usage Model and Road Control System 2.0 Infrastructure Usage Model. In both cases the models were compared with the EA model of Technology Software Components with valid components, looking for out of date technological infrastructure in the infrastructure usage models. As for model variant 1.0, the query detected one out of date technological infrastructure component, which was not included in the list of valid technological infrastructure elements. For model variant 2.0 the query detected one element, which is a supported infrastructure element, but it was not provided with the version attribute in the Technological Software Components model. This case forms a constraint to the query. Follow-up interviews revealed that some elements are not provided with version attribute in the Technological Software Components model. The query detects the lack of related infrastructure elements as well, this is why the symptom is also violated in the 2.0-version infrastructure usage model. According to results validation, two possible extensions can be made to correct the query: (1) to add the lacking version attributes in the EA models, (2) to narrow the scope of the query.

Similar to misalignment symptom S.16, misalignment symptom S.18 was also validated against the EA models of Road Control System 1.0 Infrastructure Usage Model and Road Control System 2.0 Infrastructure Usage Model. The query used the EA model of Technology Hardware Components for comparing the infrastructure usage models with the list of valid hardware components. In this query, incompatible platforms and technologies were explored. For model variant 1.0, the query detected one incompatible hardware component, which was not included in the list of valid technological infrastructure elements. However, in model variant 2.0 the symptom was not detected. This is a good example for analysing and detecting misalignment symptoms over time: While model variant 1.0 contained an incompatible element, the incompatibility was corrected over time, and for the next version of the model there was no violation of this kind of incompatibility. Follow-up interviews also confirmed that the incompatibility in model version 1.0 was corrected in model version 2.0. While the road control initiative had an incompatible infrastructure element during the progression of the project, it was later corrected and in the end, model version 2.0 lacks the incompatible element.

Misalignment symptom S.32 was validated against the EA models of Road Control Data Model OV, 1.0 and 2.0 to detect missing data owners. The validation against the original version did not detect any problem. The validation against the 1.0 and 2.0 versions both detected one data entity without a data owner. Similar to misalignment symptom S.02, a possible extension is to examine whether or not a data entity needs an owner. There must be cases when data entities do not need a data owner. This examination is not included in the query, therefore a possible extension is to alter the query to investigate this stipulation as well. Follow-up interviews on results validation confirmed that there are data entities in the road control initiative which have no data owner, ergo the query worked properly in this case.

Finally, misalignment symptom S.52 was validated against Road Control Process 1.0 and Road Control Process 2.0 to explore unused data entities. The query used the EA model of Road Control Data Model 1.0 and Road Control Data Model 2.0 respectively to compare the business process models with the list of data entities. Both the validation against 1.0 and 2.0 versions detected 2 unused data entities. Contrary to the overtime incompatibility checking in misalignment symptom S.18, the malfunction was not corrected during the progress of the initiative. The query has one major potential for extension. Similar to data usage checking, the examination can be extended to other usage checks as well. Follow-up interviews on results validation verified that there are unused data entities in the road control initiative, ergo the query worked well in this case. Interviews also confirmed that there is a need for query extension in terms of similar usage checks. Appropriate EA models have to be sorted out to detect other kinds of usage checks.

7 Conclusion and Further Research

This paper outlined public sector specific issues of alignment assessment and alignment problems. The paper discussed the topic of EAM-based analysis of misalignment problems in public sector using an existing rule-based method. The case study analysed the applicability of the framework in a public organisation. We assume that strategic alignment is a prevalent problem in any public or private organisations that can be considered from many aspects like culture, leadership, planning procedure and mechanisms, but also from the evidences of EA models and available metrics. The analysing framework presented in this paper is based on EAM models to discover symptoms of misalignment. The proposed methodology was tested in a case study of a public sector organisation, showing several misalignment issues related to the four main perspectives of strategic alignment (strategic implementation, technology leverage, technology exploitation, technology implementation). A possible future extension is to examine the correctness of the proposed methodology by objective measures using existing fit measurement methods (e.g. [1, 5]). The alignment of IT and organisations is a dynamic exercise, not easy to implement, awareness does not suffice, and actually the two main poles of alignment, strategy and technology, are drifting apart for one reason or another. The proposed method can facilitate planning by discover various alignment problems in organizations, where the complexity of the organization and the IT infrastructure hides the interdependences and misalignment symptoms. This approach, as a preliminary analysis can be used as a base for IT planning, managerial level discussion about IT, and organization design. The quality of the analysis is determined by the available set of EA models, but in many organizations sophisticated modelling and measurement practice can provide sufficient data for analysis. In public sector organizations the push towards digital transformation is not so dramatic than in the private sector, but still a major trend. IT is the inevitably necessary facilitator of public services and has a pervasive impact on the organizational configuration.

Acknowledgement.　Supported by the ÚNKP-17-4 New National Excellence Program of the Ministry of Human Capacities.

References

1. Al Bouna, B., Raad, E.J., Chbeir, R., Elia, C., Haraty, R.: Anonymizing multimedia documents. World Wide Web **19**(1), 135–155 (2016)
2. Carvalho, G., Sousa, P.: Business and information systems misalignment model (BISMAM): an holistic model leveraged on misalignment and medical sciences approaches. In: Proceedings of the Third International Workshop on Business/IT Alignment and Interoperability (BUSITAL 2008). CEUR-WS, Aachen, vol. 336, pp. 104–119 (2008)
3. Chen, H.M., Kazman, R., Garg, A.: BITAM: an engineering-principled method for managing misalignments between business and IT architectures. Sci. Comput. Program. **57** (1), 5–26 (2005)
4. Fritscher, B., Pigneur, Y.: Business IT alignment from business model to enterprise architecture. In: Salinesi, C., Pastor, O. (eds.) CAiSE 2011. LNBIP, vol. 83, pp. 4–15. Springer, Heidelberg (2011). https://doi.org/10.1007/978-3-642-22056-2_2
5. Gerber, D., et al.: DeFacto—temporal and multilingual deep fact validation. Web Semant. Sci. Serv. Agents World Wide Web **35**, 85–101 (2015)
6. Henderson, J.C., Venkatraman, H.: Strategic alignment: leveraging information technology for transforming organizations. IBM Syst. J. **32**(1), 472–484 (1993)
7. Luftman, J., Lyytinen, K., Zvi, T.: Enhancing the measurement of information technology (IT) business alignment and its influence on company performance. J. Inf. Technol. **32**(1), 26–46 (2015)
8. Niemann, K.D.: From Enterprise Architecture to IT Governance, vol. 1. Springer Fachmedien, Heidelberg (2006). https://doi.org/10.1007/978-3-8348-9011-5
9. Őri, D., Szabó, Z.: Pattern-based analysis of business-IT mismatches in EA models: insights from a case study. In: Hallé, S., Dijkman, R., Lapalme, J. (Eds.) Proceedings of the 2017 IEEE 21st International Enterprise Distributed Object Computing Conference Workshops and Demonstrations (EDOCW 2017), pp. 92–99 (2017)

10. Őri, D.: On exposing strategic and structural mismatches between business and information systems: misalignment symptom detection based on enterprise architecture model analysis. Ph.D. thesis, May 2017

11. Pereira, C.M., Sousa, P.: Business and information systems alignment: understanding the key issues. In: Proceedings of the 11th European Conference on Information Technology Evaluation, pp. 341–348 (2004)

12. Rusu, L., Jonathan, G.M.: IT alignment in public organizations: a systematic literature review. In: Rusu, L., Viscusi, G. (eds.) Information Technology Governance in Public Organizations. ISIS, vol. 38, pp. 27–57. Springer, Cham (2017). https://doi.org/10.1007/978-3-319-58978-7_2

13. Saat, J., Franke, U., Lagerström, R., Ekstedt, M.: Enterprise architecture meta models for IT/business alignment situations. In: 14th IEEE International Enterprise Distributed Object Computing Conference, pp. 14–23. IEEE Press, New York (2010)

14. Short, J.E., Venkatraman, N.: Beyond business process redesign: redefining Baxter's business network. Sloan Manag. Rev. 34(1), 7 (1992)

15. Strong, D.M., Volkoff, O.: Understanding organization-enterprise system fit: a path to theorizing the information technology artifact. MIS Q. 34(4), 731–756 (2010)

16. Venkatraman, N.: IT-enabled business transformation: from automation to business scope redefinition. Sloan Manag. Rev. 35(2), 73 (1994)

17. Versteeg, G., Bouwman, H.: Business architecture: a new paradigm to relate business strategy to ICT. Inf. Syst. Front. 8(2), 91–102 (2006)

18. Winkler, T.J.: IT governance mechanisms and administration/IT alignment in the public sector: a conceptual model and case validation. In: Proceedings of International Conference on Wirtschaftsinformatik, pp. 831–845 (2003)

19. Zachman, J.A.: A framework for information systems architecture. IBM Syst. J. 26(3), 276–292 (1987)

20. Zarvic, N., Wieringa, R.: An integrated enterprise architecture framework for business-IT alignment. White Paper (2006)

Young People's Views of Municipality Websites: Use, Attitudes, and Perception of Quality

Hanne Sørum[(✉)]

Westerdals Oslo School of Arts, Communication and Technology, Oslo, Norway
hanne.sorum@westerdals.no

Abstract. The present paper investigates public sector websites in Norway by focusing on municipalities. Norway consists of 422 municipalities each of which has its own website. To help inform the increasing investments and use of technologies within eGovernment, this study focuses on young people's perceptions of municipality websites. Today's young people constitute a key user group in the coming years. The following research questions are investigated: (1) *How frequently do young people visit municipality websites and for what reasons?* (2) *Do young people prefer physical meetings or online communication when interacting with municipalities?* (3) *How do young people perceive the quality of municipality websites, when evaluating content, design, and usability?* An online survey was conducted with undergraduate students (n = 200) in Norway. Findings suggest that young adults do not widely use municipality websites and that they visit primarily to search for specific information or use digital services. Results also suggest that young adults prefer digital interaction over face-to-face communication, and email and chat are their most favored ways to interact with the public sector. They consider paper-based communication undesirable. Participants ranked the quality of municipality websites as moderate to good but were not overwhelmingly positive. The paper ends with concluding remarks and suggestions for future research.

Keywords: Public sector websites · Municipalities · Website quality
User satisfaction · Usability · Online survey questionnaire

1 Introduction

Norway is one of many countries in which there have been major technological changes and advances over the past 20 years. These changes affect citizens in many ways, including how they use technology, communicate, solve tasks, and live their lives. Norway is a relatively small country with 422 municipalities of different size and population spread. The country consists of about 5.1 million inhabitants and is ranked the happiest country in the world [1]. Each municipality in Norway presents its own website to provide information and services to citizens and businesses. Within the private sector, 80% of all enterprises (with a minimum of 10 employees) in Norway have their own websites [2]. After the United States, Norway was the first country outside the United States to be connected to the ARPANET (1973), and today 90% of

© Springer Nature Switzerland AG 2018
A. Kő and E. Francesconi (Eds.): EGOVIS 2018, LNCS 11032, pp. 86–100, 2018.
https://doi.org/10.1007/978-3-319-98349-3_7

the population uses the internet to download/read newspapers and magazines [3], while 97% of all Norwegian households had access to the internet in 2016 [4]. Almost every citizen in the country has access to online information and services provided by the public sector. According to Goldkuhl [5]: "Citizens should always be able to reach, through the web, government agencies and also be served by them" (p. 135). Websites have thus become important conduits for the dialogue between citizens and the public sector [6], and high-quality interactions are a vital component of this dialogue. This uptake of technology puts great pressure on public sector organizations, forcing them to create a user-centric focus in development and quality improvements. Despite this pressure, digitization in the Norwegian public sector has progressed slowly. There is also a widespread issue among Norwegian municipalities that existing digital services are not being used as expected [7]. While 63% of Norwegian municipalities have set specific targets for digitizing services, only 16% have identified the effects such investments will have on citizens and businesses, and only 23% have identified the effects within the municipal enterprise [8]. A positive sign is that public sector websites, on average, had significantly higher quality in 2011 than in 2007 and increasingly focused on important quality aspects. A study conducted by Rambøll [9] on mapping the development and plans in digital business development and innovation showed that citizens perceive digital services to be effective and adequate for their needs.

Although a range of citizens likely use municipality websites, this study has chosen to focus on the perceptions of young people. Young people today use the internet a lot and have broad experience with a variety of technologies. Many of them are online frequently and are skilled in the use of social media, apps, and a range of platforms. Though they may not frequently need the information and services offered by municipalities, they most likely will in the coming years. For example, they may need information on applications for nurseries or permits for housing renovations. Today's young people constitute a key user group in the coming years, and the public sector should be interested in developing websites and digital interactions that are in line with the needs and requirements of this target group. Understanding this group will help the public sector increase website usage and user satisfaction, as well as guide digitization initiatives within eGovernment environments. To examine this area of interest, the present study addresses the following three research questions: (1) *How frequently do young people visit municipality websites and for what reasons?* (2) *Do young people prefer physical meetings or online communication when interacting with municipalities?* (3) *How do young people perceive the quality of municipality websites, when evaluating content, design, and usability?* To answer these questions, an online survey was given to undergraduate students (n = 200) at a Norwegian university college located in Oslo, the capital city.

The rest of this paper is organized as follows. Related work is described in Sect. 2 and methodology is presented in Sect. 3. Findings are presented in Sect. 4, followed by a discussion in Sect. 5. Concluding remarks are made in Sect. 6, along with suggestions for future research directions.

2   Related Work

Prior studies within the field of eGovernment have focused on issues concerning electronic service provision, and many published articles concentrate on the adoption of services from the supplier side (the government) [10]. According to Axelsson, Melin, and Lindgren [11]: "The main goals of e-government are to increase agency efficiency and offer benefits to citizens" (p. 10). To this end, users' perceptions of quality are important. The government provides services, information, and news to citizens, and citizens actively participate in dialogue with the public sector using the tools provided by public organizations [12]. Over the past ten years, the public sector has undergone many changes and has moved from offering simple online services to more complex services that create a two-way dialogue with citizens [13]. Governments in many countries other than Norway have set goals and launched strategies for developing high-quality web services and satisfaction among users. These goals and strategies are anchored in the guidelines which public and private organizations are forced to comply. Moreover, public websites (e.g., in Norway and Denmark) have for many years been ranked by quality. The quality criteria are public available and reflect aspects (e.g., usability, accessibility and content) that are important from a user's (citizen's) point of view. The aim has been to encourage public organizations to prioritize and spend resources on website quality improvements. The winners of such web awards (website ranking) are highlighted as good-practice examples and serve as inspiration to many organizations within both the public and private sectors. During the last decade, attention to improving user experiences has increased, and the use of innovative technologies has expanded dramatically. The national ranking of public websites and the many web awards are examples of that, along with the many blogs, forums, and digital societies that discuss the experiences of technology users.

Furthermore, website quality is extremely fluid and dynamic, and continuous improvements are important [14]. These truths are evidenced by the fact that both public and private organizations have invested large sums into information technology (IT) over the past decades, and budgets are only increasing [15]. Therefore, it is important to focus on users throughout the development and quality-improvement processes to ensure users' needs and requirements are considered. A vital component of interaction design is to maintain and develop usable products, which are easy to learn and effective and enjoyable to use [16]. Such design is particularly important in the public sector, which lacks competitors and holds a monopoly on most digital services. Using design principles and heuristics, as well as guidelines provided by the government, guide the public sector's digital development in the right direction. Norman [17] suggested principles that can be easily applied to the development process to make the system more user-friendly. To emphasize, when digital services are developed within the Norwegian public sector, the government explicitly states that users (citizens) and their needs must be placed in focus throughout the entire development process [18]. "For citizens, the benefits of e-government include greater service access and ease of interaction with the government; and for governments, the benefits are lower service delivery cost and a new channel to engage citizens" [19, p. 87]. eGovernment shall therefore provide values for both the citizens and the sector itself, that can be linked to efficiency, effectiveness and great user experiences. According to Krug [20], people do not read the entire content of a website but scan content they find interesting. This finding likely also applies to government websites and is important knowledge for website developers and designers. If a site's design is inconsistent or does not meet user expectations and needs, users can get confused and be forced to spend time and effort on usability concerns. Website usability and aesthetics contribute significantly to user satisfaction [21]. Despite this fact, the public sector has not made the digital leap effectively and lacks digital flexibility and choice when compared to private organizations [22]. As stated previously, public sector websites, in contrast to private ones, must commit to almost every government strategy and goal, such as government guidelines for website design and service delivery. Due to the increasing user adoption of digital services within eGovernment, we also find many examples of best practices and maturity models [23]. A study by Malik, Bhargava, and Chaudhary [6] concludes that there are few issues of usability and accessibility for public sector websites when investigating district level in India. "If e-government website design is of a professional standard with high quality, then it will promote user satisfaction and facilitate adoption" [24, p. 2]. This goal may be more important for public organizations than for private, as it is relevant to ensuring that all citizens have equal access to public information and digital services [25].

Quality evaluations and improvements to website maintenance play an important role in achieving this goal [26]. Bad website design is poor marketing for any company or organization, and great attention should therefore be given to quality evaluations and improvements [27]. We stress the importance of knowing the users and their individual needs and requirements. To assess the quality of websites, many frameworks and quality indicators have been suggested, e.g. [12, 28]. Because it ensures equal access, accessibility is also a vital component of website quality, especially within an eGovernment context [29]. Although there is consensus among scholars and practitioners on the importance of website quality, different aspects of a website have been emphasized. According to Papadomichelaki and Mentzas [30]: "The subject of e-service and website quality is very rich in context of definitions, models, and measurement instruments. Nevertheless, different quality dimensions have been proposed and there is no consensus on the component dimensions" (p. 98). Different approaches can be used to study website quality and in some studies service quality is part of this term, along with other quality aspects. However, this can also be evaluated separately. Besides that, this is a multidimensional construct, it is still developed tools to measure quality and satisfaction. Rocha [26] proposed a global framework for measuring website quality that is anchored in three dimensions: content quality, service quality, and technical quality. Each dimension consists of sub-dimensions and measures that are specific and measurable in a given context of use.

Papadomichelaki and Mentzas [30] established an instrument for measuring the service quality of public websites from the user's point of view by focusing on reliability, efficiency, citizen support, and trust. They found that each aspect had a significant influence on the perception of overall service quality. In addition, Tan, Benbasat, and Cenfetelli [31] found that high-quality websites matter for building trust among users of eGovernment services. Achieving trust is important for meeting users' need for safety and must be considered when designing any website. According to

Qutaishat [27], the following quality aspects are important: system quality, information quality, and service quality. Service quality had the strongest effect on intention to use eGovernment services, followed by service quality and information quality. The importance of each quality aspect may also depend on the type of website, the context of use, and user type and intention. Barnes and Vidgen [32] emphasized many of the same aspects of quality but divided the measures into the following categories: usability, information quality, service interaction, and overall impression. Information quality is grounded in the information systems (IS) literature; interaction and service quality from marketing, e-commerce, and IS service quality research; and usability from human-computer interaction research. Literature from various research areas is therefore important in measuring user experiences on the web and can be viewed as a discipline that draws on different subject areas. Liu, Arnett, and Litecky [33] conducted a survey among webmasters to investigate the design quality of e-commerce websites. They emphasized six quality aspects: information quality, learning capability, playfulness, system quality, system use, and service quality. Many of the same aspects apply to eGovernment sites. Oliveira and Welch [34] found variation among local governments in use of social media tools (e.g., Facebook, Twitter, and Skype) based on type of department or agency.

Both the government and the business community use social media to develop reputation. In addition, 3 out of 4 government enterprises and 3 out of 5 business enterprises use social media as a means of recruitment [35]. Findings from a study by Gregg and Walczak [36] indicate that website quality explains 49% of variation in trust for eBay sellers, and sellers with good website quality are perceived to be equally trustworthy regardless of their eBay reputations. Moreover, sellers with poor-quality websites are not perceived as trustworthy despite high eBay reputation scores. In sum, website quality is a multidimensional construct consisting of different quality attributes. Many of the same aspects are emphasized when investigating the overall user experience within the eGovernment domain and information systems in general.

3   Method

3.1   Survey Design

An online survey consisting of 17 questions was developed and distributed. The questions addressed website quality as determined by previous research, e.g. [31, 32, 37] and included the aspects of content (information quality), usability, and design (visual appearance). These are all considered important aspects of user interfaces. The study therefore strives to use quality dimensions relevant to public sector websites and examples of questions are: I think the information is easy to understand, it is easy to navigate the website and the design meets my expectations. The measurement scale ranged from "completely disagree to completely agree" and "very low to very high" (five-point scale), including the alternative "I do not know". The questionnaire also included free-text fields to allow participants to enter open-ended comments. Survey Monkey® (www.surveymonkey.com) was employed for design, collection of data, and descriptive analysis. Each survey question (except the optional open-ended comments) had to be answered before continuing to the next. For some questions, only one answer was possible, while for others it was possible to choose more than one response. To reduce the risk of errors, unclear questions, and technical challenges during the data collection process, two pilot tests were conducted before the survey was launched. The aim was to ensure that all questions were relevant and easy to understand. Only a few changes were made to the questionnaire following the pilot tests. To ensure validity the questionnaire has been developed based on relevant literature, tests are completed and feedback has been incorporated.

3.2   Data Collection

Data were collected under controlled conditions in a classroom setting. Students were invited to participate in the study before the start of a lecture, and it was clearly stated that participation was voluntary. If they were not interested in participating in the study, they were not told to provide any explanation. Participants were given a short introduction to the study and a link (web address) and were asked to log in from their own computers. As reported by SurveyMonkey®, participants required an average of 6 min to complete the questionnaire. It was quiet in the classroom during the data collection process, and there were no disturbing elements to influence the respondents. The researcher was available throughout the process to address any questions or problems. The survey was closed with 205 completed responses. Five respondents are excluded from the analyzes due to age (over 30 years) and not considered as young adults. Consequently, the dataset in the present study draws on the results from 200 respondents.

3.3   Data Analysis

After the data were collected, they were first reviewed to get an idea of how question responses were distributed on the measurement scales. Then focus turned to the three research questions addressed. The open-ended, qualitative comments provided by participants were also examined and used as a component in the findings section (Sect. 4). They are presented in the paper via direct quotation, aiming to shed light on topics not covered in the questionnaire. The tools used for analysis of the quantitative data were SurveyMonkey® and Microsoft Excel. This paper provides a descriptive analysis of the data.

3.4   Respondent Profile

The participants recruited to the study were students enrolled in a bachelor's program at a university college located in the capital of Norway (Oslo). The profile of respondents is shown in Table 1.

From Table 1, we see that males are overrepresented in the study (111 male and 89 female participants). Furthermore, because all respondents were enrolled in a bachelor's program, few had education beyond that level. Most of the respondents were in the 21- to 25-year age group (75%) and self-reported that their IT skills are better than

Table 1. Respondent profile (actual numbers with percentages in parentheses).

Gender	Male: 111 (55.50%); female: 89 (44.50%)
Age	20 years or younger: 20 (10%); 21–25 years: 150 (75%); 26–30 years: 30 (15%)
Perception of IT-knowledge	Bad: 1 (0.50%); medium good: 27 (13.50%); better than average: 105 (52.50%); very good; 67 (35.50%); I do not know: 0 (0%)

average (52.50%) or very good (35.50%). The respondent profile also confirms that our respondents were members of our target group in the present study (young adults).

4   Findings

This section is divided into three parts. Section 4.1 reports why and how often young people visit municipality websites. Section 4.2 presents the findings regarding the role of participant perception of social media and online interactions. Section 4.3 reports respondents' views on the content, design, and usability of municipality websites.

4.1   Visits of Public Websites

There are many reasons citizens visit public websites, and the frequency of visits varies. Study participants generally reported visiting municipal websites rarely. Visiting occasionally (more than once every six months) was reported by 42.50% of respondents, while 27.50% reported visiting very rarely (less than once a year). Only 13.50% reported visiting monthly and 6.50% weekly. None of the respondents visited daily, and about 10% had never visited a municipality website. These results suggest that young people generally visit municipal websites infrequently.

Regarding the reasons why young people visit this type of website, the majority (73%) visit to search for specific information, while 37% visit to apply for a digital service. Visiting to assist others in finding information and/or applying for help was reported by 23%, and 13% of respondents did not know why they visited municipal websites. Thus, searching for information and applying for services were the most common reasons for a visit, followed by helping others with these tasks. In the open comments, one respondent gave the following reason for a visit: "*I want to find information and meeting notes that I can use for political influence*" while another wrote: "*For access to different types of services (provided by the government), I have to go through the municipality's website.*" Other reasons mentioned were: searching for job opportunities, seeking information on doctors and dentists, and linking to the library. Overall, municipal websites are rarely visited by younger people.

4.2   The Role of Social Media

Digital interactions and online communication has replaced many traditional face-to-face interactions and physical meetings. Table 2 reveals the findings regarding the interaction and communication preferences of participants.

Table 2. Types of interaction preferred by respondents.

	Completely disagree	Disagree	Medium	Agree	Completely agree	Do not know
Electronic	–	–	3.50%	26.50%	69.50%	0.50%
Face-to-face	9.00%	15.00%	41.50%	19.00%	13.00%	2.50%
By phone	9.50%	12.00%	27.50%	32.00%	19.00%	–
Paper-based	50.50%	26.50%	15.00%	4.00%	3.50%	0.50%
Social media	11.00%	13.50%	31.50%	26.50%	17.00%	0.50%

As shown in Table 2, electronic communication by form, email, chat, etc. are most preferred by participants when having an interaction with the public sector, followed by communication by phone and through social media. Face-to-face interactions and paper-based communication are the least preferred alternatives. On this topic, one respondent wrote the following in the comment field: "*I prefer paper-based information, but not paper-based communication.*" This comment suggests a perceived difference between paper-based information and paper-based communication (two-way dialogue).

The public sector makes use of social media to communicate with citizens and various target groups. In the present survey, we chose to examine such interactions from a user's point of view and determine the type of interaction users prefer to have with public organizations. Table 3 shows the distribution of respondent preferences regarding the use of social media and electronic communication.

Table 3. Respondent opinions on the importance of various functions for interactions.

	Very low	Low	Medium	High	Very high	Do not know
Chat	10.50%	16.50%	21.50%	23.00%	18.00%	10.50%
Email	–	2.50%	14.50%	24.00%	51.50%	7.50%
Forum	16.50%	30.00%	24.50%	14.50%	6.00%	8.50%
Blog	18.00%	29.00%	26.00%	14.00%	6.00%	7.00%
Facebook	14.00%	18.50%	29.50%	23.00%	6.50%	8.50%
Twitter	37.50%	25.00%	17.50%	8.50%	1.50%	10.00%

From Table 3, we see that respondents generally prefer having digital interactions with public sector organizations. We also find that interaction through email is most preferred, followed by a chat with the service center or equivalent. Moreover, respondents consider a link to an organization's Facebook profile important, as well as a link to a forum for discussing municipality topics and general citizen welfare. To a lesser extent, respondents prefer a blog for reading about topics concerning the municipality. Twitter is the least preferred alternative for communication with public organizations. In the questionnaire's open comment field, Snapchat, Instagram, and Infographics were mentioned as other preferred communication channels.

4.3   Perceptions of Content, Design, and Usability

To gather information on participants' opinions about the content, design, and usability of municipality websites, participants were given the following task: log in to the website of their home municipality and spend 2–3 min becoming familiar with the content and services provided. Afterwards, they were asked to complete the questionnaire about content, design, and usability. Most respondents (65%) had visited the website before, while 26.50% were visiting for the first time and 8.50% were unsure whether they had visited previously. More male participants (55%) had previously visited the website than females (45%).

Furthermore, 39.50% of respondents knew the website address (URL), while 60.50% had to search for the address on Google. Regarding respondents' overall impression of the website (the quality level in general), the findings were distributed as follows: very bad (2.50%), bad (14%), medium (43.50%), good (35.50%), and very good (4.50%). Results also show that females were generally more positive about the websites than males. On the question *"Would you like to revisit the website?,"* 17% responded "yes," while 3.50% responded "no." The majority (77.50%) answered "only if I must," and 2% chose "I do not know." Here we find a relatively equal distribution for males and females. Moreover, in Norway, there is a requirement that public websites follow certain standards and guidelines for accessibility and universal design (WCAG). While 62% knew that public websites should be accessible to everyone in our digital society (including those with hearing impairments, color blindness, etc.), only 46.50% of respondents knew about this specific requirement, and 35% did not know either of these expectations.

Regarding the quality of information, respondents generally gave high scores and they seemed satisfied with the quality of the websites' content. All aspects of information quality received relatively equal scores, and none of them was rated remarkably low or high. However, the ratings of some aspects stood out. Respondents reported that it was easy to find relevant information and that the information was easy to understand. It is worth noting, however, that when questioned about the extent to which information is perceived to be updated (from their point of view), 16.50% answered, "do not know/have no meaning," though most ratings were generally positive. This aspect of a website may be more difficult to evaluate after only a few minutes and especially following a first visit. Somewhat weaker are the findings regarding respondents' comparison of the quality of information on municipality websites with that on other websites they visit. For this comparison, 15% answered, "do not know/have no meaning," and almost 50% answered "medium." Figure 1 illustrates the distribution of answers for each of the three quality aspects assessed in the study; content, design and usability.

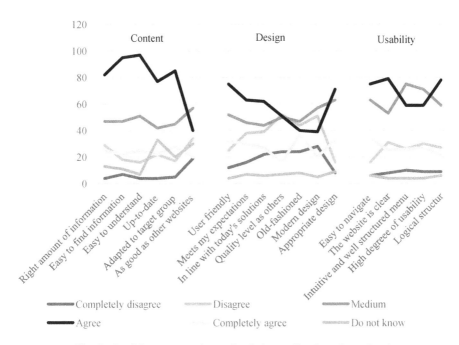

Fig. 1. Participant perceptions of website quality (actual numbers).

Regarding participant perceptions of design quality, Fig. 1 shows that the municipality websites received the highest scores on appropriateness of design and user-friendliness. While the scores on these measures are not as good as those for quality of the information, they are still relatively high. However, some aspects of design were rated worse. Though respondents found the designs appropriate for municipality websites, they considered them relatively old-fashioned, impressions which do not invite repeated use. Regarding design, one respondent wrote: *"The municipalities are not penalized for a bad website as a company does. All residents MUST use that website either they will or will not."* Another wrote: *"The design is okay, works well for what it is meant for, but could be better. Again, it is a municipal website, so do not have so much regrets."* These comments demonstrate negative attitudes about and low expectations for public websites. Regardless, participants generally found the websites easy to navigate and rated them high on usability. Ease of use is therefore given great scores, even though there are weaker results regarding the design (visual appearance).

To provide an overall impression of how respondents experienced the municipal websites, Fig. 2 shows the average scores of all answers within each of the three main quality areas distributed on a Likert-scale ranging from completely disagree to completely agree (including do not know).

Figure 2 shows that respondents were relatively satisfied with the websites overall. The distribution of these averages shows fewer responses on the lower and upper ends (completely disagree/totally agree); most respondents rated quality at the middle of the scale, with a lean to the positive end. Although results are generally positive, there is room to improve design, usability, and the quality of information and services

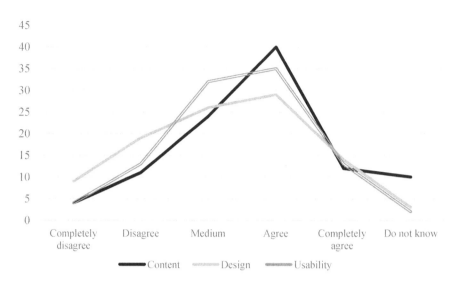

Fig. 2. Average scores for content, design, and usability based on all survey items distributed on a Likert-scale (reported in percentage).

provided. Such improvement is critical for targeting this younger group, given its great IT knowledge and frequent presence on the web and other digital channels.

5   Discussion

eGovernment aims to increase efficiency and effectiveness for both citizens and the public sector itself [11]. Over the past ten years, many changes have occurred within the public sector, and organizations have progressed from offering simple online services to facilitating two-way digital dialogue with citizens [13]. Website quality and user satisfaction are important to providing high quality interactions [16] that fulfill the goals set by the government. Most of the Norwegian population uses the internet [3] and almost all young people have access to and/or use the internet regularly [4]. The younger generation therefore has good knowledge of IT and most likely, high expectations for user interfaces, use of technologies, usability, and provision of online information and services. By focusing on younger adults, the findings of the present study reveal that respondents rarely visit municipal websites; none of the respondents visit daily. Furthermore, 10% had never visited a municipality website. When they do visit, the majority search for specific information, and/or apply for a digital service. Our findings suggest that although young people are online users, municipality websites are not among the websites they regularly visit, rather the opposite. As the main reason for visiting a municipality website, among the respondents, is closely related to information search and services, it is nearby to believe that the content presented on such websites is something the respondents do not need or must deal with on a regular basis. Therefore, to capture young people it is important to know what content they are looking for, for what purpose and how they prefer to acquire this information.

As the results also suggest that electronic communication with public organizations is most preferred by young people, followed by communication via phone and social media, we need to facilitate for high quality interactions on the web. This finding is aligned with the government's goals of profit realization (e.g. efficiency and effectiveness) and the use of digital channels for greater communication between citizens and the public sector [19]. The least preferred communication alternatives among young people are face-to-face interactions and paper-based communication, which is more time-consuming and expensive, both for individuals and the public sector itself. Most precisely, from an organizational perspective, this is another reason to increase digitization [11, 19], to create public values and benefits. Although digitization within the public sector in Norway has progressed slowly and only 23% of municipalities have identified the effects of digitization [7], the participants in this study are clear about their preference for digital communication and how they prefer to interact. Furthermore, the public sector explicitly states that citizen need is a vital factor for determining website usage and user satisfaction [9]. However, the public sector also faces challenges in making the digital leap and, compared with private organizations, lacks flexibility and choice [22]. According to these findings, if the eGovernment website design is professional and high-quality, it will foster user satisfaction and adoption [24].

Design and usability of websites, and high-quality information is considered as significant contributors to user satisfaction [27, 32]. It is important with a visually attractive user interface (inviting to use). In general, participants of the present study ranked the quality of the websites' information highly and they ranked each quality aspect comparably; none were ranked very good or very poor. Half the respondents ranked the websites as highly user-friendly. However, respondents agreed that the designs were not modern (based on respondents' views on a modern website design) and that there is room for improvement, for keeping up with the technological changes and improvements. Participants reported that it is easy to find relevant information and that the information is easy to understand. This finding is a positive sign because information quality is a vital contributor to user experiences on the web [16, 20], however, there are potential for improvements regarding website design and the art of creating a modern expression, that attracts younger users. For web designers and other facilitators/developers this may be useful knowledge in future development work, along with identifying the needs across different target groups.

Although some positive findings have been made in this study, we clearly see potential for improvements concerning the user interface, increased use of public information and services, and facilitation for digital interactions and communication between the public sector and citizens. Though it may not be appropriate to digitize all types of services (most likely not), but to the extent that it is suitable, the findings in this study may be some input to discuss. Younger people are target groups we know a lot about, at the same time, there is also much we do not know – concerning their needs and requirements, use and satisfaction with public information and digital services.

There are some limitations to this study: The participants in the survey are all students. This does not necessarily have to be a weakness, but it is worth mentioning. They are also asked to evaluate a specific website, some of them have never visited before, after a few minutes of use. Compared with a traditional usability test, the results are more superficial and not necessarily based on usage over a longer time period. In addition, using a questionnaire, it is also limited with information gained regarding usability issues and quality aspects of a website. However, this study provides some findings to follow up.

6 Conclusions

From this study's findings, the following generalizations can be made: (1) Young adults rarely visit public websites. Information and services offered on municipal websites are not relevant or of interest to them. (2) When interacting with the public sector, young people prefer online communication and digital interaction over paper-based communication and physical meetings. (3) Young adult users are in general satisfied with the quality of municipal websites, especially the quality of the information provided. They believe, however, that there is room for improvement in design and visual appearance. (4) If the public sector aims to reach young citizens, it must develop online content and design that captures this target group and facilitate communication on the users' premises.

Future studies could focus on the information and services that are relevant to young people, the difference in website satisfaction across various audiences (target groups), user design preferences, and the typical reasons for visiting municipal websites (and public websites in general).

References

1. World Happiness Report. http://worldhappiness.report/ed/2017/. Accessed 17 Jan 2018
2. SSB. https://www.ssb.no/teknologi-og-innovasjon/statistikker/iktbrukn/aar. Accessed 11 Jan 2018
3. SSB. https://www.ssb.no/teknologi-og-innovasjon/statistikker/ikthus. Accessed 11 Jan 2018
4. OECD Internet access (indicator). https://doi.org/10.1787/69c2b997-en. Accessed 17 Jan 2018
5. Goldkuhl, G.: What does it mean to serve the citizen in e-services? Towards a practical theory on founded in socio-instrumental pragmatism. Int. J. Public Inf. Syst. **3**, 135–159 (2017)
6. Malik, P., Bhargava, R., Chaudhary, K.: Assessing the effectiveness of accessibility and usability of government website at district level. Int. J. Comput. Trends Technol. (IJCTT) **49** (1), 58–70 (2017)
7. TU.   https://www.tu.no/artikler/det-star-darlig-til-med-digitalisering-i-offentlig-sektor/350723. Accessed 10 Apr 2017
8. Digi.no. https://www.digi.no/artikler/dette-er-et-desperat-rop-om-it-hjelp-fra-staten/350648. Accessed 11 Feb 2018
9. Difi.   https://www.difi.no/sites/difino/files/30.05.-kl.-09.00.-it-i-praksis-2013-lansering-digitalisering-i-offentlig-sektor-1-_1.pdf. Accessed 04 Mar 2017
10. Lee, J., Kim, H.J., Ahn, M.J.: The willingness of e-Government service adoption by business users: the role of offline service quality and trust in technology. Gov. Inf. Q. **28**, 222–230 (2011)

11. Axelsson, K., Melin, U., Lindgren, I.: Public e-services for agency efficiency and citizen benefit – findings from a stakeholder centered analysis. Gov. Inf. Q. **30**, 10–22 (2013)
12. Rodriguez, R.A., Giulianelli, D.A., Vera, P.M., Marko, I.B., Tigueros, A., Larrosa, M.: Analyzing e-governance mainstays on municipalities websites. In: Communicabaility MS 2008, Vancouver, BC, Canada, 31 October 2008, pp. 31–38 (2008)
13. Thorstensen, A., Udjus, L.: eDialogue: government innovation in Norway. In: 2011 International Conference on E-Business and E-Government (ICEE), Shanghai, China (2011). https://doi.org/10.1109/icebeg.2011.5887083
14. Wells, J.D., Valacich, J.S., Hess, T.J.: What signal are you sending? How website quality influences perceptions of product quality and purchase intentions. MIS Q. **35**(2), 373–396 (2011)
15. Mohagheghi, P., Jørgensen, M.: What contributes to the success of IT projects? In: 2017 IEEE/ACM 39th International Conference on Software Engineering Companion (ICSE-C), Buenos Aires, Argentina (2017). https://doi.org/10.1109/icse-c.2017.146
16. Preece, J., Sharp, H., Rogers, Y.: Interaction Design: Beyond Human-Computer Interaction, 4th edn. Wiley, Hoboken (2015). ISBN 978-1119020752
17. Norman, D.A.: The Design of Everyday Things (1998). ISBN 978-0-465-06710-7
18. Difi (2016). http://www.uio.no/studier/emner/jus/afin/FINF4001/h16/eg_forelesning-2016-finf-4001.pdf. Accessed 17 Jan 2018
19. Venkatesh, V., Thong, J.Y.L., Chan, F.K.Y., Hu, P.J.H.: Managing citizens' uncertainty in e-government services: the mediating and moderating roles of transparency and trust. Inf. Syst. Res. **27**(1), 87–111 (2016)
20. Krug, S.: Don't Make Me Think, Revisited – A Common Sense Approach to Web Usability. New Riders, Thousand Oaks (2014). ISBN 978-0-321-96551-6
21. Beaird, J.: The Principles of Beautiful Web Design. SitePoint Pty. Ltd., Melbourne (2007). ISBN 978-0-9802858-9-5
22. Weerakkody, V., Janssen, M., Dwivedi, Y.K.: Transformational change and business process reengineering (BPR): lessons from the British and Dutch public sector. Gov. Inf. Q. **28**, 320–328 (2011)
23. Andersen, K.V., Henriksen, H.Z.: E-government maturity models: extension of the Layne and Lee model. Gov. Inf. Q. **23**, 236–248 (2006)
24. Alshehri, M., Drew, S., Alhussain, T., Alghamdi, R.: The effects of website quality on adoption of e-government service: an empirical study applying UTAUT model using SEM. In: Proceedings of 23rd Australasian Conference on Information Systems, Melbourn, Australia, 3–5 December 2012 (2012)
25. Ministry of Modernisation (2005). https://www.regjeringen.no/globalassets/upload/fad/vedlegg/ikt-politikk/enorway_2009.pdf. Accessed 04 Dec 2017
26. Rocha, Á.: Framework for a global quality evaluation of a website. Online Inf. Rev. **36**(3), 374–382 (2012)
27. Qutaishat, F.T.: Users' perceptions towards website quality and its effect on intention to use e-government services in Jordan. Int. Bus. Res. **6**(1), 97–105 (2013)
28. Lappas, G., Triantafillidou, A., Kleftodimos, A. Yannas, P.: Evaluation framework of local e-government and e-democracy: a citizens' perspective. In: 2015 IEEE Conference on e-Learning, e-Management and e-Services (IC3e), Melaka, Malaysia (2015). https://doi.org/10.1109/ic3e.2015.7403509
29. Abdelgawad, A.A., Radianti, J., Snaprud, M.H., Krogstie, J.: Accessibility of Norwegian municipalities websites: an interactive learning environment experimental investigation. In: 2016 UKSim-AMSS 18th International Conference on Computer Modelling and Simulation (UKSim), Cambridge, UK (2016). https://doi.org/10.1109/uksim.2016.16

30. Papadomichelaki, X., Mentzas, G.: e-GovQual: a multiple-item scale for assessing e-government service quality. Gov. Inf. Q. **29**, 98–109 (2012)
31. Tan, C.-W., Benbasat, I., Cenfetelli, R.T.: Building citizen trust towards e-government services: do high quality websites matter? In: Proceedings of the 41st Hawaii International Conference on System Sciences, Hawaii (2008)
32. Barnes, S.J., Vidgen, R.T.: Data triangulation and web quality metrics: a case study in e-government. Inf. Manag. **43**, 767–777 (2006)
33. Liu, C., Arnett, K.P., Litecky, C.: Design quality of websites for electronic commerce: fortune 1000 webmasters' evaluations. Electron. Mark. **10**(2), 120–129 (2000)
34. Oliveira, G.H.M., Welch, E.W.: Social media use in local government: linkage of technology, task, and organizational context. Gov. Inf. Q. **30**(4), 397–405 (2013)
35. SSB. http://www.ssb.no/teknologi-og-innovasjon/artikler-og-publikasjoner/bruker-sosiale-medier-til-omdomme-og-rekruttering. Accessed 11 Jan 2018
36. Gregg, D.G., Walczak, S.: The relationship between website quality, trust and price premiums at online auctions. Electron. Commer. Res. **10**, 1–25 (2010)
37. Prybutok, V.R., Zhang, X., Ryan, S.D.: Evaluating leadership, IT quality, and net benefits in an e-government environment. Inf. Manag. **45**, 143–152 (2008)

Knowledge Management in the Context of e-government

Knowledge in Government: New Directions

Keynote – Extended Abstract

Roland Traunmüller[(✉)]

Johannes Kepler University Linz, Altenbergerstraße 69, 4040 Linz, Austria
`traunm@ifs.uni-linz.ac.at`

1 Knowledge and Digitalization

Digitalization is the main driver aiming at the integration of digital technologies into everyday life. The motto is making digital everything that can be digitized and converting information into digital format. One core element for growth is the avid gathering of data via automatic devices. Extensive data collections lead to the realm usually labelled with the notion Big Data. This is a term for data sets so large/complex that traditional data processing application software is inadequate to deal with them. Under the label "Big Data" convincing promises are stated yet also threats and difficulties occur underlining the dark side of development (Big Brother).

Digitalization brings an overwhelming amount of data and mastering this abundance is of utmost importance. Knowledge has become the head topic as the concepts of handling knowledge help at structuring the wealth of data. In addition, knowledge builds a bridge to connect quite diverse themes such as administrative work, legal norms, collaborative platforms, participation etc. A caveat should be added that the task of handling data in Digitalization encompasses enormous problems. In praxis, it means working with huge collections of heterogeneous data repositories, originated from different sources and with different quality, and holding data of miscellaneous semantic and type format.

Next one should stress the tight connection Digitalization and Globalization and the significance of competing developments. Their inclusion in the discussion is essential as the radical changes pertaining to Globalization exert high impacts and mutual influence. Here we cite just some megatrends: production with cyber-physical networks (IoT); traffic with autonomous driving; cities and their compliance with ecology; health with individualized medicine and tele-consulting.

2 General Features of Knowledge

Knowledge in general may be described as information combined with experience, context, interpretation, and reflection. Knowledge in general is marked by important characteristics: enriched value (more than just information); combining information (web of information); given purpose (purpose-oriented); directed towards a goal

© Springer Nature Switzerland AG 2018
A. Kő and E. Francesconi (Eds.): EGOVIS 2018, LNCS 11032, pp. 103–107, 2018.
https://doi.org/10.1007/978-3-319-98349-3_8

(goal-oriented); related to specific situation (context-sensitive); bearing relevance for somebody (subject-oriented); determining next actions (control). Concerning control loop retrospection leads back to quite early views of political cybernetics.

Knowledge is an abstract issue always connected either belonging to a person/group of persons or being embodied in artefacts (material items, structures, systems). The visibility of knowledge may be explicitly formalised as found in physical artefacts, formal rules, norms, systems etc. Implicit knowledge is in tacit, unspoken behaviour as well as in emotions, beliefs, desires and social practices.

3 Knowledge in Government

Turning to the topic of knowledge in organisations, knowledge and information stand for the decisive success factor. Knowledge is comprehended as diverse qualities, such as intellectual capital, as productive resource, as competitive factor or as instrument of power. Viewing a specific category of organisations, namely government, employment of knowledge is the dominant feature and officials may be regarded as knowledge workers par excellence.

Government has a high diversity in functions as the principal realms, legislation, public administration and justice, are quite different. Diversity grows as for every realm, various layers ought to be considered: governance as a strategic-political layer; diverse bodies as tactical layers; agencies as executive layers. Government involves numerous types of repositories. Some registers cover basic items such as persons, taxes, duties; others include geographical data. Other main categories concern legal norms and repositories containing controlling and management information.

4 Knowledge Management in Government

Objective is to manage knowledge distributed within and outside an organization with the instrument of a knowledge base. Knowledge Management emerged as a scientific discipline in the earlier 1990s. First were techno-centric methods with a focus on technology particularly concerned with enhancing knowledge sharing and creation. Then organizational methods were added dealing with questions how an organization ought to be designed for facilitating knowledge processes.

Most approaches are quasi built around such methods and tools. At least, a system for handling knowledge includes the following key elements: repositories, ontologies, content integration and tools for collaboration, knowledge dissemination and security. Repositories contain the collected knowledge while ontologies are standardized representation of knowledge, given by a set of concepts within a domain and the relationships between these concepts. A simple everyday example is a map, where the relevant ontology comprises map-symbols such as castle, church, temple, bridge, viewpoint etc.

Subsequently, some examples are given indicating current directions of knowledge in government.

5 Broadening the Range

Electronic government is about transformation: changing fundamentally the way government does what it does. The permanent e-Transformation puts the focus on diverse issues. As paradigms we cite: public governance, the law profession, commercial applications, business analysis and new registers.

Public governance in the general attracts high attention. The broad scope involves a bunch of issues: cooperative policy formulation; citizen and civil society involvement; efficient implementation of policies; a continuous evaluation of their results; an accountability of public decision makers.

Transforming the law profession deserves prominent notice. Tremendous change arises compared with earlier situations. Then technology had a smaller impact reduced to office software, key-word retrieval and internet access. Now usage of legal technology has advanced and multiplied. Consequently, the proximity to information technology will breed a new generation of law professionals.

Furthermore, the realm of commerce pursues novel ways and induces rampant changes in several segments, particularly in production, retail and finance. Government must cope with all these changes, especially in adapting/establishing regulations. For Bitcoins this means securing the taxation base in dealing with international enterprises. Novel methods offer new application as e.g. predictive analytics. Experiences from previous tax examinations will direct the assignment of future inspections.

Improved business analysis shows the power of new methods. Better recherche is enabled by intelligent retrieval extracting knowledge and insights from large and complex collections of digital data. New approaches for retrieval surpass conventional key-word directed analysis. Chiefly, the semantic background is described. In addition, better algorithms assess the actual relevance of results obtained. An example is the automated analysis of documents which is used for inspecting contracts about their legal compliance and the relevance for taxation.

Another example is novel register technology. Blockchain means using a shared, distributed, decentralized and tokenized register that allows untrusted parties to exchange legal-binding transactions. Offering document verification as well as assistance in collecting taxes are examples.

6 Citizen Information

Citizen information aims at the provision of information, advice and advocacy on a broad range of public and social services. Citizen information and referral systems include assistance in translating the questions of citizens from real life description in administrative terms and vice versa. This means to resolve conflicting demands such as balancing the system's limited explanatory capabilities with citizens' needs for explanations. Several improvements are viable, so constructing clarifying dialogues and describing illustrative scenarios. In addition, detailed knowledge (on both, on the field in question and on the interaction) can be embodied in software agents. Multimedia technology may be also used. Hereby a small annotation that citizen advice is not a one-way road. Complaint management and the collection of responses provide valuable feedback for improving administrations.

Open Government Data is a top actual issue caused by the state providing public information with the intention to create public value from such data. Public value is linked to individual and societal interests. Ways in heighten public value are manifold: efficiency brings higher outputs; transparency: sets accountability and participation may lead to more intense communities. Such marks are the main traits of good governance and these should be mirrored in the way authorities act. In OGD the fan of relevant data is broad comprising geographical coordinates, micro-census, regulations, traffic data etc. Thus, many business-related projects flourish with an opening of the Governmental data and with novel applications extracting value from such data.

7   The Power of Modelling

Modelling has become a hot topic. Modelling policy making gives support to policy makers in creating analyses and forecasts. In some way as concerning the part of common public information it is unproblematic, but it is tough about the knowledge necessary for the concrete planning. Modelling policy making may become quite complex on diverse reasons as e.g. a broad focus combined with some fuzziness. Then, often factors are only partly defined such as the bystanders and the course of negotiation. Further, it needs to deal with several gaps, so the vagueness of task descriptions. Goal is to identify and characterize problem areas and to develop visionary scenarios for enabling solutions.

Modelling norms is another application benefiting several purposes such as legal drafting or data exchange. In legal retrieval present systems are keyword-oriented and provide only little help for case-oriented tasks. There are few pilot systems for case-based retrieval use deontic logic, probabilistic measures or neuronal nets. Modelling norms has high impact for data exchange. The semantics of data is described which allows a global use of data collected at diverse agencies. Numerous projects display solutions on data carrying along their legal-administrative context. With more complex ontologies more sophisticated applications come within reach showing the huge potential of the realm.

8   E-Democracy

E-Democracy is the support and enhancement of democracy by strengthening as well representative democracy as well as direct democracy. There is a lot that technologies may spur such as reinforcing existing institutions of representative politics and improving deliberation in the public sphere and building vivid communities. The idea of empowerment means giving someone the power that he was deficient before. Hence empowerment is the red thread in many activities and leads to new forms of processes for rendering decisions and policy making. Important to state that fostering democratic participation shapes political culture very much. Hence, inducing every-day democracy in workplaces will spur community development and encourage the practice of consultation and dialogue.

Important elements are the emerging of virtual communities and the employment of collaborative tools. Some means are easy-usable and low-cost as to cite discussion fora and mailing lists. More advanced solutions are meeting support and brainstorming software. Some sophisticated tools will need experts for handling. Illustrations are simulation, visualization, argumentation systems. Modes of involvement are manifold just as to cite campaigning, planning, petitioning and law enforcement.

Campaigning encourages citizens to support actively their representatives at elections. Thus, it channels the power of public opinion to advance a progressive drive of sustainment. In e-Campaigning the tools used are uncomplicated, so writing blogs, spreading information or making fund raising web-sites. Planning processes need attention of the public and a broad awareness is fundamental. In addition, the political system gets valuable input as the expertise of citizens is being tapped. Petitioning system handle complaints or requests on certain issues. The respective legal bodies should action on the issue in question and inform the initiators of the petition on the process and outcome. In law enforcement citizens observe public life in a critical mood. The targets include: events such as elections, groups such as politicians, modes such as proper fund spending or spaces such as parks.

9   Mobile Government

Mobile Government means that citizens communicate to Government with the devices at hand. There is an urge to mobility. Maybe it is in the genes, or in our evolution or in a lifestyle we learn and adopt. Mobility is both – optional and mandatory. Connectivity is the consequence which can be realized by two ways. One way is distributing technical means for shared use, the other way is making personally owned mobile devices/items such as phones, bikes or cars. For electronic devices the ubiquity of communication is under the motto "Keep in touch with your Business" and offers several benefits: increased productivity, decreased costs or a more responsive service. An eminent advantage is that mobile devices exert considerable impact on communication patterns. It elevates the numbers of users giving feedback – a very decisive factor in some applications, so e-Marketing and e-Participation.

Connecting, Integrating and Empowering Society for Social Control Through Distance Education

Cristiano Maciel[1,2]([⊠]) [iD], Cassyra L. Vuolo[3]([⊠]) [iD],
Taciana M. Sambrano[1] [iD], Alexandre M. dos Anjos[1] [iD],
Ana Paula Kuhn[1] [iD], and Claudia Oneida Rouiller[3] [iD]

[1] Universidade Federal de Mato Grosso, Cuiabá, MT, Brazil
crismac@gmail.com, tacianamirna@gmail.com,
dinteralexandre@gmail.com,
profapaulaunemat@hotmail.com
[2] Fundação de Apoio da Universidade Federal de Mato Grosso - Uniselva,
Cuiabá, MT, Brazil
[3] Tribunal de Contas do Estado do Mato Grosso, Cuiabá, MT, Brazil
{cassyra, claudiar}@tce.mt.gov.br

Abstract. In order for a participatory democracy to exist, the population must participate in public affairs. However, exercising citizenship requires preparation, which is a top concern of Brazilian public policy management councils. The focus of this research is the articulation between the State Audit Court of the state of Mato Grosso (Tribunal de Contas do Mato Grosso – TCE-MT) and public policy management councils. This article presents the results of a combined effort of different government institutions in adopting innovative digital technology as a tool used in Distance Education to integrate and empower the community, encourage citizen control and thus generate public value. This tool allowed access to and engagement of citizens from different backgrounds and led to the construction of new concepts and ideas that are engrained in these environments.

Keywords: Distance education · Social control · Citizenship · Public value

1 Introduction

In order to enjoy a participatory democracy, it is crucial that citizens participate in public affairs [23, 29]. According to Nerling [14], community, citizenship, participation, transparency and control permeate many stages of the public policy management cycle. However, the full exercise of citizenship requires certain preparation, which is a top concern of Brazilian public policy management councils [14].

Social control is understood to be a form of sharing decision-making power between state and society regarding public policies. It constitutes one of the tools of democracy and citizenship that can be employed during both the implementation and assessment of public policies [25]. For Kuhn et al. [25], internal control aims to monitor the functions of activities performed by subordinate agencies of the

© Springer Nature Switzerland AG 2018
A. Kő and E. Francesconi (Eds.): EGOVIS 2018, LNCS 11032, pp. 108–122, 2018.
https://doi.org/10.1007/978-3-319-98349-3_9

administration by observing the constitutional principles established in the scope of public management. On the other hand, external control exerts political control, as it aims for accountability and financial legality [10]. In Brazil, it is the exclusive role of the Legislative Branch, exercised through acts that have been previously determined by the pertinent legislation, with the assistance of the audit courts of each state.

Of course, these councils are not the only instruments of democratization and social control regarding the management of public funds, but they do include in its composition an equal number of representatives of the government and civil society, whose inherent duty is to propose public policies and evaluate their results. It is only possible to monitor and supervise the government by means of public policy councils if there is proper use of information and knowledge regarding their role in participatory democracy. At this juncture, articulation takes place between the State Audit Court of Mato Grosso (Tribunal de Contas do Mato Grosso - TCE-MT) and public policy councils, which is the focus of this research. The TCE as the body responsible for scrutinizing the results of public management, with capillarity over data related to public policies to increase the effectiveness and transparency of its decisions, can empower the councils to exercise social control [26, 27].

In view of the above, this article presents the results of the combined effort of different government agencies in adopting digital innovation initiatives in Distance Education as a pedagogical tool for connecting, integrating and empowering society to generate public value for achieving social control. This successful experiment began in 2012 with the joint effort of government agencies. At the time, the TCE-MT made a pioneering decision to establish a partnership with the Federal University of the State of Mato Grosso (Universidade Federal do Estado de Mato Grosso - UFMT) through the Foundation for Support and Development of UFMT - Uniselva Foundation (Fundação de Apoio e Desenvolvimento da UFMT - Fundação Uniselva), to minister a continuing education course called "Citizenship and Social Control" by Distance Education (DE). Thus the public university is appreciated as a locus of technological knowledge and training for political citizenship [15]. The course objective was to allow citizen inclusion in participatory management processes by providing information and knowledge that encourages social empowerment and provides interface between external and social controls.

The course was held in the Virtual Learning Environment called Moodle [24]. Conducting an analysis of the process and the results of technology-mediated learning may contribute to the debate about the relevance of corporate education, allowing us to broaden our reflections on how this can be offered to society as a whole. The course proposal also indicates the possibilities and effective contributions of joints efforts from both the academia milieu and external control agencies in overcoming the challenges of training interested parties to optimize resources. Approximately 700 students, 4 content instructors, 2 information technology teachers, 40 tutors selected by UFMT, 3 coordinators and 1 supervisor of the TCE-MT actively participated in this process. The course's final assignment was the elaboration of an essay listing the community needs and relating them to specific public policies, while suggesting innovative and feasible solutions that may generate collective public value. Approximately 700 papers were presented and the 50 best texts were selected and then analyzed in the course [15].

In this case, reflections with people residing in different municipalities and from different backgrounds facilitated democratic dialogue and enabled the exchange of experiences, knowledge and information. This experience could only be possible with the use of the virtual learning environment and the incorporation of digital technologies. At the end, it was possible to understand the influence of the combination of different types of knowledge and public information that, mediated by virtual learning technology, creates access to and interaction among different actors and provides the construction of new ideas imbued in these environments from an educational point of view [16].

2 Political, Social and Legal Background

The political, social and legal background will be presented to provide deeper understanding of this conjuncture. It is possible to say that the starting point for these actions was the promulgation, in 1988, of Brazil's Federal Constitution, which created several spaces for the participation of civil society in public management at all three levels of government (municipal, state and federal). As a political-ideological measure, these spaces aim to: assure the primacy of popular sovereignty by creating conditions for citizen emancipation from state custody; establish power decentralization; and guarantee the effectiveness of social and political participation in the management of public affairs. Regarding the constitutional prerogatives related to the control of public resources, it is important to emphasize the content of Constitutional Amendment n. 19/98, which amended Paragraph 3 of Article 37 of the Federal Constitution. In addressing the forms of citizen/user participation in public administration, Constitutional Amendment n. 19/98 established a perspective of direct control of public resources in the following [4]:

"Paragraph 3 - The law shall regulate the forms of participation of users in governmental entities and in entities owned by the Government, especially as regards:

I.   claims relating to the rendering of public services in general, the provision of user services being ensured, as well as periodical assessment, both external and internal, of the quality of services;
II. the access of users to administrative records and to information about Government initiatives, with due regard for article 5, items X and XXXIII;
III. the rules of a complaint against negligence or abuse in the exercise of an office, position or function in government services."

Individual and collective actors in Brazil began to articulate amongst themselves to claim for their rights. The idea of participation is reinforced as a foundational element of citizenship and, therefore, of projects that aim to build a "participatory democracy". Peruzzotti and Smulovitz [17], who study citizen participation associated with the surveillance of public resources, argue that there is a new form of politicization developing in new democracies whose main goal is to strengthen and perfect mechanisms of control and supervision by representative institutions and that citizens affected by acts of government, in the exercise of their citizenship, should ask managers to account for their actions.

The repercussions of this situation were felt in all the power structures of the Brazilian public administration, including agencies within the system of external control. This led to a reflection on several institutional aspects, specifically on their role as democratic and republican institutions that held responsibility for initiating dialogue among new actors, above all, Brazilian citizens, who are the actors that should be exerting "social control of the public administration". In this background, the dialogue between external control and social control is welcomed in the consolidation of civil, social and political rights, which converge to enumerate the opportunities and instruments of democratization and introduce the citizen's voice in the decision-making process of public management, especially in the context of public policy budgeting.

The main event that becomes a legal reference for this interlocution was established in Article 74, Paragraph 2 of the Constitution of 1988, which considers citizens, political parties, associations or unions as legitimate parties that can legally denunciate irregularities or illegalities across the country to accountability courts (or audit courts) [3]. According to Moreira Neto [18], "Citizen control was added to the process of external control through participatory channels: social control."

The increasing interaction between state control (external control) and non-state control (social control) was included in Brazilian legislation with the Law of Fiscal Responsibility, Complementary Law 101/00, which proclaimed the requirement of balanced public finances and introduced the right to transparency and society participation in the process of elaborating public policies [19]. The Law of Information Access - Law n. 12.527/11 made transparency mandatory for all levels of government. It also implemented the requirement to publish, in official electronic websites, every information that possesses collective or general interest produced or guarded by the state [20]. This system entailed several challenges for public institutions and society. The former were now required to implement formal participation mechanisms and promote social empowerment through their information and decisions. The latter was awarded the task of exercising its role as the main interested party in the results of the state. Society was now able to demand from the state new governance structures that enable the proposition, evaluation, targeting and monitoring of public policies.

According to the United Nations Human Development Report (HDR) in 2015 [28], Brazil ranked as one of the most unequal societies in the world, representing 10th place, so public policies must be formulated and implemented to mitigate this reality and generate improvement in the quality of life of the population. Social participation in management processes strongly contributes to the establishment of more effective policies. Participatory democracy, combined with integrated action between control and regulation of society regarding decisions and results of public management, are important factors in combating social and economic inequality.

However, articulation and participation of Brazilian society in political, economic and cultural life in the country are still embryonic. Brazil is undergoing a learning stage and moment of expansion in the co-management of public affairs, in which deeper connections are sought with the state. Similarly, there are very few public institutions that adequately inform citizens, or develop concrete actions towards community integration, or encourage social empowerment, or increase opportunity for citizen "voices" to be heard in the public sphere, especially where the presence of the state is dominant.

It is precisely at this point in which there is an interface between citizens, the external control agency – the TCE-MT – and the university – UFMT.

3 Social Control and External Control: Integration

Regarding control, it is worth highlighting, in order to establish a foundation for the discussion, that this action should occur starting from the planning stage, through the execution and constant supervision of the destination of public funds. However, control cannot be left only to state entities, which suffer personnel and resource limitations, for inspection in all spheres, especially in a country with continental dimensions such as Brazil. In this sense, community participation, through its multiple representations, becomes crucial. The participation of citizens, who are at the receiving end, is crucial for maintaining permanent supervision of public affairs, a prerogative guaranteed by the Federal Constitution of 1988 [3]. The Brazilian Magna Carta creates the possibility for the citizen to exercise a form of direct democracy (of popular sovereignty). The materialization of this exercise is characterized by social control. The means of social control would be founded on the possibility of supervision of public actions. Therefore, social control could occur through legal monitoring or the individual or collective initiatives of a social group.

According to Faccioni [6], the Federal Audit Court promote the association between individuals and the public administration, insofar as it contributes to the achievement of participatory democracy, the exercise of citizenship (as a fundamental principle), and interface between external control and social control. In this context, Article 74, Para. 2 of the Federal Constitution of 1988 assigned the Federal Audit Court the role of appraising irregularities or illegalities in the Public Administration, as a response to the manifestation of citizens and civil society, as seen below [3]: "Para. 2. Any citizen, political party, association or labor union has standing under the law to denounce irregularities or illegalities to the Federal Audit Court."

As seen from the excerpt above, citizens, associations and labor unions have achieved the status of 'legitimate party'. They have been legitimated, to a large extent, to trigger an autonomous act of inspection, i.e., they can present irregularities or illegalities related to the application of public resources for external control. This content is deemed as a "complaint", contingent upon relevance, backed by the Federal Constitution. The Audit Courts, within the democratic constitutional state, are characterized as sovereign agencies, with invaluable functions to the republican and democratic order, with regards to the fiscal management of public funds and the defense of basic rights. The Audit Courts, in their role as management inspectors, are supposed to measure the results achieved by the government and the quality of public policies, seek resonation of their actions from society, and provide information that should be understood and consumed by the citizen. In this context, it should be highlighted that the accountability courts are responsible for fulfilling its constitutional obligations, but they must venture further to assure a role in the construction of democracy, so that external control, within the limits of institutional legitimacy, may produce concrete effects and real results in both the supervision of resource management and verification of public policy efficiency.

However, exercising external control to tread these paths is equally challenging as rousing society to participate. On the institutional side, there may be fear of communicating with society, as states Fernandes [7]; from the community's perspective, there may be a latent "social lethargy" that needs to be abandoned in order to "raise the expression of consciousness that reveals to be immanent in the social body, merely waiting for motivation" (p. 50). Social participation in terms of government supervision is an increasing phenomenon in Brazil. It is associated with the tendency towards a dialogic state, since there is still a long way between what is planned and what is truly in the public interest. The Audit Court should contribute to maximizing the application of scarce resources and increasing control mechanisms to encourage the participation of society in public resource management. Given that money is essential for regulating the exercise of liberty and for living with dignity, it would be unacceptable for the state not to properly manage public resources to which it has been entrusted. The legitimacy of expenditures must correlate with the satisfaction of society's claims. According to Furtado [8], legitimacy control must be associated with monitoring how popular demands are met, as a consequence of the democratic principle. For the author, it is necessary to investigate the purpose presented and the motivation offered.

Peruzzotti and Smulovitz [17], who study citizen participation associated with the supervision of public funds, argue that there is a new form of politicization developing in new democracies, and that its main objective is to strengthen and improve control mechanisms and monitoring of representative institutions. Therefore, the citizens affected by public actions should exercise their citizenship by demanding that public administrators be accountable for their actions.

External control interacting with social control is beginning to be fed with knowledge and experience from society, exercising its pedagogical and leadership role. As a result, its decisions, work methods, standards, economic and financial results, and profits obtained in improving the management, is to be published [13].

The necessary interaction of external control and social control has been the subject of international discussions by supreme audit institutions, notably Latin American Audit Institutions, and has been addressed in the last General Assemblies of the Organization of Latin American and Caribbean Supreme Audit Institutions (Olacefs)[1]. Olacefs is a privileged forum organized by audit institutions in Latin America and constitutes a space designed for integration, dialogue among participating countries, diagnosis, problem identification, and sharing of good practices that may improve external control institutions. The Federal Audit Court has been a member of Olacefs since its foundation and currently presides over its work.

The entities come together to improve results, in order to make a difference in citizens' lives. They are aware that the information they provide causes impact on the management of audited spaces and constitutes a valuable instrument of social control by allowing citizens to be informed about public affairs from a reliable source so that they can demand compliance with their claims based on recognized technical data, as states Aguillar and Roldán [1]. In this context, social control has been studied and

---

[1] http://portal.tcu.gov.br/lumis/portal/file/fileDownload.jsp?fileId=
8A8182A14DB4AFB3014DBAAB30F00590.

fostered through various statements and actions. The first reference on the possibility of citizen participation in fiscal control is contained in the Declaration of Lima, formulated at the V General Ordinary Meeting of 1995, and is referred to as a qualified and permanent source of information on the critical areas of public administration.

As discussions increase about the necessary combination of external control with social control and the encouragement of effective citizen participation in management, and with the growing recognition of the importance of the topic for Supreme Audit Institutions (SAIs), in 2009, the Technical Commission for Citizen Participation (Comissão Técnica de Participação Cidadã – CTPC) was created during the XLIII Olacefs Board of Directors Meeting. This meeting sought to establish mechanisms of articulated cooperation for the conceptualization and development of strategies designed to encourage citizen participation and social control. The idea was to share conceptual frameworks, approaches, methodologies, tools and experiences that lead to the improvement of external control in the public administration of member countries. Olacefs has agreed to disseminate, among its members, eight important principles of good governance, which will serve as a guide for its members in promoting the proper exercise of accountability, namely: 1. Accountability is the foundation of good governance; 2. Obligation of reporting and justifying; 3. Integrity of the accountability system; 4. Information Transparency; 5. Sanction in the event of non - compliance; 6. Complete legal framework for accountability; 7. Leadership of the SAI and the 8. Active Citizen Participation, with emphasis on the ability of civil society of organizing itself to exercise citizen control, as part of social accountability, in the control of legality and the efficient use of public resources [5].

Orellana [12], head of the Department of Citizen Participation of El Salvador, in a recent article in which he presents his experiences in citizen control in the government of his country, defines citizen participation as a set of actions and initiatives that contribute to boost participatory democracy by integrating a broader concept of citizenship. This right extends to all citizens as the ultimate expression of the people's sovereign power that emanates from the constitutional norms of various countries. This participation assumes the implementation of mechanisms that allow the population to access and directly suggest management policies and to execute governmental control, without the need to be part of the public administration.

4 The Extension Course: "Citizenship and Social Control"

The course was initially offered in 2013 and was attended by only 200 students. In 2017, 2,000 places were offered for the distance education course "Citizenship and Social Control", divided into 40 classes, overseen by 40 tutors and monitored by four TCE-MT employees, certified by UFMT as an extension course. This study will address only the version of the course developed in 2017. The course was ministered with the aid of partnerships, mainly developed for the purpose of dissemination, with the Association of Municipalities of Mato Grosso, municipal mayors, social observation groups, National Union of Municipal Education Directors, National Union of Municipal Education Boards, universities and colleges, public policy state and municipal councils, trade unions representing public servants and class entities that represent lawyers, engineers, accountants, social workers etc.

The guiding principle of the course considered that the Public Policy Councils constitute fundamental strategies for the effective implementation of social control, seeking public management based on constitutional principles and aimed at achieving socially desired results. The term social control was defined as participation of the community in supervising, monitoring and controlling acts performed by the Public Administration. The view is that social control is an important mechanism for strengthening the exercise of citizenship and integrating state and society.

In that sense, the main objective of the course was to train the councilors of the Municipal and State Councils, students, and members of the community to exercise social control, encouraging an interface between internal and external control. The specific objectives of the course were to: (a) view social control as contingent to democracy; (b) contribute to strengthening Municipal and State Councils and Education Boards as effective centers of social control, whose role includes suggesting means of intervention in local affairs; (c) learn and characterize the three forms of public management control (internal, external and social), identifying the responsible actors; (d) learn about the TCE and its projects and programs that were developed to stimulate social control, such as the Integrated Institutional Development Program (Programa de Desenvolvimento Institucional Integrado - PDI), the information and transparency systems, and social control actions; (e) explore the TCE website and the external control decisions related to the community's public policies; (f) learn about the budget cycle and the forms of citizen participation in the government budget process.

The main target of the course "Citizenship and Social Control", were the Councilors of federative agencies because the councils are characterized as being a victory resulting from popular claims. Balcão and Teixeira [2] define management councils as

"[...] collegiate bodies stipulated by federal legislation, composed of civil society and government representatives whose purpose is to draw up guidelines for the elaboration and approval of action plans for public policies at three levels of government: municipal, state and federal. The councils act cooperatively with the Executive Branch in formulating policies in fields such as health care, education, child and adolescent services and social work, and then allocating funds to these areas (p. 5)."

Management councils are very important because they are a response to the pressures of civil society originating from popular struggles and claims as the country undergoes re-democratization. Because they were promulgated in the context of a neoliberal avalanche of state reforms, several analysts and social movement activists discredited the councils as possibilities for real, active participation, forgetting that they were claimed and proposed by movements in the recent past. The new structures belong to the public sphere and, by virtue of law, are integrated with public agencies associated with the Executive Branch focused on specific public policies, which are responsible for advising and supporting the operation in their respective fields. They are, therefore, composed of government representatives and organized civil society [9].

The priority of the course was to minister a training process based on knowledge that is directly related to the nature of the Councils and to the main responsibilities and tasks assigned to its members. In order to do so, the curricular structure of the course was configured as three integrated modules in order to create systemized knowledge and thus enable effective social control of public policies. The course was conducted with the aid of a forum apparatus and by means of the stratification of coordinators, tutors and students. It was punctually monitored through meetings, reports, and other forms. The course load includes 100 h devoted to discussions about the importance of supervision and different types of monitoring and social and external control, in the context of defining and experiencing citizenship.

Students were approved under the condition of writing a substantial final essay. The academic work completed in class is the most representative indicator of the importance of the course. The fifty best essays were selected out of all the coursework written by the students. Ten of these were later included in a book [15], which characterized an important contribution for the audience of the student voices concerning public policies from the viewpoint of their community and background.

5   Course Analysis

Once again, the number of course applicants exceeded expectations. This time, however, more than 3,000 people registered for the course in a matter of only 5 days. Consequently, the research team had to create a student waiting list. This time, more than 1,000 students completed the course, which represented a dropout rate of 50%. Out of that pool, 679 students were approved after handing in a substantial final essay, thus receiving a certificate from the UFMT (approved by the national education board MEC). This academic production delivered in class became the most representative indicator of the new phase of the extension course. The inaugural class reached over 400 students: 458 accesses in the live broadcast and 191 accesses in the video posted on the TCE-MT website. Furthermore, out of the students who completed the course, i.e., who scored 7.0 or higher out of 10, 41% are council members, 54% are associated with Boards of Education, therefore, unsurprisingly, there were 113 teachers graduating from the course. Of the 141 municipalities located in the state MT, 122 had residents registered in the course and 89 of them had residents graduating from the course.

Among the innovations implemented in the version of the course that is described here, some were very positive, such as: (a) free access to the community, provided the students had completed at least a primary education. Consequently, the classes were composed of students with different backgrounds and heterogeneous knowledge, who resided in the state capital city, rural MT, and even in other Brazilian states; (b) the new layout of the AVA and the graphic design of the modules with easily recognized icons caught the students' attention in the "Informative Text" menu, as well as the "Study Guide", designed to provide a deeper understanding of the general operating rules of the course structure as a whole; (c) the opportunity to watch, via Facebook, the live event Consciência Cidadã (Community Awareness) and interact simultaneously, by commenting or asking questions to the participants of this event, in order to encourage social control; (d) insertion of "Learn More" menus, with additional bibliography, and "Videos" that contain themes related to those discussed in the course, both of which facilitated the understanding of the subject through another type of language, and also sought to expand the students' horizon; (e) among the functionalities inserted in the environment, one of the highlights was the insertion of some "menus" to help students in the course development, such as "Technical Support", "Tutorials" and "FAQ", aimed at solving questions posed by students by compiling the most commonly recurring questions and/or possible questions about the course; (f) the "Tutor's room" integrated the coordinators, supervisor, tutors, technical support from UFMT/UNISELVA and coordination of the TCE-MT, and in the "General Student Forum" the questions of the students on theoretical subjects and course exercises were more quickly answered.

In recent years, Distance Education (DE) has grown exponentially in Brazil and has received considerable recognition. According to Mill [11], DE benefits from the possibilities of bringing information to the individual in its singularity and in time and space (demographic unit) because, through telematics, students can access the content wherever they are and whenever they want. This creates an opportunity for communication and discussion about a specific topic.

The course presented in this paper is inserted in the context of DE expansion. The results show that the TCE-MT, in partnership with UFMT, ministered to 97% of the 141 municipalities which compose the state of MT. This means there were students from 137 municipalities effectively participating in the course. Furthermore, 26 municipalities from other states were also contemplated. It should be noted that the largest number of registered students was concentrated in the most populous municipalities. Among the students who were enrolled, there were some who had completed a basic level of education and there were also doctors who worked as public prosecutors, state tax inspectors, maintenance, homemakers, among others.

At the end of the course, the students presented the final essay, which presented important reflections about their experience while studying the respective modules. On the whole, there were approximately 700 (seven hundred) final essays. Fifty of them were previously selected, observing the structure regarding essay format, problematizing, coherence and textual cohesion. It is possible to verify that the 50 selected essays were written from 27 municipalities in the state of MT, and 38% of papers were from the Cuiabá, capital of MT (19 essays).

The essays that were analyzed demonstrated the degree of participation and also the importance of the supervision of the activities of public administrators, who are responsible for assuring that the citizens participate in the definition of priorities regarding collective interest, and who are, moreover, accountable for their actions regarding the community. With this behavior concerning citizens and control bodies, public administrators share the responsibility for managing public funds and for the results obtained. When analyzing all the selected essays, it became evident that the topics covered in the text varied immensely in terms of content. There seems to be a greater concern with public policies aimed at environmental preservation and education, sports and leisure. The analyzed essays involving public policies in education emphasized students undergoing primary school. Concern with Municipal Councils actions also appears in a significant degree. Figure 1 presents the themes addressed in the final essays of the course. Research studies are focused on the public policies of the municipalities from which the fifty selected essays were written. The greatest concern observed in the reflective texts concern policies related to housing, education, sports and leisure. It was observed that 35% of the researched topics demonstrate the need to guarantee basic living conditions with regard to citizenship rights. Perhaps it is important to emphasize that acquiring this level of increased awareness means undergoing a process of awareness towards social issues and empowerment in order to assure citizenship rights and, consequently, the exercise of full citizenship.

▪ Public policies concerning education, sports and leisure
▪ Public policies concerning women's issues, senior citizens, PwD
▪ Public policies concerning environment preservation
▪ Public policies concerning public transport and public safety

Fig. 1. Topics addressed

Another very obvious concern present in the essays refers to the public policies concerning women's issues, senior citizens, and people with disabilities. We identified 25% of the essays involved these topics. The discussions held throughout the course made it possible to raise awareness concerning minorities. It is important to highlight that issues regarding health care also appeared significantly in the reflections focused on women and senior citizens, as well as pertinent reflections on accessibility for people with disabilities. Studies show how health care has been precarious, especially when referring to women and senior citizens. In 20% of essays that addressed public policies aimed at environmental protection, there was much concern with solid waste disposal. Studies show that there are still no effective public policies that are capable of solving the problem of solid waste disposal, access to clean water, and sewage treatment. Survey results draw attention to several situations that can be considered government negligence and mention the urgent need to solve these problems. This situation becomes more evident in large urban centers, since they have a huge demographic and population concentration. Within the topics addressed, 16% of the essays were concerned with transparency and supervision of Municipal Councils. The data collected indicate that the population has not yet internalized the importance of effective participation in the various existing councils. In this context, transparency acquires expressiveness as one of the most strategic issues in Brazil's public agenda and becomes a key instrument for working with the complex relationship between citizens and their agents [27]. The effective use of information tools and technologies, especially the Internet, is extremely important when aligned with a democratic process. The Internet is an ally that is able to confer visibility and transparency to decisions and results by creating favorable conditions for access to public data. The remaining 4% of the essays were concerned with transportation and public safety. The main concern focused on the quality of public transport and safety at bus stops. In addition to the need to strengthen policies that protect public transportation users, the surveys also reveal the community wish to prioritize collective transportation in urban spaces in order to reduce the time spent commuting to and within cities.

5.1 User Satisfaction

It is important to record the analysis of feedback data answered by the participants. According to the answers of the user satisfaction survey presented to the distance education "Citizenship and Social Control" class of 2016 (CCS/2016), the presence of Supervisors and Coordinators was helpful, given that 71.5% of respondents considered the performance of the former to be excellent, and 72.6% considered the performance of the latter to be excellent 69.3% stated that the course contributed positively to their work activities, and that 77.3% rated the course as 'great' overall, and it is worth noting that zero students rated it as 'bad'.

Regarding the work of the TCE-MT, 64% of students stated they knew about the audit court and were well informed about its work. If we consider that all the work carried out by TCE with the councils started no more than four years ago, and considering the high turnover of government staff and society representatives in these spheres, 64% represents an excellent number. However, 29% of respondents informed that they had first heard about the TCE-MT through this course and 7% stated they had heard about it, but did not know about their work. For 97% of the CCS/2016 DE students, the services provided by the TCE-MT generate benefits to society and only 3% consider the opposite true. This is a fact that presents growth bias, since the knowledge index of the benefits provided by Audit Courts, in general, is very low at the national level.

This percentage also reveals that result accountability initiatives have been well received by society, that the events rendering open access of the TCE-MT to citizen participation, as part of the TCE-MT's media campaign, has succeeded in informing the community about the audit court. It is also worth mentioning the communications unit of the TCE-MT, mainly for its bold performance in social networks in the use of more inclusive language that is more relatable to the common citizen.

In a natural trend inherent to distance learning courses, 50% of the students who completed the research selected social networks as the best means of communication between the TCE and society, followed by e-mails, with 22% of followers. On the other hand, 17% said they preferred personal communication and 12% preferred contact by telephone. It should be highlighted that communication between the TCE-MT and the students was encouraged through an activity in which the students simulated a complaint to the Audit Court based on a hypothetical situation and that should contain minimal elements such as narration of the fact, identification of the responsible ones, presentation of evidence or clues etc.

The survey reveals that 39% of respondents know and are well informed about the social control actions developed by the TCE. However, 46% said that this was the first time they had heard about social control actions developed by the Court and 15% said they do not know about them. The course created opportunities for the students to be informed about TCE activities that encourage social control in the last chapter of Module I. However, there is evident need to intensify dissemination efforts in other projects.

6 Conclusion

In general, innovations greatly contribute to the success of the remodeled version of the course. The School of Accounts deserves merit for their unceasing effort to minister the course with the usual excellence that exceeds the standards of the courses normally offered by distance education.

The total numbers are significant: 2,567 people were encouraged to exercise social control through this training, with representatives in 100% of the municipalities that are members of the PDI, in addition to 22 students from other federative states.

In the context of the presented debate, we found that, through this course, students were able to acquire more significant degree of understanding of the forms of controls reserved to the public administration, such as social, external and internal control, thus promoting the institutional empowerment of public policy councils insofar as they encouraged refresher courses for council members and offered training for the citizen to become more active in the community.

In this sense, the course on Citizenship and Social Control generated important reflections on issues such as: what does becoming a citizen mean? What is my role in society? How can I contribute to improving my country's social conditions and effectively exercising citizenship? How can I make a complaint and monitor the actions designed to solve the problem? It is understood that awareness is the starting point for the citizen to rethink and transform his praxis. In this sense, we highlight the importance of the Citizenship and Social Control course in the preparation of council members and of regular citizens who can act, interact and intervene in society in order to guarantee their rights and become aware of their responsibilities. The practices executed during the development of the Course contributed significantly so that reflections and decision-making were consciously contemplated, based on existing legislation and always seeking the common interest.

It is hoped that, by becoming well informed, society members will cease to be governed as subjects in order to become active citizens who will truly influence the acts of power made on their behalf. The active and participative integration of community members as citizens, influencing and deciding public affairs, is one of the premises for the incorporation of civil society as one of the interpreters of the Constitution [21].

The history of innovation and improvement characterized by all the actors involved in the construction of this educational and deeply social project reflects, in its entirety, the same innovative and progressive line of the TCE-MT itself, which, throughout the far-reaching institutional development over the last decade, has also been able to create an extensive and valuable network of social articulation.

In the specific case of this extension course, it was the network established between the TCE-MT, the Secretariat of Institutional Articulation and Citizenship Development (SAI), School of Accounts, UFMT/Uniselva and the public policy councils that played a very active role in assuring the path towards a true participatory democracy through the exercise of social control.

The data show that, in the process of a maturing participatory democracy, both state and society are called forth to adjust to change, to build an alliance around cooperative guidelines, to engage in social and political mediation in order to follow the community agenda and to move forward towards the construction of autonomous and democratic public spheres in the field of political decisions [22].

From the point of view of social empowerment, a diverse student body in terms of educational background allows us to state that different spaces where plural discussions is engaged have been achieved in different ways. It is therefore recommended that a focus group study is conducted in order to identify these impacts and measure the effectiveness of the community voice before the public administration. Because, in a country with dimensions as wide as Brazil, which suffers from a culture of poor resource management, despite a perceived increase in society politicization, the mere existence of control agencies is not enough to combat irregularities. It is thus increasingly urgent to hear from the community and encourage society to exercise social control. We are treading new paths whose processes are undergoing improvement, but need to be implemented by public administrators, assimilated by society, and encouraged by Brazil's Audit Courts. We hope that this experience will intensify democratic and republican dialogue, which is still very incipient, albeit possible and necessary to prepare the current situation for a new horizon.

Acknowledgements. We would like to thank the UFMT, TCE-MT and Uniselva for all the support to develop and publish this research. And to the CCS DE students.

References

1. Aguillar, M.M., Roldán, E.G.: Participação cidadã no controle fiscal. Revista de La Organización Latino Americana y Del Caribe de Entidades Fiscalizadoras Superiores **8**(17), 34–40 (2015)
2. Balcão, N., Teixeira, A.C. (eds.) Controle Social do Orçamento Público, 112 p. Instituto Polis, São Paulo (44) (2003)
3. Brasil: Constituição da República Federativa do Brasil, de 1988. www.planalto.gov.br/ccivil_03/constituicao/constituicaocompilado.htm. Accessed 10 May 2017
4. Brasil: Emenda Constitucional nº 19, de 04 de junho de 1998. http://www.planalto.gov.br/ccivil_03/constituicao/emendas/emc/emc19.htm. Accessed 05 July 2017
5. Rica C.: Declaração de Assunção (2010). http://buenagobernanza.agn.gov.ar/sites/all/modules/ckeditor/ckfinder/userfilesfiles/DECLARACIO_CCN_ASUNCION_CyP.pdf. Accessed 05 July 2017
6. Faccioni, V.J.: A Sociedade e o Controle Externo. In: I Fórum do PROMOEX: Formação da Rede de Informação e Portal do Controle Externo. TCE-MG, Belo Horizonte (2006)
7. Fernandes, J.U.J.: Tribunais de contas do Brasil: jurisdição e competência, 3rd edn. Fórum, Belo Horizonte (2008)
8. Furtado. O Controle da Legitimidade do Gasto Público. In: Fórum de Contratação e Gestão Pública-FCGP, Belo Horizonte, ano 5, n. 54, pp. 7298–7301 (2006)
9. Gohn, M.G.: Conselhos Gestores e Participação Sociopolítica, 3rd edn. Cortez, São Paulo (2007)
10. Meirelles, H.L.: Direito Administrativo Brasileiro, 9th edn. Revista dos Tribunais, São Paulo (1989)
11. Mill, D.: Das inovações tecnológicas às inovações pedagógicas: considerações sobre o uso das tecnologias na educação a distância. In: Mill, D., Pimentel, N. (eds.) Educação a Distância: desafios contemporâneos. EdUFSCar, São Carlos (2010)

12. Orellana, J.S.M.: La Participación Cidadana: principio inclusivo em lãs EFS para mejorar el control fiscal. Revista OLACEFS **8**(18), 42 (2015)
13. Rocha, Z.: Os Tribunais de Contas e os desafios para a promoção do controle social. Revista do TCM-RJ **46**(11), 4–11 (2011)
14. Nerling, M.: Preparar para o exercício da cidadania, através do controle social, na Gestão de Políticas Públicas. In: Vuolo, C.L., Maciel, C., dos Anjos, A. (eds.) Educação a Distância: (In)formação em Cidadania e Controle Social, pp. 17–67. EdUFMT, Cuiabá (2017)
15. Vuolo, C., Maciel, C., dos Anjos, A.M.: Educação a Distância: (In)formação em Cidadania e Controle Social. EdUFMT, Cuiabá (2017)
16. Valente, J.A.: A espiral da aprendizagem e as tecnologias da informação e comunicação: repensando conceitos. In: Joly, M.C. (ed.) Tecnologia no Ensino: implicações para a aprendizagem, pp. 15–37. Casa do Psicólogo, São Paulo (2002)
17. Peruzzotti, E., Smulovitz, C.: Controlando la política: ciudadanos y mediosenlasnuevas democracias, pp. 23–52. Editorial Temas, Buenos Aires (2002)
18. Moreira Neto, D.F.: O planejamento e a sociedade como destinatários dos trabalhos dos Tribunais de Contas. In: Souza, A.J. (ed.) O novo Tribunal de Contas – órgão protetor dos direitos fundamentais, 2nd edn. Fórum, Belo Horizonte (2004)
19. Brasil: Lei Complementar n° 101, de 4 de maio de 2000. Lei de Responsabilidade Fiscal. http://www.planalto.gov.br/ccivil_03/Leis/lcp/Lcp101.htm. Accessed 10 Jan 2018
20. Brasil: Lei n° 12.527, de 18 de novembro de 2011. Lei de Acesso a Informação. http://www.planalto.gov.br/ccivil_03/_ato2011-2014/2011/lei/l12527.htm. Accessed 10 Jan 2018
21. Mangia, C.C.: Participação popular, cidadania e Estado Democrático de Direito. In Revista Jus Navigandi. Teresina, ano 19, n. 4094, 16 set. https://jus.com.br/artigos/29663. Accessed 26 Dec 2016
22. Raichelis, R.: Desafios da gestão democrática das políticas sociais, Política Social. Módulo 03. Capacitação em Serviço Social e Política Social. Brasília, CFESS, ABEPSS, CEAD/NED-UNB (2000)
23. Maciel, C., Garcia, A.C.B.: Modeling of a democratic citizenship community to facilitate the consultative and deliberative process in the web. In: ICEIS (3), pp. 387–394 (2007)
24. dos Anjos, A.M.: Tecnologias da informação e da comunicação, aprendizado eletrônico e ambientes virtuais de aprendizagem. In: Maciel, C. (ed.) Educação a distância: Ambientes virtuais de aprendizagem, pp. 11–57. EdUFMT, Cuiabá (2013)
25. Kuhn, A.P., Rouiller, C.O., Maciel, C.: Um olhar sobre os trabalhos dos participantes do curso a distância de cidadania e controle social. In: Vuolo, C.L., Maciel, C., dos Anjos, A. (eds.) Educação a Distância: (In)formação em Cidadania e Controle Social, pp. 173–188. EdUFMT, Cuiabá (2017)
26. Girata, N.N.H, Maciel, C.: eGov website evolution study within strategic planning. In: 15th Annual International Conference on Proceedings of the 15th Annual International Conference on Digital Government Research - dg.o 2014, pp. 69–78. ACM Press, Aguascalientes (2014)
27. de Oliveira, L.K.B., Maciel, C.: Transparency and social control via the citizen's portal: a case study with the use of triangulation. In: Kő, A., Leitner, C., Leitold, H., Prosser, A. (eds.) EGOVIS/EDEM 2013. LNCS, vol. 8061, pp. 112–124. Springer, Heidelberg (2013). https://doi.org/10.1007/978-3-642-40160-2_10
28. Connor, R.: The United Nations World Water Development Report 2015: Water for a Sustainable World, vol. 1. UNESCO Publishing, Paris (2015)
29. Karacapilidis, N., Loukis, E., Dimopoulos, S.: Computer-supported G2G collaboration for public policy and decision-making. J. Enterp. Inf. Manag. **18**(5), 602–624 (2005)

Critical Success Factors
(CSF) to Commercializing Technologies
in Universities: The Radar Framework

Jaqueline Vargas González$^{(\boxtimes)}$ ⓘ, André Luiz Zambalde ⓘ,
André Grützmann ⓘ, and Thiago Bellotti Furtado ⓘ

Federal University of Lavras, Lavras, Brazil
javargon0101@gmail.com, thiagobellotti@gmail.com,
{zamba,andre5}@dcc.ufla.br

Abstract. Universities have been considered as potential sources of scientific development; therefore, they are involved in processes of Technology Commercialization (TC), associated with licensing and transfer to the market and/or society. The goal of this work is to develop and validate an instrument for the identification and analysis of the Critical Success Factors (CSF) in the commercialization of technologies in public Universities – radar framework. A bibliometric and systematic review, and interviews with specialists, provided a theoretical and empirical foundation that consider the process, mechanisms, ways, and means of commercialization, as well as the promotion and management of marketing policies. A Radar framework was built with four dimensions and explicit indicators to evaluate the CSF in public Universities. A framework contains enough elements to be used as an instrument to identify and analyze the CSF in the TC in Public Universities. The framework characteristics are especially useful for universities monitoring the factors for the improvement of the Technology Commercialization (TC) process, setting the groundwork for future studies related to this subject.

Keywords: Universities · Innovation · Technology transfer
Technology commercialization

1 Introduction

Nowadays, the research related to technology commercialization in Universities have been increasing. It is a complex process, fundament on the licenses concession, transferring and sells [31]. In [26] defined technology commercialization as the process of transferring a technology-based innovation from the developer of the technology to an organization utilizing and applying the technology for marketable products and bring benefits to the society.

Specifically, in the University context, the process of technology transfer is directly related to the commercialization of technology. From the specialized institutes to the business sector the transfer and commercialization of technology depend on the effects of the organizational and individual variables that compose them [45]. Because it is a multidimensional, complex, multidisciplinary and inter-organizational process, for its

© Springer Nature Switzerland AG 2018
A. Kő and E. Francesconi (Eds.): EGOVIS 2018, LNCS 11032, pp. 123–135, 2018.
https://doi.org/10.1007/978-3-319-98349-3_10

monitoring and analysis it is necessary to take into account a large number of elements and factors [46].

In this way, for its proper understanding and analysis, it is necessary to take into account, elements central, which have been called critical success factors - CSF [32, 34]. In the context of universities and the commercialization of technologies (CT), CSF can be defined as a limited number of elements, factors or indicators, descriptive of strategic, culture, infrastructure and knowledge that must be considered in order to guarantee competitive performance and generation of value [4, 6, 26, 31, 37].

The CSF's offers effective support for the process of surveying, planning and monitoring information that can affect the competitive position of organizations, particularly when they are associated with instruments or models for evaluation and analysis [7]. In this sense, the main goals of this work were: (1) to carry out a systematic review of literature, associated with a review by specialists, on the CSF for the commercialization of technologies in Public Universities; (2) propose a model or instrument to measure these factors: A radar of the CSF; (3) describe a case study on the application of the CSF and the proposed radar framework in a public university of Brazil.

This research was organized as follows. First, the background and the context of commercializing technology in Universities is provided. Second, the theoretical definitions for this work are shown. Third, the methodology and the design of the investigation is described. As result, the radar framework with the critical success factors is proposed and applied in a case study. Also, research implications for future studies as well as for management practice are given.

2   Technology Commercialization – Background and Definitions

2.1   University, Intellectual Property and Innovation

In the era of knowledge economy, changing from classic university paradigm to Entrepreneurship University, associated to a Triple Helix model, is needed. The "third mission", knowledge and technology transfer to the society [18, 23, 36], is being incorporated in the university context.

In this context, the key to the diffusion, competitiveness, and growth relies on a definition of Intellectual Property (IP) and its proper understanding. Intellectual property refers to the registration of inventions; literary and artistic works; and symbols, names, and images with the purpose of commercialization. Usually, this term (IP) is classified into two categories: (a) Industrial property: includes patents for inventions, trademarks, industrial designs and geographical indications; and (b) Copyright: covers literary works, films, music, artistic works and architectural design [50].

The concepts involved in IP are intimately related to the technology commercialization process (transfer, licenses and vending). This technology refers to a set of knowledge that generates and incorporates the products, processes, and services, subject to property registration or regulation [14].

The actors, cultures, and institutions participate and interact, from property regulation to innovation. As mentioned by [43], innovation refers to new products, new processes, new markets, new sources of supply or new organization of the sector, that generate economic and social value. Economic development is influenced by innovation through the dynamic process called "creative destruction" where new technologies replace the older ones. Radical innovations generate disruption, while incremental innovations allow continuous small changes [41].

In the [35], innovation means implementation of a new product (good or service), a new or significantly improved process, a new method of marketing, or a new organizational method in the business practice, in the internal organization or in external relationships. In a new perspective, "open innovation" requires the organizational capacity to access and adopt internal or external knowledge sources in a profitable way [13].

2.2   Technology Commercialization

The University can and must contribute to innovation by developing applied research and generating useful technologies to the society. Beyond that, it should, directly or indirectly, incorporate new technologies generated both on the public or productive sector. For this to happen, the university must pay close attention to the technology commercialization process [9, 14].

In a recent literature review, the following approaches to CSF were found: Technology knowledge and innovation [28]; Technology commercialization [11, 22]; Knowledge Transfer [44, 51].

According to [40], commercialization refers to transference, a process where a country, an organization or industry adopts a technology made by another. For [15, 25], it constitutes an acquisition, development, and use of technological knowledge of a country. It is a shift of know-how, technical knowledge or technology from one environment to another [39]. Commercialization or transference refers to a process where ideas and concepts move from laboratory to a market and to the society. Technology commercialization process can be understood as the result of constant interaction among actors and heterogeneous sources. Therefore, the meaning of technology commercialization is wide and it has been discussed for a long time.

Universities can implement technology commercialization through sales, interchanges, transferences, and licenses, using specific features (incubators, spin-offs, startups, innovation on request, production, direct sales); shared media (strategic alliances, joint ventures) and through third parties (license of intellectual property assets and franchises). In this scenario, universities or research centers are suppliers and companies that produce goods and services are the customers. Everything happens in exchange for a paid rate [30, 31].

Many universities have Technology Transfer Offices (TTO) or Office for Technology Transfer (OTT) to manage the technology commercialization process. These TTOs/OTTs are created to promote the register and commercialization of useful technologies to the industries, governments, and society.

In Brazil, TTOs are denominated Innovation Technology Centers (Núcleos de Inovação Tecnológica - NIT). They are institutional sectors created to manage the intellectual property and create and promote the commercialization of research results. The NITs are particularly important to the Brazilian innovation system, since government-funded R&D in Brazil accounts for more than 63% of the total, while private capital contributes with 37% of R&D funding. A World Bank study about development, technology, and innovation notice that Brazil shows low rates transforming R&D into commercial applications, what could explain the weak collaboration among companies and universities. Hence, it is fundamental to look for understanding in the practices of technology commercialization in Brazilian Universities [20, 34].

2.3 Critical Success Factors (CSF) and Innovation Radar Chart

CSF's are internal or external aspects that should be considered by the organization to define its scope or objectives [17, 19]. Historically the CSF's answer the question "where we should focus?". When they are identified and managed, they can have a significant impact on the organization's success [5].

The identification of the CSF's is essential to the analysis of business environment, resources, and strategies. This identification must be according to the business sector, industry, and institution, so that the critical factors can help to build metrics, analyses decision or priorities [24, 29, 38].

CSF's of technology commercialization can be understood as a limited number of indicators that, if proven, will ensure an organization competitive performance [8, 27]. According to the literature, a "radar chart" is the instrument commonly used to measure the indicators. [42] propose a "radar of innovation" framework that represent twelve dimensions to measure the business innovation. These dimensions or indicators are connected with four principal axes and each dimension represents different ways to innovate.

In [12] a radar chart was tested in order to confirm its easiness of use. The authors consider that the innovation radar could help the companies to perform innovation auto-diagnosis and to identify innovation opportunities when comparing results with competitors. Also, [47] discussed the development of a framework to measure innovation. This framework is based on research of (i) [47] - PwC Wheel of innovation Excellence; (ii) [42] - Innovation radar; (iii) BCG - Senior management survey [1, 33, 42].

A framework must focus on the importance of organization strategy linked to the innovation process [47]. Results must be presented on a simple chart in order to facilitate adoption, use and understanding. The questions related to the performance indicators must be structured in different levels, in order to make the measure easier. The framework must measure tangible and intangible innovation aspects.

Finally, through innovation radar, the framework describes an innovation dashboard based on six indicators: collaboration, commercialization, concept, leader, success, and talent [47].

The radar framework associated with the CSF's and an effective measuring methodology can help the organizations to identify threats and opportunities, weaknesses and strengths in order to prioritize factors. Then, this work intends to propose a model to validate CSF associated with technology commercialization.

3   Data and Method

This work is a qualitative case study based on Systematic Literature review (SLR) and experts review. A SLR consists in searching, studying and analyzing previous studies to develop a better understanding of a particular subject. An expert review aims to gather opinions to validate knowledge on a given research topic. In this study, the SLR focused on CSFs for technology commercialization in the Brazilian public university context. For the experts review, key people from universities were asked to review the results of the SLR. The results allowed them to refine data and propose an instrument consisting of questions related to CSFs for technology commercialization to be used in the case study. It is worth mentioning that a qualitative case study allows to deepen the understanding on CSFs from the reality of a chosen organization.

SLR (Table 1) helped identify the most cited papers and their authors, countries and journals with a higher number of publications related with technology commercialization. The timeframe was from 1990 to 2016, claring the US Bayh-Dole Act influence. The articles were analyzed to verify useful contributions to the subject, focusing on the success factors. The following categories were found: Management and Strategy, Organizational, Technical and Individual. Each category has CSFs related to technology commercialization.

Table 1. Research Systematic Literature Review (SLR) process

Purpose	Identify the success factors of technology commercialization
Survey data	699 papers (127 selected and 572 discarded papers)
Selected data (responded)	127 papers
Method	SLR (Systematic Literature Review)
Timeframe	1990–2016
Keywords	Technology transfer, technology commercialization, University*, licensing and patents (Languages: English, Portuguese and Spanish)

The study allowed them to identify the critical factors affecting technology commercialization success. In addition, experts were asked to analyze the factors and the proposed categorization from the literature review.

In the first round, five professionals from a Brazilian public university Innovation Technology Center were contacted: two professors, two researchers and one technical manager. The experts were selected based on the following criteria: (a) doctorate degree, (b) research line related to this work, and (c) availability and interest to contribute to this research. Each professional agreed to receive an instrument consisting of open-ended questions concerning to CSFs and its categories. A content analysis [3] was performed on the written opinions and suggestions of the experts.

In the second round, ten experts were asked to analyze and validate the categories and the critical success factors. All of them are teachers in a Brazilian public university located in Minas Gerais, Brazil. The contributions of each specialist were transcribed and analyzed using the content analysis techniques proposed by [3]. The results were refined resulting in the Critical Success Factors presented at Table 2 (Sect. 4.1. Results and discussion) and in the variables showed on Table 3 (Sect. 4.2. Results and discussion). Following, the radar chart presented in Fig. 1 (Sect. 4 Results and discussion) was proposed.

An instrument for data collection was built based on the previous data. Each factor was split up in two questions using the Likert-scale. A questionnaire was used to perform the case study in this research (the questionnaire can be found at http://bit.ly/2KKoudk). In future studies, the instrument will be used for data collection from a larger number of Brazilian public universities.

4   Results and Discussion

4.1   CSF Systematic Literature Review

The Critical Success Factors for the technology commercialization in public universities were elaborated from a literature review process (Table 2).

Table 2. Critical success factors (CSFs) for the technology commercialization in public universities.

Categories	Factors
Management and strategy	Licensing strategies
	Technological transfer mechanisms
	Intellectual property rights
	Companies creation
Organizational	University, institutional, governmental policies
	Business experience
	Business development culture
	Culture of innovation
Technical	Understanding technological needs
	Nature of technology
	University-business liaisons
	Attributes of technological inventions
Individuals	Scientific quality
	Technological aptitude
	Individual characteristics of researchers
	Research reputation

The categories and their supporting authors are presented below:

A. Management and strategy: strategies, processes, mechanisms, and structure for technology commercialization in the universities [16, 26, 48, 49];
B. Organizational: managerial and political aspects in addition to the culture towards innovation and commercialization [2].

C. Technicians: nature of technologies and market needs [21, 26, 27];
D. Individuals: characteristics related to the knowledge domain and profile of the teachers, students, and technical staff [10, 12, 21, 26, 28, 52].

4.2   Experts Review and Radar Chart

The CSFs from the literature review were submitted to experts from Knowledge Management, Entrepreneurship, Innovation, and Marketing areas for analysis and revision. The specialists analyzed the terms correctness and the factors' appropriate validity and categorization. Also, experts were asked to propose changes or additions to presented factors and categories. In this sense, after the experts reviews a new table was created (Table 3) containing categories, acronyms, factors, and names for the variables to be used in the data collection instrument.

Table 3. CSFs for technology commercialization in public universities after experts review.

Category	Acronym	Factors	Variables
STRATEGY AND MANAGEMENT	SAM	Public and governmental policies	SAM01
		Strategy and strategic planning	SAM02
		Top management involvement	SAM03
		Intellectual property	SAM04
CULTURE AND STRUCTURE	CAS	Organizational culture	CAS01
		Entrepreneurial training	CAS02
		Technology support	CAS03
		Entrepreneur support	CAS04
MARKET AND TECHNOLOGIES	MAT	Market orientation	MAT01
		University-industry relationship	MAT02
		Quality and applicability of technologies	MAT03
		Diffusion of technologies	MAT04
INDIVIDUAL COMPETENCES	ICO	Scientific production reputation and quality	ICO01
		Innovation know-how	ICO02
		Researchers entrepreneurial profile	ICO03
		Real world problem-solving competences	ICO04

After defining categories, factors and variables, the framework "CSFs for technology commercialization in public universities" (Fig. 1) was proposed. The framework consists of 16 variables that will help to perform the case study. The radar chart will be created from field data collected using the questionnaire. Each variable has a set of closed-ended questions using a five points Likert scale (1 - Totally disagree to 5 - Totally agree).

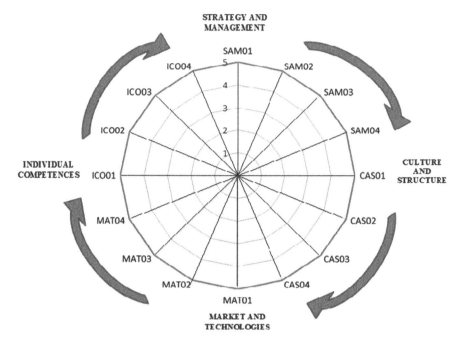

Fig. 1. CSFs for technology commercialization in public universities (radar chart).

4.3   Case Study – Brazilian Public University

The case study was conducted from January to February 2018 within an Office for Technology Transfer (OTT) in a Brazilian public university located in Minas Gerais, Brazil (called University 1).

4.4   Office for Technology Transfer

The OTT is the department responsible for the policies of technological innovation and the intellectual protection of the knowledge generated within the university. It is linked to the research process, collaborating with professors, researchers, and technical staff. One of its main objectives is to disseminate the importance of the research in the University 1. The structure of Office for Technology Transfer at University 1 is the following: General Coordinator, Intellectual Property Coordinator, and Technological Park Coordinator.

In accordance to the industrial property laws, University 1 elaborated a resolution of the Board of Education, Research and Extension which governs its intellectual property policy. This resolution provides characteristics for determining the ownership and profits division from technology transfer within University 1.

4.5   CSFs Radar in OTT-University 1

Figure 2 shows the opinion of the five respondents from the OTT at University 1 regarding the CSFs categorization and its items.

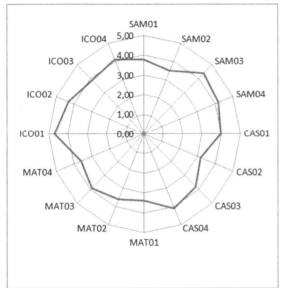

VARIABLE	VALUE	AVERAGE
SAM01	3.80	
SAM02	3.50	
SAM03	4.40	
SAM04	4.20	3.98
CAS01	4.00	
CAS02	3.20	
CAS03	3.80	
CAS04	4.10	3.78
MAT01	3.40	
MAT02	3.60	
MAT03	3.90	
MAT04	3.60	3.63
ICO01	4.70	
ICO02	4.30	
ICO03	3.90	
ICO04	4.10	4.25

Fig. 2. CSFs radar of the University 1.

The results of CSF in OTT-University 1 show that the highest value is associated to ICO01 (Scientific production reputation and quality) and the low value item is the CAS02 (Entrepreneurial training). In the category Strategy and Management (SAM) the Organizational strategy (SAM02) was the lowest average, while the highest average was the Top management involvement (SAM03). The Culture and Structure lowest value was Entrepreneurial training (CAS02) and the highest was Entrepreneur support (CAS04). For Market and Technologies the lowest average was Market orientation (MAT01) and the highest was Quality and applicability of technologies (MAT03). In the category Individual Competences, the lowest average was Researchers entrepreneurial profile (ICO03) while the highest was scientific production reputation and quality (ICO01).

The highest average was found in the Individual Competencies category, which can indicate that the human factor is key to develop technology commercialization. Scientific production reputation and quality (ICO01) it is considered of special importance by respondents. They mentioned that the university reputation can work as a brand that shows trust to society and to the organizations.

5 Conclusion

The main research goal was to present an empirically validated framework of CSFs for technology commercialization in public universities. After a systematic review of literature and an experts review, CSFs radar was described to be used in a case study.

The data analysis allowed knowing the perception of respondents about the pertinence and relevance of the CSFs categories proposed in this work. The radar chart provides a graphical view of the data. This chart can be used by a public university to map out its situation and compare to other institutions.

The CSFs categories and subcategories definition showed good results, according to the respondents perception. This was evidenced by the scores awarded to each subcategory, thus those scores were used to find out the average of each category.

The literature review found no previous research that uses the radar chart for the analysis of CSF for technology commercialization. Nevertheless, the results of this study can be used for further research.

The ability to visualize the institution's situation concerning CSFs is one of the reasons and motivations pursued when identifying CSFs. Also, this study provides an opportunity to provide tools to monitor strengths and weaknesses, gather information that can help improvements, and adapt procedures. Besides those, increased competitiveness and grounds to formulate strategies and tools towards decision-making are desired.

Although beyond the scope of the current research, the analysis of CSF can provide substantial knowledge to manage the initiatives of the universities OTTs. The proposed radar framework need additional experimental tests and analysis to map out the technologies commercialization capabilities. By using the CSF framework, the Universities can focus on particular aspects of their technology commercialization capabilities through the efficient use of the scarce resources of the organization. Thus, the OTTs can identify items and categories of the CSF framework that need improvements. Monitoring of how organizations improve their technology commercialization capabilities can add value to innovation research.

This work come with its limitations given the small number of respondents in a single institution from a specific country. However, an extension to the study is planned with more universities in Brazil and Mexico, so internal and external validity can be tested in a large and heterogeneous sample.

Acknowledgments. The authors would like to thank the National Council for Scientific and Technological Development (CNPq - Brazil) - Process CHSSA 444072/2015-2, the Minas Gerais State Foundation for Research Development (FAPEMIG–MG–Brazil), and the Organization of American States (OAS-COIMBRA) for the financial support.

References

1. Andrew, J.P., Haanaes, K., Michael, D.C., Sirkin, H.L.: Measuring Innovation 2009: The Need for Action – A BCG Senior Management Survey. The Boston Consulting Group (2009). www.bcg.com/documents/file15484.pdf
2. Antonites, M.: Assesing antecedents of entrepreneurial activities of academics at South African Universities. Int. J. Innov. Manag. **20**, 1650058 (2016)
3. Bardin, L.: Análise de Caonteúdo-Content Analysis. Edicoes, Lisbon (2006)
4. Bortolussi, S.: Gestão de propriedade intelectual em Universidades: Análise do desempenho da Universidade Federal de Minas Gerais no processo de Tranferência de Tecnologia. Encontro nacional de Engenharia de Produção. Fortaleza, Brasil, Outubro de 2015
5. Bullen, C., Rockart, J.: A prime on critical Success Factors. Center for Information Systems Research Sloan School of Management No. 69, Masssachusetts Institute of technology (1981)
6. Calderón-Martínez, G.: Patentes en Instituciones de Educación Superior en México. Revista de la Educación Superior **43**(170), 37–56 (2014)
7. Caralli, R.: The critical success factors method: establishing of foundation for enterprise security management. Technical report CMU/SEI-2004-TR-010-ESC-TR-2004-010 (2004)
8. Carayannis, E.A.: Technology commercialization in entrepreneurial universities: the US and Russian experience. J. Technol. Transf. **41**, 1135–1147 (2016)
9. de Lima, C., Rochade, O.: Análise do radar da innovação no segmento de bares e restaurantes da regiaõ metropolitana de Natal-RN. Revista Eletrônica de Ciências **9**(3), 175–193 (2016)
10. Chang, Y.C.: The determinants of academic research commercial performance: towards an organizational ambidexterity perspective. Res. Policy **38**, 936–946 (2009)
11. Chatterjee, D., Sankaran, B.: Commercializing academic research in emerging economies: do organizational identities matter? Sci. Public Policy **42**, 599–613 (2015)
12. Chen, J.: Defining and measuring business innovation: the innovation radar. Kellogg School of Management Working Paper (2010)
13. Chesbrough, H.: Managing Open Innovation in Large Firms. Fraunhofer Institute for Industrial Engineering, Stuttgart (2013)
14. De Benedicto: Apropriação da inovação em agrotecnologias:estudo multicaso em Universidades Brasileiras. Tese (Doutorado em Inovação) UFLA (2011)
15. Derakhshani, S.: Negotiating technology transfer agreements. World Exec. Dig. **8**(5), 47–49 (1987)
16. Dias, A.A.: Como a USP transfere tecnologia? Organizações Sociedade **21**, 489–507 (2014)
17. Didriksson, A.: La universidad desde su futuro. Pro-Posições **15**, 63–73 (2004)
18. Etzkowitz, H.: The evolution of entrepreneurial university. Int. Technol. Glob. **1**, 64–77 (2004)
19. Ferguson, C.R., Dickinson, R.: Critical success factors for directors in the eighties. Bus. Horiz. **25**(3), 14–18 (1982)
20. Fernandes Jr., O., Oliveira, E.: A inovação faz a diferença - Como o Brasil pode tirar melhor proveito das pesquisas tecnológicas. In: Desafios do desenvolvimento. BNDES, Brasília-Brasil (2007). http://ipea.gov.br/desafios/index.php?option=com_content&view=article&id=1466:catid=28&Itemid=23
21. Fukugawa, N.: Knowledge creation and dissemination by Kosetsushi in sectoral innovation systems: insights from patent data. Scientometrics **109**, 2303–2327 (2016)

22. Goldstein, H.B.: University mission creep? Comparing EU and US faculty views of university involvement in regional economic development and commercialization. Ann. Reg. Sci. **50**, 453–477 (2013)

23. Gómez, J., Mira, S.I.: Las Spin Offs Académicas como vía de Transferencia Tecnólogica. Economía Industrial **366**, 61–72 (2007)

24. Jk, L., Av, B.: Identifying and using critical success factors. Long Range Plan. **17**(1), 23–32 (1984)

25. Kanyak, E.: Transfer of Technology from Developed Countries: Some Insights from Turkey. Quarum Books, Westport (1985)

26. Kirchberger, M.A., Polh, L.: Technology Commercialization: a literature review of success factors and antecedents across different contexts. Technol. Trans. **41**, 1077–1112 (2016)

27. Kumar, U.U.: Critical success factors in technology transfer from government laboratories to private sector: a study based on Canadian Federal Government Departments. In: ASAC (2007)

28. Lee, J.: University reputation and technology commercialization: evidence from nanoscale science. J. Technol. Trans. **41**, 586–609 (2016)

29. Martins, H.: Metodologia qualitativa de pesquisa. Educação e Pesquisa, São Paulo **30**(2), 289–300 (2004)

30. Medellin, E.: Construir la Innovación: gestión tecnológica en la empresa. SigloXXI, México (2013)

31. Molero, K.: Comercialización de tecnologia como estrategia del consejo de fomento en la Universidad del Zulia. Trabajo de grado presentado como requisito pata obtener grado de Magíster Scenciarium en Planificación, p. 147, Maracaibo (2013)

32. Morioka, S.: Análise de fatores críticos de sucesso de projetos em uma empresa de varejo. Trabalho de Formatura - Escola Politécnica da Universidadede São Paulo. Departamento de Engenharia de Produção, São Paulo, Brasil (2010)

33. Morris, L.: The innovation master plan: the CEO's guide to innovation. Innovation Academy, Walnut Creek (2011)

34. Oliveira, H.V., Sá, V.C.: Identificação e análise dos fatores críticos de sucesso: o caso da Master Produções e Eventos. Revista de Admininstração de Roraima - RARR, Ed 2, vol. 1, pp. 41–66. Boa Vista - RR - Brasil, 1°. Sem 2012 (2012)

35. Oslo Manual: Guidelines for collecting and Interpreting Innovation Data: Directrices para la recogida e interpretación de información relativa a Innovación. OCDE y Eurostat, Madrid: Comunidad de Madrid Consejería de Educación Dirección General de Universidades e Investigaciónn de información relativa a Innovación (2005)

36. Padilla, D.À.: Factores determinantes de la transferencia tecnologica en el ámbito Universitario. La perspectiva del investigador. Dialnet, Economía Industrial, pp. 91–106 (2010)

37. Pérez-Hernández, P., Calderón-Martínez, G.: Análisis de los Procesos de Comercialización de tecnología en dos Instituciones de Educación Superior Mexicanas. J. Technol. Manag. Innov. **9**, 196–209 (2014)

38. Rockart, J.: Chief executive define their own data needs. Harv. Bus. Rev. **57**(2), 81–93 (1979)

39. Roessner, J.D.: What companies want from the federal labs. Issues Sci. Technol. **10**(1), 37–42 (1993)

40. Rogers, E.M.: Diffusion of Innovations, 5th edn, p. 2003. Simon & Schuster, Inc., New York (2003)

41. Sabater, J.G.: Manual de Transferencia de tecnología y Conocimiento. Instituto de transferencia de tecnología y conocimiento, España (2010)

42. Sawhney, M., Wolcott, R.C., Arroniz, I.: The 12 different ways for companies to innovate. MIT Sloan Manag. Rev. **47**(3), 75–81 (2006)
43. Schumpeter, J.: The theory of economic development (s.d.). https://books.google.com.br/books?id=-OZwWcOGeOwC&printsec=frontcover&hl=es#v=onepage&q&f=false. Transaction Publishers, United Staes of America (2004, tenth printing)
44. Siegel, D.S., Wright, M., Lockett, A.: The rise of entrepreneurial activity at universities: organizational and societal implications. Ind. Corp. Change **16**, 489–504 (2007)
45. Silva Santiago, C.V.: Análisis de los factores que influyene ne l éxito de la transferencia tecnológica desde los institutos tecnológicos a las Pymes: los casos de España y Brasil. J. Technol. Manag. Innov. **1**, 57–70 (2006)
46. Sira, S.: Letter to the editor: factors affecting the universitary technoogy transfer processes to promote effective and efficient interaction with externa sectors. Revista Ingeniería UC **23**(2), 223–236 (2016)
47. Skerlj, T.: Measuring innovation excellence: measurement framework for PWC's wheel of innovation excellence concept (s.d.). In: Human Capital without Borders: Knowledge and Learning for Quality of Life; Proceedings of the Management, Knowledge and Learning International Conference, pp. 221–229. ToKnowPress (2014)
48. Suvinen, N.K.: How necessary are intermediary organizations in the commercialization of research? Eur. Plan. Stud. **18**, 1365–1389 (2010)
49. Valente, L.: Hélice tríplice: metáfora dos anos 90 descreve bem o mais sustentável modelo de sistema de inovação. Conhecimento Inovação **6**, 6–9 (2010)
50. WIPO: Acesso em Feb de 2017 (s.d.). What is Intellectual Property. http://www.wipo.int/edocs/pubdocs/en/intproperty/450/wipo_pub_450.pdf
51. Wood, M.: Does one size fit all? The multiple organizational forms leading to successful academic entrepreneurship. Entrep. Theory Pract. **33**, 929–947 (2009)
52. Wu, Y.W.: Commercialization of university inventions: individual and institutional factors affecting licensing of university patents. Technovation **36**, 12–25 (2015)

Semantic Technologies and the Legal Aspects

PrOnto: Privacy Ontology for Legal Reasoning

Monica Palmirani[1(✉)], Michele Martoni[1], Arianna Rossi[1],
Cesare Bartolini[2], and Livio Robaldo[2]

[1] University of Bologna, CIRSFID, Via Galliera 3, 40121 Bologna, Italy
{monica.palmirani,michele.martoni,
arianna.rossi15}@unibo.it
[2] SnT - Interdisciplinary Centre for Security, Reliability and Trust,
Université du Luxembourg, JFK Building, 29, Avenue J.F. Kennedy,
1855 Luxembourg City, Luxembourg
{cesare.bartolini,livio.robaldo}@uni.lu

Abstract. The GDPR (GDPR, REGULATION (EU) 2016/679 OF THE
EUROPEAN PARLIAMENT AND OF THE COUNCIL of 27 April 2016 on
the protection of natural persons with regard to the processing of personal data
and on the free movement of such data, and repealing Directive 95/46/EC
(General Data Protection Regulation)) introduces the self-assessment of digital
risks and the modulation of duties on the basis of the impact assessment analysis, including specific measures that intend to safeguard the data subject's
human dignity and fundamental rights. Semantic web technologies and legal
reasoning tools can support privacy-by-default and legal compliance. In this
light, this paper presents a first draft of a legal ontology on the GDPR, called
PrOnto, that has the goal of providing a legal knowledge modelling of the
privacy agents, data types, types of processing operations, rights and obligations. The methodology used here is based on legal theory analysis joined with
ontological patterns.

Keywords: Semantic web · Legal reasoning · Legal ontology
Checking compliance

1 Introduction

The GDPR *(General Data Protection Regulation)* introduces a common legal framework for all the EU member states with the aim of harmonizing their privacy principles
and the application of these principles inside the Digital Single Market. One of the
main newly introduced instruments is the self-assessment of the digital risks and the
modulation of the duties on the basis of the impact assessment analysis, including
specific measures to safeguard the data subject's human dignity and fundamental rights.
The audit and the compliance checking are instruments to guarantee *privacy-by-design*
during software development (*ex-ante* phase) and the prompt detection of violations
(*ex-post* phase) when they occur [7]. For this reason, semantic web and legal reasoning
techniques can support the application of privacy-by-default principles in the day-by-
day operative tasks of public administrations, companies and non-profit organizations.

© Springer Nature Switzerland AG 2018
A. Kő and E. Francesconi (Eds.): EGOVIS 2018, LNCS 11032, pp. 139–152, 2018.
https://doi.org/10.1007/978-3-319-98349-3_11

In this light, there is the urgent need to model a legal ontology of the privacy and data protection regulation, which must not be limited to the GDPR and which can be extended to other jurisdictions, in order to define the legal concepts in these legal frameworks and the relationships among them. This paper presents the first draft ontology on the GDPR, called PrOnto (Privacy Ontology), that aims to provide a legal knowledge modelling of the privacy agents, data types, processing operations, rights and obligations. The goal of this ontology is to support legal reasoning and check compliance by using defeasible logic theory (LegalRuleML standard [3] and SPINDle engine [13]), as opposed to exclusively improve information retrieval on the web.

2   Related Work

Different authors from the semantic web community [2, 12, 17, 23, 24] have developed privacy ontologies for specific goals. For instance, the HL7 privacy ontology [15, 16] is oriented to manage health data for electronic health records; others are oriented to secure messaging among automatic systems in the Internet of Things ecosystem, whereas others are oriented to manage the data flow in the linked open data environment or on the blockchain. However, there exists no legal ontology of privacy principles of the theory of law and foundational concepts that is able to support legal reasoning and check compliance. Those functionalities require a precise modelling of the rights and obligations using deontic operators and, at the same time, a modelling of the actors and the processing operations described in the normative prescriptions. For this reason, PrOnto takes inspiration from different existing ontologies and from the methodology of ontology design pattern [9]. We have used several other ontologies:

1. **ALLOT:** this ontology implements the Akoma Ntoso Top Level Classes (TLCs) as a formal OWL 2 DL and allows to connect the data and document classes with the FRBR ontology [5].
2. **FRBR:** FRBR is an ontology that implements the FRBR model [18].
3. **LKIF Core:** Action.owl is an ontology that represents actions in general, i.e., processes that are performed by an agent. We use in particular lkif:Agent to model lkif:Organization and lkif:Person [6].
4. **LKIF Core:** Role.owl is an ontology to describe typologies of roles (epistemic roles, functions, person roles, organisation roles). We use in particular lkif:Role [6].
5. The **Publishing Workflow Ontology** (PWO) is a simple ontology written in OWL 2 DL for the characterization of the main stages in the workflow associated with the publication of a document (e.g., being written, under review, XML capture, page design, publication on the Web). We reuse the workflow pattern to model the different types of processing of personal data [10].
6. **Time-indexed Value in Context** (TVC) is an ontology pattern that allows to describe scenarios in which someone (e.g., a person) has a value (e.g., a particular role) during a particular time and for a particular context. We use this portion of ontology to connect the event with value, context and time parameters [19].

7. **Time Interval** (TI) is an ontology design pattern that enables the description of periods of time that are characterised by a starting date and an ending date. We use this ontology to manage the time interval [19].

3   Methodology: MeLOn

We developed PrOnto by using an interdisciplinary approach called MeLOn (Methodology for building Legal Ontology), which has been already used with success to develop several legal ontologies. The MeLOn methodology was built to design legal ontologies, considering the great difficulties that legal experts encounter when they must define a model of the reality using the ontological techniques. Protégé was used frequently in the past in the legal community, but with the result to produce a large number of classes, one for each legal term, because the legal expert is not usually familiar with the modelization of the reality using classes, relationships and attributes. The Glossary method is too language-oriented. The foundational approach is too abstract and too little applicative, even if DOLCE [11] is used as skeleton for the final checking.

The MeLOn methodology is composed of ten steps that can be recursively applied:

1. **Describe the goal of the ontology.** In this step, the team describes the research questions that the ontology intends to cope with. It is also important to select two or three use-cases where the ontology is helpful. For PrOnto we defined the following goals:
    - (i) to model data protection legal norms starting from legal texts but including also social norms, practitioner opinions or social behaviours;
    - (ii) to build a legal ontology that is usable for legal reasoning;
    - (iii) to build a legal ontology that is usable for web of data and information retrieval.
2. **Evaluation indicators.** We define some parameters/indicators to evaluate the ontology according to the goals (step 1). In the PrOnto ontology, we selected the following criteria based on the existing state of the art [4];
    - (i) **coherence:** the axioms of the ontology can't create inconsistency or contradictions;
    - (ii) **completeness:** the domain is adequately covered by the ontology and the main concepts are included;
    - (iii) **efficiency:** the ontology is technically sound, concise and the reasoning is computable in reasonable time, and it is based on patterns;
    - (iv) **effectiveness:** the ontology covers the most important queries about the domain and the end users find it helpful to resolve applicative situations;
    - (v) **usability:** the end users find the ontology clear, understandable, easy to use, close to the main terminology used inside of the community, sefl-explained.
    - (vi) **agreement:** the grade of agreement and acceptance of the ontology in the legal expert community.
3. **State of the art survey.** We have checked the state of the art in order to reuse existing ontologies, ontology patterns [14], and other existing domain vocabularies.

4. **List all the relevant terminology.** We produce a glossary with the most relevant legal terms extracted from normative documents, case-law, contracts, or any other legal source. In particular, we included all the legal definitions.

5. **Use usable tools.** We use tools that are close to the legal experts such as tables or UML diagrams in order to model the knowledge-base of the legal domain. Legal experts can use the Graffoo tool[1] that allows to use graphical instruments and to transform the UML into OWL/XML serialization.

6. **Refine and optimize.** The serialization into OWL by Graffoo [8, 21] or UML is not optimal for the efficiency and the coherence, therefore the axioms are added manually by an ontology expert in order to check the coherence.

7. **Test the output.** The ontology is tested by legal experts using a web interface in order to evaluate the completeness, effectiveness and usability.

8. **Evaluate the ontology.** We use the OntoClean method to polish the ontology and apply the criteria of point 2 to provide metrics. A set of SPARQL queries are prepared and the output is measured.

9. **Publish the document** with the LODE tool[2] [20].

10. **Collect feedbacks** from the community in order to reach the agreement criteria.

The method must be repeated at least three times and transparently published online.

4   PrOnto Modules

PrOnto consists of different modules: (i) documents and data, (ii) actors and roles, (iii) processing and workflow, (iv) legal rules and deontic formula, (v) purposes and legal bases (Fig. 1).

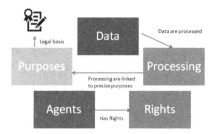

Fig. 1. Modules of PrOnto ontology

---

[1] http://www.essepuntato.it/graffoo/, http://www.yworks.com/en/products/yfiles/yed.

[2] http://www.essepuntato.it/lode.

Some document and data are referred to the data subject. Data subject is a *role* of an *agent* (physical person). Data is processed following a given *workflow* plan of actions. When executed, each action assumes specific temporal parameters (e.g., the processing's interval of time), context (e.g., jurisdiction where the data processing is carried out), and value (e.g., place where the data processing is performed). The data processing must be performed according to a *legal basis* that provides the lawfulness of the processing. Each *processing* activity involves a controller, a processor, and other actors. Each actor has obligations or rights, for instance the data subject has rights related to the data protection. These rights and obligations are linked to documents where the norms appear: terms of use, information, privacy policies, consent forms.

4.1 Data and Document

Data protection involves data and documents in a twofold manner: data are the object of the regulation and the target of its protection, and also the source of information to regulate the relationships between the different agents (e.g., controller, processor, etc.) using privacy, informed consent, contracts, codes of conduct, law, case-law and any other legal document. The data and the documents are documental sources; using the FRBR ontology, we model their representations over time by reusing a robust design pattern already adopted for the publication process [22]. Data are defined in categories according to the GDPR: personal data, non-personal data, anonymized data, pseudonymised data (Fig. 2).

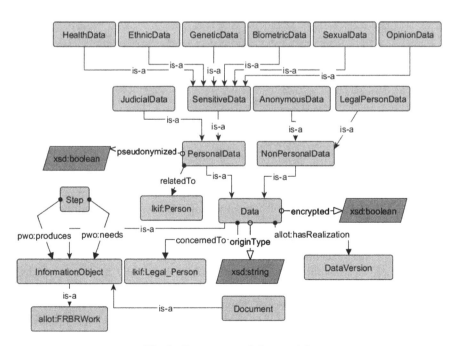

Fig. 2. Document and data module

4.2   Agent and Role

One of the most frequent errors in legal ontology design is to confuse agents and roles. In PrOnto we clearly distinguish the two classes. Physical persons and organizations are agents, but we include into the agent class also IT organizations or artificial intelligence and software or robots. An agent could play multiple roles related to different processing activities and contexts. Additionally, a controller could act as processor or third party with respect to a separate processing. Each role is fixed in a given period of time that is joined with the time version of the dataset and the duration of the data processing. The role is authorized by an event that assigns it to the agent (see Fig. 3). The role is modelled in subclasses like DPO (data protection officer), controller, processor, third party, representative, recipient, data subject, supervisory authority, Member State. Other roles are defined by the deontic legal rules such as bearer or counter party.

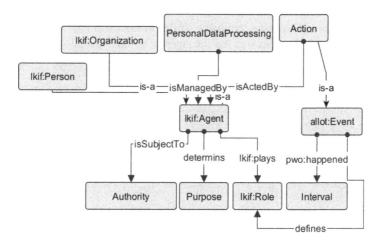

Fig. 3.   Agent and role module

4.3   Data Processing

When we model human activities, we need to model workflows as a sequence of steps that uses some resources in input and produces some outcomes. However, a workflow is composed of two parts: the plan to do something (e.g., workflow) and the concrete sequence of actions actually performed (e.g., execution of the workflow). In the GDPR, it is especially important to distinguish the plan (e.g., Impact Assessment Plan made of steps) from the real execution (e.g., data breach event and counter measurement enacted), which is constituted by a set of actions. Especially in the compliance checking scenario, there is the need to have a plan that conforms to the law and to provide counter measures in case of violation during the actual execution (e.g., remedies). For this reason, we have used the Publishing Workflow Ontology (PWO) as the basis to model the data processing ontology module. PWO incudes workflow and executed workflow. *PersonalDataProcessing* is a subclass of Workflow with several attributes: *transparency, fairness, lawfulness* that are Boolean value that a legal reasoning process could set up. Personal data processing is also planned for being eligible for a given period of time (*isValid*), also in accordance with the purpose (*isBasedOn*). *PersonalDataProcessingExecution* is a subclass of *WorkflowExecution*. The workflow execution involves actions. The actions [1] are a kind of *event* that are described by temporal parameters (e.g., interval) and context values (Time-indexed Value in Context - TVC). The Action class in PrOnto also has an important attribute for storing the status of *breachness*: the action is prone to configure a data breach event. One of the values of the action is the place where the event occurs (e.g., within the EU borders) and the *jurisdiction* (e.g., Regional competence). Other values and statuses can be added in order to enrich the context description (see Fig. 4).

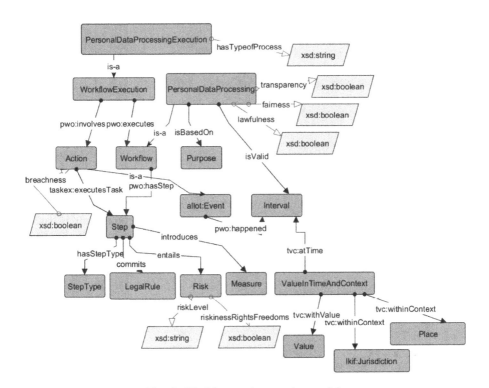

Fig. 4. Workflow and processing module

For instance, we take the category of all the actions that produce a "deletion" according with the Article 17 of GDPR. Technically speaking, it is not easy to isolate the exact moment and level of deletion (e.g., logical deletion or physical erasure – see Fig. 5), but under the legal point of view we can include in this category the following behaviours: a temporary deletion, a permanent deletion including the backup copies in cloud computing, destruction of the physical device, anonymisation of the data, and finally the pseudoanonymisation of data with double password access and kept in a secure place (e.g., safe). However, there are situations in which it is difficult to ensure a total erasure (e.g., blockchain), and the anonymisation techniques do not guarantee 100% security of de-identification [25]. For these reasons, PrOnto distinguishes between different levels of delete actions: PermanentErasure, Destroy e Anonymise. The deletion action is also activated when the processing expires. When the purpose and the valid period expires, the ontology can execute the deletion action.

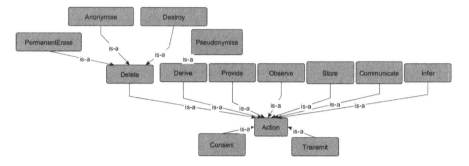

Fig. 5. Action module

4.4 Purposes and Legal Basis

The GDPR permits the processing of personal data only in the light of several lawful purposes. The purposes must be supported by a legal basis (Article 6 – Lawfulness of processing). For this reason, we have introduced a *lawfulness* status as a Boolean data property of the *PersonalDataProcessing* class. Each personal data processing is based on a *Purpose*. In this way, a rule engine, based for instance on a rule language like LegalRuleML, can return this value after the rule reasoning process (Figs. 6 and 7).

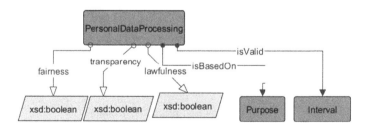

Fig. 6. Lawfulness status and legal basis relationship

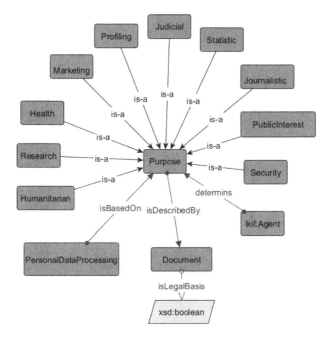

Fig. 7. Purpose class and subclasses

4.5 Deontic Operators

The modelling of legal norms needs deontic operators such as right, obligation, permission and prohibition. From the point of view of the GDPR, it is very relevant to also include violation/compliance as the status where an obligation or a prohibition is violated or is compliant. The deontic operators are connected to temporal parameters, and to a jurisdiction as well, in case some rights are effective only in a certain domestic regulation. This part of the PrOnto ontology allows us to model the necessary predicates to implement legal rules. This module is an extension of the LegalRuleML meta model, which allows us to synchronize the legal rule language modelling with the ontology.

Each step commits a LegalRule that is made up of Deontic Specifications (Fig. 8).

The Right and Obligation classes are detailed in subclasses according to the GDPR. Right is connected to a permission. In this manner, we can track the permission connected with a specific right such as the right to access (e.g., permission to use a PET – Privacy-enhancing technology), whilst obligation is connected to violation or compliance. We are thus able to make queries like the following: give me all the obligations of the controller (X) that were violated in a given interval $[t_x, t_y]$ (Figs. 9 and 10).

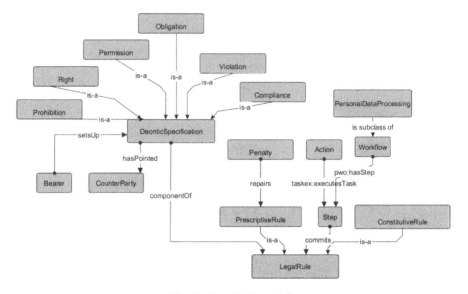

Fig. 8. LegalRule module

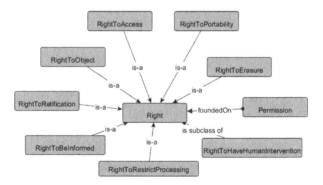

Fig. 9. Right classes

The ontology in this module also intends to model the relationships between deontic rules, actors' rights and obligations, obligations and permissions, and violation/compliance. This modelling allows to populate the ontology, or to create RDF triples, in order to perform queries like the following: "give me all the data processing that has been violated by some actors in a given time". This knowledge is processed by the rule engine, but transformed into individuals in the ontology (or RDF triples) without the need to query to the rule engine each time.

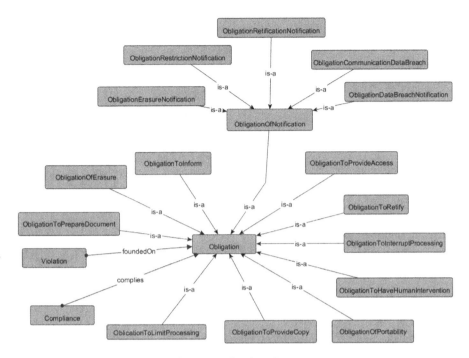

Fig. 10. Obligation classes

5 Evaluation

The evaluation is carried out inside the Cloud4EU European project PCP[3] that intends to provide legal compliance checking systems for eGovernment services that are delivered across the cloud. We are currently in the phase of testing PrOnto on three different scenarios related to school services. PrOnto is also used inside the MIREL European project[4] and the DAPRECO Luxembourgish project[5].

An example of the use of PrOnto is presented hereafter.

---

[3] http://www.agid.gov.it/cloudforeurope.

[4] http://www.mirelproject.eu/.

[5] https://wwwen.uni.lu/research/fstc/computer_science_and_communications_research_unit/research_projects/data_protection_regulation_compliance.

a. Give me all the personal data processing performed by company X in the role of controller valid in [t₁, t₂].	SELECT ?pdp
	WHERE {
	    ?pdp :isManagedBy _:c .
	    [lkif:plays _:c ;
	        rdfs:label "X"] .
	    ?pdp :isValid [
	        time:hasBeginning [rdfs:label "t1"] ;
	        time:hasEnd [rdfs:label "t2"]
	    ] .
	}

b. Give me all the communications connected with of a given step K in the PersonalDataProcessing.	SELECT ?a ?pdp
	WHERE {
	    ?a a :Action .
	    ?a taskex:executesTask _:s .
	    ?pdp pwo:hasStep _:s .
	    _:s rdfs:label "K" .
	}

The previous queries produce important results to check the GDPR obligations and facilitating a dynamic self-assessment. We suppose that a software manages documentation, registry of processing, DPIA information, etc. (e.g., software provided by the French CNIL – Commission Nationale de l'Informatique et des Libertés[6]). If such a software is connected with PrOnto ontology, we can check for GDPR compliance throughout all the lifecycle of the personal data, using advanced legal reasoning tools or SPARQL end-points.

6   Conclusions and Future Work

Several privacy ontologies exist (e.g., HL7 for eHealth, PPO for Linked Open Data, OdrL for modelling rights, etc.) in the state of the art but are not integrated with deontic logic models usable for legal reasoning. PRONTO intends to integrate different levels of semantic representation: document and data modelling to support the semantic web information retrieval, in particular Linked Open Data (e.g., SPARQL queries); workflow and processing to support the planning of privacy policy and possibly also BPMN modelling for system design (e.g., privacy-by-design); rights and obligations to enable the legal reasoning using rule languages (e.g., LegalRuleML and compliance checking); human-centric approaches to favour the visualization and the presentation of the privacy-related legal principles and concepts in different contexts and towards different targets.

---

[6] https://www.cnil.fr/en/open-source-pia-software-helps-carry-out-data-protection-impact-assesment.

This is a long-term research. We intend to proceed with the modelling and optimization of the formal ontology and to evaluate it with a large number of use-cases. In the meantime, we believe that such an ontology has to be negotiated with a large community, in order to create a consensus and to place those results into a standardization body for the future governance (e.g., OASIS, W3C). In the future, it is also necessary to develop specific profiles, one for each specific national law, or by thematic domain (e.g., Privacy in IoT, Privacy in AI, etc.).

Acknowledgement. This work was partially supported by the European Union's Horizon 2020 research and innovation programme under the Marie Skłodowska-Curie grant agreement No 690974 "MIREL: MIning and REasoning with Legal texts" and by the Luxembourg National Research Fund (FNR) CORE project C16/IS/11333956 "DAPRECO: DAta Protection REgulation COmpliance".

References

1. Abrams, M.: The origins of personal data and its implications for governance. https://papers.ssrn.com/sol3/papers.cfm?abstract_id=2510927
2. Ashley, K.: Artificial Intelligence and Legal Analytics New Tools for Law Practice in the Digital Age. Cambridge University Press, Cambridge (2017)
3. Athan, T., Governatori, G., Palmirani, M., Paschke, A., Wyner, A.: LegalRuleML: design principles and foundations. In: Faber, W., Paschke, A. (eds.) Reasoning Web 2015. LNCS, vol. 9203, pp. 151–188. Springer, Cham (2015). https://doi.org/10.1007/978-3-319-21768-0_6
4. Bandeira, J., Bittencourt, I., Espinheira, P., Isotani, S.: FOCA: a methodology for ontology evaluation, arxiv (2016)
5. Barabucci, G., Cervone, L., Di Iorio, A., Palmirani, M., Peroni, S., Vitali, F.: Managing semantics in XML vocabularies: an experience in the legal and legislative domain. In: Proceedings of Balisage 2009 (2010)
6. Breuker, J.A.P.J., et al.: OWL ontology of basic legal concepts (LKIF-Core). Estrella: Deliverable 1.4., AMSTERDAM, UVA, 2007, p. 138 (2007)
7. Casalicchio, E., Cardellini, V., Interino, G., Palmirani, M.: Research challenges in legal-rule and QoS-aware cloud service brokerage Future Gener. Comput. Syst. **78**, 211–223 (2016)
8. Falco, R., Gangemi, A., Peroni, S., Shotton, D., Vitali, F.: Modelling OWL ontologies with Graffoo. In: Presutti, V., Blomqvist, E., Troncy, R., Sack, H., Papadakis, I., Tordai, A. (eds.) ESWC 2014. LNCS, vol. 8798, pp. 320–325. Springer, Cham (2014). https://doi.org/10.1007/978-3-319-11955-7_42
9. Gandon, F., Governatori, G., Villata, S.: Normative requirements as linked data. In: JURIX 2017. IOS Press (2017)
10. Gangemi, A., Peroni, S., Shotton, D., Vitali, F.: The publishing workflow ontology (PWO), ISO (2016). http://www.semantic-web-journal.net/content/publishing-workflow-ontology-pwo
11. Gangemi, A., Guarino, N., Masolo, C., Oltramari, A., Schneider, L.: Sweetening ontologies with DOLCE. In: Gómez-Pérez, A., Benjamins, V.R. (eds.) EKAW 2002. LNCS (LNAI), vol. 2473, pp. 166–181. Springer, Heidelberg (2002). https://doi.org/10.1007/3-540-45810-7_18

12. Gharib, M., Giorgini, P., Mylopoulos, J.: Towards an ontology for privacy requirements via a systematic literature review. In: Mayr, H.C., Guizzardi, G., Ma, H., Pastor, O. (eds.) ER 2017. LNCS, vol. 10650, pp. 193–208. Springer, Cham (2017). https://doi.org/10.1007/978-3-319-69904-2_16

13. Governatori, G., Hashmi, M., Lam, H.-P., Villata, S., Palmirani, M.: Semantic business process regulatory compliance checking using LegalRuleML. In: Blomqvist, E., Ciancarini, P., Poggi, F., Vitali, F. (eds.) EKAW 2016. LNCS (LNAI), vol. 10024, pp. 746–761. Springer, Cham (2016). https://doi.org/10.1007/978-3-319-49004-5_48

14. Hitzler, P., Gangemi, A., Janowicz, K., Krisnadhi, A.A., Presutti, V.: Ontology Engineering with Ontology Design Patterns: Foundations and Applications. IOS Press, Amsterdam (2016)

15. http://wiki.hl7.org/index.php?title=Security_and_Privacy_Ontology

16. http://www.hl7.org/implement/standards/product_brief.cfm?product_id=348

17. http://www.w3.org/Privacy/

18. IFLA Study Group on the FRBR: Functional requirements for bibliographic records (2009). http://www.ifla.org/publications/functional-requirements-for-bibliographic-records. Accessed 7 May 2017

19. Peroni, S., Palmirani, M., Vitali, F.: UNDO: the United Nations system document ontology. In: d'Amato, C., et al. (eds.) ISWC 2017 Part II. LNCS, vol. 10588, pp. 175–183. Springer, Cham (2017). https://doi.org/10.1007/978-3-319-68204-4_18

20. Peroni, S., Shotton, D., Vitali, F.: The live OWL documentation environment: a tool for the automatic generation of ontology documentation. In: ten Teije, A., et al. (eds.) EKAW 2012. LNCS (LNAI), vol. 7603, pp. 398–412. Springer, Heidelberg (2012). https://doi.org/10.1007/978-3-642-33876-2_35

21. Peroni, S.: A simplified agile methodology for ontology development. In: Dragoni, M., Poveda-Villalón, M., Jimenez-Ruiz, E. (eds.) OWLED/ORE -2016. LNCS, vol. 10161, pp. 55–69. Springer, Cham (2017). https://doi.org/10.1007/978-3-319-54627-8_5

22. Peroni, S., Shotton, D.: The SPAR ontologies. To appear in Proceedings of the 17th International Semantic Web Conference, ISWC2108 (2018 under publication). https://w3id.org/spar/article/spar-iswc2018/

23. Proceedings of the 5th Workshop on Society, Privacy and the Semantic Web - Policy and Technology (PrivOn2017) co-located with 16th International Semantic Web Conference (ISWC 2017), Vienna, Austria, 22 October 2017. CEUR Workshop Proceedings 1951, CEUR-WS.org 2017. http://events.linkeddata.org/ldow2011/papers/ldow2011-paper01-sacco.pdf

24. Samavi, R., Consens, M.P.: Publishing privacy logs to facilitate transparency and accountability. J. Semant. Web **50**, 1–20 (2018)

25. Deleting personal data. https://ico.org.uk/media/for-organisations/documents/1475/deleting_personal_data.pdf

Semantic Interoperability of Multilingual Language Resources by Automatic Mapping

P. Schmitz[1], E. Francesconi[1,2(✉)], N. Hajlaoui[1], B. Batouche[1], and A. Stellato[3]

[1] Publications Office of the European Union, Luxembourg City, Luxembourg
enrico.francesconi@publications.europa.eu
[2] Institute of Legal Information Theory and Techniques of CNR (ITTIG-CNR),
Rome, Italy
francesconi@ittig.cnr.it
[3] Department of Enterprise Engineering, University of Rome Tor Vergata,
Rome, Italy

Abstract. The PMKI project is an European Commission action aiming to create a public multilingual knowledge management infrastructure to support e-commerce solutions in a multilingual environment. Such infrastructure will consist in a set of tools able to create interoperability between multilingual classification systems (like thesauri) and other language resources, so that they can be easily accessible through a Web dissemination platform and reusable by small and medium-sized enterprises (SMEs), as well as by public administrations. In this paper the standards used to represent language resources and a methodology for automatic mapping between thesauri, based on an information retrieval framework, are presented.

Keywords: Semantic interoperability · Language resources
Information retrieval · Semantic mapping · Ontolex-Lemon

1 Introduction

Language barriers in the EU make the European market fragmented and decrease its economic potential. Particularly small and medium-sized enterprises (SMEs) are currently at a disadvantage compared to big companies to approach European and global markets for the high cost of providing multilingual services. The EU institutions aim to overcome language obstacles and increase cross-border e-commerce by building open multilingual tools and features free of charge.

For this reason the European Commission, through the ISA[2] program[1], launched a pilot project on creating a public multilingual knowledge management infrastructure (PMKI project). It is aimed to support e-commerce solutions in a

---

[1] ISA2: Interoperability solutions for public administrations, businesses and citizens (https://ec.europa.eu/isa2/home_en).

A. Kő and E. Francesconi (Eds.): EGOVIS 2018, LNCS 11032, pp. 153–163, 2018.
https://doi.org/10.1007/978-3-319-98349-3_12

multilingual environment by creating a set of tools, based on semantic Web technologies, to facilitate the development of multilingual facilities able to improve cross border accessibility of digital services and e-commerce solutions. In practical terms, overcoming language barriers on the Web means creating multilingual lexicons (as vocabularies, thesauri, taxonomies, semantic networks), establishing links between concepts, as well as using them to support the accessibility of services and goods offered through the Internet.

This paper presents an overview of the PMKI project (Sect. 2), the standards adopted, based on the Ontolex-Lemon model for language resources (Sect. 3) and their interoperability (Sect. 4). A semi-automatic methodology for establishing semantic interoperability based on an information retrieval framework is then proposed (Sects. 5, 6, 7). Finally, some experiments on the application of such methodology to a gold-standard data set of matching concepts (Sects. 8, 9) and some conclusions (Sect. 10) are reported.

2   The PMKI Project

PMKI aims to implement a proof-of-concept infrastructure able to expose and to harmonize internal (European Union institutional) and external multilingual lexicons aligning them in order to facilitate interoperability. Moreover, the project aims to create a governance structure for a possible public service, in order to extend systematically the infrastructure by integrating supplementary public multilingual taxonomies/terminologies. The need to have a public and multilingual platform with a role of hub able to collect and share language resources in standardized formats is essential to guarantee semantic interoperability of digital services. For instance, such platform is missing in CEF.AT[2], while it would provide an advantage for the development of machine translation systems, in particular for domain-specific ones (tender terminology, medical terminology, etc.). A platform like PMKI may represent a *one-stop-shop* harmonized multilingual lexicons repository at European level.

Complementary to the European Language Resource Coordination (ELRC[3]) action, which aims at identifying and gathering language and translation data, the PMKI platform aims firstly to harmonize multilingual language resources making them interoperable, then to integrate supplementary public multilingual taxonomies/terminologies in a standardized representation.

3   Standard Representation of Language Resources

With the advent of the Semantic Web and Linked Open Data, a number of models have been proposed to enrich ontologies with information about how

---

[2] https://ec.europa.eu/digital-single-market/en/automated-translation.

[3] ELRC: the European Language Resource Coordination action launched by the European Commission as part of the CEF.AT platform activities, to identify and gather language data across all 30 European countries participating in the CEF programme. More information can be found here: http://www.lr-coordination.eu/.

vocabulary elements have to be expressed in natural language. These include the Linguistic Watermark framework [1,2], LexOnto [3], LingInfo [4], LIR [5], LexInfo [6] and Monnet lemon [7]. The lemon model envisions an open ecosystem in which ontologies and their lexicons co-exist, published as data on the Web.

In 2012, the OntoLex W3C Community Group[4] (OntoLex) was chartered to define an agreed specification informed by the aforementioned models, whose designers are all involved in the community group. The OntoLex Group published its final report[5] defining the OntoLex-Lemon model [8]: a suite of RDF vocabularies (called modules) for the representation of ontology lexicons in accordance with Semantic Web [9] best practices. The modules of OntoLex-Lemon cover aspects such as morphology, syntax-semantics mapping, variations, translation, and linguistic metadata. This rich linguistic characterization of ontologies is unattainable with widely deployed models on the Semantic Web (e.g. RDFS and SKOS-(XL) labels), and it enables a wide range of ontology-driven NLP applications (e.g. knowledge verbalization, semantic parsing, question answering...) [10]. Outside of its original scope, the OntoLex-Lemon model (and its predecessors) has been also used to represent and interlink lexicons, lexical-semantic resources and, in general, language resources in the Linguistic Linked Open Data (LLOD) cloud [11]. For such characteristics, OntoLex-Lemon has been adopted to represent language resources within the PMKI project. The OntoLex-Lemon model is primarily based on the ideas found in Monnet lemon, which was already adopted by a number of lexica [12–14]. More specifically, OntoLex-Lemon consists of a number of vocabularies corresponding to different

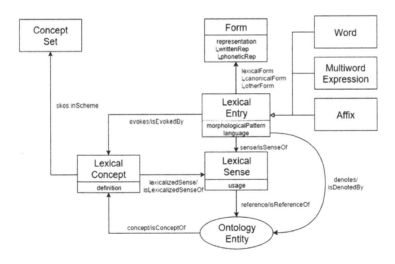

Fig. 1. The OntoLex Core data model

---

[4] Ontology-Lexica Community Group: https://www.w3.org/community/ontolex/.

[5] Lexicon Model for Ontologies: Community Report, 10 May 2016: https://www.w3.org/2016/05/ontolex/ (last consulted: 03/04/2018).

modules: core, synsem, decomp, vartrans, lime. The core module (Fig. 1) retains from Monnet lemon the separation between the lexical and the ontological layer (following [15,16]), where the ontology describes the semantics of the domain and the lexicon describes the morphology, syntax and pragmatics of the words used to express the domain in a language. A lexicon consists of lexical entries with a single syntactic class (part-of-speech) to which a number of forms are attached (e.g. the singular/plural forms of a noun), and each form has a number of representations (string forms), e.g. written or phonetic representation. While an entry can be linked directly to an entity in an ontology, usually the binding between them is realized by a lexical sense resource where pragmatic information such as domain or register of the connection may be recorded. Lexical concepts were introduced in the model to represent the "semantic pole of linguistic units, mentally instantiated abstractions which language users derive from conceptions". They are intended to represent abstractions in existing lexical resources such as synsets in wordnets.

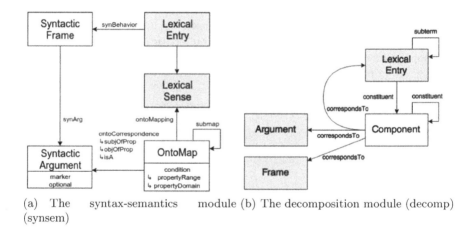

(a) The syntax-semantics module (synsem)

(b) The decomposition module (decomp)

Fig. 2. The OntoLex modules

The synsem module (Fig. 2(a)) allows to associate a lexical entry with a syntactic frame (representing a stereotypical syntactic context for the entry), while an ontology mapping can be used to bind syntactic and semantic arguments together. The decomp module (Fig. 2(b)) is concerned with the decomposition of a lexical entry into its constituents (i.e. tokens). Components are instances of a dedicated class, which in turn correspond to lexical entries. This indirection allows recording inside a component information such as the fact that the entry "autonomo"es occurs with feminine gender inside "comunidad autonoma"es. We can also represent parse trees, by subdividing a component into its constituents. Because of the lack of space, we will not introduce vatrans and lime, but necessary information about them will be provided briefly later on. Additionally, [17] describes the design of (a candidate-release version of) LIME under the perspective of metadata-based discovery and exploitation of linguistic information in different tasks, including ontology mediation [18]. While Semantic Web practitioners recognized the benefits of linguistic information, linguists in turn acknowledged that the adoption of Semantic Web technologies could benefit the publication and integration of language resources. This led to the formation of the Linguistic Linked Open Data (LLOD) cloud. There is thus a convergence of interests and results between these two communities. Unsurprisingly, recent discussions on OntoLex-Lemon were focused on improving its suitability to encode (legacy) language resources, departing from its original focus on ontology lexicons.

4   Semantic Interoperability Types in PMKI

PMKI aims to implement the following two types of semantic interoperability between language resources

- Semantic resources lexicalization (for example enriching thesaural concepts with lexical information)
- Conceptual mapping between semantic resources (for example identifying matching concepts in different thesauri).

In this work we have focused the attention on formalizing the conceptual mapping between semantic resources, in particular between thesauri, and to implement a semi-automatic procedure to establish mapping relation between concepts of two different thesauri.

5   Thesaural Mapping Formal Characterization

Conceptual mapping in PMKI is a problem of thesaural concepts alignment, having only thesaurus schema available (*Schema-based mapping* [20]). In this case thesaurus mapping is the problem of identifying the conceptual/semantic similarity between a descriptor (represented by a simple or complex term[6]) in a source thesaurus and candidate descriptors in a target thesaurus.

A vast literature exist in this field [19–21] combining different approaches, in [22] the schema-based Thesaurus Mapping ($\mathcal{TM}$) problem has been characterized as a problem of Information Retrieval ($\mathcal{IR}$): the aim is to find concepts in target thesaurus, better matching the semantics of a concept in a source thesaurus. The isomorphism between $\mathcal{TM}$ and $\mathcal{IR}$ ($\mathcal{TM} \equiv \mathcal{IR}$) can be established once we consider a source concept as a *query* of the $\mathcal{IR}$ problem, and a target concept as a *document* of the $\mathcal{IR}$ problem.

Therefore, the $\mathcal{TM}$ problem can be viewed and formalized, like the $\mathcal{IR}$ problem, as a 4-uple $\mathcal{TM} = [D, Q, F, R(\boldsymbol{q}, \boldsymbol{d})]$ [23] where:

---

[6] for example *Parliament* is a simple term, *President of the Republic* is a complex term.

1. D is the set possible representations (*logical views*) of a concept in a target thesaurus (a document to be retrieved in the $\mathcal{IR}$ problem);
2. Q is the set of the possible representations (*logical views*) of a concept in a source thesaurus (a query in the $\mathcal{IR}$ problem);
3. F is the framework of concepts representation in source and target thesauri;
4. $R(\boldsymbol{q}, \boldsymbol{d})$ is a ranking function, which associates a real number with $(\boldsymbol{q}, \boldsymbol{d})$ where $\boldsymbol{q} \in Q, \boldsymbol{d} \in D$, giving an order of relevance to the concepts in a target thesaurus with respect to a concept of a source thesaurus.

In this framework the implementation of a thesaurus mapping procedure is represented by the instantiation of the previous 4 components.

6   Logical Views (Q and D) of *Descriptors* and Matching Framework (F)

Mapping between thesaural concepts is a process which aims at matching concept semantics rather than their lexical equivalences.

In PMKI thesaural concepts are represented by the SKOS model included in OntoLex-Lemon. In traditional thesauri, concepts are *descriptors* and *non-descriptors* represented by different terms (`skos:prefLabel` and `skos:altLabel`, according to SKOS) expressing the same meaning. More precisely, each meaning is expressed by one or more terms[7] in the same language (for instance 'pollution', 'contamination', 'discharge of pollutants'), as well as in different languages (for instance, the English term 'water' and the Italian term 'acqua', etc.). Moreover, each term can have more than one sense, i.e. it can express more than one concept. Therefore, to effectively map thesaural concepts, term (simple or complex) semantics has to be captured and represented.

In $\mathcal{IR}$ a query is usually constructed as a context (set of keywords) able to better represent the semantics of a query. Similarly, in $\mathcal{TM}$ the semantics of a thesaural concept is conveyed not only by its terms, but also by the context in which the concept is used, as well as by the relations with other concepts. In $\mathcal{TM}$ problem, Q, D and F are exactly aimed at identifying logical views and related framework for concept representations able to better capture the semantics of terms in source and target thesauri, as well as to measure their conceptual similarity.

In this work we propose to represent the semantics of a thesaural concept by a vector $\boldsymbol{d}$ of binary[8] entries composed by the term itself, relevant terms in its definition, in the alternative labels, as well as terms of directly related thesaural concepts (broader, narrower, related concepts).

Firstly a vocabulary of normalized terms from target thesaurus is constructed, where 'normalization' in this context means string pre-processing,

---

[7] Linguistic expressions by single or multi words.

[8] Statistics on terms to obtain weighted entries are not possible since document collections are not available (*schema-based thesaurus mapping*).

in particular stopwords eliminations and word stemming/lemmatization procedures. In order to implement such pre-processing steps, the word stemming/lemmatization procedures provided by the java-based Elasticsearch libraries are used[9].

Being T the dimension of such vocabulary, both source and target concepts d are represented in a vector space of T-dimension ($d = [x_1, x_2, \cdots, x_T]$); the entry x_i gives information on the presence/absence of the corresponding i^{th} vocabulary term among the terms characterizing the concept d. In Fig. 3 a binary vector representation of a Eurovoc concept is sketched. In such representation the framework F is composed of T-dimensional vectorial space and linear algebra operations on vectors.

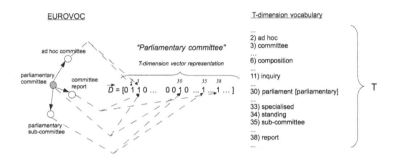

Fig. 3. T-dimension vectorial representation of a thesaural concepts d.

7   The Proposed Ranking Function (R)

Having represented the semantics of thesaural concepts as a binary vector, their similarity can be measured as the related binary vectors correlation, quantified, for instance, as the cosine of the angle between them

$$sim(q, d) = \frac{q \times d}{|q| \cdot |d|} \qquad (1)$$

where $|q|$ and $|d|$ are the norms of the vectors representing concepts in source and target thesauri, respectively.

In order to classify a couple of concepts as an instance of the set of matching concepts (represented by one of the skos:mappingRelation), a heuristic threshold $Th \in [0, 1]$ is set as decision surface, so that:

$$\text{if } sim(q, d) \geq Th \Rightarrow (q, d) \in \text{skos} : \texttt{mappingRelation} \qquad (2)$$

---

[9] https://www.elastic.co/guide/en/elasticsearch/guide/current/stemming.html.

8 Interoperability Assessment Through a "Gold Standard"

In this work a thesaurus mapping case-study is proposed, including three thesauri of interest for the European Union institutions. The thesauri are EUROVOC, ECLAS, STW. EUROVOC is the main EU thesaurus containing a hierarchical structure with inter-lingual relations. It helps to coherently and effectively manage, index, and search information of EU documentary collections, covering 21 fields. ECLAS is the European Commission Central Libraries thesaurus[10], covering 19 domains. STW[11] is the Thesaurus for Economics of the German National Library of Economics, bilingual thesaurus for representing and searching for economics-related content. It covers almost 6.000 subject headings in English and German and more than 20,000 synonyms.

The evaluation of the mapping procedure is based on a "gold standard" data set, namely an ideal collection of conceptual mappings expected by humans. To build the "gold standard" data set, an intellectual activity has been carried out by a group of experts dealing with EUROVOC as pivot thesaurus. The experts have established exact match relations between EUROVOC descriptors and the descriptors of ECLAS and STW, respectively. Specific guidelines have been given to the experts [24] to establish relations of type `skos:mappingRelation`, including `skos:exactMatch`, `skos:closeMatch`, `skos:narrowMatch`, `skos:broadMatch` relations. The complete "gold standard" dimension is reported in Table 1.

Table 1. The "gold standard" of matching concepts

Thesauri	Couples of matching concepts
EUROVOC-ECLAS	4099
EUROVOC-STW	2959
Total number of matches	**7058**

9 Experimental Results

A set of experiments for thesaural conceptual mapping is carried out over the "gold standard". The experiments have been carried out using English as the pivot common language of all the three thesauri (anyway the approach is independent of the languages or of their combination, as long as they are the same for source and target resources). These experiments aimed at establishing the optimal similarity threshold, representing the best percentage of matching prediction, in terms of combination of *Precision* and *Recall* (*F-measure*), as well as *Accuracy*, of the cosine distance concept matching predictor. In Table 2 the

---

[10] http://ec.europa.eu/eclas/.
[11] http://zbw.eu/stw/.

detailed results of different experiment runs are reported, obtained by heuristically adapting the similarity threshold Th aiming at optimizing the automatic predictions quality over the gold-standard. The best results in terms of F-measure and Accuracy have been obtained using a similarity value threshold $Th = 0.3$, so that the mapping procedure is the best compromise between having a good level of Recall (so to include in the prediction the most part of actually matching concepts) and accuracy, while not decreasing too much in Precision.

Table 2. Precision (P), Recall (R), F-Measure (F) and Accuracy (A) results of the matching concepts prediction according to different values of similarity thresholds (Th)

Similarity threshold (Th)	Eurovoc–Eclas				Eurovoc–STW			
	P	R	F	A	P	R	F	A
0.60	98.89	64.41	80.17	82.70	99.50	52.91	69.09	75.87
0.50	98.32	77.24	86.51	87.50	98.46	72.21	83.32	85.26
0.40	90.43	87.16	88.77	88.55	94.29	85.54	89.70	89.99
0.30	**88.36**	**90.73**	**89.53**	**88.99**	**91.45**	**92.30**	**91.88**	**91.68**
0.20	86.53	92.47	89.40	88.63	88.02	96.02	91.84	91.31

10   Conclusions

The PMKI project aims to establish interoperability between language resources. While the OntoLex-Lemon model has been used to represent linguistic resources for the Semantic Web, two types of semantic interoperability are forseen: lexicalization and conceptual mapping. In this paper an approach for establishing automatic interoperability between language resources by semantic mapping of thesaural concepts has been presented. The preliminary results have shown satisfactory performance of the matching predictor. As future development we aim to implement a machine learning approach to set the matching decision surface on the basis of examples of matching concepts, as illustrated in [22].

References

1. Pazienza, M.T., Stellato, A., Turbati, A.: Linguistic watermark 3.0: an RDF framework and a software library for bridging language and ontologies in the semantic web. In: Proceedings of the 5th Workshop on Semantic Web Applications and Perspectives (SWAP 2008), Rome, Italy (2008)
2. Oltramari, A., Stellato, A.: Enriching ontologies with linguistic content: an evaluation framework. In: Proceedings of OntoLex 2008, Marrakech, Morocco (2008)
3. Cimiano, P., Haase, P., Herold, M., et al.: LexOnto: a model for ontology lexicons for ontology-based NLP. In: Proceedings of the OntoLex 2007 Workshop (2007)

4. Buitelaar, P., Declerck, T., Frank, A., et al.: LingInfo: design and applications of a model for the integration of linguistic information in ontologies. In: Proceedings of OntoLex 2006, Genoa, Italy (2006)
5. Montiel-Ponsoda, E., Aguado De Cea, G., Gómez-Pérez, A., et al.: Enriching ontologies with multilingual information. Nat. Lang. Eng. **XVII**(3), 283 309 (2011)
6. Cimiano, P., Buitelaar, P., McCrae, J., et al.: LexInfo: a declarative model for the lexicon-ontology interface. Web Semant. Sci. Serv. Agents World Wide Web **IX**(1), 29–51 (2011)
7. McCrae, J., Aguado-De-Cea, G., Buitelaar, P., et al.: Interchanging lexical resources on the semantic web. Lang. Resour. Eval. **XLVI**(4), 701–719 (2012)
8. McCrae, J., Bosque-Gil, J., Gracia, J., et al.: The Ontolex-Lemon model: development and applications. In: Proceedings of eLex 2017 conference, pp. 19–21 (2017)
9. Berners-Lee, T., Hendler, J.A., Lassila, O.: The semantic web: a new form of web content that is meaningful to computers will unleash a revolution of new possibilities. Sci. Am. **CCLXXXIV**(5), 34–43 (2001)
10. Cimiano, P., Unger, C., McCrae, J.: Ontology-based interpretation of natural language. Synth. Lect. Hum. Lang. Technol. **VII**(2), 1–178 (2014)
11. Chiarcos, C., Nordhoff, S., Hellmann, S. (eds.): Linked Data in Linguistics. Spinger, Heidelberg (2012). https://doi.org/10.1007/978-3-642-28249-2
12. Borin, L., Dannells, D., Forsberg, M., et al.: Representing Swedish lexical resources in RDF with lemon. In: Proceedings of the ISWC 2014 Posters & Demonstrations Track, Riva del Garda, Italy, pp. 329–332 (2014)
13. Navigli, R., Ponzetto, S.: BabelNet: the automatic construction, evaluation and application of a wide-coverage multilingual semantic network. Artif. Intell. **CXCIII**, 217–250 (2012)
14. Eckle-Kohler, J., Mccrae, J., Chiarcos, C.: Lemonuby-a large, interlinked, syntactically-rich lexical resource for ontologies. Semant. Web **VI**(4), 371–378 (2015)
15. Buitelaar, P.: Ontology-based semantic lexicons: mapping between terms and object descriptions. In: Huang, C.R., Calzolari, N., Gangemi, A., et al. (eds.) Ontology and the Lexicon. Cambridge University Press, Cambrige (2010)
16. Cimiano, P., Mccrae, J., Buitelaar, P., Montiel-Ponsoda, E.: On the role of senses in the ontology-lexicon. In: Oltramari, A., Vossen, P., Qin, L., Hovy, E. (eds.) New Trends of Research in Ontologies and Lexical Resources. Theory and Applications of Natural Language Processing, pp. 43–62. Springer, Berlin (2013). https://doi.org/10.1007/978-3-642-31782-8_4
17. Fiorelli, M., Stellato, A., McCrae, J.P., Cimiano, P., Pazienza, M.T.: LIME: the metadata module for OntoLex. In: Gandon, F., Sabou, M., Sack, H., d'Amato, C., Cudré-Mauroux, P., Zimmermann, A. (eds.) ESWC 2015. LNCS, vol. 9088, pp. 321–336. Springer, Cham (2015). https://doi.org/10.1007/978-3-319-18818-8_20
18. Fiorelli, M., Pazienza, M.T., Stellato, A.: A meta-data driven platform for semi-automatic configuration of ontology mediators. In: Proceedings of the Ninth International Conference on Language Resources and Evaluation (LREC 2014), Reykjavik, Iceland, pp. 26–31, May 2014
19. Resnik, P.: Disambiguating noun groupings with respect to WordNet senses. In: Armstrong, S., Church, K., Isabelle, P., Manzi, S., Tzoukermann, E., Yarowsky, D. (eds.) Natural Language Processing Using Very Large Corpora. Text, Speech and Language Technology, vol. 11, pp. 77–98. Springer, Dordrecht (1999). https://doi.org/10.1007/978-94-017-2390-9_6

20. Shvaiko, P., Euzenat, J.: A survey of schema-based matching approaches. In: Spaccapietra, S. (ed.) Journal on Data Semantics IV. LNCS, vol. 3730, pp. 146–171. Springer, Heidelberg (2005). https://doi.org/10.1007/11603412_5
21. Lacasta, J., Nogueras-Iso, J., Falquet, G., Teller, J., Zarazaga-Soria, F.J.: Design and evaluation of a semantic enrichment process for bibliographic databases. Data Knowl. Eng. **88**, 94–107 (2013)
22. Francesconi, E., Bartoloni, G.: Sharing knowledge by conceptual mapping: the case of EU thesaural interoperability. In: Proceedings of the JURIX Conference, pp. 17–26. IOS Press (2010)
23. Baeza-Yates, R., Ribeiro-Neto, B.: Modern Information Retrieval. Addison Wesley, Boston (1999)
24. Liang, A.C., Sini, M.: Mapping AGROVOC and the Chinese agricultural thesaurus: definitions, tools, procedures. New Rev. Hypermedia Multimed. **12**(1), 51–62 (2006)

The Right to Know and Digital Technology: Proactive and Reactive Transparency in the Italian Legal System

Fernanda Faini[✉] and Monica Palmirani

CIRSFID - Interdepartmental Centre for Research in the History,
Philosophy and Sociology of Law and in Legal Informatics,
University of Bologna, Bologna, Italy
{fernanda.faini,monica.palmirani}@unibo.it

Abstract. In this paper we take the vantage point of the law as a prism through which to observe the new relation that has taken shape between public sector bodies and the citizenry in view of the knowledge enabled by digital technologies. More to the point, we analyse the right to know vis-à-vis the government and its institutions, assessing the way the changes brought about by technology in the digital space are reshaping digital rights, entrusted with striking a new and complex balance between citizens and the government.

We will specifically address the right to access government data. To this end we will consider the way the law has evolved in Italy, with a focus on Legislative Decree 97/2016 and the deep changes it has made to Legislative Decree 33/2013, providing tools for greater transparency and knowledge of government activity and administration. We highlight the deep transformation that has resulted from these changes, affecting the legal relationship between public sector bodies and citizens.

Keywords: Transparency · Right to know · Public sector information
E-government · Open government

1 Introduction

In Italy, regulatory developments led to the last transparency reform brought by the Legislative Decree No. 97 of 25 May 2016, which gave form and substance to the freedom of information with regard to Italian institutions.

Previously the rules provided for procedural transparency, which can only be activated in presence of objective and subjective conditions, and which, consequently, did not constitute a real freedom for anyone to know.

The paper aims to analyze the current tools of the Italian legal system that allow transparency and the right to know. The Italian case, in fact, differs from other countries; for example, by recalling different orders, the United States of America,

© Springer Nature Switzerland AG 2018
A. Kő and E. Francesconi (Eds.): EGOVIS 2018, LNCS 11032, pp. 164–174, 2018.
https://doi.org/10.1007/978-3-319-98349-3_13

England and France provide for a proactive transparency, that is expressed in the publication, and a reactive transparency, which translates into a single form of access.

In 1966 the United States adopted the *Freedom of Information Act*, modified and integrated over the years[1]: the access regime is "open to all" (without subjective limitations and without motivation) and is accompanied by the provision of broad proactive transparency. The *Office of Government Information Services* (OGIS) oversees compliance with US law.

The United Kingdom was inspired by this model and adopted in 2000 the *Freedom of Information Act* (FOIA) and, in 2002, the specular *Freedom of Information* (Scotland) *Act*. The right to access information is broad, without subjective limitations and without obligation of motivation; there is no list of information subject to mandatory publication, but the administrations must realize and disclose publications schemes indicating the types of information that will be published. An authority is provided for the regulation, the *Information Commissioner's Office* (ICO).

In France the law No. 78-753 provides for the freedom of access to administrative documents (not mere information) as the right of every person to information, to be exercised without obligation to state reasons; the administration is not required to communicate documents that are already the subject of public disclosure. Compliance with the regulations is guaranteed by the *Commission d'accès aux documents administratifs* (CADA).

In Italy, instead, the system is more complex, also due to the legislative evolution and revolution that characterizes it, and today consists of different types of access, based on different aims and articulated in a different way, on which the paper will focus, in order to examine the current face of transparency in Italy [3, 4, 11–13, 16].

2 The Right to Know: Its Evolution in the Italian Legal System

Transparency is the key tool by which to guarantee open access to government information, so as to make sure that the government's administration is accountable to its citizens, and in such a way as to enable the latter to fully participate in the political process.

The principle of transparency has increasingly become a focus of interest in Italian law, especially in recent years.

As early as 1990—with Law No. 241 of 7 August 1990, amended in 2005—transparency entered the Italian legal system as the principle on which rests the government's administrative activity:[2] it configures itself as the guarantee that all those who are entitled to access information about such activity can in fact do so.[3] But the

---

[1] The *Electronic Freedom of Information Act* (e.g. EFOIA) of 1996, which adapted the text to the possibilities offered by new technologies, is particularly relevant.

[2] Art. 1(1) of Law 241/1990, as amended by Law No. 15 of 11 February 2005, which places transparency next to the principles requiring that administrative activity be economical, effective, impartial (a criterion that was added in with Law No. 69 of 18 June 2009), and open to public scrutiny.

[3] Title V of Law 241/1990 is devoted to the right to access administrative documents.

law also evolved in such a way as to expand the scope of transparency, which now encompassed access to information regardless of one's legal status, for it is conceived as a principle by which to ensure that access to information is general and widespread [14].

The principle of transparency has in the meantime made headway with the spread of information and communications technology: the Internet can make information available to broad swaths of the population, making it possible to easily access the information at any time from almost any geographic location, giving information a kind of currency it has never before seen. This is why the principle transparency has been deeply embedded into the Italian Digital Administration Code, formally identified as Legislative Decree No. 82 of 7 March 2005. The same code was subsequently amended by expanding the range of information subject to mandatory publication, a case in point being Law No. 69 of 18 June 2009, under which compliance with the obligation to ensure transparency is achieved once an administrative agency publishes the information at issue on the Web.[4]

A significant turning point came with the so-called Brunetta Reform (under Enabling Law No. 15 of 4 March 2009 and the relative Legislative Decree No. 150 of 27 October 2009), considering that it reshapes the organization and management of civil servants by introducing the concept of total disclosure, while providing for forms of widespread oversight in checking compliance with the principles of impartiality and effectiveness (economy and efficiency in the provision of public services)[5] [8, 20]. Over the years, several provisions, directives, and guidelines have been issued, and the transformation has been remarkable: this includes the changes that Legislative Decree No. 235 of 30 December 2010 made to Legislative Decree 82/2005, expanding the toolkit for ensuring transparency, while looking to make them more effective [9].

The next step in this legislative evolution came with the so-called Transparency Decree (Legislative Decree No. 33 of 14 March 2013), giving effect to the so-called Anticorruption Law (Law No. 90 of 6 November 2012): this decree took a melange of provisions that had accreted over the years as legislators introduced various standards under which public sector bodies were required to ensure that their information was transparent and publicly and widely available, and reshaped these provisions and obligations into a substantially reconfigured design [17].

In turn, the Transparency Decree recently received a significant reconfiguration under Legislative Decree No. 97 of 25 May 2016, giving effect to the so-called Madia Reform: the outcome has been what some have referred to as an Italian Freedom of Information Act [6].

---

[4] Art. 32 of Law 69/2009.

[5] Art. 4(1) of Law 15/2009 and Art. 11(1) of Legislative Decree 150/2009 (the latter was subsequently repealed by Legislative Decree 33/2013). See M. Savino, "Il FOIA italiano: La fine della trasparenza di Bertoldo," *Giornale di diritto amministrativo* 5 (2016): 593ff., making the point that "full access was an impossible conceit from the outset, considering that only the information subject to mandatory publication public information was deemed public (accessible online)".

3 Proactive Disclosure: Publication

The body of transparency provisions enacted before 2013 was gappy and with a good deal of overlap, and it was not equipped with meaningful enforcement mechanisms: the result had been a good deal of noncompliance. An attempt to address these issues was made with Legislative Decree 33/2013 [19].

To this end, Legislative Decree 33/2013 reframed the obligation of public disclosure by distinguishing four broad classes of obligations, concerning (i) the organization and activity of public sector bodies; (ii) the use of public resources; (iii) the delivery of government services; and (iv) so-called "special sectors":[6] the Web becomes the main tool of transparency, which public sector bodies comply with by making the records, information, and data relating to their activity and organization publicly available on their websites.[7] This has been described as proactive disclosure.

Legislative Decree 33/2013 regulates a specific section of a government agency's homepage called *Amministrazione Trasparente* (Transparent Administration), requiring that it contain all the data, information, and records subject to compulsory publication and defining the layout of this transparent administration section, in such a way that public sector bodies all have a coherent and familiar interface:[8] under Article 54 of Legislative Decree 82/2005, the transparent administration section must contain the data specified in Legislative Decree 33/2013, as well as all data required under current legislation.

The principle of transparency rests on a solid constitutional foundation, which forms the basis of its construction and is amenable to broad interpretation: this constitutional basis makes transparency a sort of meta-principle serving the purpose of furthering the aims of a series of other constitutional principles [1, 2].[9]

Legislative Decree 33/2013 also provides some enforcement tools giving government the power to exercise oversight over the compliance of its own public sector bodies and to issue fines for noncompliance.[10] In particular, the decree contains a

---

[6] Special sectors include public works, service, and procurement contracts; zoning and urban planning; and the national health service. As much as the Transparency Decree effects an overhaul of transparency obligations, some of these obligations are not addressed in the decree but are set forth in other legislation, both prior and subsequent, a case in point being Arts. 1(2) and 4(2) and (6) of Legislative Decree No. 198 of 20 December 2009, setting forth the public disclosure obligations pertaining to class action lawsuits.

[7] Art. 2(2) of Legislative Decree 33/2013.

[8] Arts. 2(2) and 9(1) of Legislative Decree 33/2013. The layout required for the transparent administration section is outlined in Annex A.

[9] Art. 1(2)(3) of Legislative Decree 33/2013 and Art. 1(36) of Law 190/2012.

[10] These tools are contained in particular in Arts. 43ff., Title VI, of the Transparency Decree. Oversight is entrusted to outside agencies and to officials both inside and outside each public sector body, examples being the *responsabile per la trasparenza* (transparency officer), *organismi indipendenti di valutazione* (OIV, or independent assessment organisms), and the Autorità Nazionale Anticorruzione (ANAC, or National Anticorruption Authority). Noncompliance is among the elements taken into account in laying nonfeasance charges on civil service executive officers, who may also be held responsible for reputational damage to the agencies they work for, and who, in any event, face the prospect of a pay cut when it comes to assessing their pay-for-performance and their overtime pay (Art. 46); the decree also provides fines for specific cases.

public oversight tool called *accesso civico* (public access), making it possible for anyone to (a) request records, information, and data that are not publicly accessible even though they are subject to public disclosure, and (b) obtain such access free of charge and without having to state a reason for the request (Art. 5 of Legislative Decree 33/2013, previously also in Legislative Decree 97/2016).[11]

This meant that Legislative Decree 33/2013, prior its reform by Legislative Decree 97/2016, did not strictly provide for a right to government information, considering that its main tool, namely, public access (*accesso civico*), could only be used in cases of noncompliance, to access records, data, and information that public sector bodies failed to make public even though they were legally required to do so. This meant that there was no transparency for any of the information that was not subject to public disclosure: it was up to each public sector body to make such choices at its own discretion, and the governing law remains that of the right of access set forth in Law 241/1990, under which no request for information can be made without (a) showing a legitimate interest in such information and (b) stating a reason for the request. This effectively amounts to a conditional "right to know" [2, 8].

In view of these shortcomings, and in an international context where many countries around the world have freedom of information acts protecting the right to know, and also in response to pressure from citizen groups,[12] the Italian government issued Legislative Decree 97/2016, which under the powers delegated to the executive by Article 7 of Law 124/2015, modified the Transparency Decree (Legislative Decree 33/2013) so as to guarantee an authentic public right to know that citizens can exercise to access government information.

Under the amended law, transparency is understood as "full access to the data and records held by administrative public sector bodies, in the interest of protecting the rights of citizens, promoting citizen participation in the government's administrative activity, and favouring broad-based oversight of the government's institutional functions and its use of public resources."[13] To this end, Legislative Decree 97/2016 made deep changes to Legislative Decree 33/2013. These include (*i*) making it easier to comply with public disclosure requirements;[14] (*ii*) introducing stricter standards governing public spending and government contracting and staffing;[15] (*iii*) granting greater powers to the Autorità Nazionale Anticorruzione (the National Anticorruption Authority, or ANAC for short);[16] (*iv*) making officials subject to greater responsibilities and stiffer penalties [18, 20].[17] In order to simplify public disclosure requirements, the amended law gives public sector bodies the option to comply by linking to the databases

---

[11] See M. Savino, "Il FOIA italiano", commenting that the civic access tool (*accesso civico*) has effectively become a dead letter.

[12] Especially the *Foia4italy* initiative (at www.foia4italy.it), which drew the support of more than thirty associations in Italy.

[13] Art. 1(1) of Legislative Decree 33/2013.

[14] The need to streamline the disclosure procedure emerged as a result of recognizing right to know as a basic right (a topic we will take up in the next section).

[15] Arts. 4-bis and 14 of Legislative Decree 33/2013.

[16] Arts. 3(1-bis)(1-ter) and 8(3-bis).

[17] These aims of Legislative Decree 97/2016 are outlined in the accompanying explanatory document.

listed in Annex B of Legislative Decree 33/2013, having previously filled these databases with the data, information, and records that are subject to public disclosure.[18]

The most important innovations concern the right of access known as *diritto di accesso civico*.

4 Reactive Disclosure: *Accesso Documentale* (Access to Records), *Accesso Civico Semplice* (Simple Public Access), and *Accesso Civico Generalizzato* (Broad Public Access)

Next to *proactive* disclosure—where government agencies make public records available without responding to requests from the public—we have *reactive* disclosure, which is precisely the latter of the two circumstances, where publication comes in response to a request [7, 10, 12].[19]

In this regard, Legislative Decree 97/2016 innovated on Legislative Decree 33/2013 in significant ways, notably by (*i*) introducing a new way to access information (*accesso civico generalizzato*) and (*ii*) expanding the public's right to know in relation to the government and its agencies. For this reason this 2016 decree has come to be known as the Italian Freedom of Information Act (FOIA).

Legislative Decree 97/2016 has no effect on Law 241/1990 or on the right of access to records set forth in this law, which as a result stands as valid law,[20] but it does affect the public's right of access set forth in Legislative Decree 33/2013. As a consequence, there are three forms of access now in force in Italy as tools of reactive disclosure: (1) access to records (*accesso documentale*), pursuant to Law 241/1990, which stands as valid law; (2) "broad public access" (*accesso civico generalizzato*), pursuant to Legislative Decree 33/2013 and introduced by Legislative Decree 97/2016; and (3) what is now called "simple public access" (*accesso civico semplice*), which is the previously recognized right of access that can be exercised in response to failure of a government agency to comply with public disclosure requirements [8, 15].

These changes have proven necessary in order to make sure that the right to know is fully protected.

4.1 *Accesso Documentale* (Access to Records)

Indeed, the right of access to records (*accesso documentale*), as set forth in Law 241/1990, configures a right to know that, as previously noted, is conditional, in that there are two essential conditions that need to be met before it can be exercised: the first of these (Art. 22) is that in order to request access to government-held records, and regardless of whether you are acting in a private or a public capacity, you need to show a

---

[18] Art. 9-bis(2) of Legislative Decree 33/2013, introduced by Legislative Decree 97/2016.

[19] See the opinion the Italian Consiglio di Stato (an administrative court) issued on the design of what would have become Legislative Decree 97/2016: Opinion No. 00515/2016 of 24 Feb. 2016 (decided at a meeting of 18 Feb. 2016).

[20] Art. 6(11), Legislative Decree 97/2016.

legitimate interest in the records you are requesting, an interest having a direct, concrete, and current bearing on the protected legal status that access to the records may jeopardize; the second condition is that you need to state a reason for your request (Art. 25).

The distance that separates this scheme from the freedom of information principle can also be appreciated in the blanket-oversight restriction, where the law prohibits access aimed at subjecting the overall activity public sector bodies to broad oversight (Art. 24(3) of Law 241/1990). The system for exercising the right of access to administrative government records is one of retrieval and review: this means that once a request is made— and it must be made to the administrative agency that produced the records being sought and is currently holding them—the agency has thirty days to retrieve and review the records, and if no reply is received after this thirty-day period, the request is understood to have been rejected (on the principle that administrative silence amounts to a tacit rejection). Article 24 further constrains this right under broad exclusions and limitations needed to protect private and public interests: the main grounds here are secret of state, statistical confidentiality, trade secret, and personal data protection.[21]

4.2   *Accesso Civico Semplice* (Simple Public Access) and *Accesso Civico Generalizzato* (Broad Public Access)

It is a different set of premises that inform the right of access known in Italy as *accesso civico generalizzato* (broad public access), which acts in conjunction with the *accesso civico semplice* ("simple public access") that was in force before the overhaul of transparency law.

The basic principle (set forth in the enabling act authorizing the law through which this right was enacted) is that of freedom of information.[22] As stated in the law, this freedom "must be exercised consistently with all pertinent legally protected public and private interests and is guaranteed by way of (a) public access (*accesso civico*) to records, information, and data concerning the organization and activity of public sector bodies and (b) public disclosure of such information."[23]

Under the right of access referred to as *accesso civico generalizzato* (broad public access), access to administrative government data and records is not restricted to the data and records that have not been made publicly available even though they are subject to mandatory public disclosure (*accesso civico semplice*), and anyone may request access to such information without stating a reason for the request [20].[24] Indeed, this form of access (*accesso civico generalizzato*) is intended to "favour broad

---

[21] In the event of a rejection, whether tacit or express, or in the event of administrative delay, applicants have the option of appealing to a regional administrative court or to have the case reviewed by an ombudsman with proper jurisdiction or by the Commissione per l'Accesso ai Documenti Amministrativi (Commission for Access to Administrative Records).

[22] Art. 7(1)(h) of Law 124/2015.

[23] Art. 2(1) of Legislative Decree 33/2013 (my translation).

[24] Art. 5(1–2) of Legislative Decree No. 33/2013. Savino, "Il Foia italiano" (n. 4): "This new right introduces an essential framework that retains previous forms of by which to access government-held data—the procedural form (1990) and the civic form (2013)—even though they are bound to become redundant."

oversight over the performance of institutional functions and the use of public resources."

Unlike the right of access set forth in Law No. 241/1990, as just noted, broad public access (*accesso civico generalizzato*) is not subject to the conditional constraint requiring requesters to state a reason why they are seeking access to the information they are requesting, nor is it subject to the limit that rules out the ability to access government-held information in the interests of broad oversight:[25] access requests need only identify, the data, information, or records for which access is sought, and they can be submitted either remotely (over the Internet) or to any of a set of administrative bureaus specified in the statute.[26]

Once an access request, the public sector body in question has thirty days to respond: the principle of silence as tacit rejection therefore does not apply, and any rejection must be accompanied by a statement explaining its grounds, which must in turn have a legal basis.[27] The onus of proof—explaining the reasons for any denial of access—therefore falls on the government.[28] Indeed, under the law, access requests may be rejected only if access would prove "concretely prejudicial" to the legally protected public or private interests set forth in Art. 5-bis. The exclusions provided under this rule have been interpreted in legal commentary as numerous, overbroad, and in some cases too open-ended [5, 18, 20].[29] In this regard, Italy's National Anticorruption Authority (ANAC), in agreement with the Italian Data Protection Authority, and in keeping with the opinion of the Conferenza Unificata, has issued a set of operating guidelines (under Determination No. 1309 of 28 Dec. 2016) defining all public-access exclusions and limits.[30] The ANAC guidelines contain what it terms "strict exemptions," under which the law specifically requires public sector bodies to deny access requests: these cases concern state secrets (classified information) and information that cannot be accessed and circulated. In addition the guidelines contain

---

[25] Art. 5(3) of Legislative Decree 33/2013.

[26] Access requests are free of charge, but a fee may be charged to cover any costs the administrative agency in question may incur to make copies of the records being sought. Art. 5(3–4) of Legislative Decree 33/2013.

[27] Art. 5(6) of Legislative Decree 33/2013.

[28] Requesters who are denied access have the option of appealing to a regional administrative court, or they may have the case reviewed by the transparency officer within the agency itself. In cases involving local government entities, they can also settle the matter out of court by recourse to an ombudsman (Art. 5(7–8) of Legislative Decree 33/2013).

[29] See, among others, E. Carloni, "Se questo è un FOIA: Il diritto a conoscere tra modelli e tradimenti," *Rassegna Astrid* 4 (2016), 9ff., and B. Ponti, *Nuova trasparenza amministrativa*. For a contrary view, see M. Savino, "Il FOIA italiano", arguing that "the number and formulation of the legally protected interests specified in the decree are consistent with the prevailing standard. The list of ten public and private interests specified in Article 5-*bis* looks a lot like the lists found in most FOIAs across Europe, and indeed may even be narrower. It must also be pointed out that the differences between the Italian list and those found in the European Union are or marginal import" (my translation).

[30] Art. 5-bis of Legislative Decree 33/2013. These changes took effect on 23 June 2016, after which time public sector bodies and all other entities and officials concerned were given six months to make the adjustments necessary for compliance (Art. 42(1) of Legislative Decree 97/2016).

relative or qualified exemptions, in cases where access to the requested information would be "concretely prejudicial" to any one or more of the legally protected public or private interests listed in the ANAC guidelines. This determination is made under specific causational and temporal criteria stating (*i*) when an access request would cause a protected interest to be prejudiced and (*ii*) how much time must elapse before there is no longer any danger of prejudicing the protected interests of the persons or entities concerned.

The legally protected *public* interests concern (a) public security and order; (b) national security; (c) national defence and military operations; (d) international relations; (e) the national political system and the country's financial and economic stability; (f) criminal investigations and prosecutions; and (g) government inspections. The *private* interests instead fall under three headings: (a) personal data protection under applicable law; (b) secrecy of correspondence; and (c) a natural or legal person's economic and commercial interests, including intellectual property, copyright, and trade secrets.

The ANAC guidelines, along with others, have clarified that requests cannot be exploratory: public sector agencies cannot be asked to gather information that is not in their possession or is out of scope; it is possible, however, to make requests of broad scope, so long as they do not cast a net so wide that the resources needed to satisfy them would interfere in the ability of an agency to do its work. The guidelines addressed at the agencies include recommendations that they set up internal procedures for different types of requests, as well as a dedicated FOIA office, and that they keep a register of such requests organized by type, in such a way as to facilitate ANAC's oversight. The guidelines also address the question of exemptions (information not subject to public disclosure) and include an annex providing operational guidance.

The law thus sets a "reactive disclosure" standard providing several forms of access. Among these (pursuant to Legislative Decree 97/2016) is the broad form of access known as *accesso civico generalizzato*, through which Italy brings its freedom of information framework into line with the international model [12].[31]

5 Conclusions

In the Italian doctrine there have been criticisms of the current reform, which focused, in particular, on aspects such as the absence of penalties for administrations in the case of confirmed illegitimate denials of access, the extent of the envisaged exclusions, the difficulty of applying the regulations for the administrations and the lack of an independent authority to which the implementation process is entrusted: these profiles may constitute possible shortcomings to the effectiveness of the provisions [5, 7, 12, 20]. Added to this there are potential difficulties in the application resulting from the

---

[31] In the previously cited opinion on this legislative decree (at n. 21), the Consiglio di Stato speaks of "reactive disclosure" precisely to describe the disclosure of government data on request. Here we have a shift from the *need* to know the *right* to know that in the Italian legal system amounts to a Copernican revolution proper, as a result of which—using a phrase that was much beloved by Filippo Turati—the transparent public sector can really begin to look like a "glass house."

complexity of the discipline and the need to coordinate different access tools, in particular Access to Records and Public Access.

Despite these perplexities concerning the application and the connected effectiveness of the instrument, the introduction of the generalized civic access right has made mention of the recognition of freedom of information also in Italy, as in many other countries in the world, which for some time have provided for the right to know in relation to institutions even if, for the most part, with the provision of a single form of access.

Although the Italian system suffers a certain complexity, the right to know is now protected in our system as a fundamental right, unlike the past which provided for procedural transparency confined by the existence of specific normatively foreseen conditions. While in the past it was the citizen who had to demonstrate the possession of the legitimate conditions, now with the Broad Public Access the administration has to prove that there are grounds for exclusion against knowledge: therefore it is acceptable to consider that the legislative decree No. 97 of 2016 constitutes the Freedom of Information Act of the Italian legal system [10, 12, 20].

References

1. Califano, L., Colapietro, C. (eds.): Le nuove frontiere della trasparenza nella dimensione costituzionale. Editoriale scientifica, Napoli (2014)
2. Carloni, E.: I principi del codice della trasparenza (artt. 1, commi 1 e 2, 2, 6). In: Ponti, B. (ed.) La trasparenza amministrativa dopo il d.lgs. 14 marzo 2013, n. 33, 38ff. Maggioli, Rimini (2013)
3. Carloni, E.: Le Linee guida del Garante: protezione dei dati e protezione dell'opacità. Giornale di diritto amministrativo **11**, 1113ff. (2014)
4. Carloni, E. (ed.): L'amministrazione aperta. Regole strumenti e limiti dell'open government. Orizzonti di diritto pubblico. Maggioli, Rimini (2014)
5. Carloni, E.: Se questo è un FOIA. Il diritto a conoscere tra modelli e tradimenti. Rassegna Astrid **4**, 9ff. (2016)
6. Carotti, B.: La riforma della pubblica amministrazione - L'amministrazione digitale e la trasparenza amministrativa (commento alla legge 7 agosto 2015, n. 124). Giornale di diritto amministrativo **5**, 625–629 (2015)
7. Cudia, C.: Appunti su trasparenza amministrativa e diritto alla conoscibilità, no. 12, pp. 1–10 (2016). GiustAmm.it
8. D'Urgolo, G.: Trasparenza e prevenzione della corruzione nella P.A.: la recente introduzione del Freedom Act of Information (FOIA) nell'ordinamento italiano, no. 3, pp. 1–14 (2017). GiustAmm.it
9. Faini, F.: Dati, siti e servizi in rete delle pubbliche amministrazioni: l'evoluzione nel segno della trasparenza del decreto legislativo n. 235 del 2010. In: Tiscornia, D. (ed.) Open data e riuso dei dati pubblici, pp. 1–2. Informatica e diritto (2011)
10. Faini, F.: Internet e il diritto a conoscere nei confronti delle pubbliche amministrazioni. In: Passaglia, P., Poletti, D. (eds.) Nodi Virtuali, legami informali: Internet alla ricerca di regole, pp. 337–350. Pisa University Press (2017)
11. Faini, F., Palmirani, M.: The right to know through the freedom of information and open data. In: Dečman, M., Jukić, T. (eds.) Proceedings of the 16th European Conference on e-Government, pp. 54–62. ACPI (2016)

12. Furiosi, E.: L'accesso civico generalizzato, alla luce delle Linee Guida ANAC, no. 4, pp. 1–21 (2017). GiustAmm.it
13. Garante per la protezione dei dati personali (Italian Data Protection Authority), Linee guida in materia di trattamento di dati personali, contenuti anche in atti e documenti amministrativi, effettuato per finalità di pubblicità e trasparenza sul web da soggetti pubblici e da altri enti obbligati, Rule No. 243 of 15 May 2014 (Official Gazette No. 134 of 12 June 2014), doc. web 3134436 (2014)
14. Merloni, F. (ed.): La trasparenza amministrativa. Giuffrè, Milano (2008)
15. Monea, A.: La nuova trasparenza amministrativa alla luce del d.lgs. 97/2016. L'accesso civico. Azienditalia, no. 11, p. 1040ff. (2016)
16. Palmirani, M., Martoni, M., Girardi, D.: Open government data beyond transparency. In: Kő, A., Francesconi, E. (eds.) EGOVIS 2014. LNCS, vol. 8650, pp. 275–291. Springer, Cham (2014). https://doi.org/10.1007/978-3-319-10178-1_22
17. Ponti, B. (ed.): La trasparenza amministrativa dopo il d.lgs. 14 marzo 2013, n. 33, Rimini, Maggioli (2013)
18. Ponti, B. (ed.): Nuova trasparenza amministrativa e libertà di accesso alle informazioni, Rimini, Maggioli (2016)
19. Savino, M.: La nuova disciplina della trasparenza amministrativa. Giornale di diritto amministrativo **8–9**, 795ff. (2013)
20. Savino, M.: Il Foia italiano. La fine della trasparenza di Bertoldo. Giornale di diritto amministrativo **5**, 593ff. (2016)

Open Data and Open Innovation

Quality Issues of Public Procurement Open Data

Csaba Csáki[1(✉)] and Eric Prier[2]

[1] Corvinus University of Budapest, Budapest, Hungary
Csaki.Csaba@uni-corvinus.hu
[2] Florida Atlantic University, Fort Lauderdale, Fort Lauderdale, FL, USA
eprier@fau.edu

Abstract. The previous decade has witnessed numerous open data initiatives by various levels of government around the globe to promote transparency and accountability. One crucial area is government spending or public procurement. This paper reports on an attempt to utilize purchasing data published under the international open data program of the European Union aimed at making available all expenditure data over certain thresholds from 33 European countries. The data had been planned to be used in research aimed at investigating spending and contract awarding patterns within the EU. However, the structure and quality of the data as it has been published in CSV format leave questions about accountability, and this paper serves as a functional primer warning beginner-users of the experientially-based issues of utilizing this and other open data. Key messages include that given its size and complexity this dataset is not for the faint of heart and that no current quality frameworks appear readily able to help.

Keywords: Open data · Data quality · Open data quality · Public procurement Open data challenges · Open data case study

1 Introduction

The concept and associated practices commonly known as 'open data' have been around for well over a decade [3], and its availability emanates for the "right to information," or more generally, "freedom of information" [6, 22]. In terms of government practices, the open data movement is grounded on the assumption that data provided by governments should promote economic, social, and political transformation [33]. Therefore, in a democratic context, society is better off with the data than without the data. Recently, open data initiatives have fallen more broadly under the umbrella of Electronic Government [6, 7, 13]. Such open government programs encompass the utilization of government websites to access public data and public information by civil society [13, 16, 21, 35].

Generally, open data (OD) refers to various government initiatives that make both public data and information in the public sphere available to be to used and repurposed for whatever reason, but primarily to promote political and governmental accountability. While researchers of open data often emphasize their potential advantages [6],

© Springer Nature Switzerland AG 2018
A. Kő and E. Francesconi (Eds.): EGOVIS 2018, LNCS 11032, pp. 177–191, 2018.
https://doi.org/10.1007/978-3-319-98349-3_14

the open data initiatives are not without negative undertones [19, 39]. For example, maintaining national security or protecting the privacy of citizen data limits the availability of certain types of data for public consumption. Furthermore, [37] found that datasets made available by governments typically suffer from poor data quality (DQ). Research on open data quality (ODQ) issues focuses on providing frameworks of quality dimensions or recommendations about ODQ measurements [11, 38]. Most data quality characteristics are technology related and only a few studies have addressed the user side of the open data equation [11]. This is surprising because while data and information produced in the public sphere is more and more being shared, little research looks specifically at the quality requirements of new end-users and how these groups can repurpose the data to spur economic development.

For the purpose of this exploratory case study the focal point is the Tenders Electronic Daily (otherwise known as TED), the public procurement open data portal of the European Union (EU). Based upon the conceptual contours of the principles of open data, it is assumed that the TED data is 'open' in a strict sense. *The goal of this research is to examine the quality of the TED data from the point of view of an inexperienced end-user.* While the current research avoids a critique of open data initiatives, it is nonetheless intended to raise awareness about data and information quality issues as they relate to debates about the ostensible openness promised by e-Government (e-Gov). The premise here is that governments not only have a responsibility of making public data freely available, but it must also ensure that the data provided is free of defect and easily usable in order to reach intended benefits.

The article is organized as follows. First it looks at the place of open data in e-Gov and in public procurement (PP). This is followed by a brief overview of data quality frameworks. The next section looks at the dataset and its context – followed by some methodological ground work. The core part of the paper is an overview of the various challenges experienced with the target open datasets, and the final section provides some conclusions and recommendations to enhance the quality of the TED dataset.

2   Open Data in the Public Sector

Governmental webportals have become a key interface between citizens and governments even in less developed countries [23, 24] and indeed they are now important elements of successful public administration in nearly all societies. While well-designed online services are able to open up government process and strengthen the link between citizens and various policy and administrative actors [6], accountability requires providing answers and remaining responsible to others who have a legitimate claim to demand an account [4]. Meeting these goals assumes a requisite level of openness whereby non-government actors (the public) have mechanisms to know what governmental actors are doing. Thus, data about governmental behavior may be used to hold actors of the public sphere accountable for their actions (or inactions). Yet, even with the tremendous growth of the internet, research conducted by [37] found that less than 8% of countries in its survey provided data on government budgets and spending and public sector contracts under open formats and open license agreements. According to [1], open data needs to be available online; machine-readable; available in bulk so that it can be downloaded as one dataset and easily analyzed; free of charge; and open-licensed so anyone has permission may reuse the data.

Since more and more data generated in various public policy domains are being captured, digitized, and stored, it would be difficult to argue for completely shielding such digital records from public scrutiny in democratic regimes for at least three reasons. First, transparency goals are perceived to be enhanced through improved accessibility, which in turn can promote transactional efficiencies and better planning, as well as greater accountability [17]. Second, specific areas such as public expenditures on goods and services (i.e. public procurement) that are used to fulfill public sector objectives, obligations, and activities in the pursuit of desired policy outcomes [26] could be subject to the eye of the public thereby warranting better planning and delivery, as well as promote greater business access and enhance competition. Finally, even when governments provide data in an open environment, data must be accessible by the right person at the right time in a concise and meaningful manner.

However, in order to clearly achieve these closely associated goals, users of open public data must be confident that the data is free of defects and that they are able to utilize the data to make informed decisions. However, accessibility and usability – as well as other issues associated with open data – have gained increasing scrutiny [11]. To better understand these matters, it is worthwhile to look at the concepts and practices of data quality with a special focus on quality interpretation of open data.

3   Data and Information Quality

It is important to remember, that data are simply facts or figures, not information. Only when data are contextualized to make them meaningful or useful is data transformed into what is commonly called information. In general, all DQ problems will result in information quality (IQ) problems when the data are utilized. In addition, problems with the context or presentation of the data can also result in IQ problems. For example, a poorly formatted report can lead the user to misunderstand the data provided, even when the data itself is accurately captured, and this will result in issues with the quality of the information.

DQ can be an elusive concept even when it comes to describing everyday products or service delivery – and the meaning of this term in the context of digitized data can be especially challenging [36]. There are different frameworks from which data quality issues can be assessed. Adopting a technical view mandates associating information quality with the accuracy of the information in products such as databases [18]. This may be viewed as 'data system quality', looking at issues surrounding timeliness of update, system reliability, system accessibility, system usability and system security [12]. Another, the machine readability approach [10] is concerned with linking, finding, relating and reading information typically using automated processes [28], and characteristics considered include number of formats, traceability, automated tracking, use of standards, trustworthiness, authenticity or provenance. Perhaps the most commonly used definition of user side IQ interprets the term as 'fit-for-use' [34]. However, informational quality defined this way remains a relative construct whereby data considered appropriate for a given use may not display acceptable attributes in another setting [30]. Furthermore, fit-for-use does not immediately allow for ready measurability and it requires additional detail in order to be operationalized [11]. Moreover, the literature's appreciation of specific characteristics of IQ reveal, that the number, definition, and measurability of recommended features or dimensions varies widely [29].

Potential IQ criteria may also be classified based on whether they are related to the user, the information itself or its manipulation [20]. Even though the use and application of these frameworks expand, they tend to remain focused on the underlying technical and data aspects of IQ. Ultimately, however, it is the user who must decide between qualitatively good and poor information and whether there is an acceptable level of quality required to achieve certain objectives [5]. Indeed, [15] distinguishes accuracy, authority, currency and novelty as quality dimensions, while [24] differentiated information quality based on accessibility, actual value, completeness, credibility, flexibility, form, meaning over time, relevance, reliability, selectivity and validity.

With this background, it becomes apparent that there are compounding complications from using numerous dimensions to address information quality by considering the following three examples: (1) the Extended ISO Model [32] presents thirty-two IQ characteristics sorted into six categories; (2) the Product and Service Performance Model for Information Quality (aka. PSP/IQ) [14] distinguishes two quality types and then maps sixteen IQ dimensions into four IQ classes; and (3) [8] lists twenty-eight dimensions of information systems quality grouped into five categories.

Considering a user-centric perspective of the Internet, information quality would identify the degree to which information is suitable for doing a specific task by a particular user in a certain context [9]. [2] then characterized IQ as the user's reaction to the characteristics of output information versus the user's information requirements.

4 Quality in the Realm of Open Data

It is safe to assert that users of open data seek information which may or may not be readily available in the published open dataset. It is also easy to imagine that given the context, quality expectations for open data might dramatically diverge from data and informational quality issues associated with private data and there may be additional considerations that are special to open data. For example, open data must have some level of recognized trust associated with it anchoring its value proposition in accountability [23], therefore, utilizing data from public websites presumes some level of legitimacy on the part of the immediate publisher. Thus open data quality may require a different approach that may be distinguished from more traditional data quality discussions. At the same time, although various streams of ODQ discussions do emphasize different issues, most tend to mirror the DQ literature.

One ODQ approach considers technical abilities and issues raised deviate little from those associated with general DQ investigations. So while they are concerned about the processes and outcomes of producing and managing datasets as well as about corresponding technical standards, the ODQ literature also considers the timeliness of data. i.e. whether data are out-of-date [2]. Another stream is centered on the availability and accessibility of various categories of data. As an example, the Open Data Barometer [7] raises awareness about the gap between data haves and have-nots on several different availability measures of open datasets around the world. Other related concerns cover whether intended audiences are aware of the availability of relevant datasets and even if they are, whether data is easy to find. Finally, it is customary to ask about the value of open data, which, in general terms considers the needs of end-users [11]. However regardless of the approach, there is a tendency to favor characteristics that are measurable. The current disposition of open data quality characteristics is aptly demonstrated by the work of [38] who, in pursuit of the measurability of ODQ, define and operationalize 68 metrics along 6 dimensions.

The Linked Open Data (LOD) movement concentrates on provenance that may enrich the context of open data [25]. Key principles concern the traceability and informational links about the source, the structure of data provenance, linkages to individual elements and linking provenance records. Therefore, dimensions such as origin, attribution, traceability, accessibility and presentation can provide evidence for supporting the assessment of quality, including reliability and trustworthiness.

To summarize, although there are various approaches and frameworks in the existing ODQ literature, the proliferation of approaches and frameworks surrounding general information or open data quality inadequately prepares naïve researchers who venture into the realm of actually using open data. While there are many frameworks and specific cases of individual issues, there appears to be no systematic overview of these potential issues and how they may impact the research of newcomers to open data – and what to do about it. The intention hereafter is to adopt and apply ODQ theoretical frameworks to an important European open dataset on public procurement.

5   The Case of Tender Electronic Daily in the EU

5.1   The Context

The authors' motives for utilizing open data lay in the search for information regarding the potential impacts of public procurement on various societal outcomes, and the open data initiative of the European Union (EU) appeared to be a good place to start. As part of its broader e-Government initiative the European Commission (EC) offers a single point of access (https://data.europa.eu/) to a growing range of data covering EU bodies and member states. By providing free access to data, the EC aims to promote transparency and through that accountability. "The European Union Open Data Portal" (http://data.europa.eu/euodp/en/data/) is the main point of entry to an increasing number of datasets generated or controlled by various EU bodies, while "The European Data Portal" (https://www.europeandataportal.eu/) offers public sector information originated in the member states (and affiliated countries).

One key component of this initiative is the Tenders Electronic Daily dataset (http://ted.europa.eu/) comprised of public procurement data. The stated goal is to make European government procurement more accessible. Data come from the official online version of Supplement 32 to the Official Journal of the European Union, which publishes all public procurement made in EU member states that meets criteria stipulated in the EU regulation for procurement. Other than the twenty-eight EU members, five affiliated countries also publish tender and award notices in the TED Journal to gain access to the EU market – these are Iceland (IS), Liechtenstein (LI), The Former Yugoslav Republic of Macedonia (MK), Norway (NO) and Switzerland (CH). Data in the Journal are collected from standardized public procurement forms as required by the corresponding EU Directive (Directives 2014/18 and 17) and their Annexes. The obligation to tender and thus become part of the TED dataset depends on the type of contracting authority (such as central or local governments that are governed by public law, or European institutions and agencies) and the value of the planned purchase (if it falls above minimum threshold amounts depending on the object and type of contract such as for goods, services, or works). At the time of download, the open data files stored information captured from the contract notices reported in standard forms #2, #4, #5, or #17. These forms announce information concerning a future purchase (i.e. call for tender). In addition, the data files also report contract award notice information on the outcomes of the procurement obtained from standard forms for public procurement #3, #6 or #18 [31]. Data in the TED Journal is entered through online forms, one notice at a time. To appreciate the scope of the activities captured in this data, TED publishes over half a million awards per year for about 420 billion Euro of value.

5.2   The Actual Data

The current study utilizes data from the TED open data website where bulk European public procurement data (https://data.europa.eu/euodp/en/data/dataset/ted-csv) is published annually. Each dataset is published in csv format using UTF-8 coding and it contains data regarding the version of the XML schema definition (XSD) used. There are two types of data records – calls and awards – and each has annual files (with file names in the format of "TED_CAN_2015.csv". The TED open data is very complex because the csv data files are embedded with three levels of procurement information: (a) contract notices or calls for tender (CN); (b) contract award notices i.e. announcements about the result (CAN); and (c) contract awards each stating who won parts of a call within a given award notice (CA). While the process of public procurement is inherently complicated, for now it should suffice to state that one and occasionally two (or rarely more) CNs lead to one CAN, but one CAN may lead to one or more CAs associated with it (this is because a CN may have a preliminary notice, while a single call may have several parts or lots with each leading to a separate contract being awarded). All data files were downloaded January 17, 2017. Due to documented concerns over maintaining consistency of reporting and the procurement standard forms from which the data are captured, only data from 2009 to 2015 is considered in this case study. The total size of the fourteen different data files is approximately 2.13 GB consisting of over 4.5 million records. The datasets are accompanied by a codebook [31] that serves as a guide: contract notice datasets (CN) have 54 fields, while award datasets (CAN/CA) have 50 fields – some fields are not in the original form but generated during csv output.

6   Methodological Considerations of the Exploration

The original intent concerned the analysis of the TED open data and the authors expended a lot of effort reading, manipulating, and documenting the various EU TED open data files trying to better understand their complex structure. Data was loaded into various tools in order to explore the potential advantages and shortcomings of utilizing this open data. However, leaving aside the results achieved in analyzing the data files (actual statistical data is reported in [27]), several nagging questions continued to haunt this process: (a) What should various users of open data expect in terms of operational results of utilizing this type of data? (b) What challenges might they face when attempting to utilize open data – especially for the first time? (c) What common issues might arise in accessing open data and for what contingencies should scholars need to prepare themselves? (d) How can one judge the status of a dataset before investing substantial effort to ready it for use? Interestingly, a considerable search of appropriate resources revealed a substantial gap in the literature finding no practical help to address these questions. In other words, there appears to be no general primer or users' guide on how to approach open data. This article reports the experience of utilizing an important open dataset in the hope that others may benefit from the experience.

At its core this research uses the TED dataset as a single case and focuses on the journey of actually utilizing open data. The report here may be categorized as a self-reflective anthropological study: it shares the experiences how the journey unfolded – but it is done so not with the rigor of a 'participant observation' or 'action research' approach, but instead it is a reflection on the process and may be considered more properly as a storytelling documentation. What makes this case especially appropriate is that this data is mandated by EU law and regulations and it is a result of iterative cycles of policy-making. One of the highest public sector ideals remains transparency and this dataset is chosen exactly because it is intended to be an example of quality open data that is supposed to be, by its nature, transparent. A set of commonly-available software tools were utilized including MS Excel, MS Access (Office 2010 on Win7 OS), SPSS (v22.2), Oracle Database (11g Release 11.2.0.4) with SQL Developer interface (v4.1.5). Regarding the default language setting of the MS Windows operating system (and through that the MS Office package) the authors used English (North American) and Hungarian. The tools had been used to understand and manipulate the dataset in order to eliminate errors, discover operational issues, and to understand the nature of the data beyond mere reading and statistical summaries.

While the report and its comments below have been organized in a segmented chronological path that follows a natural progressive timeline of the steps one normally takes to explore new data, it also considers the corresponding key characteristics identified in the literature above to judge DQ and ODQ:

Find the data: concerned with awareness and availability;
Download: focuses on accessibility;
Open, Load, Check: looks at ease of access and readability characteristics;
Transform: deals with technical qualities of the data;
Assessment: this step is about the structure and content of the dataset;

Linking: this is where traceability is investigated;
Manipulate: this step is about ease of use and usability characteristics;
Interpret and analyze: quality in use, value, and fit-for-purpose.

7 Journey into Open Data: A Beginner's Account

Find the Data: Having worked in the public procurement research area for over a decade, researchers involved have been aware of the availability of data related to public sourcing in numerous countries around the globe. They have used the TED Journal extensively at the official single-search site until July 2016, when the European Commission itself has published machine-readable csv bulk extracts of the TED data on its open data portal.

Download: As mentioned earlier, the granularity of the data at the file level is one year, but an integrated file covering seven years is also available. The files are in csv format and the individual file sizes span from 100 MB to 1.6 GB. None of these posed any issues during download with a normal Internet connection. The official TED Journal on the other hand offers individual notices as well as daily digests (in zipped xml format) – the size of which is typically 150 MBs per month.

Open, Load, Check: Even though the format is standard csv, initial opening of the first file using Excel resulted in unstructured lines with no segmentation (i.e. each line was rendered into one cell instead of recognizing the columns). It quickly turned out that the language setting of the MS Windows OS impacts how Excel reads data, namely, the Regional and Language settings determine the default field separator. Using English as a default enables Excel to read the data correctly and separate out the fields. But even when the lines were properly segmented into fields, some of the text was scrambled. In fact, reading the file into SPSS or Access – and later adding it to an Oracle DB – resulted in the same often unreadable text with strange, meaningless characters. The problem appears to have been rooted in the encoding schema: the csv files use UTF-8 which needed to be specifically defined. In Excel the solution was to 'import' the csv instead of simply opening it, as then it was possible to define the encoding schema. But in Access for UTF-8 character coding the language setting should not be English or Hungarian, but 'All'. Essentially the csv file requires the so called BOM character for font mixing as EU members may use any of the official languages for PP announcements. As a last point, although expected file sizes were reported at the download page, there was no ready documentation explaining how many lines of data should be correctly read in the csv files. Hence users have no reliable information that precisely describes a "properly" imported file.

Transform: Once the data is readable in full format without loss or damage, the user has to consider the issue of data types. The original dataset as published does not carry datatypes. While Excel has a limited capability to differentiate between a few datatypes such as Text, Date or Number, the csv format does not carry such information (Excel would automatically assign a datatype though when the csv file is opened – if nothing else it uses the "General" type as a default). On the other hand, many database or data management tools would offer a range of types, and this set might be quite sophisticated. It is noteworthy that each tool utilized in this project had its own special names and options – with Oracle having a different approach compared to Access or SPSS. In fact, Oracle is known for having a unique stance on datatypes. Furthermore, each tool used herein had a different take on the 'Date' type. All of the tools (Access, Oracle, and SPSS) offer automatic type recognition and also make suggestions regarding the potential maximum size or length of relevant types (such as integer or text). Although it might sound like a minor concern, much effort was spent struggling with fields of 'Date' type. This is mostly because there is no unique standard for storing date/time values, each tool offered different options which unnecessarily complicated what should be simple conversions. For example, the Hungarian version of Access refused to accept the (given TED) English date format, e.g. it would not take 'DD.MMM.YY' or 'DD-MMM-YY', instead, it would require 'YYYY.MM.DD'. Oracle had similar issues while also accepting only a limited set of formats.

Another technical issue concerned the length of text fields. Interestingly, should one choose the wrong length for text, Access would truncate fields with longer size while Oracle would reject such records fully – all of which suggests that knowing the longest possible text field is important. Needless to say though, choosing a very large value for all fields would result in a much larger database file requiring more storage and more memory to manipulate the data.

Assessment

Modifications and Cancellations. Without going into the details of PP operations, it should suffice to know that changes to or cancellation of procedures require special steps such as using appropriate forms in a certain way. The same is true for unsuccessful procedures. However, there were differing practices followed how to use the forms. To rectify this situation, the content and use of EU PP forms have changed in 2014 and new forms were also created. When a contracting authority modifies the contractual condition, a modification to an existing contract notice leads to a new entry (called 'Additional Information' using form #14) which may or may not require a new contract notice identification number (CN ID). On the other hand, actual contract cancellations are only captured through 'cancellation notices' which after 2014 require a new form (#02). Further, unsuccessful procedures under the new directives should not be canceled but instead contracting authorities should use the relevant CAN form reporting 'no award'. But not all member states have started to follow the changes at the same time. This has led to inconsistences over time and discrepancies within the same year. All of this ambiguity produces continuity problems within the dataset because those countries which have not yet ratified the new directives into national law were still using the old forms. Problematically, all of these contingencies were not readily clear from documentation at the website, and it is currently unknown how the algorithm generating the csv files has taken this into consideration.

Missing Values. According to the TED documentation available at the website [34], the connection between the two types of records – calls and awards – in the csv files is made using a special ID field called FUTURE_CAN_ID – a field that had been added to CN records during the generation of the csv file. This field is often left empty which makes data quality checking problematic. For example, the consolidated 2009–2015 CN files showed that 66% of this field was empty across that time period.

Of course, there are often legitimate reasons for this including the fact that the call might have been cancelled (no winner was announced), or the procedure had not yet concluded at the time of publication. Unfortunately, it is also possible that the cancellation was not recorded or improperly done so, thus leaving the user of the data with the assumption that the call is still open. All of this suggests that currently there is no means to establish this state, unless one goes back to the source database searching on each individual call in question, which is, of course prohibitive. On the other hand, it is possible that the cancellation generates a new csv record when it officially should not – at least not under the new form regime. Moreover many FUTURE_CAN_IDs point to documents that will be published in the future e.g. in 2016 but the open data file of that year had not been made available at the time of download. Therefore, assuming that one would not individually search and download relevant notices from the TED DB using the interactive TED data website, certain types of analysis are either not possible; incomplete; or subject to both validity and reliability issues. This further suggests that although procurement accountability would often require an easy connection of calls to awards, the generated csv files make this difficult in many ways. In addition, there are other potential problems associated with real missing values in numerous other fields. Of course, many of these missing data fields are concentrated in non-key or non-essential data elements such as national contract ID or the national code of the authority. But when needed, the lack of data values in these fields would cause problems in case of statistical analysis targeting those specific fields.

Multiple Values in One Field. Perhaps a greater cause for concern lays in the situation when there are multiple values in one field. This happens in these csv data files in two ways: in the column reporting additional CPV codes and in the column announcing winners. The former issue can be resolved with some text manipulation whenever such statistics are required, but the latter one is more complicated because it requires numerous lines of software code to separate this information out into individual values. In public procurement, more than one winner may occur in several cases: as a result of using a framework agreement a dynamic purchasing system; in the case of contract separation into lots; and when the call notice has different parts. In the case of lots, there should be one "contract award" with a unique "CONTRACT_AWARD_ID" affiliated with the same CAN ID. However, for the other two cases, different authorities (in different countries) appear to have established different standards.

Link: As mentioned, the dataset has two main parts, calls (CNs) and corresponding awards (CANs and its awards), and they are presented separately for each ear. Each part has its own datastructure (represented by a specific header row in the corresponding csv file). However, evidence had been found that the FUTURE_CAN_ID linking this two parts is often generated inappropriately. Not simply is the value wrong, but during the generation of the annual csv CN file new records were created that have no meaning in the original TED DB. Manual investigation of several such cases lead to the conclusion that the csv generating algorithm connects together otherwise unlinked CN and CAN items of the same contracting authority. It would be hard to calculate the number of these false lines, but the proportion may be several percent annually. One potential reason for this might be the use of the new forms. Without other means of confirmation (e.g. manual check) there is essentially little confirmable traceability between the two parts of the dataset.

Manipulate: Similarly, ease of use appeared to depend on the same three matters as 'transformation': the format of the file (csv), the tools required to work on the data (various tools had been tried), and the structure of the data in the files. The difficulties experienced due to language settings and date formats kept coming back during the analysis of the data whenever data had to be transferred between research sites using different language settings or needed to be loaded from one application to another. Although the data structure is described in a guide, a deep understanding of the meaning of various fields required extensive knowledge of not only public procurement but also specific details of EU procedures. This was further complicated by the fact that the csv fields often did not fully reflect either the fields in the TED DB or the original forms contracting authorities required to use when submitting data related to calls and contract results. Even the guide did not explain the mapping between these three formats which further required additional effort in connecting the dots whenever a new research question was asked from the datasets. The fact that data is published in non-normalized form also required attention when making statistical calculations (due to multiplication of field values over numerous records and also because one CAN may have more than one CA associated with it each resulting in one CSV record).

Interpret: Considering the complexity of the dataset as well as the issues and problems discussed so far it would not be an exaggeration to state that doing any kind of analysis (even basic statistics) utilizing this open data required a lot of preparation and careful attention including a lot of manual data cleansing. Again, intimate domain knowledge (in this case of European public procurement formalities) was essential beyond studying the codebook. Perhaps the most obvious recurring issue that will infect any data analysis using this open dataset is the problem of missing values across numerous fields. In some cases a simple visual browsing of the file was enough to see that certain records had missing values, while in other cases the statistics revealed a number of 'no value' items. Whether the missing value was a result of the way csv files were generated or that data had not been entered at all (the latter is most likely) is not known. As previously mentioned, missing data raises validation concerns and can be difficult to detect because cancellation of calls appears to not always be reported consistently. Consider that over the period of 2009–2015 60% of the calls (452,078 of 754,378) had no reported outcome (i.e. had no award indicated and yet was not cancelled either).

8 Discussion and Insights for Open Data Newcomers

This case study offers a cautionary tale to those new to open data – and does so with a clear warning: one should be careful to spend time and effort preparing any project that intends to utilize large sets of open data. While the quality of actual datasets may differ widely, this study documents at least three seemingly unrelated skills that are needed to appropriately utilize open data when attempting research that intends to rely on it: data management skills; expertise in software applications, as well as domain knowledge and expertise. The result of this case study suggests the following set of generalized issues that end-users consider when preparing to work with open data.

- Find the data (availability): check for the data source to be authentic and whether the data is up to date and if it came with adequate and up-to-date description and sufficient documentation;
- Download (accessibility): open data may come in many different formats and its size could be large and is often composed of several files or parts;
- Open, Load, Check (readability): make sure that you have several tools available and that their settings fit the requirements of the data format – if something does not look right, try different language, coding and location settings;
- Transform (technical qualities of the data): open data often looks different in different tools and transformation of different formats might be necessary - special support or expertise may be required to decide which tool fits best (don't stick with a tool just because that is the only one you know). Loading the data into any management tool requires several steps of preparation such as assessing the types and sizes of fields as well as obtaining and applying the proper settings during the load;
- Assessment (content, structure): while using the guide if available, be careful - there might be errors, missing information, or the data structure might be so complex that substantial domain expertise might be required to understand both the meaning and the structure of the data;
- Link (traceability): open data is rarely standalone and is often composed of several parts or related/connected datasets. It has (should have) references within the area covered, but it might use references to other sets (i.e. country codes, national abbreviations etc.): pay special attention and double check all such references for correctness;
- Manipulate (ease of use, usability): search out and find explanation for duplicates, missing values or even missing or omitted fields;
- Interpret, analyze (use, value, fit-for-purpose): depending on the issues uncovered during the earlier steps, the researcher might need to reconsider the questions that could be meaningfully answered from the dataset in actual use (which often differs from the intended use); special attention should be paid to any generated statistical results which obviously depend on records/fields/values.

9   Conclusions and Potential Future Directions

Open Data initiatives have gained considerable momentum in many countries, and this has been mirrored by increased attention in academic research – especially concerning data quality. While a few frameworks have been put forward on how to assess open data quality and what measures to utilize, studies investigating actual cases are lacking. This case study utilized procurement data from EU countries to demonstrate potential generalized hazards likely to be found in open data relevant to a variety of academic fields, and the experience recounted here provides useful insights to others planning to work with open government data for the first time. The discussion lays the groundwork how to more clearly think about open data issues in the future. For example, there is often a recursive loop in how scholars conceptually think about the quality of data and information: modeling social processes – in this case, procurement – involves varying levels of data which in turn influences how data and informational quality is conceived. For instance, filling out forms is actually data generation of the procurement process. However, when the forms are transformed into flat csv files, the data in the forms may be distorted. Given the centrality of a procurement outcome in an open dataset that is devoted to making this government spending more transparent, surely this calls for a more complete documentable explanation by the authorities providing the data.

In sum, this article provides a functional practical guide by explaining how the relevant literature examines specific issues that are often discussed in isolation from real-world experience. What makes this study different is filling the gap between theory and practice for researchers of open data by illuminating potential issues and providing applicable solutions for beginners and veterans alike. The eight general issues described here go beyond offering differential measures of quality and instead, prepares researchers with warnings and tips on how to think about navigating the open data ocean.

Acknowledgments. This paper has been written with the support of the National University of Public Service in the framework of the priority project KÖFOP-2.1.2-VEKOP-15-2016-00001 titled "Public Service Development for Establishing Good Governance" - Ludovika Digital Governance Research Group. The authors wish to thank the staff of the European Commission for use of the TED csv dataset and also acknowledge the contribution of Prof. Clifford McCue of Florida Atlantic University.

References

1. ACWG – Anti Corruption Working Group of G20: Anti Corruption Open Data Principles. http://www.g20.utoronto.ca/2015/G20-Anti-Corruption-Open-Data-Principles.pdf. Accessed 21 Jan 2018
2. Bailey, J.E., Pearson, S.W.: Development of a tool for measuring and analyzing computer user satisfaction. Manag. Sci. **29**(5), 530–545 (1983)
3. Blakemore, M., Craglia, M.: Access to public-sector information in Europe: policy, rights, and obligations. Inf. Soc. **22**(1), 13–24 (2006)
4. Bovens, M., Goodin, R.E., Schillemans, T. (eds.): The Oxford Handbook of Public Accountability. Oxford University Press, Oxford (2014)
5. Chai, K., Potdar, V., Dillon, T.: Content quality assessment related frameworks for social media. In: Gervasi, O., Taniar, D., Murgante, B., Laganà, A., Mun, Y., Gavrilova, M.L. (eds.) ICCSA 2009. LNCS, vol. 5593, pp. 791–805. Springer, Heidelberg (2009). https://doi.org/10.1007/978-3-642-02457-3_65
6. Chun, S.A., Shulman, S., Sandoval, R., Hovy, E.: Government 2.0: making connections between citizens, data and gov. Inf. Polity **15**(1–2), 1–9 (2010)
7. Davies, T. Open Data Barometer, Global Report (2013). http://www.cocoaconnect.org/publication/open-data-barometer-2013-global-report. Accessed 13 Jan 2017

8. Dedeke, A.: A conceptual framework for developing quality measures for information systems. In: Proceedings of the 5th International Conference on Information Quality, pp. 126–128 (2000)
9. Emamjome, F.F., Rabaa'i, A.A., Gable, G.G., Bandara, W.: Information quality in social media: a conceptual model. In: Proceedings of the Pacific Asia Conference on Information Systems (PACIS 2013). AIS Electronic Library (AISel), Seoul (2013)
10. Erickson, J.S., Viswanathan, A., Shinavier, J., Shi, Y., Hendler, J.A.: Open government data: a data analytics approach. IEEE Intell. Syst. **28**(5), 19–23 (2013)
11. Frank, M., Walker, J.: User centred methods for measuring the quality of open data. J. Commun. Inform. **12**(2), 47–68 (2016)
12. Fox, C., Levitin, A., Redman, T.C.: Data and Data Quality: Total Data Quality Management Research Program. Sloan School of Management, MIT, Boston (1995)
13. Jaeger, P.T.: The endless wire: E-government as global phenomenon. Gov. Inf. Q. **20**, 323–331 (2003)
14. Kahn, B.K., Strong, D.M., Wang, R.Y.: A model for delivering quality information as product and services. In: Proceedings of the 1997 Conference on Information Quality, Cambridge, MA, pp. 80–94 (1997)
15. Klobas, J.E.: Beyond information quality: fitness for purpose and electronic information resource use. J. Inf. Sci. **21**(2), 95–114 (1995)
16. Kraemer, K.L., King, J.L.: Information technology and administrative reform: will the time after e-government be different? http://www.crito.uci.edu. Accessed 10 Dec 2016
17. Leipold, K.: Electronic Government Procurement (e-GP) opportunities & challenges. Talk given at the Congress at Annual Session of UNCITRAL in Vienna, 9–12 July 2007. http://www.uncitral.org/pdf//english/congress/Leipold.pdf. Accessed 10 Dec 2016
18. Levitin, A., Redman, T.: Quality dimensions of a conceptual view. Inf. Process. Manag. **31**(1), 81–88 (1995)
19. Martin, S., Foulonneau, M., Turki, S., Ihadjadene, M., Paris, U., Tudor, P.R.C.H.: Risk analysis to overcome barriers to open data. Electron. J. e-Gov. **11**(1), 348–359 (2013)
20. Naumann, F., Rolker, C.: Assessment methods for information quality criteria. In: Proceedings of the 5th International Conference on Information Quality, Humboldt-Universität zu Berlin, Institut für Informatik, pp. 148–162 (2000)
21. Norris, F.D., Lloyd, B.A.: The scholarly literature on e-government: characterizing a nascent field. Int. J. Electron. Gov. Res. **2**(4), 40–56 (2006)
22. OECD [Organisation for Economic Co-operation and Development]: Recommendation of the Council for Enhanced Access and More Effective Use of Public Sector Information (2008). https://legalinstruments.oecd.org/Instruments/ShowInstrumentView.aspx?Instrument ID=122. Accessed 10 Dec 2017
23. OECD: Trust and Public Policy: How Better Governance Can Help Rebuild Public Trust, OECD Public Governance Reviews. OECD Publishing, Paris (2017)
24. Olaisen, J.: Information quality factors and the cognitive authority of electronic information, In: 1989 Proceedings of a NORDINFO Seminar, pp. 91–121. Taylor, London (1990)
25. Pignotti, E., Corsar, D., Edwards, P.: Provenance principles for open data. In: Proceedings of DE 2011 (2011)
26. Prier, E., McCue, C.P.: The implications of a muddled definition of public procurement. J. Publ. Procure. **9**(3&4), 326–370 (2009)
27. Prier. E., Prismakova, P., McCue, C.P.: Analysing the European Union's tender electronic daily: possibilities and Pitfalls. Int. J. Procure. Manag. (forthcoming)
28. Rula, A., Zaveri, A.: Methodology for assessment of linked data quality. In: Proceedings of the 1st Workshop on Linked Data Quality at the 10th International Conference on Semantic Systems, LDQ@SEMANTiCS 2014 (2014)

29. Scannapieco, M., Catarci, T.: Data quality under a computer science perspective. Arch. Comput. **2**, 1–15 (2002)
30. Tayi, G.K., Ballou, D.P.: Examining data quality. Commun. ACM **41**(2), 54–57 (1998)
31. TED: TED Processed Database: Notes & Codebook, Version 2.2. http://data.europa.eu/euodp/repository/ec/dg-grow/mapps/TED(csv)_data_information.doc. Accessed 20 Jan 2017
32. van Zeist, R., Hendriks, P.: Specifying software quality with the extended ISO model. Softw. Qual. J. **5**(4), 273–284 (1996)
33. Verhulst, S., Young, A.: Open data impact when demand and supply meet key findings of the open data impact case studies. GovLab (2016). http://odimpact.org/files/open-data-impact-key-findings.pdf. Accessed 18 Dec 2017
34. Wang, R.Y., Strong, D.M.: Beyond accuracy: what data quality means to data consumers. J. Manag. Inf. Syst. **12**(4), 5–33 (1996)
35. World Bank: Definition of E-Government. http://documents.worldbank.org/curated/en/527061468769894044//pdf//266390WP0E1Gov1gentina1Final1Report.pdf. Accessed 20 Feb 2018
36. Wormell, I.: Information quality: definitions and dimensions. In: Proceedings of a NORDINFO Seminar, Royal School of Librarianship. Taylor, London (1990)
37. WWWF, World Wide Web Foundation: Open Data Barometer, 2nd edn (2015). http://opendatabarometer.org/assets/downloads/OpenDataBarometer-SecondEdition-PressRelease.pdf. Accessed 21 Jan 2018
38. Zaveri, A., Rula, A., Maurino, A., Pietrobon, R., Lehmann, J., Auer, S.: Quality assessment methodologies for linked open data. Semant. Web J. **1**(5), 1–31 (2012)
39. Zuiderwijk, A., Janssen, M., Choenni, S., Meijer, R., Alibaks, R.S.: Socio-technical impediments of open data. Electron. J. e-Gov. **10**(2), 156–172 (2012)

Open Data Research Challenges in the EU

Csaba Csáki[(⊠)] and Andrea Kő

Corvinus University of Budapest, Budapest, Hungary
{Csaki.Csaba,Andrea.Ko}@uni-corvinus.hu

Abstract. Although the concept of 'open data' has been around for some time, it has gained more attention in the public sphere over the last decade. This momentum has attracted the interest of 'mainstream' e-Government researchers as well, what is well indicated by the increased number of papers addressing the topic. Even though this interest seemed to be declining two-three years ago, the idea of reusing public sector data provided new ammunition to do research into this phenomenon. This paper relies on the latest literature and relevant studies to review the research area of open government data and to offer recommendations regarding potential research directions that could advance our understanding of the challenges facing the reuse of public sector information.

Keywords: Open data · Open government data · Open data reuse
Open data research agenda · Open data research questions

1 Introduction

Providing 'open data' has become a key element in the e-Government arsenal in support of transparency and accountability [8, 22]. Its primary purpose is to make available specific sets of data and information produced by various public sector entities or controlled by governmental organizations typically through Internet outlets [29]. One typical example of open government data (OGD) is data related to public expenditures and procurement – including calls for tender, contracts, purchase items and prices as well as general spending data – published both during purchasing processes and retrospectively. But there is a large amount of data related to other areas such as data generated during various legal, official or administrative processes or while executing various government tasks and functions. Beyond their primary purpose (i.e. being used during public sector processes) these data sets are worthy of additional value generation [23]. Reusable public sector data may be related to economic, social, societal, demographic or health matters, but certain legal, judicial, or property/real estate registry data may also have potential for added value [3]. Utilizing public sector data in innovative, marketable services has become a successful practice in several countries over the last few years [29]. Accordingly, scientific interest in this area has increased as well [52]. There have been several models and interpretive frameworks put forward or had been reused – such as the application of the ecology metaphor to address the complexity of the open data arena in general and to describe the relationships among its actors in particular [21]. Although there are various research efforts moving along different directions to explore the questions related to the reuse of OGD

© Springer Nature Switzerland AG 2018
A. Kő and E. Francesconi (Eds.): EGOVIS 2018, LNCS 11032, pp. 192–204, 2018.
https://doi.org/10.1007/978-3-319-98349-3_15

[46, 52], it is still not clear what the important trends and open questions are for the next decade. This paper attempts to propose important and promising research areas and questions within the open data domain.

The paper is organized as follows. After this introduction the paper reviews the history of OGD in an international context with special focus on the European Union. This is followed by a review of the most popular and relevant scientific models and frameworks. After the discussion of our research approach and methods, the fourth section starts with a presentation of research areas based on most recent literature. This is followed by our own proposal of areas concluded from an analysis of key research papers. The main part of the discussion concludes with specific research questions proposed for the areas identified. The paper concludes with a summary of the most relevant theoretical findings and practical recommendations.

2   Open Government Data

2.1   A Brief History of Open Government Data

The idea to push for open government and to make public sector data available is not new. Indeed, in the US it was already raised in the 50s of the last century that the government should be 'open' – at least in a legal sense [37]. The primary goal was to achieve better accountability, and according to the argument this required that government data should be more accessible as well. This expectation can be found in the principles of freedom of information or in the legal (and constitutional) requirements of 'right to information' [22], which was the dominant motivation to request access to public sector information or data 'owned' by state or government entities. Over the last two decades – on the back of the spreading use of the Internet – the idea of open data has gotten new fuel from the technology backed e-Government initiative and during the turn of the millennium governmental (data) portals were created in several countries [42]. Strictly speaking the term 'open data' as an expression with special meaning may be dated from the 2006 manifesto of the Open Knowledge Foundation [7, 35], although that call was mainly a generic proposal, as it also concerned scientific and other data. Data may be called 'open' if it is freely accessible in machine readable format and it is (legally) free to be used, reused, or redistributed for any purpose [35] – typically assuming that the source is attributed and the results are shared [29]. Open government data as a special area on its own emerged towards the end of the first decade of this century when it was brought into focus as part of the (rejuvenated) open government movement [2, 34]. The core of the open government concept is that citizens have the right to get access to data, information and documents generated by governments as well as to public sector procedures involved [8]. Over the last decade more and more countries have initiated their own open government program and a result the number of accessible datasets has increased considerably [3, 7, 42]. At the same time – and this is especially true for data possessed by governments and their institutions – the real value of open data lies in their further reuse and utilization, mainly because OGD makes several commercial service-oriented endeavours possible, even for businesses that don't own any data [29]. This implies that commercial utilization gets higher emphasis on top of strengthened social, societal, and political requests, with the latter aimed at increasing the participation of citizens in democratic and governmental decision making processes. In the context of the European Union, the Public Sector Information (PSI) program of the European Commission started in 2003 [18] initiated a push for OGD publication, while the Digital Agenda initiative of 2010 [15, 16] has moved towards a framework encouraging the socio-economic utilization of data such published.

2.2   Open Data and Its Reuse in the European Union

The first significant appearance of the open data concept at the Union level came as early as the late 90s as the Commission already recognized the secondary value of public sector information and named data to be a key resource [14]. Later, in the so called Public Sector Information (aka PSI) directive (Directive 2003/98/EC) the Commission encouraged member states to make public sector information available for re-use by third parties as much as possible [18]. Prior to this legal statement the question of data openness was left to the member states to regulate. The directive aimed to catalyse the development of new services through providing public sector data at low price with supportive conditions [22]. The European Commission promoted open data initiatives again in its Digital Agenda for Europe program initiated in 2010 [14, 17]. The 2013 amendment (Directive 2013/37/EU) broadened the scope of the directive with the "*open data, unless*" standpoint [19]. The expectation was that the availability of public data stimulate the secondary use of such data, which not only promotes government transparency but supports information industries as well. The potential value that may result from the re-use of open public sector information in Europe is huge: it is estimated to be between €27 billion [9] and €68 billion [40, 47].

However, there are roadblocks to fulfil this potential. For example, van Loenen et al. [47] call the related EU *data protection legislation* a "*very hungry caterpillar*", which cause problems for the successful execution of the EU digital agenda through obstructing the implementation of open government data policies for mapping data in the EU. Furthermore, Ződi [51] – while reviewing the implementation of the PSI directive in Hungary – identifies additional factors that could hinder the success of the directive. He considers copyright issues, proprietary data formats, and overpricing as serious challenges to overcome, and also adds, that it is difficult to calculate marginal costs. He notes, that public sector entities as data owners has no motivation to share their data or, when they enter the market on their own, they have an unfair advantage.

Several aspects of the Open Government Data area has been addressed during the EGOVIS conference series [24–27]. Martin et al. [30] present open data ecosystem approach implemented in BE-GOOD European program. BE-GOOD is an Interreg VB NWE project aiming to unlock, re-use and extract value from Public Sector Information (PSI) to develop data driven services in the area of infrastructure and environment. The authors developed a new open data ecosystem framework, which is based on the analysis of existing open ecosystem models. They introduced a new role called stimulator and a new stimulating function into the open data ecosystem concept. The main specificity of the stimulator function is that it involves thinking about and influencing the ecosystem. The stimulating function then has a decisive role in risk management within the ecosystem. The new approach was customized for public procurement context.

Palmirani et al. [36] discussed the Open Government Data legislation framework in force in the Italian legal system. Their paper provide an overview of an empirical research conducted on Italian Municipal web sites (covering 35 portals) to investigate the connection between the Open Government Data legislation and the Italian Transparency Act.

Schmitz et al. [43] presented a pilot project on Linked Open Data (LOD) and e-Participation, promoted by the European Parliament and developed by the Publications Office of the European Union (OP). They detailed the main features of LOD and an e-Participation platform based on open source and semantic web technologies. The main goal of the project was to allow citizens to actively participate in public consultations within the EU decision-making process. Their solution gives citizens the possibility to participate in the preparation of documents throughout the law-making process, for example participants may make comments and amendments on each document fragment, or express their sentiment on them.

Hansen et al. [20] analyzed the background, extent and expected impact of the Danish open government data initiative. Their research focused on the role of open public sector information as a major step towards a digital society. They applied the principles of the Open Government Data initiative as a discussion framework for the Danish approach to open government data. They draw attention to the observation that open government data is just one factor in promoting innovation, while human resources, like skilled specialists and researchers, entrepreneurship, and venture capital are perhaps more important.

According to the literature review, researchers discuss open data and the related issues mainly from policy or technical point of view. A few papers deal with other considerations, like organizational challenges, but a holistic view of related potential research questions and problems is missing.

3 Frameworks and Models Proposed for the Research of Governmental Open Data

It was put forward already in the 90s that the process and activities of managing (organizational) data may be compared to the manufacturing and logistics processes of physical products [49]. This lead to the rise of the 'data supply chain' concept that was built around the production-delivery-consumption metaphor of creating, recording, storing, and using data.

The first data-transparency solutions appearing under the e-Government banner handled the issue mainly from a technical point of view and offered 'platforms' where (certain) governmental data could be published. This actually meant a one directional approach. The next step, still rooted in the technical approach to e-Gov, created 'portals' that typically offered APIs (interfaces) which allowed an avenue to pose queries in a specific language. This was followed by the more interactive 2.0 solutions that allowed for feedback as well [10, 11].

The main goal of the data supply chain approach was to enable the application of the quality assurance models developed for manufacturing processes [50]. This idea has resurfaced in the context of OGD almost two decades later in the work of Groth [13] who considered the important questions of who is responsible for the quality (and problems) of data and how to properly manage the sources of data collection. In this regard the data supply chain starts with the creation of data which then can be passed on and may be combined with other data (or datasets). In addition, data may go through various transformations until it gets to its final user [28].

Combining different types of data and data coming from differing sources forms the basis of the Big Data approach, where this combination of types and sources contributes to the creation of added value [31]. This gives way to the application of the value chain metaphor to data, similarly to the value chain of industrial production [41]. Indeed, the data value chain model fits well with the question of open data reuse, since the final goal of OD reuse is the creation of socio-economic value through the development of OD-based new, innovative services. One potential criticism of both the data supply and data value chain is that they consider the movement of data along a linear model. Consequently, there are arguments for a more life-cycle like approaches to the understanding of the nature of data use – including open data (see for example [38]). The main contribution of the data life-cycle models is that the producers of data are consumers of it at the same time and vice versa – from a different point of view (considering a different source). To simplify, one may say that while the supply chain and life-cycle models of data focus on the connections between suppliers and consumers (supply and demand), the value chain interpretation considers the context as well and its focus is on the process/activities of transforming data elements in order to produce higher level information in support of a given goal.

While the static platform and portal solutions of e-Gov (mentioned earlier) allow for the publication of data primarily from the point of view of public sector actors (as a responsibility or legal-regulatory expectation), the option to reuse open data brings into the picture a few new actors on the 'consumer' side in order to generate higher added value [8]. Such roles include data providers (participants who provide better – easier, more organized – access to open data), the data cleansers, and service developers among others [29]. One should also consider that the added value is often not the final goal, the impact achieved is more important, which might manifest itself in the form of economic advantage or social well-being [7]. Trying to understand these more complex roles lead researchers to the application of the 'ecosystem' approach to open data, and this model has gained momentum over the last few years [52]. So much so, that now it is a dominant stream in open data research papers [45]. Considering the origins of the ecosystem approach to data, it is rooted in data (and information systems) 'ecology', but it must be noted that the original literature using the ecosystem model to describe relationships in the open data area did not provide a clear definition (or none at al) and there is no common, accepted notation how to depict open data ecosystems (roles, processes and relationships in them). This resulted in the diverging set of building blocks (and corresponding notations) used by various authors building on the ecosystem metaphor to explain various aspects of the open data phenomenon. The principles of ecology were already applied during the turn of the millennium to understand and explain the issues of organizational information sharing [12, 33].

Ecology is the *"scientific study of the processes influencing the distribution and abundance of organisms and the transformation and flux of energy and matter"* ([12], p. 74). In this regard information ecology means *"a system of people, practices, values, and technologies in a particular local environment"* ([33], p. 49) and studying information ecologies implies the description and understanding of the elements of such systems and their relationships. Therefore, the goal is to identify and describe roles, tasks, and relationships as well as to show their change and evolution over time in a given environment. In their forward looking book Davenport and Prusak [6] identified the following elements of an information ecology: outside environment, organizational environment, information environment and within them stakeholders, strategy, culture and behaviour, principles and rules, processes, and finally (technological) architecture. This vision is embraced by the ecosystem approach, which for open data first has been used by Parsons et al. [38]. Based on the data lifecycle model they defined an 'information ecosystem' as *"the people and technologies collecting, handling, and using the data and the interactions between them"* (p. 557). This metaphor has since been appropriated and applied by others. As a critique it should be noted that neither the roles and actors of an (open data) ecosystem nor its processes has achieved an acceptable level of standardization yet, and there is no widely accepted framework.

Considering the literature of open data research (with its dominant organizational interest and diverging focus) as well as the current state of the art of open data models (including the uncertainty surrounding the various interpretations and models), it appears useful to establish a holistic research framework that offers clear and well defined (sub)areas and allows for the posing of relevant questions worthy of scientific interest.

4   Methodological Considerations

4.1   Research Questions

According to the aim of the research and based on the literature reviewed, three research questions have been formulated: (1) Which frameworks and corresponding holistic dimensions would be relevant in restructuring the main research areas identified by the literature review? (2) What are the decisive research areas in the "open data" research domain? (3) What are the recent, important open research questions in the European "open data" research? The rest of the paper will address these research questions and provide answers for them in Sect. 6 – based on the methodological approach discussed in the next Subsection.

4.2   Research Strategy: Systematic Analysis of Literature

The selected research method is literature review based, as suggested by vom Brocke et al. [48]. Their framework for literature reviewing has five phases: (1) definition of review scope; (2) conceptualization of topic; (3) literature search; (4) literature analysis and synthesis; (5) research agenda. The first step (definition of review scope) is a critical one as it determines the subsequent phases. To clarify the definition of review scope, Cooper's taxonomy [5] could be applied. It has six dimensions: research focus, goal, organization, perspective, audience and coverage. The vom Brocke research framework was applied in the following way. The review scope is open data domain. In the first step, the Cooper taxonomy was used as well. Research focus is the overview of open government data related research outcomes. The goal is a critical but reconstructive review of the related literature. Issues consider were mainly conceptual, while the perspective followed is a neutral representation. Target audience includes scholars and practitioners, and the coverage is representative (in the sense of the vom Brocke approach, as the whole corpus of literature is represented through a sample selection). The second step of vom Brocke framework is conceptualization of topic, which can be performed by using terminology, taxonomy or ontology. They suggest collecting the key terms in this step and defining them, which was covered in the second and third sections above. The third step is the search of the literature. A search of English language articles and books was executed in both the Scopus database and in Google Scholar using "open government data" (483) in conjunction with each of the following terms (the number inside the parentheses indicates hits in Scopus – double checked in Scholar): "literature review" (89), "research agenda" (98),, "taxonomy" (24), "overview" (84), "history" (32) or "research framework" (2). From the resulting pool those articles from the last fifteen years were kept which: a) presented research questions and orientations; (b) provided terminology or taxonomy; (c) dealt with historical overview; (d) included literature review; (e) discussed the regulatory environment. The original pool consisted of 127 items which was manually reduced to 10. In the literature analysis and synthesis step two experts processed the articles and structured them according to the aspects and dimensions detailed in Table 1.

5   Research Areas in the Open Data Literature

Scientific papers fitting the above conditions consider open data related research questions from the point of view of several research fields. During the last fifteen years or so there have been numerous attempts to review the history of the open data area and to sketch its potential future.

Arzberger et al. [1] were among the first to address the questions of open data reuse scientifically. Their study was supported by OECD and investigated the opportunities arising from opening up research results financed through public funds. It recommended five areas in connection to the accessibility of public sector data: technological, institutional and managerial, financial and budgetary, legal and policy, and cultural and behavioural. Harrison et al. [21] put the concept of open government into the centre of their research and claimed four areas as important: policies and practices, users (civil society and business), technology and innovation, as well as context (which may include legal, regulatory, and economic environments). Within these areas they proposed seven topics to be relevant in relation to open data: the process of identifying data of interest, setting priorities for data collection, collecting data, publishing data, utilizing data, value creation, and sustainability. Lindman et al. [29] focused their research efforts on understanding the services built on open data and their research proposal listed challenges grouped into seven categories: information, technologies,

Table 1. Open data research areas in relevant literature

Areas	Arzberger et al. [1]	Harrison et al. [21]	Lindman et al. [29]	Munk et al. [32]	Zuiderwijk et al. [52]	Davies and Perini [7]	Charalabidis et al. [4]	Kankanhalli et al. [23]	Styrin et al. [45]	Susha et al. [46]	Areas of this paper (Sect. 6)
History of open data						+					f
Politics				+	+	+					a
Policy, regulatory, and legal (environment)	+	+		+	+	+	+		+	+	a
Financial and budgetary	+										a
Organization, management (e.g. readiness, motivation)	+			+	+	+	+			+	b
Culture and behaviour (preparedness)	+	+				+				+	b
Practice and execution (operations)		+			+	+			+		b
Processes and activities								+			b
Participants and roles (stakeholders, collaboration)		+	+	+					+	+	b, e
Users, consumers (use)			+		+		+				e
Technology and infrastructure (standards)	+	+	+		+		+	+			c
Information			+							+	c
Data management									+	+	c
Products and services			+								d
Innovation					+						d
Impact, value, profit						+	+			+	e
Society					+						e
Theory				+	+			+			f
Domains, applications								+			d, e

processes and activities, products and services, participants, customers, and environment. While investigating open data related innovation Zuiderwijk et al. [52] – while reviewing relevant literature – proposed seven research perspectives: legislative, political, social, economical, institutional, operational, and technical. They identified three main research directions based on these perspectives: theory and development; rules, use, and innovation; as well as infrastructure and technologies. Davies and Perini [7] investigated the impact of open data initiatives and identified four areas on which to concentrate their efforts: the history of open data, evaluating readiness, implementation case studies, and impact analysis. Charalabidis et al. [4] reviewed several research programs (among them four of the above five) and constructed thirty-five topics under four umbrella areas (management and policies, infrastructures, use and value, and interoperability). According to Styrin et al. [45] there are three focal points within the open data domain, namely government policy and practice, data management, and handling stakeholders. One of the latest open data research program has been put together by Kankanhalli et al. [23] where they put forward three research directions: domain-specific studies, investigating the application of tools, and finally theoretical foundation and research methodologies used. The study recently published by Susha et al. [46] considered the collaboration between sectors which lead them to propose a taxonomy for the open data domain. This taxonomy introduces fourteen dimensions (within two groups): data sharing (in it type, content, administrative level, diversity of data providers, support, and the level of access) and data usage (target audience, user selection, policy problems, incentives, continuity of collaboration, outcome, collaboration among users, and purpose of use). In the context of *Europe* Munk et al. [32] reviewed research challenges of open data in Hungary within the framework of the European Union directives and phrased questions grouped into three areas: conceptual challenges and questions of interpretation; the complex relationships of national and union level regulations; and the analysis of application areas (this latter including questions of semantics and technology, among others).

The range of areas appearing in the above papers has been summarized in Table 1 (augmented with the coding of the areas proposed later in this paper).

6   Research Areas Proposed – and Research Questions Identified

Considering the research areas and directions discussed by the literature and the dominance of technical and organizational issues in research outcomes, we suggest a more holistic approach in research areas discussion, which include the following elements:

(a) *Context:* considers policy, regulations, legal background, and other environmental elements such as governance (including non-organizational public service issues);
(b) *Organizational aspects of the public sphere:* participants, roles, decisions, processes, and other organizational issues belong here – as well as specific case studies, country status reports and related analysis;
(c) *Technology and data:* this area covers platforms, standards, data typology, questions of data quality, frameworks of data quality assessment, availability (scope of data accessible), usability, and linked open data (including issues related to provenance);
(d) *Reuse:* this addresses the (direct) utilization of open data, questions of innovation, and value added services;
(e) *End users:* this not only includes users of open data, but covers the investigation of (actual) societal and economic impact;
(f) *Theory:* discussions over theoretical foundations, questions of terminology, modelling issues, and historical overview belong here – not to mention research agendas.

For each area above this research proposes a few nagging, important or timely questions – considering both the literature as introduced and discussed above as well as the analysis of open data in the EU.

Context: (1) What are the most important elements of the regulatory environment and how are they connected (e.g. what areas are being covered and do they overlap; how the Union/Commission level relates to national laws)? (2) What are the main IT applications identified by the regulatory environment as being key in supporting end-users?

Organizational aspects of the public sphere: (1) What approaches and solutions have been applied in EU countries for open government data management and what best practices exist? (2) What would be a suitable maturity model to compare these practices?

Technology and data: (1) What are the typical open data architectures, and what would be their advantages and disadvantages? (2) What are the relevant standards and how are they related? (3) How can end-user services and applications support the wider utilization of semantic technologies? (4) How can the quality of open government data be measured? (5) How would it be possible to identify the reasons of open data quality problems and how can those problems be resolved?

Reuse: (1) What reusability models exist and how can they be evaluated? (2) How added value may be captured and measured? (3) How can we interpret 'innovation' in this context?

End users: (1) What societal impacts may be identified? (2) How would it be possible to increase the efficiency and effectiveness of the results in order to provide better services using open data (this relates to the technological and organizational areas too)?

Theory: Open data related literature is conceptually rich, but these concepts have different definitions, interpretations in some cases and not always have been applied in the same manner. There are projects aimed at developing a common terminology, taxonomy or ontology of this domain (e.g. [39] or [44] and see also http://data.europa. eu/euodp/en/linked-data), but these projects are isolated and don't take into account national specialities. Related research questions: (1) What is the most suitable research methodology when developing terminology, taxonomy, or ontology for OGD? (2) How can we evaluate the existing terminologies, taxonomies and ontologies and what is their 'quality'? (3) What are the options to integrate the existing terminologies, taxonomies and ontologies? (4) How can we customize and utilize the existing terminologies, taxonomies and ontologies in local/national environments?

7   Summary and Further Research

The growth in the 'data industry' has been explosive over the last few years. Indeed, the majority of digital information stored today has been produced over the last few years. Accordingly, more and more research projects put data related challenges into the centre of their interest – and the question of open government data is no exception. The goal of the study presented here was to provide an overview of the OGD research areas based on most recent publications, structure these areas, and offer recommendations regarding potential future research directions. This paper reviewed the theoretical background of governmental open data and presented the most important interpretive frameworks and models of this field. Analysing key documents and articles related to open data in the European Union (at the Union level) highlighted the dominance of policy and technology related approaches, but also identified the trend towards an end-user perspective (mostly through an organizational focus). However, beyond these frames, there appears to be no holistic handling of this important field end-to-end. Therefore, this paper attempted to provide such a holistic research picture. As a key contribution, Sect. 5 has presented an overall set of criteria how the OGD field is segmented according to literature. This has led to a new, structured set of research areas, with specific research questions posed in each. These questions were formulated based on the relevant literature with the aim of enriching the area's potential to deliver new insights. Within the open data research areas identified, there is an increasing interest towards the questions of reuse and societal impact. Consequently, this study has expanded on the analysis of the open data field and reframed the related research efforts. Regarding future direction, our own interest is primarily focused on questions of OD theory, the application of the ecosystem approach and the challenges of improving the quality of open data.

References

1. Arzberger, P., et al.: An international framework to promote access to data. Science **303** (5665), 1777–1778 (2004)
2. Bates, J.: The strategic importance of information policy for the contemporary neoliberal state: the case of open government data in the United Kingdom. Gov. Inf. Q. **31**(3), 388–395 (2014)
3. Center for Open Data Enterprise: Open Data Impact Map Report (2016). http://opendataenterprise.org/map/reports/May2016Report.pdf. Accessed 3 Mar 2018
4. Charalabidis, Y., Alexopoulos, C., Loukis, E.: A taxonomy of open government data research areas and topics. J. Organ. Comput. Electron. Commer. **26**(1–2), 41–63 (2016)
5. Cooper, H., Hedges, L.V., Valentine, J.C. (eds.): The Handbook of Research Synthesis and Meta-Analysis. Russell Sage Foundation, New York (2009)
6. Davenport, T.H., Prusak, L.: Information Ecology: Mastering the Information and Knowledge Environment. Oxford University Press, New York (1997)
7. Davies, T., Perini, F.: Researching the emerging impacts of open data: revisiting the ODDC conceptual framework. J. Community Inform. **12**(2), 148–178 (2016)
8. Dawes, S.S., Helbig, N.: Information strategies for open government: challenges and prospects for deriving public value from government transparency. In: Wimmer, M.A., Chappelet, J.-L., Janssen, M., Scholl, H.J. (eds.) EGOV 2010. LNCS, vol. 6228, pp. 50–60. Springer, Heidelberg (2010). https://doi.org/10.1007/978-3-642-14799-9_5
9. Dekkers, M., Polman, F., te Velde, R., de Vries, M.: Measuring European public sector information resource. Final report of study on exploitation of public sector information - Benchmarking of EU framework conditions (2006)
10. DiNucci, D.: Fragmented future. Print **53**(4), 32 (1999)
11. De Kool, D., Van Wamelen, J.: Web 2.0: a new basis for e-government? In: Proceedings of the 3rd International IEEE Conference on ICTTA, pp. 1–7 (2008)
12. Fedorowicz, J., Gogan, J.L., Ray, A.W.: The ecology of interorganizational information sharing. J. Int. Inf. Manag. **13**(2), 73–85 (2004)
13. Groth, P.: Transparency and reliability in the data supply chain. IEEE Internet Comput. **17** (2), 69–71 (2013)
14. EC - European Commission: Public sector information: a key resource for Europe, COM (98)585, Brussels (1999). http://aei.pitt.edu/archive/00001168/. Accessed 4 June 2018
15. European Commission: A digital agenda for Europe, Communication to the European Parliament, the Council, the European Economic and Social Committee, and the Committee for the Regions, COM 245 final (2010)
16. European Commission: Digital Agenda: Turning government data into gold (2011). http://europa.eu/rapid/pressReleasesAction.do?reference=IP/11/1524&format=HTML&aged=0&language=EN&guiLanguage=en. Accessed 20 May 2015

17. European Commission: Open data: an engine for innovation, growth and transparent governance, Communication to the European Parliament, the Council, the European Economic and Social Committee, and the Committee for the Regions, COM 882 final (2011)
18. European Parliament and Council: Directive 2003/98/EC of the European Parliament and of the council of 17 November 2003 on the re-use of public sector information. OJ L, 345, 90 (2003)
19. European Parliament and Council: Directive 2013/37/EU of the European Parliament and of the council of 26 June 2013 amending Directive 2003/98/EC on the reuse of public sector information. OJ L, 175, 1 (2013)
20. Hansen, H.S., Hvingel, L., Schrøder, L.: Open government data – a key element in the digital society. In: kő, A., Leitner, C., Leitold, H., Prosser, A. (eds.) EGOVIS/EDEM 2013. LNCS, vol. 8061, pp. 167–180. Springer, Heidelberg (2013). https://doi.org/10.1007/978-3-642-40160-2_14
21. Harrison, T.M., Pardo, T.A., Cook, M.: Creating open government ecosystems: a research and development agenda. Future Internet 4(4), 900–928 (2012)
22. Janssen, K.: The influence of the PSI directive on open government data: an overview of recent developments. Gov. Inf. Q. 28(4), 446–456 (2011)
23. Kankanhalli, A., Zuiderwijk, A., Tayi, G.K.: Open innovation in the public sector: a research agenda. Gov. Inf. Q. 1(34), 84–89 (2017)
24. Kő, A., Leitner, C., Leitold, H., Prosser, A. (eds.): Technology-Enabled Innovation for Democracy, Government and Governance, vol. 8061. Springer, Heidelberg (2013). https://doi.org/10.1007/978-3-642-40160-2
25. Kő, A., Francesconi, E. (eds.): Electronic Government and the Information Systems Perspective, vol. 8650. Springer, Heidelberg (2014). https://doi.org/10.1007/978-3-319-10178-1
26. Kő, A., Francesconi, E.: Electronic Government and the Information Systems Perspective, vol. 9265. Springer, Heidelberg (2016). https://doi.org/10.1007/978-3-319-22389-6
27. Kő, A., Francesconi, E. (eds.): Electronic Government and the Information Systems Perspective, vol. 10441. Springer, Heidelberg (2017). https://doi.org/10.1007/978-3-319-64248-2
28. Li, P., Wu, T.Y., Li, X.M.: Constructing data supply chain based on layered PROV. J. Supercomput. 73(4), 1509–1531 (2017)
29. Lindman J., Rossi, M., Tuunainen, V.: Open data services research agenda. In: Proceedings of HICSS-46, pp. 1239–1246 (2013)
30. Martin, S., Turki, S., Renault, S.: Open data ecosystems. In: Kő, A., Francesconi, E. (eds.) EGOVIS 2017. LNCS, vol. 10441, pp. 49–63. Springer, Cham (2017). https://doi.org/10.1007/978-3-319-64248-2_5
31. Miller, H.G., Mork, P.: From data to decisions: a value chain for big data. IT Prof. 15(1), 57–59 (2013)
32. Munk, S., Fleiner, R., Micsik, A., Sikolya, Zs., Nyáry M.: Kapcsolt nyílt kormányzati adatok és kutatásuk keretei Magyarországon. Pro Publico Bono – Magyar Közigazgatás, vol. 4, pp. 144–169 (2014, in Hungarian)
33. Nardi, B.A., O'Day, V.: Information Ecologies – Using Technology with Heart, chapter 4, pp. 49–57. MIT Press, Cambridge, London (1999)
34. Obama, B.: (U.S. Executive Office): Open government directive (2009). http://www.whitehouse.gov/sites/default/files/omb/assets/memoranda_2010/m2010/m10-06.pdf. Accessed 7 Aug 2017
35. Open Knowledge Foundation: Open Knowledge Definition (2006). http://www.opendefinition.org/. Accessed 7 Sept 2017

36. Palmirani, M., Martoni, M., Girardi, D.: Open government data beyond transparency. In: Kő, A., Francesconi, E. (eds.) EGOVIS 2014. LNCS, vol. 8650, pp. 275–291. Springer, Cham (2014). https://doi.org/10.1007/978-3-319-10178-1_22

37. Parks, W.: The open government principle: applying the right to know under the constitution. George Wash. Law Rev. **26**(1), 1–22 (1957)

38. Parsons, M.A., et al.: A conceptual framework for managing very diverse data for complex, interdisciplinary science. J. Inf. Sci. **37**(6), 555–569 (2011)

39. Pattuelli, M.C., Provo, A., Thorsen, H.: Ontology building for linked open data: a pragmatic perspective. J. Libr. Metadata **15**(3), 265–294 (2015)

40. Pira International Ltd., University of East Anglia, and KnowledgeView Ltd.: Commercial exploitation of Europe's public sector information. Final report for the European Commission Directorate General for the Information Society (2000)

41. Porter, M.E.: Competitive Advantage: Creating and Sustaining Superior Performance. Simon and Schuster, New York (1985)

42. Sáez Martín, A., De Rosario, A.H., Del Carmen Caba, M.: An international analysis of the quality of open government data portals. Soc. Sci. Comput. Rev. **34**(3), 298–311 (2016)

43. Schmitz, P., et al.: Linked open data and e-Participation in the EU law-making process. In: Kő, A., Francesconi, E. (eds.) EGOVIS 2016. LNCS, vol. 9831, pp. 79–89. Springer, Cham (2016). https://doi.org/10.1007/978-3-319-44159-7_6

44. Southwick, S.B., Lampert, C.K., Southwick, R.: Preparing controlled vocabularies for linked data: benefits and challenges. J. Libr. Metadata **15**(3–4), 177–190 (2015)

45. Styrin, E., Luna-Reyes, L.F., Harrison, T.M.: Open data ecosystems: an international comparison. Transform. Gov.: People Process Policy **11**(1), 132–156 (2017)

46. Susha, I., Janssen, M., Verhulst, S.: Data collaboratives as a new frontier of cross-sector partnerships in the age of open data: taxonomy development. In: Proceedings of the 50th Hawaii International Conference on System Sciences, pp. 2691–2700 (2017)

47. van Loenen, B., Kulk, S., Ploeger, H.: Data protection legislation: a very hungry caterpillar: the case of mapping data in the European Union. Gov. Inf. Q. **33**(2), 338–345 (2016)

48. vom Brocke, J, Simons, A., Niehaves, B., Riemer, K., Plattfaut, R., Cleven, A.: Reconstructing the giant: on the importance of rigour in documenting the literature search process. In: Proceedings of ECIS 2009, Paper 161 (2009)

49. Wang, R.Y., Storey, V.C., Firth, C.P.: A framework for analysis of data quality research. IEEE Trans. Knowl. Data Eng. **7**(4), 623–640 (1995)

50. Wang, R.Y., Strong, D.M.: Beyond accuracy: what data quality means to data consumers. J. Manag. Inf. Syst. **12**(4), 5–33 (1996)

51. Ződi, Zs.: Elvek és valóság Európában: a PSI-irányelv érvényesülésének problémái. In: Sáry, P. (Szerk) Jogtörténeti és jogelméleti tanulmányok. Miskolc, Miskolci Egyetemi Kiadó, pp. 174–185 (2015 in Hungarian)

52. Zuiderwijk, A., Helbig, B., Gil-García, J.R., Janssen, M.: Innovation through open data - a review of the state-of-the-art and an emerging research agenda. J. Theor. Appl. Electron. Commer. **9**(2), 1–8 (2014)

Platforms of Ideas Management and Open Innovation: The Crowdstorm Approach Applied to Public University in Brazil

Karen Moreira Vilas Boas$^{(\boxtimes)}$(iD), Andre Luiz Zambalde(iD),
Paulo Henrique de Souza Bermejo(iD), Thiago Bellotti Furtado(iD),
Rodrigo de Freitas Santos(iD), and Andre Grützmann(iD)

Federal University of Lavras, Lavras, Minas Gerais, Brazil
karen_vilasboas@hotmail.com, zambaufla@gmail.com,
paulobermejo@next.unb.br, thiagobelloti@gmail.com,
rodrigotkd23@gmail.com, andre5@dcc.ufla.br

Abstract. In the current globalized scenario, open innovation applied to the public sector is becoming increasingly prominent. This model allows organizations to achieve greater breadth of ideas, which, coupled with internal practices, expand the field of solutions to problems in society. Therefore, glimpses the adoption and use of technological platforms for the management of ideas and open innovation, in order to promote greater relationship and collaboration between governments and citizens. In this context, considering the potential contributions of technological platforms and crowdstorm processes in promoting innovations and improvements in organizations, the present work tries to understand the processes of adoption, implantation and use of a technological platform of ideas management associated with crowdstorm processes, applied to a public university in Brazil. The main objective is to describe the project, here called "Open University: Innovative Solutions", involving all the processes related to the implantation and use of the PremioIdeia® Technology Platform associated with the crowdstorm approach in a Public University in Brazil. The numbers associated with the project and the themes challenges evidence that crowdstorming brought benefits to the university, such as a greater appreciation of collaborations, the commitment of participants and also a greater interaction among students, teachers and university management. Based on this, it is suggested that projects of this nature can be carried out in other public universities in order to meet a specific demand for academic and administrative improvements and, in this way, promote the growth and evolution of the country's public universities.

Keywords: Platforms · Ideas management · Crowdstorm · Public university

1 Introduction

In the current globalized scenario, open innovation applied to the public sector [1] is becoming increasingly prominent. There is interest of society and citizens to participate in the planning and development processes of governments as a way to deal with the crisis and the poor performance of public managers [2].

© Springer Nature Switzerland AG 2018
A. Kő and E. Francesconi (Eds.): EGOVIS 2018, LNCS 11032, pp. 205–217, 2018.
https://doi.org/10.1007/978-3-319-98349-3_16

Seeks out social participation through open innovation [3], in other words, the acquisition of information and external knowledge, based on collaborations from citizens, aiming at ensuring greater objectivity, legitimacy and support for propositions, government projects and actions [4].

According to [5], the open innovation model allows organizations to achieve greater breadth of ideas, which, coupled with internal practices, expand the field of solutions to problems in society.

Therefore, glimpse the adoption and use of technological platforms for the management of ideas and open innovation, in order to promote greater relationship and collaboration between governments and citizens [6].

Platforms, according to [7] refers to a new model of technological artifact to connect people, organizations and resources in an interactive ecosystem in which incredible amounts of value can be created and exchanged. These should incorporate specific technologies and techniques, such as cloud computing, social networking, gamification, co-creation, coopetition, and the do-it-yourself approach.

In the public sector, one of the purposes of the platforms is to strengthen the relationship between citizens and managers, fostering the creation of value for society. When the relationship and collaboration of a relatively large number of representatives of a particular population (citizens) are sought, the *crowdstorm* process is characterized [8].

In this context, considering the potential contributions of technological platforms and crowdstorm processes in promoting innovations and improvements in organizations, it is very clear the importance of these when applied to the public sector, with the purpose to prospect innovations associated with citizen participation.

Therefore, for the present work, the question that is presented concerns the understanding of the processes of adoption, implantation and use of a technological platform of ideas management associated with crowdstorm processes, applied to a public university in Brazil.

The main objective is to describe the project, here called "Open University: Innovative Solutions", involving all the processes related to the implantation and use of the PremioIdeia® Technology Platform associated with the crowdstorm approach in a Public University in Brazil.

The article was organized as follows: in addition to this introduction, the next section presents a literature review on technology platforms, open innovation in the public sector and the crowdstorm; in the third section the methodology is presented, followed by the results and discussion in Sect. 4. Finally, in Sect. 5 we have the conclusion of the study and suggestions for future work.

2   Theoretical Background

2.1   Technological Platforms

According to [7], platforms correspond to a new technological artifact that uses technology to connect people, organizations, and resources in an interactive ecosystem in which incredible amounts of value can be created and exchanged. These typically incorporate technologies and techniques such as cloud computing, social networking, gammatization, co-creation, coopetition, and the "do it yourself" approach [7, 9].

Cloud computing refers to the use of the memory capacity, processing and computation of shared and interconnected computers and servers through the Internet. Organizations do not need to invest heavily in infrastructure. The opportunity for co-creation, that is, clients, collaborators, partners, citizens and guests, participates in processes such as generation of ideas and products, collaboration and sharing data and information [10–12].

The social networking approach allows you to enjoy, comment and share ideas. These activities can generate points for users participating in a platform and be associated with gamification [13, 14].

A dispute that can occur in a chain of business and even among departments within the same organization, grounding the coopetition, that is, the cooperation allied to the competition [15, 16].

Finally, platform technology can be installed and configured by users or organizations themselves. It's the concept of "it youself - DIY" [17].

Each platform works differently, attracts different types of users and creates different forms of relationship and value. Examples of platforms are: Amazon, Linkedin, Uber and Udemy. Specifically, in the context of the management of ideas and innovation, for example: PremioIdeia; Vocoli and Brighteo.

While in the private sector the use of technological platforms focused on management of ideas and innovation is usually centered on the development of new products or on the improvement and innovation of processes and services. In the public sector these platforms are associated with the terms "open innovation" [18] and "social participation" [19], that is, citizen participation is sought in solving problems and generating value for the society [20, 21].

The fact is that the use of platforms for generating ideas and innovation in the public sector may have a myriad of positive benefits, including improving awareness of social problems, more effective practices based on the knowledge of citizens and increasing trust between government and citizens [22].

2.2 Open Innovation and Public Sector

The organizations recognize that innovation is one of the most important paths to success, with which they can increase their performance and promote their survival in competitive environments [23, 24].

Specifically, in the public sector, innovation focuses on improving services and adding value in terms of benefits to society [3], and can be leveraged through open innovation.

The innovation model was presented by [18]. According to the second author, the beginning concept is based on the idea of an organization that can not innovate in an isolated way since they depend of many partnerships to get ideas and resources. Open innovation can be considered as a new approach to improvement, characterized by the opening of the frontiers of organizations, providing the establishment of cooperation and sharing of technologies and knowledge with partners, research institutions and universities.

In the public sector, the practice of opening up the innovation process involving citizens, for example, can be characterized as social participation and includes, besides the advantages of the concept of open innovation itself, the possibility of directly addressing the real needs of citizens, promoting the alignment of people's interests with the government [25].

In social participation, the objective is to obtain information and external knowledge, based on collaborations from citizens aimed at guaranteeing greater legitimacy and better support for government actions [4].

According to [25], social participation increases the flexibility of formulated policies, directing government efforts to the real needs of society. In addition, the inclusion of more individuals in decision-making processes opens up a wider range of perspectives on the issues discussed, providing opportunities for innovative solutions [18].

Through technological platforms for generating ideas and innovation, citizens can collaborate in solving problems related to public lighting, traffic, road infrastructure, building defects, breaches, and others [6].

Examples of technological platforms of innovation associated with crowstorming [8] are those used by governments such as Singapore and the United States [26], or by public institutions such as the Military Police of Minas Gerais - Brazil [12, 27] and the Ministry of Education of Brazil [28].

One of the main goals is to interact with society in the search for solutions and value creation. It introduces the idea of co-government, one of the most complex challenges in the field of public management.

Therefore, the questions range from who and how to participate or collaborate to the legitimacy of the organs as an effective and continuous expression of society. Considering that this debate is broad and controversial, it is argued that whatever the channels or forms, the criteria require a widely discussed and consensual policy [3].

It is precisely in this context that the technique or process of crowdstorming approach [8] will be explained in the next section.

2.3   Crowdstorming

In today's context of globalization, where innovation is related to an increasingly connected world, open innovation engages, connects, and integrates various strategies [29].

The application of open innovation with the purpose of generating innovative ideas characterizes, as already commented, a process of crowdstorm, term determined by [8] based on the observation of challenges of ideas realized by diverse organizations.

There is in the crowdstorm an open and mass collaborative approach, somewhat different from crowdsourcing, considered a way to leverage the collective intelligence of communities, particularly online, to meet business objectives.

Created by [30], the term crowdsourcing was based on the word outsourcing, meaning outsourcing - a formal commitment to problem solving or service delivery. Therefore, the first (crowdstorm) differs from the second (crowdsourcing) because there is no formal requirement associated with citizen commitment, but rather a collaboration for the generation of ideas, solutions and value. Therefore, crowdstorming is a "brainstorming" and discussions around the same problem [8, 29].

In Fig. 1, we have the illustration of the life cycle of the crowdstorm, according to [8].

The Crowdstorming requires an excellent management. It has at its heart the PDCA method - Plan, Do, Check and Act [31, 32].

Fundamentally, this method allows: the participation of all people in proposing solutions to the proposed challenges; the standardization of language and the improvement of communication; the understanding and collaboration of each in the effort for innovation; continuous learning and improvement; the selection and creation of innovation project portfolios, the improvement in the absorption of the best practices of collaboration, idea generation and innovation [31–33].

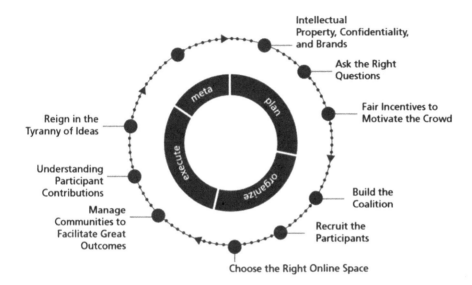

Fig. 1. Life cicle of the crowdstorm [8].

3 Methodology

This article is classified as applied, descriptive and qualitative. It is based on bibliographic review and documentary research.

The applied approach concerns a current and technological research based on the use and analysis of a platform for the management of ideas and innovation (Premioideia®) adopted by a Brazilian public university.

The nature is descriptive, as it reports the characteristics of the application of the artifact (platform) to the organization under study (University), demonstrating its results [34].

First, a normative bibliographical review involving the terms management of ideas and innovation, open innovation in the public sector, social participation and crowdstorm was carried out.

In the sequence a documentary research was carried out, aiming at raising and describing the scenario of application of the technological platform of ideas and innovation management to the University.

Documentary research consists of the analysis of documents (written materials, collected data and iconographic elements) that have not been studied analytically, or that can be reexamined by another perspective, in order to obtain complementary interpretations [35], to produce new knowledge and to elaborate new ways of understanding a phenomenon [36]. Documents can be primary - produced by people who have experienced the event or secondary - produced by people not directly involved with the event, and who have already been somehow analyzed, for example, research reports.

In the present work the documents are characterized as primary, being data-based (themes-challenges, ideas, tastings and comments) directly collected by the Technological Platform for the management of ideas and innovation (Premioideia®) based on themes-challenges of proposed by the managers of the Public University to the university community (students, teachers, employees and guests).

The campaign to apply the challenges from the Premioideia® platform to the University community was called "Open University: Innovative Solutions". It was composed of 11 themes-challenges that were active for a period of 6 months (06/2015 to 11/2015).

The Premioideia® is a platform for managing ideas and innovation where, from an initial planning of the organization, the themes-challenges, scores and awards are defined, so that the organization citizens (students, employees, teachers and guests) can respond to these themes-challenges in order· to solve them. The answers of these collaborators (the ideas) can be liked, commented and shared by the participating colleagues. With this, they are being punctuated in a gamification process. In the end, those with the highest number of points are ranked, reaching the winner, who receives the prize. In addition, the University creates, through internal and particular selection of ideas, a portfolio of innovative projects based on this process of social participation and collaboration.

The aim of this work is to present a descriptive and step-by-step description of all the stages and results of the application of the Premioideia® Platform within the "Open University: Innovative Solutions" Campaign, considering all the themes-challenges and innovation, entrepreneurship, internationalization, scientific publications, quality of services provided, quality of undergraduate education, avoidance of undergraduate courses, sustainability, transparency and auditing, and university and society relations.

4   Results and Discussion

The "Open University: Innovative Solutions" project was promoted by a Brazilian Federal University from 05/2015 to 11/2015, in partnership with the Ideideia® Management and Innovation Platform. In this section will be described the rules, actors, artifacts, steps and results obtained in the realization of the project.

4.1   Rules, Actors and Artifacts

The challenge "Open University: innovative solutions" was carried out in the contest modality, with 11 themes-challenges proposed to the University community presented at Table 1.

Table 1. Challenge themes of the project "Open University: innovative solutions".

Challenge theme	Question
Internal communication	What is your idea for improving communication between sectors, departments and people at the University?
Organizational structure	What is your idea to improve the organizational structure of the University?
Evasion in undergraduate courses	What is yours ideas to reduce evasion in undergraduate courses at the University?
Innovation and Entrepreneurship	What is your idea to boost the development of innovations and entrepreneurship at the University?
Internationalization	What is your idea to create new internationalization opportunities for the University and to improve existing ones?
Scientific publications	What is your idea to boost the actions and results of the University Publishing Company?
Quality of services	What is your idea to improve the performance evaluation of technical-administrative staff and teachers in order to ensure quality work?
Quality of undergraduate education	What is your idea to improve undergraduate teaching at the University?
Sustainability	What is your idea to advance the promotion of sustainability at the University, reducing costs without compromising quality and growth?
Transparency and audit	What is your idea to improve internal control processes in the University?
University and society	What is your idea to enhance the intensification of the interaction between university and society?

The participants were teachers, students, employees and collaborators who registered on the project web page. Thus, they could present ideas as well as evaluate (enjoy or dislike) and enhance (comment) ideas of others, accumulating points. The score was specified in 5 points for idea creation, 1 point for another idea likes and 1 point for comment. On the other hand, when a participant enjoys the ideas of another participant, the participant receives 15 points (one time). In the situation of the participant "not liking" an idea, no points are computed.

In the end, the presented ideas, regardless of their classification or awards, may be developed or not by the University. In this process there is a virtual social network for generating ideas and open innovation.

On the other hand, were also registered by the University the Pro-rectors, sectors, departments and student entities. When entering the system the participant informs which Pro-rectory, sector, department or entity is linked. This sector or department also receives points and wins prizes. Here we have a process of co-optation, that is, innovation considering a "healthy competition" between sectors of an educational organization.

In the sequence, the web page of the project "Open University: Innovative Solutions" as the front-end and the Premioidea® Platform as back-end (see Fig. 2) are used as artifacts.

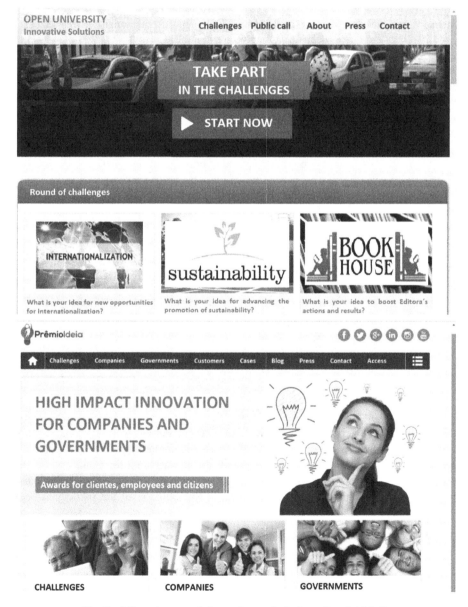

Fig. 2. Life web page of the project and platform Premioideia®.

Today's technologies, necessary for a broad and quality project, associated with ideas management and innovation are present in the context of the challenges and the platform, such as: cloud computing, social networks, gamification, co-creation.

The project was also placed on mobile devices (application). So, instead of entering the challenge site, it was possible to access it directly from the phone or tablet, in just one click, through an internet connection.

4.2 Planning and Execution

The project "Open University: Innovative Solutions" has an innovative collective space for proposing solutions that contribute to decisions anchored in the teaching, research and extension tripod. The fact is that when the management model of a university seeks collaboration and commitment to results, ideas can, for example, guide strategies and institutional plans.

In the context of planning execution, the project was divided into phases, these being associated with the crowdstorm approach. The main phases were as follows:

Phase 1: Definition of Objectives.

Identify the needs of the University and establish the objectives of the project. Eleven themes were defined and for each of these themes a question was asked to explore innovative ideas.

Phase 2: Beginning of the Challenge.

The project was organized as a competition. Through a public call (n° 01/2015) made by the rectory on 05/27/2015, the 11 challenges were launched.

Phase 3: Qualitative Evaluation.

All the ideas posted underwent an administrative evaluation, so that the viability of implementation is verified. On 06/18/2015, a technical committee to accompany the project met to evaluate the status of the tender and start the technical evaluation phase of the proposals. Each Pro-Rector or sector involved in the challenges evaluated the ideas suggested following a set of criteria such as applicability, feasibility and cost. Each idea posted gained an indication of stars, in its status, which signaled the relevance of its application and also the benefits to the University. The five-star ideals represented high-impact, high-input suggestions.

Phase 4: End of the challenge.

The challenges were closed on 07/31/2015. The three participants who until then were able to mobilize more support for their ideas (obtaining more tastings and comments) were the winners.

Phase 5: Provisional Disclosure of Results.

The provisional result of the challenges was announced on the platform, University page and on social networks on 08/12/2015.

Phase 6: Period of appeal.

According to the edict, the challenge provided a deadline of two days for the presentation of an appeal, which took place from August 13 to August 20,

Phase 7: Disclosure of Final Results.

Finally, on 21/08/2015, the final result of the challenges was announced. As individual participants, three university students were considered. Among the Pro-Rectorates,

Departments and Sectors, the Law Department was the winner; and among the student organizations, the University's Junior Informatics Company was the winner.
Phase 8: Awards.

The winners' official awards were made in a ceremony attended by the university community and open to other interested parties.

4.3   Synthesis of Results

The challenge was then opened for participation on 05/27/2015 and ended on 07/31/2015, totaling approximately 2 months of participation. The total involvement of 2,546 people was registered, with 4,409 ideas posted, 352,187 tanned and 155,858 comments. The mobilization involved more than 90% of the departments, sectors and pro-rectors, in addition to 105 student organizations.

The theme that attracted the greatest number of ideas was "Sustainability", with 584 suggestions (13.2%), followed by the theme "Quality of Undergraduate Education", with 570 suggestions (12.9%) and "Internationalization" with 508 ideas (11.5%).

The other themes, as shown in Fig. 3, reached the following scores: University and Society: 492 ideas - 11.2% of the total; Evasion in undergraduate courses: 449 - 10.2%; Scientific Publications: 412 - 9.3%; Innovation and Entrepreneurship: 394 - 8.9%; Internal Communication: 326 - 7.4%; Quality of Services Provided: 235 - 5.3%; Organizational Structure: 220 - 5%; and Transparency and Audit: 219 - 5%.

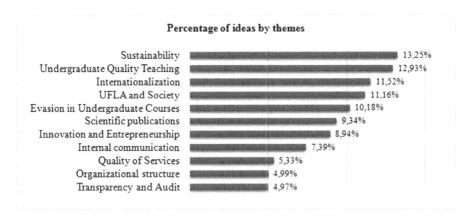

Fig. 3. Percentage of ideas by themes-challenges - Open University Project.

In the evaluation of the Rector of the University the public consultation is an important tool of shared management, mainly for giving opportunity to all the people to express their ideas and to contribute to the improvement of the University. The Rector's main statement was as follows: "I am sure that many ideas will be implemented and management will be further improved." The result, according to the leader, represents the collective effort of students, teachers and administrative technicians, committed to the ideals of the university. "The objective of offering another collective space for proposing solutions that contribute to shared management and also promote greater integration has been achieved."

It is important to emphasize that the presented ideas, regardless of their classification or awards in the project, can be implemented or not by the University, after analyzing their legal, financial and operational feasibility, among others.

5   Conclusions

The present described the planning and execution of a project involving technological platform of ideas management, social participation, open innovation and crowdstorm. A contribution that applies to theory and practice of innovation in the public sector, more specifically in public universities.

In the context of the adoption and use of technologies associated to innovation and social participation, emphasis should be placed on the presence of technologies and techniques such as cloud computing, social networks, gamification, co-creation, coopetition, crowndstorm and "do it youself".

As for the numbers, associated with the project and the themes challenges, they are promising. The involvement of 2,546 people was registered. There were 4,409 posted ideas, 352,187 tanned and 155,858 comments. A mobilization that involves more than 90% of the Pro-rectors, departments, sectors and student representations. The topics with the greatest number of ideas were "Sustainability", "Quality of Undergraduate Education" and "Internationalization".

Through the documented testimonies shortly after the completion of the project "Open University: innovative solutions" it was possible to observe that this one fulfilled its role. The number of ideas generated by the challenge was significant and the academic community worked hard to collaborate and participate, demonstrating their interest in actions that contribute to improvements in the University.

It was not the objective of the work to verify the content of the ideas and if these were effectively implemented. However, this may constitute a future study. The fact is that crowdstorming brought benefits to the university, such as a greater appreciation of collaborations, the commitment of participants and also a greater interaction among students, teachers and university management.

Based on the observed benefits, it is suggested that projects of this nature can be carried out in other public universities in order to meet a specific demand for academic and administrative improvements and, in this way, promote the growth and evolution of the country's public universities.

From the point of view of the empirical contribution, digital crowdingstorming platforms involving citizen participation are expected to become common practices in other institutions as a way of generating innovative ideas and solutions, thus stimulating innovation.

Acknowledgement. The authors would like to thanks the National Council for Scientific and Technological Development (CNPq - Brazil) - Process 402789/2015-6 and the Minas Gerais State Foundation for Research Development (FAPEMIG - MG - Brazil) for the financial support.

References

1. Brabham, D.C.: Motivations for participation in a crowdsourcing application to improve public engagement in transit planning. J. Appl. Commun. Res. **40**(3), 307–328 (2012)
2. Murray, R., Caulier-Grice, J., Mulgan, G.: The Open Book of Social Innovation, p. 2. National Endowment for Science, Technology and the Art, London (2010)
3. Lee, S.M., Hwang, T., Choi, D.: Open innovation in the public sector of leading countries. Manag. Decis. **50**(1), 147–162 (2012)
4. Ferrarezi, E., Oliveira, C.G.: Reflexões sobre a emergência da participação social na agenda das políticas públicas: desafios à forma de organização burocrática do Estado (2012)
5. Vanhaverbeke, W., Van de Vrande, V., Chesbrough, H.: Understanding the advantages of open innovation practices in corporate venturing in terms of real options. Creat. Innov. Manag. **17**(4), 251–258 (2008)
6. Hilgers, D., Ihl, C.: Citizensourcing: applying the concept of open innovation to the public sector. Int. J. Public Particip. **4**(1), 67–88 (2010)
7. Parker, G.G., Van Alstyne, M.W., Choudary, S.P.: Platform Revolution: How Networked Markets Are Transforming the Economyand How to Make Them Work for You. WW Norton & Company, New York (2016)
8. Abrahamson, S., Ryder, P., Unterberg, B.: Crowdstorm: The Future of Innovation, Ideas, and Problem Solving. Wiley, Hoboken (2013)
9. Yang, J., Adamic, L.A., Ackerman, M.S.: Crowdsourcing and knowledge sharing: strategic user behavior on Taskcn. In: Proceedings of the 9th ACM Conference on Electronic Commerce, pp. 246–255. ACM, July 2008
10. Glott, R., Husmann, E., Sadeghi, A.-R., Schunter, M.: Trustworthy clouds underpinning the future internet. In: Domingue, J., et al. (eds.) FIA 2011. LNCS, vol. 6656, pp. 209–221. Springer, Heidelberg (2011). https://doi.org/10.1007/978-3-642-20898-0_15
11. Hofstetter, R., Aryobsei, S., Herrmann, A.: Should you really produce what consumers like online? Empirical evidence for reciprocal voting in open innovation contests. J. Prod. Innov. Manag. **35**(2), 209–229 (2018)
12. dos Santos, A.C., Zambalde, A.L., Veroneze, R.B., Botelho, G.A., de Souza Bermejo, P.H.: Open innovation and social participation: a case study in public security in Brazil. In: Kő, A., Francesconi, E. (eds.) EGOVIS 2015. LNCS, vol. 9265, pp. 163–176. Springer, Cham (2015). https://doi.org/10.1007/978-3-319-22389-6_12
13. Paliokas, I., Tzallas, A., Katertsidis, N., Votis, K., Tzovaras, D.: Gamification in social networking: a platform for people living with dementia and their caregivers. In: 2017 IEEE 17th International Conference on Bioinformatics and Bioengineering (BIBE), pp. 574–579. IEEE, October 2017
14. Baumöl, U., Hollebeek, L., Jung, R.: Dynamics of customer interaction on social media platforms. Electron. Mark. **26**(3), 199–202 (2016)
15. Li, Z.: Disintermediation and co-opetition in platform ecosystems and modern value chains. Doctoral dissertation (2015)
16. Mantena, R., Saha, R.L.: Co-opetition between differentiated platforms in two-sided markets. J. Manag. Inf. Syst. **29**(2), 109–140 (2012)
17. Snake-Beings, E.: The DiY ['Do it yourself'] Ethos: a participatory culture of material engagement. Doctoral dissertation, University of Waikato (2016)
18. Chesbrough, H.W.: Open Innovation: The New Imperative for Creating and Profiting from Technology. Harvard Business Press, Boston (2006)

19. Alayed, F.: Citizen adoption of technology mediated social participation systems. In: Proceedings of the 18th International Conference on Supporting Group Work, pp. 250–251. ACM, November 2014
20. Verma, R.K., Kumar, S., Ilavarasan, P.V.: Government portals, social media platforms and citizen engagement in India: some insights. Procedia Comput. Sci. **122**, 842–849 (2017)
21. Martins, T.C.M., de Souza Bermejo, P.H., de Souza, W.V.B.: Open innovation for citizen coproduction. In: Kő, A., Francesconi, E. (eds.) EGOVIS 2015. LNCS, vol. 9265, pp. 177–188. Springer, Cham (2015). https://doi.org/10.1007/978-3-319-22389-6_13
22. Gaventa, J., Barrett, G.: So what difference does it make? Mapping the outcomes of citizen engagement. IDS Work. Papers **2010**(347), 01–72 (2010)
23. Bigliardi, B., Galati, F.: Innovation trends in the food industry: the case of functional foods. Trends Food Sci. Technol. **31**(2), 118–129 (2013)
24. Inauen, M., Schenker-Wicki, A.: The impact of outside-in open innovation on innovation performance. Eur. J. Innov. Manag. **14**(4), 496–520 (2011)
25. Irvin, R.A., Stansbury, J.: Citizen participation in decision making: is it worth the effort? Public Adm. Rev. **64**(1), 55–65 (2004)
26. Linders, D.: From e-government to we-government: defining a typology for citizen coproduction in the age of social media. Gov. Inf. Q. **29**(4), 446–454 (2012)
27. Martins, T.C.M., Bermejo, P.H.S.: Open social innovation based on idea crowdsourcing. In: 11th European, Mediterranean & Middle Eastern Conference on Information Systems, Big Data in the Era of Cloud Computing and Social Media, Doha, Qatar (2014)
28. de Souza, W.V.B., et al.: Using crowdstorm to prospect innovations in federal institutions of education in Brazil to reduce its consumption of electric energy. In: 2016 49th Hawaii International Conference on System Sciences (HICSS), pp. 2819–2828. IEEE, January 2016
29. Hopkins, R.: What is crowdsourcing? In: A Guide to Open Innovation and Crowdsourcing, vol. 1, pp. 5–14, Kogan Page, London (2011)
30. Howe, J.: The rise of crowdsourcing. Wired Mag. **14**(6), 1–4 (2006)
31. Sobek II, D.K., Smalley, A.: Understanding A3 Thinking: A Critical Component of Toyota's PDCA Management System. CRC Press, Boca Raton (2011)
32. Falconi, V.: O verdadeiro poder. INDG Tecnologia e Serviços Ltda, Nova Lima (2009)
33. van Loon, Y.: http://ywanvanloon.com/lets-crowdstorm-by-elon-musks-hyperloop-inspired-by-justdirk/. Accessed 10 Feb 2018
34. Vergara, S.C.: Projetos e relatórios de pesquisa em administração. 16. Atlas, São Paulo (2016)
35. Godoy, A.S.: Pesquisa qualitativa: tipos fundamentais. Revista de Administração de empresas **35**(3), 20–29 (1995)
36. Sá-Silva, J.R., de Almeida, C.D., Guindani, J.F.: Pesquisa documental: pistas teóricas e metodológicas. Revista brasileira de história & ciências sociais, **1**(1) (2009)

E-government Cases - Data and Knowledge Management

Emerging Data Governance Issues in Big Data Applications for Food Safety

Salvatore Sapienza and Monica Palmirani[(✉)]

University of Bologna, CIRSFID, Via Galliera 3, 40121 Bologna, Italy
{salvatore.sapienza2,monica.palmirani}@unibo.it

Abstract. The food industry and food safety authorities show an increasing interest in Big Data applications. On the one hand, Big Data strengthens data storage, data mashup, and methodology of risk assessment; on the other hand, the presence of risks and challenges linked to Big Data demands for future-proof solutions. While business practices and academic literature have already identified ways of exploiting the value of large collections of data, emerging governance issues including data sovereignty, competition, privacy and data donations, call for further analysis.

Keywords: Big Data · Food safety · Data governance · Emerging issues
Risk assessment

1 Introduction

As with other research areas, current trends in the agri-food domain highlight a growing interest in the collection and the use of Big Data. As the FAO's Sustainable Development Goals point out, the "Data Revolution" is reshaping the way in which policymakers interact with the agri-food industry, biotechnology research, and food security when implementing policies towards sustainability [1]. Among the areas positively affected by Big Data, food safety plays a crucial role in achieving FAO's commitment to promote the human right to qualitatively adequate food [2]. Therefore, Big Data is likely to represent a gateway to further develop a data-driven approach to food safety risk assessments [3].

This study departs from two premises. First, while the positive effects of Big Data can be achieved only through the collaboration of multiple stakeholders involved in the food safety domain, conflicting interests pertaining to the protection of Big Data as a valuable commercial asset hinder the finding of shared data governance. Secondly, although food consumption data is needed to understand how individuals and food interact, this information may reveal health status, thus requiring due attention to the safeguard of fundamental rights, including appropriate security measures. In this paper, three intertwined lines for further research are identified: first, the one related to the sovereignty and the exchange of information between different jurisdictions; secondly, the area related to the interferences between data ownership and the exchange of information performed by the corporations involved in this domain; lastly, the sphere connected to the cooperation between individuals and food safety assessors.

© Springer Nature Switzerland AG 2018
A. Kő and E. Francesconi (Eds.): EGOVIS 2018, LNCS 11032, pp. 221–230, 2018.
https://doi.org/10.1007/978-3-319-98349-3_17

Following this introduction, Sect. 2 describes the research question and the research methodology. While Sect. 3 summarises modern uses of large datasets in food safety, Sect. 4 introduces cutting-edge technologies whose adoption by safety assessors is reasonably foreseeable. Section 5 illustrates the data governance issues that emerge from the discussion among food safety authorities, their stakeholders, and other interested parties. Lastly, final considerations summarise the findings of the previous sections and make recommendations for future work.

2   Research Questions and Methodology

Several clashing interests emerge from the use of Big Data for food safety purposes, thus originating specific issues whose impact has not been fully analysed. While the outcome of some technologies—including genetically modified organisms and nanotechnology—is currently under the scrutiny of prominent scholars, this short study raises open questions and possible lines of research to identify emerging and undetected data governance issues.

Big Data applications currently employed by risk assessors are grounded on the practices developed within corporations and academia. Therefore, this paper has been drafted following a technology-driven approach that illustrates the connections between food safety authorities, the food industry, other industry sectors, and the academic community. This research methodology has been developed by selecting two kinds of innovative practices.

On the one hand, the selected Big Data applications rely upon or produce large and structured quantities of data gathered from multiple sources. In this domain, heterogeneous datasets are vital to reduce the presence of gaps in data and bias in data model design and to achieve a higher level of precision in the risk assessment. On the other hand, Big Data applications under scrutiny require the joint efforts of a plurality of actors to exploit the potential of this data. Since data originates from multiple sources, a certain degree of collaboration is needed to appreciate the benefits of Big Data. Conversely, those applications which neither compute large quantities of data, nor involve multiple sources and entities, are out of the scope of this paper.

The need of future-proof solutions raises the urgency of discussing both traditional Big Data practices already employed by risk assessors and possible future applications whose adoption is likely to occur in the near future. Accordingly, the following sections categorise the selected Big Data techniques in line with this approach.

3   Current Big Data Applications for Food Safety

Current research has already identified several ongoing applications of Big Data in food safety [4]. For the purposes of this paper, "Big Data" will refer to the use of collections of data characterised by Volume, Velocity, Variety and Veracity used to extract Value[1].

---

[1] http://www.ibmbigdatahub.com/infographic/four-vs-big-data.

This paper adopts an economically-neutral definition of Value. In other words, it should be understood as any advantage in the food safety risk assessment that can result in an increase in speed, precision, forecast reliability, and cost.

3.1 Data Analytics in the Food Safety Domain

Despite its business nature, data warehousing is a consolidated trend in the context of food safety. World Health Organisation's (WHO) "FOSCOLLAB" project enables users to access food safety data and information from multiple existing sources: Joint FAO/WHO Expert Committee on Food Additives (JECFA), Joint FAO/WHO Meeting on Pesticide Residues (JMPR), and WHO Collaborating Centres Database. FOSCOLLAB and its related databases are easily accessible through a digital platform. The European Food Safety Authority (EFSA) Data Warehouse has been active since 2015. Data related to zoonotic diseases, antimicrobial resistance, foodborne outbreaks, pesticide residues, chemical contaminants, and chemical hazards are accessible through an online access point. The platform has been developed to strengthen scientific progress by granting access both to the general public and food safety professionals, including EFSA's stakeholders and researchers. Similarly, the EFSA Comprehensive European Food Consumption Database collects data pertaining to food consumption in the EU. As regards the United States, the Food & Drug Administration (FDA) has opted for a different approach by making the data warehouse available to the public through its APIs. Since this accessibility method can be cumbersome to the general public, FDA web pages contain links to third parties' platforms. However, the number of apps pertaining to food safety seems quite limited.

This relevance of this large amount of information available for analysis is illustrated by Memorandum of Understanding signed by the EU European Chemicals Agency (ECHA) and EFSA. It reinforces their commitment of "[e]xploring the application of modern technology (e.g. artificial intelligence, machine learning and data mining)" which rely upon Big Data to spread their positive effects [4]. As the Open Data Institute has pointed out, data gaps and bias in the design of data analysis models constitute potential concerns when the aforementioned techniques are employed [5].

3.2 GIS-Based Approaches to Food Outbreaks Analysis

Geographic Information Systems' (GISs) practical implementations in food safety have been widely researched. The combination of geospatial data and analyses conducted on plants, foods, and feed has proven to be helpful in tracing the origins and preventing the spread of diseases.

A sample of the studies conducted using GIS-based approaches confirms their potential applications in identifying vulnerabilities in the food supply chain [6], forecasting contamination of crops on a regional basis [7], and identifying correlations between *Escherichia coli O157:H7* and vegetable production [8]. Food safety authorities are willing to adopt GIS-based assessment methodology. The GIS-iRisk project results from the joint efforts of the FDA and NASA. It correlates GISs with predictive risk-assessment models to forecast when, where, and under what conditions risks for human health may emerge from crop contamination. Similarly, EFSA's

PERSAM software has been developed to predict the environmental concentration of pesticides in soil, in accordance with the guidelines adopted by the experts of the EFSA Pesticide Panel [9].

3.3   Whole Genome Sequencing for Foodborne Pathogens Identification

Whole Genome Sequencing (WGS) is rapidly reshaping the process of identifying and characterising foodborne pathogens. While previous techniques used to analyse only the biological components of the molecule under scrutiny, WGS is a universal methodology that can be appropriate for monitoring human/animal health and food [10].

Food safety authorities in Western countries are prioritising the adoption of WGS. The UK Food Safety Authority Chief Scientific Adviser's Science Report describes a successful case of WGS application in countering the Salmonella outbreak in 2014. WGS methodology corroborated the previous research by confirming the genetic link between UK cases and German eggs, thus identifying the source of the outbreak [11]. The US FDA is leading this paradigm shift by implementing GenomeTrakr Network, a decentralised network of laboratories whose main aim is to identify pathogens through WGS. GenomeTrakr Network consists of sixty-three private and public facilities, placed inside and outside the US. In June 2014, EFSA adopted a positive resolution on the immediate implementation of the WGS of foodborne pathogens for the protection of public health. EFSA stressed that, EU private and public entities involved in healthcare should strengthen their collaboration with international counterparts to harmonise the use of WGS [12].

4   Future Big Data Applications for Food Safety

This section outlines innovative ideas for future applications of Big Data within the food safety domain. Even though some proofs-of-concept have already been published, their full deployment requires time and effort and should thus be considered a long-term goal. These examples contribute to identifying possible emerging issues in data governance, therefore promoting the adoption of future-proof solutions.

4.1   Automated Text Analysis of Scientific Opinions

Existing literature demonstrates the advantages of analysing textual digital information using both linguistic and statistical methodologies for food safety purposes. Both news related to foodborne outbreaks and academic research on pathogens are the most observed sources of information. On the one hand, IBM FoodSIS adopts a machine learning algorithm based on a supervised ranking system that retrieves and classifies food incidents news on behalf of the National Environment Agency of Singapore [13]. On the other hand, text mining may be used in the identification of emerging chemical and biological risks from previous studies published in academic journals [14]. To the author's knowledge, the potential of automated text analysis in risk assessment documents published by food safety authorities - including the open-access and free of charge EFSA Journal, i.e. the repository of EFSA's scientific opinions - is largely undiscovered. For instance, potential outcomes may consist of predicting trends in the use of chemical substance by analysing their recurrence in EFSA's opinion, identifying argumentative patterns in these documents, and simplifying scientific concepts to improve readability for the general public.

4.2 IoT, Smartphones and Social Media for Real-Time Food Consumption and Food Alerts

The number of food-related features in Internet-of-Things (IoT) devices is increasing. In 2017, EFSA launched a tender to explore 'collaborative models' for data gathering[2], thus confirming its interest in exploring decentralised methods of data collection which may include some of the devices discussed in this section.

Through third-party softwares, Amazon Echo suggests recipes for the user to cook, and as a result, gathers real-time food consumption data. This device is also widely used to manage users' grocery lists, thus helping to predict food consumption in the near future with a high level of certainty.

As with IoT devices, smartphone applications may be used to analyse consumers' behaviour. The FoodProfiler (formerly, Food Intake) is a mobile app developed by Wageningen University & Research to collect food consumption data directly from users [15]. User profiling allows to compare clusters of participants, to identify product combinations, and to analyse consumption trends. Positive outcomes may be expected from this research methodology since it combines the use of handy devices, a short recall time, and low burdens for the participant.

Lastly, a small body of literature has discussed the use of social media as food-related communication tools both in regular times [16] and in the course of emergencies [17]. Studies have confirmed the possibility of retrieving overweight and diabetes rates from a large corpus of tweets containing food-related hashtags [18]. New paradigms in gathering consumption data may consist of automatic identification of food in photos uploaded to social media. MIT's artificial intelligence algorithm Pic2Recipe! is able to identify the presence of food in pictures and retrieve the recipe[3].

While the potential of this data to predict consumers' attitudes is currently exploited only by private entities, some beneficial outcomes may result from the submission of consumption data to safety assessors directly from individuals. Moreover, beneficial effects in terms of trust and confidence may emerge from a closer engagement of consumers in the risk assessment processes.

4.3 Blockchain and Food Traceability

Blockchain is deemed to have a disruptive impact in many sectors, including financial services, human resources, and intellectual property. The potentiality of this technology in the food safety domain is currently under discussion both in academia and the tech industry. On the one hand, academic studies have modelled supply chain traceability

---

[2] https://etendering.ted.europa.eu//cft/cft-display.html?cftId=2827.

[3] http://news.mit.edu/2017/artificial-intelligence-suggests-recipes-based-on-food-photos-0720.

systems based on Blockchain and RFID [19]; on the other hand, IBM and Walmart have implemented two Blockchain pilots for the traceability of mangos and pork alongside the whole supply chain[4]. This research found several benefits both for consumers and the food industry. First, the improvement of track capabilities for the industry can result in a faster response for food recalls; secondly, the increase in transparency of the supply chain discourages frauds and illegal activities; thirdly, Blockchain is able to reduce compliance costs.

5 Emerging Issues for Data Governance

While the previous sections have identified current and future Big Data applications in the domain of food safety, this part introduces the emerging issues originated by these technologies for which forward-thinking policy solutions should be adopted.

'Data governance' consists of "the organization and implementation of policies, procedures, structure, roles, and responsibilities which outline and enforce rules of engagement, decision rights, and accountabilities for the effective management of information assets" [20]. This paper adopts a holistic approach defining data governance as "legal, ethical, professional and behavioural norms of conduct, conventions and practices"[5]. This perspective is grounded on the coexistence of the heterogeneous entities involved (academia, food industries, food safety authorities, and general public) that bring different views of governance together, thus calling for a broad definition of this term.

5.1 Data Sovereignty and International Food Data Exchange

Different approaches to the collection, the storage, and the use of data may result in non-inclusive policies implemented by regulative authorities belonging to different jurisdictions. While these conceptual resistances could lead to unintended forms of 'data protectionism', gathering data from multiple sources is crucial to perform a valid risk assessment through gaps minimisation and bias reduction. The global challenge raised by international information sharing requires the definition of peculiar regulations that satisfy all the stakeholders and comply with the internal rules adopted by each competent authority. Therefore, international information sharing platforms should be modelled according to access rules that balance the ownership of data with the general interest to an efficient risk assessment.

Alongside these practical reasons in support of international data exchange, ethical justifications could lead to a paradigm shift in the understanding of data sovereignty. On the one hand, global efforts aimed to the safeguard of the human right to adequate food and sustainability should be grounded on shared findings which could be implemented by joint data analysis. On the other hand, bearing in mind the absence of

---

[4] https://www-01.ibm.com/events/wwe/grp/grp308.nsf/vLookupPDFs/6%20Using%20Blockchain%20for%20Food%20Safe%202/$file/6%20Using%20Blockchain%20for%20Food%20Safe%202.pdf.

[5] https://royalsociety.org/ ~ /media/policy/projects/data-governance/data-management-governance.pdf.

technological infrastructures and the generally low levels of expertise, the sharing of information with emergent nations is desirable to reduce the digital divide between developing and developed countries.

5.2   Information Sharing and Competition in the Food Industry

Alongside cross-sectorial intellectual property regulations, both EU law and contractual agreements between data suppliers and EFSA grant the ownership of data to the originator [21], thus preventing a co-ownership situation or the entering into a license agreement. Previous research has observed that ownership can be broken into two facets, i.e. data protection and confidentiality. On the one hand, data protection applies to data submitted to support an application (e.g. to place a novel food on the market). It aims to protect the competitive position of the originator by denying the use of the same data for a subsequent applicant. On the other hand, confidentiality preserves the commercial value of data by not granting access to data submitted by the originator [22]. Two main arguments can be brought in favour of a different balance between transparency and secrecy of data.

On the one hand, the presence of concurring legislations that grant multiple layers of protection to data ownership might be reflected in uncertainties in the legal framework, thus leading to a self-restricting approach to the routine use of Big Data applications. As regards WGS, for instance, EFSA clearly concluded that "the legal and official systems are not yet adapted to the large-scale application of WGS to support food safety policies (and) legal obstacles are to be expected and a careful balance must be struck between the desirable complete openness from a food safety point of view and the privacy and related concerns that necessitate confidentiality" [12].

On the other hand, as regards the protection of the commercial value of data, the urgency of avoiding unfair monopolies by creating competitive markets for data calls for further investigation. French and German competition authorities have already underlined some important lines of research and identified potential solutions [23]. Their impact in the food industry should be discussed in light of the public interest in sustainability, transparency, and safeguard of fundamental rights related to food.

5.3   Privacy and Security Issues in Consumption Data Donations

The donation of non-personal data is a common practice in the food safety domain. 'Calls for data' are regularly published by risk assessment authorities to perform evaluations concerning fields where additional information is needed. The need of forward-thinking governance solutions and the entry into force of the EU General Data Protection Regulation[6] (GDPR) raise the urgency of regulating personal data donations [24]. As shown, consumption data can be used to predict overweight and diabetes rates,

---

[6] Regulation 2016/679 of the European Parliament and of the European Council of 27 April 2016 on the protection of natural persons with regard to the processing of personal data and on the free movement of such data, and repealing Directive 95/46/EC [2016] OJ L 119.

thus being subsumed to 'health data', one of the special categories of data subject to a stricter regime as regards data processing conditions and obligations under the GDPR[7]. The privacy of individuals involved in food safety pertains to the broader area of academic research that deals with the use of personal data in the scientific research, whose relevance is highlighted by the abundance of the literature on this topic.

On the one hand, as shown in the previous sections, individual data donations can be implemented as regards consumption data. The possible definition of data gathered from IoT, smartphones and social media under the category of health data poses privacy-specific questions and security risks due to the use of personal devices that can reveal sensitive information related to the data subject. On the other hand, developing a regulatory framework to encourage data donations from private companies to public bodies involved in food safety is a further challenge. Breaching data protection rules may expose the donors to liability, thus leading to an overprotective attitude that might limit donations. At the same time, the philanthropic nature underlying data donations should not suggest a less protective approach to safeguard measures, especially in light of the sensitive nature of processed data.

6   Final Considerations

Current Big Data applications are reshaping the way in which food industries, academia, food safety authorities, and consumers interact, collaborate, and fulfil their duties. Furthermore, possible future implementations present immense opportunities for these entities as regards the active engagement of all these actors. As shown, the flow of information between the food industry, consumers and food safety authorities raises open questions towards data sovereignty, competition, privacy within data sharing processes. Providing effective solutions to these issues is crucial to the implementation of the new applications discusses above. Maximising the positive outcomes of the cutting-edge technologies already in use requires clear data governance policies. Ultimately, the role of Big Data as a powerful instrument to protect and safeguard the fundamental rights pertaining to food and sustainability should be enhanced by policymakers.

Further research may explore two areas: on the one hand, bearing in mind the need of future-proof solutions, monitoring the development of future Big Data applications is crucial to understand to which extent new technologies interfere with stakeholders' interests. On the other hand, further work is needed to understand how technical measures could enable all the involved entities to protect their interests without undermining the other stakeholders.

---

[7] Recital 15 of the GDPR defines health data as the one "pertaining to the health status of a data subject which reveal information relating to the past, current or future physical or mental health status of the data subject [and] any information on, for example, a disease, disability, disease risk [...] of the data subject independent of its source".

References

1. FAO: FAO and the SDGs Indicators: Measuring up to the 2030 Agenda for Sustainable Development (2017)
2. FAO: Voluntary Guidelines to support the progressive realization of the right to adequate food in the context of national food security, adopted by the 127th Session of the FAO Council (2004)
3. Strawn, K.L., et al.: Big Data in food safety and quality. Food Technol. **69**, 42–49 (2015)
4. Memorandum of Understanding Between the European Chemicals Agency (ECHA) and the European Food Safety Authority (EFSA) (2017)
5. Open Data Institute: Helping organisations navigate ethical concerns in their data practices (2017)
6. Beni, L.H., Villeneuve, S., LeBlanc, D.I., Delaquis, P.: A GIS-based approach in support of an assessment of food safety risks. Trans. GIS **15**(s1), 95–108 (2011)
7. Öcal, M., Kaya, I.A.: Food safety and GIS applications. In: 2015 Fourth International Conference on Agro-Geoinformatics (Agro-Geoinformatics), pp. 85–90 (2015)
8. Cooley, M., et al.: Incidence and tracking of *Escherichia coli O157:H7* in a major produce production region in California. PLoS ONE **2**, e1159 (2007)
9. Decorte, L., Joris, I., Van Looy, S., Peelaerts, W., Bronders, J.: Software tool for calculating the predicted environmental concentrations (PEC) of plant protection products (PPP) in soil: final report. EFSA Support. Publ. **11** (2014)
10. FAO–WHO: Applications of Whole Genome Sequencing in food safety management (2016)
11. FSA: Chief Scientific Adviser's Science Report Issue Three: Whole-genome sequencing of Foodborne Pathogens (2016)
12. EFSA Scientific Colloquium N°20: Whole Genome Sequencing of food-borne pathogens for public health protection (2014)
13. Kate, K., Chaudhari, S., Prapanca, A., Kalagnanam, J.: FoodSIS. In: Proceedings of the 20th ACM SIGKDD International Conference on Knowledge Discovery and Data Mining - KDD 2014, pp. 1709–1718. ACM, New York (2014)
14. Lucas Luijckx, N., van de Brug, F., Leeman, W., van der Vossen, J., Cnossen, H.: Testing a text mining tool for emerging risk identification. EFSA Support. Publ. **13** (2016)
15. van den Puttelaar, J., Verain, M.C., Onwezen, M.C.: The potential of enriching food consumption data by use of consumer generated data: a case from RICHFIELDS. In: Proceedings of the 10th International Conference on Methods and Techniques in Behavioral Research, pp. 82–87. Dublin City University, Dublin (2016)
16. Shan, L., et al.: Interactive communication with the public: qualitative exploration of the use of social media by food and health organizations. J. Nutr. Educ. Behav. **47**, 104–108 (2015)
17. Regan, Á., Raats, M., Shan, L., Wall, P., McConnon, Á.: Risk communication and social media during food safety crises: a study of stakeholders' opinions in Ireland. J. Risk Res. **19**, 119–133 (2014)
18. Fried, D., Surdeanu, M., Kobourov, S., Hingle, M., Bell, D.: Analyzing the language of food on social media. In: Proceedings of the 2014 IEEE International Conference on Big Data, pp. 778–783. IEEE Press, New York (2014)
19. Feng, T.: An agri-food supply chain traceability system for China based on RFID & blockchain technology. In: Proceedings of the 13th International Conference on Service Systems and Service Management (ICSSSM), pp. 1–6. IEEE Press, New York (2016)
20. Ladley, J.: Data Governance. Morgan Kaufmann, Waltham (2012)
21. Kocharov, A.: Data ownership and access rights in the European Food Safety Authority. Eur. Food Feed Law Rev. **5**, 335–346 (2009)

22. Holle, M.: The protection of proprietary data in novel foods. Eur. Food Feed Law Rev. **5**, 280–284 (2014)
23. Bundeskartellamt: Autorité de la concurrence: Competition Law and Data (2016)
24. Taddeo, M.: Data philanthropy and individual rights. Mind. Mach. **27**, 1–5 (2017)

BI End-User Segments
in the Public Health Sector

Rikke Gaardboe and Tanja Svarre[(✉)]

Aalborg University, 9000 Aalborg, Denmark
gaardboe@business.aau.dk, tanjasj@hum.aau.dk

Abstract. In public health services, business intelligence (BI) is used by medical secretaries, nurses, doctors and economists. Although some research has investigated the use of information systems in this regard, the results have been inconclusive. One explanation could be unobserved heterogeneity. This paper aims to apply use and task characteristics as well as perceptions of BI quality and user characteristics to characterize BI usage based on end-user segments. The finite mixture partial least squares (FINMIX-PLS), Kruskal-Wallis test and Bonferroni post-hoc test are used to provide a clear picture of the characteristics affecting the use of BI. The user segments are estimated using a sample of 746 BI users from 12 public hospitals and their administrations. The results highlight three segments that are primarily characterized by differences in task compatibility, BI experience and education. Only 16.5% of the respondents fit the definition of a BI user found in the extant literature. The remaining 83.5% represents new user types. This research in progress contributes to the extant BI literature by identifying new types of BI users and by showing how critical success factors differ by user types. As user types are identified using a quantitative method, qualitative studies could be applied to extend the understanding of the various types.

Keywords: Business intelligence · User segmentation · FIMIX-PLS
Public health

1 Introduction

Public health is increasingly facing demands to deliver more efficient and effective care, and this trend is transforming one of the largest sectors in the global economy [1]. Notably, Parate and Dunbar [2] find that hospitals with integrated information systems have higher operating and total margins. In general, the public health sector has relatively underdeveloped information systems [3]. Moreover, much health-related data is now digitized rather than kept in hard copy [4]. The public health sector has always generated large amounts of data due to record-keeping, compliance, regulatory and patient-care requirements [5]. The shift to digitalization allows for the analysis and merging of data through the use of business intelligence (BI) systems. Wixom and Watson [6] define BI as "an umbrella term that is commonly used to describe the technologies, applications, and processes for gathering, storing, accessing, and analysing data to help users make better decisions".

© Springer Nature Switzerland AG 2018
A. Kő and E. Francesconi (Eds.): EGOVIS 2018, LNCS 11032, pp. 231–242, 2018.
https://doi.org/10.1007/978-3-319-98349-3_18

BI holds promising potential for the public health sector, as improved health-related information can be used to better understand patients' medical histories as well as drug-drug interactions [7]. Moreover, Gotz and Borland [1] emphasize that data-driven health systems help doctors to make more precise diagnoses, develop more personalized treatment plans, identify patients at risk and analyse medical outcomes. In addition to the clinical benefits of BI, these systems offer administrative benefits, such as lower costs, enhanced quality and resource optimization [3].

Information systems (IS) are critical organizational resources. The users of these systems and the ways in which they use them affect whether their implementation is successful [8]. This also applies to BI systems. A significant amount of research focuses on the factors that influence users' decisions to adopt and use certain technologies. However, few articles centre on how certain user segments utilize information technologies based on their needs and preferences [9]. Factors with an indirect impact on the use of IS include task compatibility [10–12], task significance [13], technology experience [11, 14], information quality [15], system quality [15, 16], organizational role [17], education [17], age [17] and gender [18]. To understand users' needs, users within a segment must be as homogeneous as possible and there must be heterogeneity between segments [9]. Such segmentation can help researchers understand the factors that affect use and assist organizations in understanding how to implement various technologies best. In the extant literature, BI end-users are typically described as highly educated managers or controllers [19]. However, the purpose of this paper is to examine general BI end-users to gain a broader picture of their characteristics. By means of structural equation modelling techniques (PLS) we identify possible end-user segments in the public health sector to gain a deeper understanding of specific user groups within the health domain. Amongst others, a deeper understanding may be useful in tailoring implementing, teaching, and support on the basis of use variations.

In Sect. 2, we discuss BI end-user segment characteristics based on a literature review. In Sect. 3 we present the data-collection process as well as the three statistical tools used in the paper: finite mixture partial least squares (FIMIX-PLS), the Kruskal-Wallis test and the Bonferroni post-hoc test. Our assessment of the measurement model as well as the user segments and their differences are presented in Sect. 4. In Sect. 5, we discuss the findings, limitations and the potential for further research.

2   Identifying the Characteristics of BI End-User Segments

A recent review shows that research on BI has focused on structure and technology rather than tasks and people [20]. The review identifies how critical success factors (CSFs) within Leavitt's task construct (e.g., task difficulty, task interdependence, task significance, task variability and task specificity) and people construct (e.g., gender, age, education, organizational role and organizational tenure) have not been empirically investigated as BI success factors. These factors are essential for describing and characterizing end-users. Furthermore, the papers that examine BI end-users pay little attention to the differences among specific sub-groups of end-users in public health [7].

For example, few researchers have looked into such user segments as nurses or hospital administrators [21]. In fact, most studies view users as a homogenous group.

In 1992, DeLone and McLean were looking for a more integrated view of IS success. It was a reaction to the existing perspective of IS success as being represented at the influence level with one variable (user satisfaction or use) [22]. The result of their research was the I/S success model [22]. In 2003, they updated the model to include system quality, information quality, service quality, intention to use, system use, user satisfaction, and net benefits. Service quality and net benefits were extensions of the original IS success model. The question of "What are the independent variables?" remained unanswered until Petter, DeLone and McLean published their literature review in 2013. In that review, they classified the independent variables related to I/S success (e.g., system quality, information quality, service quality, use, intended use, user satisfaction and net benefit). The authors used Leavitt's [23] diamond to map the model's independent variables, such that the task, structure and people constructs contained the independent variables, and the technology construct represented the dependent variable [8].

In this study, we examine whether it is possible to detect unobserved heterogeneity in BI use among end-user segments in the public health sector. Thus, we will apply a structural equation modelling technique to identify user segments among a variety of BI end-users in order to be able to identify differences and similarities. We focus on a subset of the constructs in order to understand the relationships among specific sets of users (Leavitt's [23] people construct), their tasks (Leavitt's [23] task construct) and their use of BI technologies (Leavitt's [23] technology construct). In Petter et al. [8], the task construct consists of the following variables: task compatibility (the task fits with the IS), task difficulty (the task is challenging for the user), task interdependence (the task is independent of other tasks), task significance (the task is essential to the organization), task variability (consistency between the task and work processes) and task specificity (the link between IS and the task is clear). In our study, we use all of these variables except task variability to represent the task construct, as the aim of the study is to measure and compare the specific end-users' tasks rather than to adopt the process perspective as represented by the task-variability variable. The people construct is used to characterize the segments identified in the analysis.

In Petter et al. [8], the people construct is represented by several variables: attitudes toward technology, attitudes towards change, enjoyment, trust, computer anxiety, self-efficacy, user expectation, technology experience, organizational role, education, age, gender and organizational tenure. As the purpose of the paper is to characterize users, we focus on the following variables: technology experience, organizational role, education, age, gender and organizational tenure.

Finally, the technology construct in Petter et al. [8] concerns the variables of system quality, information quality, service quality, intention to use, use, user satisfaction, individual impact, and organizational impact. In this regard, the focus is on the individual end-user and his or her use of BI. For that reason, we focus on the information-quality and system-quality variables, and on use. Our hypotheses are as follows: H1: There is a positive relation between task compatibility and use, H2: There is a positive relation between task interdependence and use, H3: There is a positive relation between task significance and use, H4: There is a positive relationship between task difficulty and use, H5: There is a positive relation between task specificity and use, H6: There is a positive relationship between information quality and use, H7: There is a positive relation between system quality and use, H8: There is a positive relationship between experience and use, H9: There is a positive relationship between job and use, H10: There is a positive relationship between education and use, H11: There is a positive relationship between gender and use, and H12: There is a positive relationship between age and use.

3 Research Methodology

The current work has been a part of a larger project [42]. The focus of the current work is on end-user segments. We used a survey to explore the distribution of the variables outlined in Sect. 2. A questionnaire was designed to measure the 12 independent constructs and 1 dependent construct. In April 2017 the questionnaire was distributed through an online survey program (Typeform). BI end-users at 12 Danish public hospitals and related hospital administrations received an email asking for their participation. That e-mail, which contained a link to the questionnaire, was sent to all registered, web-enabled BI end-users (4,232 in total). 1,351 responses were received. Of these respondents, only 746 had actually used the BI system. The responses from the actual users form the basis of the statistical data analysis.

The purpose of the questionnaire was to uncover users' perceptions of BI quality, as well as task characteristics and demographic characteristics. One or more items measured each construct. The items listed in Table 1 are based on questions that have been used, tested and validated in other research, and they were derived from two reviews of literature on IS success [8, 20]. Most items were measured using a five-point Likert scale.

For data analysis, we used several statistical tools. First, we analysed the measurement model of a structural model using PLS, which is a structural equation modelling technique [24]. Subsequently, we relied on the FINMIX-PLS technique to investigate the unobserved heterogeneity in the structural model. The technique, which was introduced in 2002 [25] and improved in 2016 [26], allows for the simultaneous estimation of model parameters and individuals' segment affiliations [27]. However, the method suffers from the limitation that it cannot find heterogeneity in measurement models. Finally, we characterized the resulting segments based on the central tendencies of the variables and by comparing them by Kruskal-Wallis test [28]. We used this nonparametric test because the use construct was not normally distributed. Bonferroni [28] was used for the post-hoc test. To compute FINMIX-PLS, we used Smart-PLS (version 3.2.7), while we used SPSS version 25 for the other tests.

Table 1. Constructs and items to be measured

Item	Question
BacAld01	What is your age?
BacJob01	What kind of job do you have?
BacKoen01	What gender are you?
BacUdd01	What is your latest completed level of education?
Expire02	How would you rate your familiarity with BI? [29]
InfQua01	Data are displayed in a consistent format in BI [30]
InfQua02	In BI data have high validity [30]
InfQua03	Other employees in the organization also think the data have a high validity in BI [30]
SysQua01	BI is easy to learn [31]
SysQua02	BI is easy to use [32]
SysQua03	Information in BI is easy to understand [30]
TaskCom01	This information is useful for my work [30]
TaskCom02	This information is complete for my needs [30]
TaskCom03	This information is relevant to our work [30]
TaskCom04	This information is sufficiently up-to-date for my work
TaskDif01	BI makes it possible to produce complex reports [33]
TaskInt01	If I am not making the reports, one or more employees of my organization can't complete their work [33]
TaskSig01	The reports I prepare in BI is an important part of my work [33]
TaskSig02	I make decisions based on the reports I draw up in BI [33]
TaskSig03	My reports produced in BI are important for other employees at my organization [33]
TaskSig04	Other people make decisions based on my reports prepared in BI
TaskSig05	My reports made in BI are important for stakeholders outside my organization
TaskSpe02	My reports in BI can be made in more ways than one [34]
Use01	What is the approximate share of your total work that you have used [BI] to solve for the past month? [22]

4   Results

Before we separated end-users into groups based on their use of BI, we followed Hair et al.'s [35] guidelines to test the measurement model for the significance of outer loading, internal consistency, convergent validity and discriminant validity. As indicated in Table 2, all multi-item constructs exhibit satisfactory results. Single item constructs are not reported, as they all have the value of 1.

In terms of the structural model, the relation between experience and use is positive and significant at the 0.001 level. Furthermore, the relation between task significance and use is also positive and significant at 0.001. The links between the rest of the variables and use are insignificant. In addition, 19.9% of the variance in the "use" construct is explained. In the following, we refer to this model as the "global model".

Table 2. Structural model of outer loading, internal consistency, convergent and discriminant validity of items.

Construct	Item	Outer loading	Cronbach alpha	Composite reliability	AVE
Information quality	InfQua01	0.716	0.774	0.851	0.657
	InfQua02	0.883			
	InfQua03	0.827			
System quality	SysQua01	0.901	0.826	0.898	0.748
	SysQua02	0.933			
	SysQua03	0.745			
Task compatibility	TaskCom01	0.843	0.817	0.875	0.638
	TaskCom02	0.817			
	TaskCom03	0.699			
	TaskCom04	0.828			
Task significance	TaskSig01	0.826	0.776	0.844	0.529
	TaskSig02	0.770			
	TaskSig03	0.767			
	TaskSig04	0.772			
	TaskSig05	0.431			

To identify the appropriate BI end-user segments, we applied the FIMIX-PLS approach found in Hair et al. [36]. As suggested by Matthews et al. [37], we identified the appropriate number of segments by running the FIMIX-PLS algorithm, beginning with two segments. In order to determine the number of segments, we used the following fit indices: modified Akaike's information criterion with a factor of 3 (AIC3), consistent Akaike's information criterion (CAIC) and normed entropy statistics (EN) [26]. Sarstedt and Ringle [38] suggest selecting a segment number at which AIC3 and CAIC are minimal, and the normed entropy statistic has a maximum value. The minimum recommended sample size is 10 times the structural path [35]. In this case, n > 120. The optimal number of segments if selected from fit indices is four (AIC3 = −923072/CAIC = −669262/EN = 0.968). However, one of the segments has an n less than 120. Therefore, we selected three segments. We then ran the Kruskal-Wallis test and the post-hoc Bonferroni test with the aim of determining the differences between the segments.

Table 3 shows the differences in the construct values, while Table 4 shows the central tendency of variables for the three segments identified. The analysis of the three segments suggests that the majority of users in segment 1 are 40–49 years of age and have completed a vocational education (e.g., as a medical secretary). They generally do not have managerial responsibilities and they have limited experience with BI. Segment 2 is similar to segment 1, but these users have a higher educational level. In other words, the majority of users in segment 2 have professional bachelor's degrees (e.g., in nursing or physical therapy). Segment 3 mainly consists of men ages 40–49 with a masters' degree (e.g., in economics). A substantial part of users in segment 3 have managerial responsibilities and these users are more experienced with BI than users in segments 1 and 2.

Table 3. Segments characteristics and differences calculated by Kruskal-Wallis and Bonferroni tests. In Bonferroni, we report the highest p-value for the relation between the two related segments. * = (p < 0.05), ** = (p < 0.01), *** = (p < 0.001).

Segments	Kruskal-Wallis test	Bonferroni post-hoc test		
		1	2	3
Number of respondents		420	203	123
Percent of respondents		56.3	27.2	16.5
R^2		1	0.537	0.997
Use	Reject***	Equal	Low***	Equal
Task compatibility	Reject***	Medium*	Low*	High*
Task interdependence	Reject**	Equal	Equal	High**
Task significance	Reject***	Equal	Low*	Equal
Task difficulty	Reject**	Equal	Equal	High**
Task specificity	Retain	Equal	Equal	Equal
Information quality	Reject***	Equal	Equal	High***
System quality	Reject***	Equal	Equal	High***
Experience	Reject***	Medium**	Low**	High**
Job	Reject***	Equal	Equal	High*
Education	Reject***	Low*	Medium*	High***
Gender	Reject***	Equal	Equal	Low***
Age	Retain	Equal	Equal	Equal

None of the segments demonstrates a high frequency of BI use in their daily work. Segments 1 and 3 have a median value of 1, which corresponds to 25% of their working hours. Segment 2 has a median value of 0, which corresponds to a very low frequency of use relative to total work hours. Despite the low frequency of use, segments 1 and 3 rate task significance above medium (mean of 3.2 for both segments on a 1–5 scale of agreement), while segment 2 has a mean of 2.8. This suggests that despite the low use frequency in all three segments, they agree that the BI-related tasks are somewhat essential to the organization.

The task-significance construct consists of four items concerning the significance of BI-related tasks within the organization and one concerning their significance outside the organization. The responses show that external significance is rated lower than internal significance. In fact, if the fourth item is removed from the task-significance construct, the means for all three segments increase. Therefore, the three segments view the tasks as particularly crucial within their organizations.

Task difficulty concerns whether BI enables the organization to handle complicated tasks. In this regard, segments 1 and 2 are similar to typical agreement assessments (3.0 and 2.9, respectively). Segment 3 rates the construct significantly higher with a mean of 3.2. Thus, segment 3 handles more challenging tasks than segments 1 and 2. This is not surprising, as users in segment 3 have generally completed more education than those in segments 1 and 2, which should generally enable them to handle tasks that are more complex.

Table 4. Central tendency of variables of the three segments identified by the FIMIX-PLS algorithm

Segments	1 (n = 420)	2 (n = 203)	3 (n = 123)
Use (median)	1	0	1
Task compatibility (mean)	3.4	3.2	3.6
Task interdependence (mean)	2.3	2.1	2.5
Task significance (mean)	3.2	2.8	3.2
Task difficulty (mean)	3.0	2.9	3.2
Task specificity (mean)	3.2	3.2	3.4
Information quality (mean)	3.0	2.9	3.3
System quality (mean)	2.5	2.4	2.8
Experience (mean)	2.3	2.1	2.8
Age (mean)	3.2	3.3	3.3

For all three segments, task interdependence is rated as below medium, indicating that the BI users do not delay colleagues' tasks with their BI outputs and that BI tasks are delimited. Interdependence is lowest in segment 2 with a mean of 2.1. Segment 3 has a higher degree of task interdependence with a mean of 2.5, while the mean for segment 1 is 2.3. This fits well with task difficulty, which is higher for segment 3 than for the two other segments.

With regards to the assessment of task specificity, there is no significant differences among the segments – all three segments rate task specificity slightly above medium with values of 3.2, 3.2 and 3.4, respectively. The same agreement is not found for task compatibility, as segment 2 has a significantly lower rating of 3.2. Segment 3 is significantly higher in this regard than the two other segments with a rating of 3.6, while the mean for segment 1 is 3.4. Again, the higher assessment from segment 3 corresponds to the segment's higher assessments for both task difficulty and task interdependence. This implies that compatibility rises as task difficulty and task interdependence increase.

We find no significant differences between segments 1 and 2 for information quality or system quality. Information quality is rated at 3.0 and 2.9, respectively, while the corresponding figures for system quality are 2.5 and 2.4. Segment 3 receives significantly higher ratings for these two constructs (3.3 for information quality and 2.8 for system quality). This means that users in segment 3 value the ability of the BI system to support task resolution and they understand the potential of the BI information to a greater extent than users in the other segments.

5   Discussion and Concluding Remarks

We have used FIMIX-PLS, the Kruskal-Wallis test and a Bonferroni post-hoc test to determine the different BI user segments in public health. When users are not divided into segments, only 19.9% (R^2) of variance in use is explained. When the BI end-users are divided into three segments, the R^2 increases to 100% (segment 1), 54.7%

(segment 2) and 99.7% (segment 3). Thus, R^2 rises significantly when the user types are segmented. This indicates that critical success factors may vary among user types. It also illustrates the potential of using PLS-FIMIX to identify segments of users in BI survey datasets. Thus, PLS can be used to identify unobserved segments in BI end-user studies that may differ from the general understanding of a BI user.

The user segments are based on user characteristics, such as BI experience, usage, age, gender, education and job type. In addition, we used users' perceptions of BI quality and task characteristics. Three user types were identified: medical secretary (segment 1), clinical (segment 2) and analyst (segment 3). The three segments significantly differed on three constructs: task compatibility, experience and education.

Traditionally, BI users have been described as leaders with a higher education who use IT [19]. Negash and Gray [39] characterize users as familiar with spreadsheets, while [43] characterize BI users as managers or controllers. Madsen [7] identifies three BI end-user segments in the healthcare sector: managers, clinicians and analysts. Moreover, Madsen [7] point out, that user types should be perceived as a continuum. In this study, we found three user segments, each of which had an education level that would fit particular labels (i.e., medical secretary, clinical and analyst). Some of the users with higher education in the last category may also be leaders. The difference between Madsen's [7] segmentation and the one presented here may reflect the fact that we have focused on BI end-users. End-users may differ from BI information users, as some users extract BI reports that are passed on to different stakeholders in the organization. One interesting finding presented here was that the typical analytical user constituted only 16.5% of respondents, while other user types constituted the remainder. One explanation of this finding could be our focus on web-enabled BI, which is BI that can be accessed through a browser [40]. This platform does not necessarily meet advanced users' needs for functionality, which may explain the low response rate from this segment. In terms of the focal context of public hospitals, it is surprising that elected politicians are not users of BI. Chen, Chiang and Storey [41] emphasize BI's democratic potential. However, in the context studied here, the technology is not used to create transparency or offer decision support on a political level.

In this study, different users were segmented into groups, and we found that the factors associated with BI success differ by group. A major success factor is user involvement. An understanding of the different BI end-user segments makes it possible for those responsible for BI to ensure that all types of users are involved in, for example, the prioritization of change requests or new data needs. As mentioned above, the users differ in terms of how they perceive the fit between BI and their tasks. Notably, task compatibility, which is a major factor in the success of BI, can be enhanced by incorporating the different user types. Another significant success factor is user education. As discussed above, segment 3 encompasses typical BI users, as these users are familiar with Excel, which has an important influence on BI. Furthermore, this segment has stronger IT skills. As the other user types have different characteristics, user education should fit the focal group to ensure the maximum benefit and help achieve a higher degree of BI success.

As the impact of the critical success factors on BI success depends on user characteristics, critical success factors should be seen in the light of user types rather than as generic solutions. Our analysis has shown that user segments exist in BI and that critical success factors need to be adapted to these segments.

This paper makes two main contributions. First, we have identified three user types and a usage pattern that is not recognized in the extant BI literature. This may change the discussion regarding BI users. Second, we have used a unique combination of three statistical tests to identify users and the differences between user groups.

Like any study, this study suffers from several limitations. We focused on 12 Danish public hospitals. Denmark assigns a "personal number" to each person living in Denmark, which allows for the combination of data on an individual level across all public sector IT systems. The use patterns presented above should therefore be seen in this light. In addition, all 12 public hospitals used the same source systems and the same BI system. Therefore, future research should focus on different BI systems in different organizational contexts. Moreover, in this study, users are grouped through statistical calculations. To gain a deeper understanding of users and user segments, qualitative studies should also be conducted. Such studies might, for example, involve think-aloud tests, semi-structured interviews or focus groups.

References

1. Gotz, D., Borland, D.: Data-driven healthcare: challenges and opportunities for interactive visualization. IEEE Comput. Graph. Appl. **36**, 90–96 (2016)
2. Parente, S.T., Dunbar, J.L.: Is health information technology investment related to the financial performance of US hospitals? An exploratory analysis. Int. J. Healthcare Technol. Manag. **3**, 48 (2001)
3. Mettler, T., Vimarlund, V.: Understanding business intelligence in the context of healthcare. Health Inform. J. **15**, 254–264 (2009)
4. Raghupathi, W., Raghupathi, V.: Big data analytics in healthcare: promise and potential. Health Inf. Sci. Syst. **2**, 3 (2014)
5. Raghupathi, W.: Data mining in health care. In: Kudyba, S. (ed.) Healthcare Informatics: Improving Efficiency and Productivity, pp. 211–223. Taylor & Francis, Abingdon (2010)
6. Wixom, B., Watson, H.: The BI-based organization. Int. J. Bus. Intell. Res. **1**, 13–28 (2010)
7. Madsen, L.: Healthcare Business Intelligence: A Guide to Empowering Successful Data Reporting and Analytics. Wiley, Hoboken (2012)
8. Petter, S., DeLone, W., McLean, E.R.: Information systems success: the quest for the independent variables. J. Manag. Inf. Syst. **29**, 7–62 (2013)
9. Schacht, S., Morana, S., Urbach, N., Maedche, A.: Are you a Maverick? Towards a Segmentation of Collaboration Technology Users (2015)
10. Agarwal, R., Prasad, J.: The role of innovation characteristics and perceived voluntariness in the acceptance of information technologies. Decis. Sci. **28**, 557–582 (1997)
11. Dishaw, M.T., Strong, D.M.: The effect of task and tool experience on maintenance CASE tool usage. Inf. Resour. Manag. J. **16**, 1–16 (2003)
12. Dishaw, M.T., Strong, D.M.: Extending the technology acceptance model with task–technology fit constructs. Inf. Manag. **36**, 9–21 (1999)
13. Lim, E.T.K., Pan, S.L., Tan, C.W.: Managing user acceptance towards enterprise resource planning (ERP) systems – understanding the dissonance between user expectations and managerial policies. Eur. J. Inf. Syst. **14**, 135–149 (2005)

14. Lawrence, M., Low, G.: Exploring individual user satisfaction within user-led development. MIS Q. **17**, 195–208 (1993)
15. Fitzgerald, G., Russo, N.L.: The turnaround of the London ambulance service computer-aided despatch system (LASCAD). Eur. J. Inf. Syst. **14**, 244–257 (2005)
16. Caldeira, M.M., Ward, J.M.: Understanding the successful adoption and use of IS/IT in SMEs: an explanation from Portuguese manufacturing industries. Inf. Syst. J. **12**, 121–152 (2002)
17. Burton-Jones, A., Hubona, G.S.: Individual differences and usage behavior. Data Base **36**, 58–77 (2005)
18. Oliver, L.W.: Research integration for psychologists: an overview of approaches. J. Appl. Soc. Psychol. **17**, 860–874 (1987)
19. Grublješič, T., Jaklič, J.: Business intelligence acceptance: the prominence of organizational factors. Inf. Syst. Manag. **32**, 299–315 (2015)
20. Gaardboe, R., Svarre, T.: Business intelligence success factors: a literature review. J. Inf. Technol. Manag. **29** (2018)
21. Sharifian, R., Askarian, F., Nematolahi, M., Farhadi, P.: Factors influencing nurses' acceptance of hospital information systems in Iran: application of the Unified Theory of Acceptance and Use of Technology. Health Inf. Manag. J. **43**, 23–28 (2014)
22. DeLone, W.H., McLean, E.R.: Information systems success: the quest for the dependent variable. Inf. Syst. Res. **3**, 60–95 (1992)
23. Leavitt, H.J.: Applied organizational change in industry: structural, technological and humanistic approaches. In: March, J. (ed.) Handbook of Organizations, pp. 1144–1170 (1965)
24. Hair, J.F., Ringle, C.M., Sarstedt, M.: PLS-SEM: indeed a silver bullet. J. Market. Theory Practice **19**, 139–152 (2011)
25. Herrmann, A., Hahn, C.H., Johnson, M.D., Huber, F.: Capturing customer heterogeneity using a finite mixture PLS approach. Schmalenbach Bus. Rev. **54**(3), 243–269 (2002)
26. Hair, J., Sarstedt, M., Matthews, L.M., Ringle, C.M.: Identifying and treating unobserved heterogeneity with FIMIX-PLS: part I – method. Eur. Bus. Rev. **28**, 63–76 (2016)
27. Ong, C.-S., Lai, J.-Y.: Gender differences in perceptions and relationships among dominants of e-learning acceptance. Comput. Hum. Behav. **22**, 816–829 (2006)
28. Aczel, A.D.: Complete Business Statistics. Wohl Publishing, Morristown (2012)
29. Batenburg, R., Van den Broek, E.: Pharmacy information systems: the experience and user satisfaction within a chain of Dutch pharmacies. Int. J. Electron. Healthcare **4**, 119–131 (2008)
30. Lee, Y.W., Strong, D.M., Kahn, B.K., Wang, R.Y.: AIMQ: a methodology for information quality assessment. Inf. Manag. **40**, 133–146 (2002)
31. Lewis, J.R.: IBM computer usability satisfaction questionnaires: psychometric evaluation and instructions for use. Int. J. Hum.-Comput. Interact. **7**, 57–78 (1995)
32. Wang, Y.-S., Liao, Y.-W.: Assessing eGovernment systems success: a validation of the DeLone and McLean model of information systems success. Gov. Inf. Q. **25**, 717–733 (2008)
33. Morgeson, F.P., Humphrey, S.E.: The Work Design Questionnaire (WDQ): developing and validating a comprehensive measure for assessing job design and the nature of work. J. Appl. Psychol. **91**, 1321–1339 (2006)
34. Daft, R.L., Macintosh, N.B.: A tentative exploration into the amount and equivocality of information processing in organizational work units. Adm. Sci. Q. **26**, 207–224 (1981)
35. Hair, J., Hult, T., Ringle, C., Sarstedt, M.: A Primer on Partial Least Squares Structural Equation Modeling (PLS-SEM). SAGE Publications Inc., Thousand Oaks (2017)

36. Hair, J.: Advanced Issues in Partial Least Squares Structural Equation Modeling. SAGE, Los Angeles (2018)
37. Matthews, L.M., Sarstedt, M., Hair, J.F., Ringle, C.M.: Identifying and treating unobserved heterogeneity with FIMIX-PLS: Part II – a case study. Eur. Bus. Rev. **28**, 208–224 (2016)
38. Sarstedt, M., Ringle, C.M.: Treating unobserved heterogeneity in PLS path modeling: a comparison of FIMIX-PLS with different data analysis strategies. J. Appl. Stat. **37**, 1299–1318 (2010)
39. Negash, S., Gray, P.: Business intelligence. In: Handbook on Decision Support Systems, vol. 2. pp. 175–193. Springer, Heidelberg (2008). https://doi.org/10.1007/978-3-540-48716-6_9
40. Gaardboe, R., Sandalgaard, N., Sudzina, F.: The importance of task compatibility for web-enabled business intelligence success in e-government. (2017). Presented at the
41. Chen, H., Chiang, R.H., Storey, V.C.: Business intelligence and analytics: from big data to big impact. MIS Q. **36**, 1165–1188 (2012)
42. Gaardboe, R.: Kritiske succesfaktorer for business intelligence - i kontekst af den offentlige sektor. Aalborg Universitetsforlag, Aalborg (2018)
43. Gaardboe, R., Sandalgaard, N., Nyvang, T.: An assessment of business intelligence in public hospitals. IJISPM – Int. J. Inf. Syst. Project Manag. 5–18 (2017)

Workload Balancing in the Hungarian Public Administration

Péter József Kiss[(⊠)] and Gábor Klimkó

MTA Information Technology Foundation, Budapest, Hungary
mtaita@t-online.hu

Abstract. The current *modus operandi* of the Hungarian public administration does not allow on-demand (dynamic) workload balancing. Underlying assumptions taken for granted that block the road to improvement are identified and a possible improved model is presented. There are two necessary conditions for workload balancing; the implementation of central registers (databases) of the involved entities (resources, cases etc.) and the establishment of an allocation (or matching) mechanism. The paper concludes with a detailed architectural view on the list of registers needed and regulated electronic e-government services.

Keywords: E-government enterprise architectures · Workload balancing
Public administration efficiency

1 Introduction

Public administration in Hungary is expected to meet two political objectives: both the standard of services offered to citizens must improve continuously and cost reduction is expected at the same time. However, the actions taken to rationalize public administration have not brought results capable of satisfying both objectives, partly since real processes of the Hungarian public administration have never been scrutinized in the necessary depth [1].

Act CL of 2016 on General Public Administration Procedures, which is effective from 2018 in Hungary, contains deadlines as short as eight calendar days for certain administrative procedures; within this length of time two days are obviously not workdays [2]. Since a significant part of the administrative procedures is not or cannot yet be automated, a suitable number of civil servants are required to comply with this provision of the law. This requirement might lead to an increase in the total number of Hungarian civil servants, but wage costs represent a significant part of the total costs incurred by public administration, consequently an increase in personnel numbers would contradict the political objective of cost reduction. Taking into consideration that for the sustainable operation of Hungarian public administration it is realistic to expect the wages of the civil servants to be comparable to what is attainable in the private sector, cutting down the number of civil servants would be the only way to ensure the wage fund.

There are detailed discussions in the literature on the management tools available to improve the performance of public administration, but they focus mainly on the

© Springer Nature Switzerland AG 2018
A. Kő and E. Francesconi (Eds.): EGOVIS 2018, LNCS 11032, pp. 243–257, 2018.
https://doi.org/10.1007/978-3-319-98349-3_19

improvement attainable through the *modus operandi* [3, 4]. A novel possibility for progress is to reconsider the management and workload balancing elements of the operating model of the Hungarian public administration; a base of rock solid assumptions which up till now have been considered untouchable. Note that it was earlier recognized in Hungary that a new model of public administration was necessary to achieve any real change in Hungary [5]. The changes in the Hungarian e-government since 2011 brought the availability of several electronic services that together form an architecture that enables to build a model that might fulfil both political objectives mentioned above.

2   Problem Statement

Two factors influenced the emergence of the organisational structure of the Hungarian public administration. This structure evolved on a distributed, geographical basis due to the local knowledge and local actions (on-site inspections, hearings, etc.) required for the procedures; governability required a distributed structure, too. The organizational structure of the Hungarian public administration was earlier typically split by function (central offices, their regional organisations) that resulted in segmented and wasteful operation. The transformation of the Hungarian regional public administration system started in 2010, which, from the aspect of governance comprises of twenty county level, and from the aspect of the practical organisation of administration of 200 (county, district offices) public administration organisations [6]. However, even when documents are submitted electronically to the administration, the above mentioned transformation is based mainly on the traditional, paper-based administration procedures where the location (of the case) does play a role during processing.

There are, however, two reasons why it is not desirable to handle together governance and operational requirements. On the one hand, there was an increasing demand even in case of face-to-face client services for case processing to be independent of location. The implementation of the so-called "Government Windows" means that there is not only one "competent authority" from the point of the client. Most of public administration cases can now be initiated at any Government Window [6]. This approach, however, would only represent a qualitative change if it were not limited to the initiation of a case (submission of applications) but it was extended to the complete processing. Still, the positioning of the Government Windows shows clearly the direction of the development.

An uptake in using electronic government services, however, could result in qualitative change. Dependence on location will lose all meaning as the internet provides equal access from all points of the world and the receipt of submitted applications could be centralised. For paper-based applications this has already been implemented in several areas, there is the so-called "Unified Governmental Document Management System", where all received paper-based documents (applications) are centrally digitized and scanned versions are forwarded to the proper authorities that are selected on a geographic basis [7]. Forwarding the accompanying digitized documents to the "appropriate" county or district office happens currently without any actual preprocessing. This practice makes workload balancing and any real improvement in the efficiency of public administration impossible.

It should be noted at this point that solely the fact, that civil servants (for the sake of simplicity we shall call them *clerks*) read electronic documents instead of paper-based documents, cannot be considered as an improvement. The approach considering paper savings as a major advantage is completely mistaken. It is more difficult for the clerks to manage the electronic than the paper-based form of the applications. More efficient work requires targeted, customized support (specialised system), which in practice assumes central implementation (and not different systems) for the whole administration. If we change the *modus operandi* of the model using the availability of on-line access and the e-government services developed in recent years, we could open new ways for improving the efficiency of the Hungarian public administration.

2.1   The Traditional Processing Procedure

The following figure illustrates the simplified traditional processing procedure:

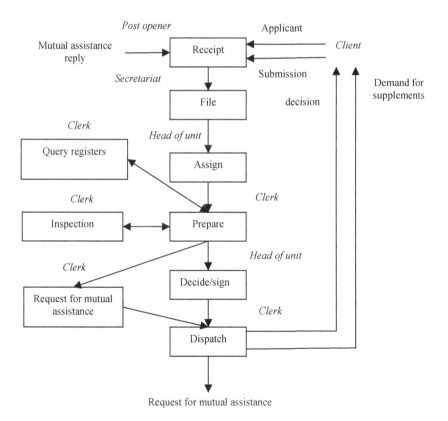

Fig. 1. Traditional processing in public administration.

Actors in the traditional processing system all work in the same organisation and the location of case processing is selected at the receipt of the application, typically based on geographic competence. The only step bound to a physical location is the (on-site) inspection in this procedure!

2.2   Improving the Traditional Processing Procedure

Note that even for activities that are currently location-bound, technical developments open new solutions for public administration. For example, if the client applies for permission for some minor construction work (i.e. installing a window in a loft), instead of an on-site inspection, it could be sufficient to transmit a picture from a smartphone according to the clerk's instructions. Another example may be the case of an agricultural application where a picture made by a drone forwarded to the district office could do the job. In these examples, the information needed for the decision can be derived from the application itself and from the registers operated by public administration with the only exception of the on-site inspection.

In most public administration cases on-site inspection is not required or does not apply. Due to the very large number of cases, at present the administrative procedure does not rest on the civil servant's memory. A civil servant working at a county office could be living in a different district (settlement) from the citizen who submitted the application, thus the need for local knowledge of the clerk does not generally apply. It is not even sure, that (within a government office) the same clerk will handle a subsequent application of the same client. Thus, the allocation of tasks based on geographical jurisdiction is not a necessary element in processing an application.

3   Workload Balancing and Its Preconditions

The problem of workload balancing, i.e. matching capacities and demand is a well-known and managed problem in industrial production. A factory disposes of a specified amount of resources (e.g. machines for the sake of simplicity) and offers a well-defined product portfolio. Certain machines are needed for manufacturing these products in a determined sequence and for a determined period. If we consider the result of case processing in public administration as a product, then one of the required resources is the clerk whose participation is necessary for a given time period to conclude a case.

3.1   Blocking Factors of Workload Balancing in Public Administration

In this analogy clerks are one of the major resources of processing in public administration. A clerk possesses a limited number of competencies. It is clear that different competencies are required for different types of cases (e.g. a land office case is completely different from a case related to epidemics), therefore the acting organisations (e.g. an office for a county) must have an adequate amount of each competency. The available capacities must satisfy the demands posed by the actual case processing. Note that we have the unrealistic assumption here that the cases are initiated evenly and so the necessary capacities for their processing can be set to a stable level. Evidently, capacities cannot be sized for peak demand (due to the principle of pursuit for saving public funds), moreover, it is not possible to plan for the increase in workload caused by any eventual change in legislation. Another factor that has a significant effect on the workload of a public administration organisation is the possible fluctuation of the local population, that is, the number of clients in time (think of the difference in the number of inhabitants in a resort between summer and winter). We need such an approach that can match the changing workload and at the same time the available free capacities of the organization concerned.

However, the analogy mentioned above between industry and public administration, is misleading as there are two basic differences:

- for optimizing (matching the demand and the capacities) in a factory one can collect the orders and batch process them, while this possibility is rather limited in public administration;
- A factory often manufactures for a warehouse – at least in the case of complex pieces, semi-finished products – anticipating the orders to ensure short delivery times. This action, except for material parts, is not applicable in public administration at all.

These differences do not prevent the application of certain elements of workload balancing used in the industrial world in public administration. (Note here that this is a typical New Public Management (NPM) approach and though some authors claim that NPM is outdated, we do not agree with that statement [9]).

Let us consider the example of those who are engaged in logistics; their job is to allocate separate resources (e.g. cars and loaders) to satisfy dynamically changing demands. The underlying basis of their work is the accurate tracking of resources, the up-to-date knowledge of free capacities and the possibility of dynamic allocation (the possibility of notifying cars and loaders where to go, what the job entails). These assumptions differ radically from the current management approach used in the Hungarian public administration.

Figure 2 shows the allocation process of cases in the Hungarian public administration. There are a total of twenty (county level) government offices and 197 district offices under them; their different departments process the cases (applications). The structure of the departments (organisational units) is identical, differing only in the number of civil servants. The allocation of an application to an acting organisational unit is predefined (typically based on the submitting client's address). This shows that workload balancing when allocating cases to civil servants is possible only at the level of organisational units (characteristically departments). Thus, not even the seasonal differences between settlements (occurring for instance due to the cases generated by the vacationers) can be evened out. In Fig. 2, $Clerk_1$ working at office GO_{20} in unit OU_1 might also have the competence required to process the case submitted by $Client_2$, but in the allocation of the case this possibility is not even considered.

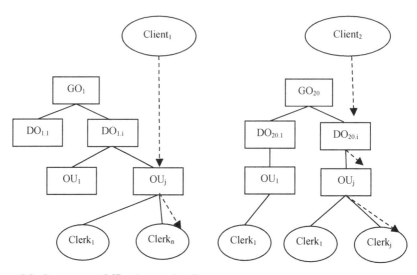

GO: Government Office (county level)
DO: District Office
OU: Organisational Unit

Fig. 2. Allocation process of cases to clerks in Hungarian public administration

If, however, we follow the logic used in an industrial company, we should take the approach shown in Fig. 3.

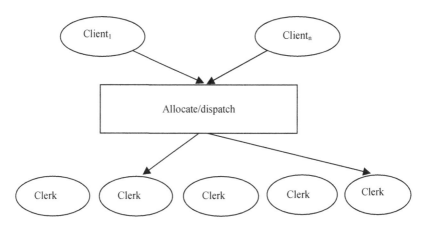

Fig. 3. Allocation process of cases to clerks that follows logic used in industry

The difference is that in public administration the competences required for case processing are not recorded at the operative level (specific competencies of individual civil servants, for instance knowledge of building regulations). Instead, a static service background is built where even the workload already allocated is not recorded. In public administration the tasks (applications) are received by the "competent" organisational unit and the allocation of the tasks is the responsibility of the head of the unit. This mechanism disregards the fact that there could be other organisational units performing the same tasks with free capacities and that there could be individuals capable of performing the task in question. An organisation focused on efficiency should consider the totality of identical resources in the allocation of tasks.

Thus, the current operating model of the Hungarian public administration hinders optimal workload balancing from two aspects:

- case allocation for processing is not based on the actual workload of the capacity and
- the competencies needed for service are statically embedded in the organisation thus further reducing flexibility.

It is necessary to emphasize the role of competency management. The traditional human resource approach in public administration focuses on the qualifications of the clerks, but this does not necessarily reflect expertise and proficiency in different areas. The importance of competence is often cited in literature [8, 10].

When one uses the term "competence", it is important to note that besides the so-called general competencies (discussion skills, group work, etc.) the term also refers to expertise acquired in different specialised areas. The education system in the Hungarian public administration lacks individual, targeted and customized short-term trainings in specialised fields in many areas; it also lacks exams to prove the acquirement of specialised knowledge. For example, it is not at all complicated to issue a simple property deed, still the knowledge of the administrative procedure is required to be able to do this, not to mention doing it without supervision. This example shows that qualification alone (e.g. a specialised exam) is sufficient to enable a person to perform tasks first under guidance and subsequently to perform them alone, but an impersonal system is unable to determine if a person has the necessary experience in the specific subtask. At present, heads of units in government offices have this information concerning competence of their clerks and they allocate cases to them on that basis. A more detailed knowledge of the competencies of individual clerks would provide more room for the heads of units (and not only the line manager) to do this.

Workload balancing as such does not require the knowledge of personal competencies, but without it optimal matching is possible only at the level of organisational units (e.g. among the 197 district offices). Competence management at the level of *all* civil servants would allow clerk level allocation. For these reasons, we will now present a model based on the known competences of each Hungarian civil servant that ensures a higher level of optimization. Note that this approach does not exclude a practical implementation optimising down to the level of the organisational unit based on specific indicators.

3.2   Workload Balancing in the Hungarian Public Administration and the Supporting Information Technology

We will show that the operating model of Hungarian public administration could be modified to follow the workload balancing principles used in industry, but this modification requires a different approach in the use of supporting information technology.

The current supporting technology does not require central record keeping, neither does it need a single point of entry for case management as it is possible to address the competent office directly. In comparison, a model capable of workload balancing in public administration, that is, matching demands and free capacities, requires the supporting technology components shown in Fig. 4.

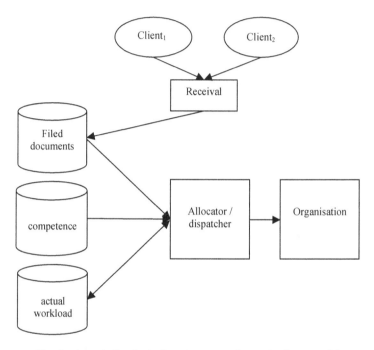

Fig. 4. A centralized, single entry supporting technology model

Thus, while the traditional model follows the "government organization → organisational unit → clerk" sequence, the modified model starts from the examination of competencies and workload.

The approach must be in line with governance requirements of public administration organisations as the accountable persons are the heads of county government offices, heads of units etc. and the work of the clerks has to be supervised. Furthermore, it is also necessary to consider the tasks that are geographically constrained (e.g. reviews, on-site inspection, etc.) during the allocation process. We are going to show that an enhanced matrix organisation could provide these harmonization requirements.

The opportunities stem from the use of, as well as the problems associated with the possible use of matrix organisation (in public administration) is discussed in the literature, see e.g. Kuprenas [11]. If we use the traditional matrix organisation in public administration, then at least there is need for one head of unit who allocates cases for each case type, as shown on Fig. 5.

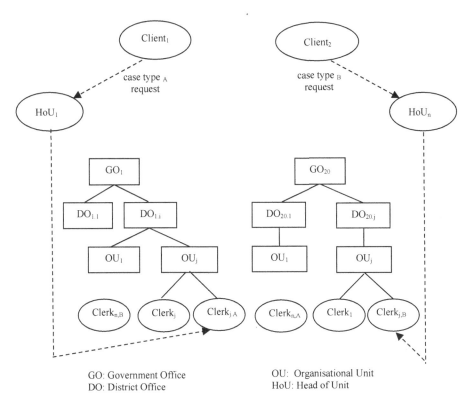

Fig. 5. The role of case type managers when a traditional matrix organization is used in public administration

According to the model in Fig. 5. the authorised heads of units are allowed to allocate tasks to clerks with the necessary competence regardless of the organisation they belong to (case types "A" or "B" in the figure, the competence of the clerk is shown in the lower indexes of $Clerk_{j,A}$ and $Clerk_{jB}$); that is why it is not indicated in the figure to which government offices HoU_1 and HoU_n work for. However, cross-allocation of tasks contains subjective, human decisions which may generate conflicts in the system. The management of these conflicts would annul the advantage created by the better utilisation of capacities. This way applying the traditional matrix organisation would not improve efficiency of public administration, thus a new approach is needed. Figure 6 shows an enhanced structure, which could be named "virtual matrix":

In Fig. 6 an automated case dispatcher system, the so-called "workload manager" forwards cases to the clerks. To enable the workload manager to work effectively a necessary condition is to provide it with objective data.

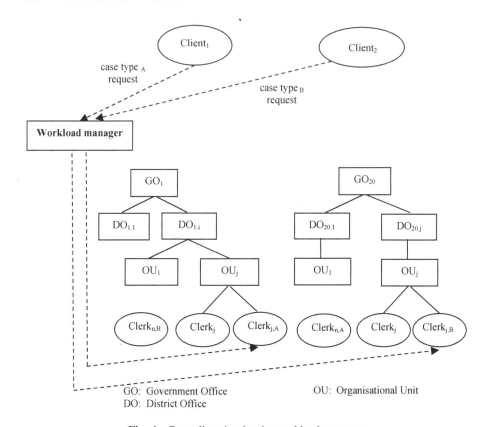

Fig. 6. Case allocation by the workload manager

4 Implementing Workload Balancing in the Hungarian Public Administration

The basic conditions of workload balancing in public administration, as pointed out before, are

- central registers (databases) of the involved entities (resources, cases etc.) and
- the establishment of an allocation (or matching) mechanism.

A comprehensive electronic connection between the client and the public administration organization is not required, though it would clearly make the situation easier. By using the previously mentioned central digitisation service ("Unified Governmental Document Management System"), it can be ensured that the competent authorities receive each case in electronic form. The implementation of workload balancing in public administration (too) depends mainly on the supporting electronic services, but there are other components that provide organizational functions, too.

We will now describe in more detail the two basic conditions for implementing workload balancing. The following components are required:

1. **Central and integrated register of competences of Hungarian civil servants.** The human resource system must keep a record of the competencies as well as the capacities of each civil servant for each case type. This register must be accessible to all public administration organisations that are involved in the workload balancing process.

2. **Central and integrated database of cases.** Note that this is a necessary precondition for ad-hoc case allocation and it is different from the document and case filing by an organisational unit, or even from the office level filing and the formal practice of document transfer/acceptance.

3. **Central register of current workload of clerks.** A case can only be allocated (delegated) to a clerk if at that time that person has the capacity to deal with it. For example, if a clerk has to conduct on-site inspection at any given location or has to conduct a hearing, these are obligations to be performed at fixed times involving other persons; therefore that clerk cannot be considered as recipient of another case at the same time. This means that, all the jobs of the clerks must be recorded and made available for the workload manager program.

4. **A central task allocation/dispatch program - the workload manager - that distributes the workload.** The allocation mechanism should preferably use a rule-based learning system (instead of individually programmed algorithms). The workload manager could apply the following evaluation criteria for case allocation:

   - the required competence for the case,
   - free capacity (time) until the deadline of the case,
   - work already allocated,
   - processing events preceding the case,
   - local (geographical) knowledge (if relevant) and
   - supplementary rules (e.g. value limit, etc.).

5. **Supervision by the head of unit.** In order to safeguard the quality of public administration, case processing based on automated workload balancing cannot dispense with the supervision of the local head of unit. In on-line work (teleworking) the limited possibility for supervision is a well-known problem; it is necessary to setup the professional control of tasks allocated by the virtual level for the virtual matrix organisations, too.

6. **A competence development and control system.** Automated task allocation presumes that the allocating system could use real, existing competencies of the clerks. This requires a training and testing structure where the necessary competencies of the clerks are developed, monitored and controlled.

The first three components are registers that enable task allocation (see also Fig. 4); the fourth is based on the previous components. The fifth indicates the need for human supervision and the last prescribes an enhanced education and training system for the clerks.

4.1   Implementing Workload Balancing in the Hungarian Public Administration: An Architectural View

We listed the necessary components for workload balancing in the Hungarian public administration, but these are just the foundations for implementation. We have not dealt with such issues as how will a client initiate a case; how will he submit his documents and how will these in turn be processed by the administration.

In Hungary a set of - both in legal and technical terms – well-defined e-government services, called Regulated Electronic e-government Services (REeGS), have been being developed since 2012 that are the building blocks of the Hungarian Governmental Service Oriented Architecture [12]. REeGS are defined and characterized in Act CCXXII of 2015 on Electronic Administration and the General Rules of Trust Services [7]. An implementation of workload balancing can be based on REeGS complemented with additional management and organisational measures.

Figure 7 summarizes an architectural view of these components that together form a supporting background implementing workload balancing in the Hungarian public administration (note that REeGS communicate through a Central Governmental Service Bus).

- **Personalised Case Processing interface:** this REeGS provides the submission of electronic forms to public administration for natural persons.
- **Central Arrival Agent** is a REeGS for the control and registration related to the acceptance of applications (its further development is needed so that it would be applicable for workload balancing).
- **Electronic Document Store** is an already available REeGS, but different government offices and specialised systems do not use it as much as they could. Though the transfer of documents stored in separate systems is technically also a possible solution, this service is more suitable from the aspect of safe storage of authentic copies and the central control of authorisations.
- **Central Workload Manager** that allocates/dispatches workload. The allocation mechanism should use a rule-based learning system, as it is difficult to plan the real effects of implementing workload balancing in public administration. Also, consequences of incidental events (e.g. mass demand for the fast processing of a certain type of case due to unexpected external circumstances) can be planned only inaccurately. Note here that the automated case allocation cannot be all encompassing, there is still need for human supervision. The smallest number of conflicts generated by the transition from the traditional processing model of public administration to the model of workload balancing will occur if case allocation first covers only the capacities (determined in view of available time and persons) offered by the local head of unit. This would reduce gradually the possibility to allocate their own cases. An incremental approach should be used regarding case types during the implementation of the new model, too. The best is to start with low volume cases.
- **Central Human Resource System:** a system is required that stores the competencies of the civil servants down to the detailed competence requirements of the specific administrative procedures and administrative actions. The current HR system in the Hungarian public administration does not meet this requirement.

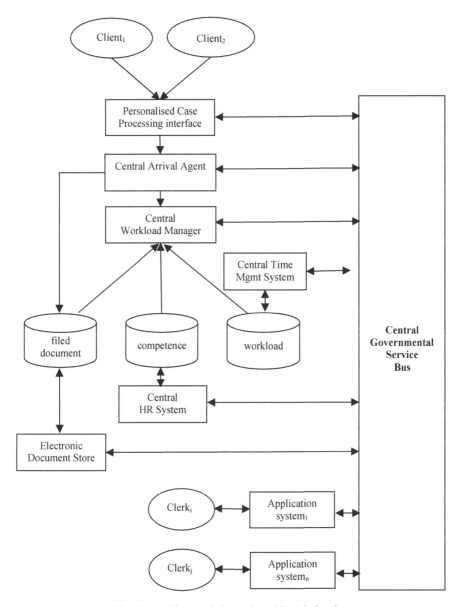

Fig. 7. Architectural view of workload balancing

- **Central Time Management System:** it is necessary to develop a central system that supports (particularly monitors) activities of all Hungarian clerks who are expected to work in case processing. At present, only time booking for the client services in Government Windows is supported as a service. A far more comprehensive system is required.

- The current case management systems, which characteristically support work-flow, should be complemented or collated with the Central Workload Manager.

Electronic forms need to be developed for different types of cases, where the data required to decide on the competencies necessary to process the case will be entered. E-mail, or a general text form application that only the clerk can interpret correctly are not suitable forms of electronic contact from the aspect of operating efficiency in public administration. To ensure the efficiency of internal operation all types of cases should have their own case-specific electronic form.

5 Conclusions

We described the basic conditions of workload balancing in Hungarian public administration as the implementation of central registers (databases) of the involved entities (resources, cases etc.) and the establishment of an allocation (or matching) mechanism. We also showed that the operating model of the Hungarian public administration could be modified to implement workload balancing.

This change, however, requires a different approach in the use of the supporting information technology. The existing REeGS, complemented with a proper automated allocation (or matching) system and with additional management and organisational measures could provide a basis for workload balancing.

We did not deal with the possible impacts of introducing workload balancing as that would require a more detailed and quantitative inquiry down to the level of specific case types. Note that the limitations of our efficiency-driven proposals have not been scrutinized from the point of legislation, political governance and organisational culture, either.

References

1. Gyula, A.: A közigazgatási szervezés és technológia fejlődése Magyarországon (The Development of Public Administration Organisation and Technology in Hungary). Ph.D. thesis, Doctoral School of the Faculty of Law, University of Pécs (PTE) (2012)
2. Act CL of 2016 on General Public Administration Procedures. https://net.jogtar.hu/jogszabaly?docid=a1600150.tv&dbnum=62&getdoc=1. Accessed 17 Mar 2018
3. Boyne, G.A.: Sources of public service improvement: a critical review and research agenda. J. Public Adm. Res. Theory **13**(3), 367–394 (2003). https://doi.org/10.1093/jopart/mug027
4. van Dooren, W., Bouckaert, G., Halligan, J.: Performance Management in the Public Sector. Routledge, Taylor at Francis Group, London (2015)
5. OECD: OECD e-Government Studies: Hungary 2007, OECD Publishing, Paris (2007). http://dx.doi.org/10.1787/9789264030527-en
6. OECD: Public Governance Reviews. Hungary: Towards a Strategic State Approach (2015). http://www.oecd.org/publications/hungary-towards-a-strategic-state-approach-9789264213555-en.htm
7. Act CCXXII of 2015 on the General Rules for Electronic Administration and Trust Services. Available in Hungarian at http://njt.hu/cgi_bin/njt_doc.cgi?docid=193173.338642. Accessed 12 Dec 2017

8. Szabó, S.: Competency management in the HR management of public service. Mil. Sci. Rev. **9**(2), 367–376 (2016). http://epa.oszk.hu/02400/02463/00031/pdf/EPA02463_hadtudo manyi_szemle_2016_02_367-376.pdf
9. De Vries, M., Nemec, J.: Public sector reform: an overview of recent literature and research on NPM and alternative paths. Int. J. Public Sector Manag. **26**(1), 4–16 (2013). http://dx.doi. org/10.1108/09513551311293408
10. op de Beeck, S., Hondeghem, A.: Competency management in the public sector: three dimensions of integration. Paper for the IRSPM Conference 2010, Berne, Switzerland, 7–9 April (2010). https://soc.kuleuven.be/io/pubpdf/IO06060041_OpdeBeeckSophie%20_ 20100407_IRSPM.pdf
11. Kuprenas, J.A.: Implementation and performance of a matrix organization structure. Int. J. Project Manag. **21**(1), 51–62 (2003)
12. Kiss, J.K., Kiss, P.J., Klimkó, G.: Towards a model of client-driven access to public e-services. In: Kő, A., Francesconi, E. (eds.) EGOVIS 2015. LNCS, vol. 9265, pp. 117–131. Springer, Cham (2015). https://doi.org/10.1007/978-3-319-22389-6_9

Meeting the Migration Challenges at Local Governance Level by Small Scale Population Projections

Henning Sten Hansen(✉)

Aalborg University Copenhagen,
A.C. Meyers Vaenge 15, 2450 Copenhagen, Denmark
hsh@plan.aau.dk

Abstract. Migration is a hot topic all over Europe these years mainly due to the wars in Syria, Afghanistan and Iraqi creating large flows of refugees. In addition, people in Africa migrate towards Europe as a consequence of unemployment, poverty, and climate changes. Also, within Europe, there has been challenges related to the free movement of people within the European Union, and the immigration of mainly Eastern European into UK has been mentioned as one of the main reasons to Brexit. Thus, in order to be prepared to meet the challenges related to migration, a decision-support tools is needed to handle immigration in an efficient but also human way. The current research describes how detailed population projections – dividing immigrants into different groups depending on their origin, can provide a sound foundation for decision making in the municipalities, which is the end destinations for the immigrants.

Keywords: Migration · Refugees · Population projections · Digital governance

1 Introduction

The European Union is facing many challenges: the after-effect of the economic and financial crisis nearly ten years ago, Brexit, the confrontation with Russia and Trumps America. However, the perhaps biggest crisis from a EU citizens point of view originates from the movement of people from Africa and the Middle East towards Europe.

During 2015 about 4.7 million people immigrated to one of the 28 EU Member States, of which estimated 2.7 million immigrants were coming from non-EU Members States[1]. With more than 1.5 million immigrants Germany reported the highest number of immigrants in 2015 followed by the other major EU countries: UK, France, Spain, and Italy. Looking at the immigration figures relative to the size of resident population, Luxembourg with 42 immigrants per 1000 inhabitants experienced the highest immigration rates in 2015. Thus, migration and refugees have been on top of the political agenda in most European countries. Therefore, most European governments promise their citizens, that the immigration politics will be tough and to prohibit foreigners to pass the borders. Even between normally friendly neighbours like Denmark, Sweden

---

[1] http://ec.europa.eu/eurostat/statistics-explained/index.php/Migration_and_migrant_population_statistics#Migration_flows.

© Springer Nature Switzerland AG 2018
A. Kő and E. Francesconi (Eds.): EGOVIS 2018, LNCS 11032, pp. 258–269, 2018.
https://doi.org/10.1007/978-3-319-98349-3_20

and Germany have now introduced border control with police to send back people without legal permission to enter their countries. In some Eastern European countries like Hungary, the situation is even worse by building border fences. Even EU citizens are not always welcome in other EU countries, although they have the rights to seek job all-over the European Union. However, nobody with respect for democracy and human rights can just look passive to migrants and refugees drowning in the Mediterranean Sea. Thus, solutions must be found, and this paper will try outline ways of mitigating the negative effects of international migration.

The end destinations for the migrants and refugees are in the municipalities around Europe. Integrating people from other countries with different language, culture, family structure, educational backgrounds may be a major challenge. Recent analyses from Denmark illustrates these challenges – particularly in municipalities with high rates of foreign immigrants.

Therefore, the aim of this research is *to build a numerical model to carry out forecasts of future migration and refugee flows to municipalities.* The model is currently being tested in several Danish municipalities – small as well as big, and the first experiences seems positive. After this introduction follows a description of the background for the migration challenges, and a description of how to model international migration. In the next chapter the results of using the developed model are presented and discussed. Finally, a conclusion on the developed method, and an outline of further research to improve the model.

2 Background and Theory

The so-called Arabic Spring and not at least the Syrian civil war has created a significant increase in the number of refugees driven by the war and other dramatic events. Thus, the number of refugees moving towards Europe and applying for asylum has increased from 627 thousand in 2014 to about 1.3 million in 2015 and 2016[2]. Due to different arrangements between the EU and Turkey, the number of people applying asylum decreased to about 700 thousand. Syria was by far the main contributor to the large number of asylum applicants in the EU with 15.5% in 2017 followed by Iraqis and Afghanis with 7% each. In the fourth-place Nigeria came in with 6%[2].

The main destinations for the applicants in 2017 was Germany (31%), Italy (20%) and France (14%), and although the number of asylum applicants are not large relative to the total population, the result was panic in many countries, and even being the most important topic in the general elections in many European countries during the last 3–4 years. Considering the expected high population growth in Africa by doubling the total population before 2050[3] a continuous pressure towards Europe is expected.

---

[2] http://ec.europa.eu/eurostat/statistics-explained/index.php/Asylum_statistics.

[3] https://www.prb.org/2016-world-population-data-sheet/.

2.1 Drivers for Migration

The traditional explanations of causes for migration is based on push-pull effects as defined by Lee [1]. He suggested, that in bot area of origin and destination may be factors, that attain and attract people (pull factors) and factors that repel people (push factors) In addition the migration decisions may also be influenced by potential 'so-called intervening obstacles existing between origin and destination – for example the great Sahara Desert.

However, the push-pull effects ignore that migration will only take place, if the people have the resources and ambitions to migrate [2]. Therefore, peoples access to social networks, education, knowledge and media increases people's aspirations and capabilities to migrate. Thus, most migrants do not move from the poorest to the wealthiest countries, and generally the middle-income countries have higher emigration levels that the poorest countries [2]. This is confirmed by the fact that skilled and relatively wealthy people are overrepresented among the long-distance international migrants trying to enter Europe. Poorer people on the other hand tend to move over shorter distances – from for example rural areas to nearby larger cities.

In addition to these migrations based on people's aspirations for a better life, we can soon expect an increased migration from Africa towards Europe due to climate change. Africa is the most vulnerable continent to climate change, and recent research indicates tripling the number of migrants from Africa towards Europe before 2050 – solely due to climate change [3].

2.2 Migration Patterns

Migration into Denmark has shown a steady increase during the last 10 years. According to Statistics Denmark [4] the immigration into Denmark in 2016 was 94,365 persons of which 24 pct. were Danish citizens. The immigration in 2016 was 16,482 persons above the average for the latest 10 years. The emigration from Denmark in 2016 was 61,078 persons providing a net migration into Denmark at 33,287 persons. Compared with a little birth surplus at 8,790 in 2016 the net emigration is responsible for a little increase in the total Danish population.

Out of a Danish population at 5,748,769 by the end of 2016, the net migration only accounts for 0.6 pct. In addition, there is a general wish by governments that the population development is balanced or with a little increase. Nevertheless, the immigration into Denmark as well as other European countries impose several challenges mainly due to the composition of the immigrants. Danish citizens only accounts for 642 of the net migration leaving 32,645 immigrants from foreign countries. The major parts of the immigrants come from western countries represents 60%, while non-western countries represent 36% of the immigrants. Faroe Islands and Greenland accounts for 4% of the immigrants. Figure 1 illustrates the migration development for the five years between 2012 and 2016.

This figure clearly illustrates the growing immigration from western as well as non-western countries during the five years period, while emigration is more or less stable although a little increase can be observed in both groups of origin. The age profile for

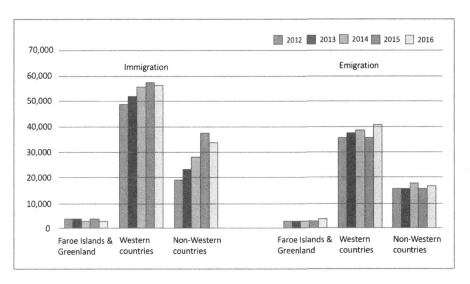

Fig. 1. Immigration and emigration after country of origin - after [4]

immigrants corresponds to the general pattern for migrations with a top in the 20–30 age interval and a secondary top in the 0–10 age interval.

In addition to this temporal development, an uneven spatial distribution can be observed. The map in Fig. 2 illustrates the net migration of foreign citizens to municipalities, and an obvious dispersed pattern can be observed. However, the larger Danish municipalities Copenhagen, Aarhus, Aalborg and Odense have a higher net migration from outside Denmark compared to the other municipalities.

2.3   Data

The main data source for the current work has been the Danish Central Person Register (CPR), which was originally developed in 1968 but its roots go back to 1924, where the first Danish Population Register was established [5]. The CPR data used are highly confidential and are obtained through a special permission from the Danish Ministry of Health.

This register is updated daily through the municipal registration of people, and their demographic transitions. All registered persons have a unique person identification number made up of 10 digits, where the first 6 digits refers to the birthday, and the last 4 digits represent a serial number, of which the last digit indicates the sex of the person. The most important information contained in CPR is Name, Address, Marital status, and Place of birth. The raw ASCII file utilised in the current population projection research includes the following columns: code for demographic event type, personal identification number, primary address, and secondary address. The two addresses are necessary to register migration events.

The Danish address system has traditionally been managed by the municipalities, but since the beginning of the century an address reform aiming at standardisation and quality improvements was launched, and a central address register was established [6].

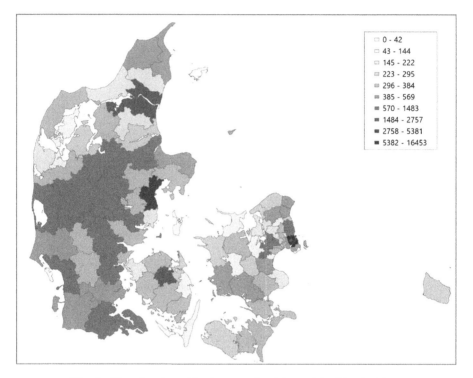

Fig. 2. Net migration of foreigners to Danish municipalities in 2017.

Each address is composed of the following elements: a municipality code, a road code, a house number plus eventually a letter. Also, floor number and side are included. Thus, a unique identification of each residential unit is available. Besides, the Address Register contains an x-coordinate and a y-coordinate. Thus, the Address Register facilitates the assignment of spatial reference to the events in the CPR.

As mentioned above the population projection model deals with people within districts and not individuals. Therefore, a district map is needed. Generally, most municipalities have subdivided their territory into smaller units – e.g. statistical districts, school districts etc. Alternatively, a neutral subdivision using grid squares can be used. First of all, the municipality should subdivide their territory into a system of districts, which are flexible enough to adapt to needed changes in for example the school structure. Therefore, the municipalities are encouraged to define a spatial subdivision, so the basic population projection districts can easily be aggregated into larger districts regarding school planning, elderly care planning etc. This means quite many – often several hundred - small districts.

Assigning district identifications to each person can thus be performed through a two-step procedure. First, spatial references are assigned to the persons in CPR through an attribute join between Central Personal Register and the Address Register with the address as join key. Second the new point-based CPR can be assigned district identifications through a point-in-polygon operation. Finally, we can summarise the state of population and the various demographic events into a set of tables with age representing the columns and districts representing the rows. However, in order to maintain the statistical quality of the coefficients described above, we have defined much larger so-called parameter districts for the purpose of estimating the different migration coefficients as well as the fertility and mortality level coefficients. Generally, the number of parameter districts are rather low (less than ten), and the basic districts entering a parameter district are characterised by similar demographic properties. However, defining the parameter districts is a tough and time-consuming exercise, but not at least a very important one, because the quality of the derived coefficients is much dependant on this task.

3   Systems Design and Development

This chapter describes the design and development of the small-scale population projection system. The systems requirements and overall design has been developed through cooperation with several Danish municipalities, having day to day experiences with the challenges they are facing in the integration of foreign immigrants, and the knowledge need about the near future in order to make decisions.

3.1   Local Scale Population Projections

The future population development is generally referred to as either population projections or population forecasts. A projection is a rather strict calculation of the future population based on a certain set of assumptions. Thus, the results of a projection show the future population development, if the set of assumptions is correct. Population forecasts are closely related to population projections by adding a probability dimension. In this context, a population forecast can be defined as the most likely of several population projections (scenarios). Very often a population forecast is a combined result of numerical results and political decisions, where for example the city council decides which of several projections shall be nominated to be the official population forecast for that particular local authority.

The current implementation employs the gross-migration method – i.e. handling immigration and emigration separately - instead of the often-used net-migration method. There are two reasons for choosing the gross-migration method. First, a separate modelling of in- and out-migration facilitates a more detailed analysis of the modelling results in order to identify potential errors behind strange looking results. Second, the net-migration method is criticised for making growing areas grow faster, and declining areas decline faster [7–9].

The population projection model applied is based on the cohort-component principle and can be described by the following general population equation, where the superscript d refers to the district:

$$P_{t+1,i,s}^{d} = P_{t,i,s}^{d} + B_{s}^{d} - D_{i,s}^{d} + I_{i,s}^{d} - O_{i,s}^{d} + \Delta H_{i,s}^{d}$$

The variables $P_{t,i,s}$ and $P_{t+1,i,s}$ refer to the population of sex s, age i at the time t and $t + 1$ respectively. B_s is the number of new-born boys ($s = 1$) and girls ($s = 2$), whereas $D_{i,s}$ denotes the number of deaths for each age group and sex. The last two variables $I_{i,s}$ and $O_{i,s}$ refer to Immigration and Emigration. The last term ΔH refers to changes in the population within a district due to changes in the stock of dwellings. Due to the requirements among the end users in for example the Childcare and Education department, the population is divided into 1-year cohorts. Below, the various components are described. The Births (B) and Deaths (D) components are rather straight forward to estimate, and a detailed description can be find in [10]. Also, the emigration component is estimated in the same way as in the former paper.

3.2   Modelling the Migration Component

The main focus in the current paper on immigration of foreigners into municipalities requires a detailed modelling of this component. Our earlier attempts to analyse and model population development into Danish municipalities just divided immigration into each district by the following three categories: (a) internal migration within districts, (b) internal migration between districts, and (c) immigration from outside the municipality (from other municipalities and the rest of the world) [10]. However, further analysis showed up, that better performance and accuracy could be obtained by further subdividing the external immigration component into three groups: (a) immigration from other Danish municipalities, (b) immigrants from foreign countries excluding refugees, and (c) refugees. The main driver behind this development was the huge increase in refugees about three years ago requiring a new approach the immigration modelling.

The immigration to a given municipality from all other Danish municipalities IM is estimated by the following formula

$$IM_{t+1,i,s} = \sum_{j=1}^{n} P^j_{t,i,s}\, im^j_{i,s}$$

where im is an empirical derived age and sex specific immigration coefficient, which is estimated from observed historical immigration data. The coefficient is calculated as the ratio between observed immigration and population for each age (a), sex (s) and municipality (j).

The immigration from foreign countries excluding refugees (IF) is estimated by the following formula

$$IF_{t+1,i,s} = P_{t,i,s}\, if_{i,s}$$

where if is an empirical derived age and sex specific immigration coefficient, which is estimated from observed historical data on immigration from foreign countries – excluding refugees. The coefficient is calculated as the ratio between observed immigration for each age (a), sex (s). At the moment we consider all immigrants of foreign origin as just one group although they certainly have different demographic behaviour.

Handling refugees is done in a very different way. All asylum applicants are handled centrally by the Ministry of Integration, and after receiving the status legal refugees they are distributed by the ministry to the Danish municipalities. Thus, it is not possible to make projections about the future number of refugees into a given municipality based on historical data but requires a different approach. The Ministry of Integration send out one year ahead its proposal for the distribution of refugees among the municipalities for the coming year, but there is no indication of the amount and distribution for the following years. All refuges are required to stay at least three years in their first destination municipality. Afterwards they can move freely around.

The way we have handled the refugee component in our model is by providing qualified guess about the number of refugees in the future years, and then multiplying the number of refugees with the historical age and sex distribution for refugees in the given municipality. Afterwards the programme will distribute the refugees among the different districts based on the population size of the individual districts – the larger population the larger share of refugees. We have provided an additional option for distributing the refugees among districts by enabling the municipality staff to explicitly allocate refugees to districts through a provided table. This is particular relevant if the staff for example already has defined appropriate accommodation for the new refugees.

The last step is to create a pool with all immigrants into the given municipality. The internal emigrants constitute one part of this pool, due to the requirement of balance between internal emigration and internal immigration. The other part of the immigration pool is made of external immigration – the external immigration from other municipalities, the external immigration from other countries, and the refugees. This immigration pool is divided into the districts based on 'demand' due to emigration from the individual districts and due to deaths in the individual districts. Again this 'demand' is coefficient driven based on historical data.

3.3 Implementation of the Model

Based on the model described above, we have developed a software application to carry out the modelling and populations forecasts. It is developed using the Delphi Developing tool, which generally creates rapid executables by supporting parallel programming. The model is rather complicated and with many districts the execution time is an important parameter. The programme is also designed so, at can handle several scenarios based on different prerequisites. Thus, the demographic development during the previous ten years may show an increasing trend or a decreasing trend, and in both cases, it would be convenient to analyses different alternatives, and assess their appropriateness for being the main scenario for decision making.

3.4 Results

Aalborg had by the end of 2017 211,237 inhabitants - thus being the third largest municipality in Denmark. Aalborg has experienced a steady increase in immigrants from foreign countries during the last ten years – and many of these immigrants are university students. All coefficients are based on data for the period 2004–2017, which provide good opportunities to achieve robust coefficients. The contribution of the different coefficients can be weighted individually, so 'strange' years due to the financial crisis in 2009–2011 can be given lower weights when estimating the coefficients.

Calculation a population projection for Aalborg municipality for the 11 years period from 2007–2017 provides the following overall results (Fig. 3). This is a baseline scenario expecting the same immigration and emigration as an average of the previous 5 years, where all years are assigned the same weights. The migration balance goes towards zero indicating a more or less stable population. Although, the discussion on refugees, the total number of refugees is nearly invisible with about 100 new refugees per year.

However, if we look into the spatial distribution of foreigners there are major differences between the different districts in Aalborg. Aalborg municipality is subdivided into 342 districts of varying size. The map illustrates number of foreign immigrants and not relative numbers. When talking about the challenges integrating foreign pupils into Danish school classes or to find appropriate jobs, we believe, that the actual number is more useful than relative numbers. It is obvious, that the highest number of foreign immigrants are concentrated in the city of Aalborg (in the middle of the map). Most of the foreign immigrants are in the age interval between 18 and 35 years old with a top around age 23–24. The second frequent age group is in the age interval between 0 and 5 years old (Fig. 4).

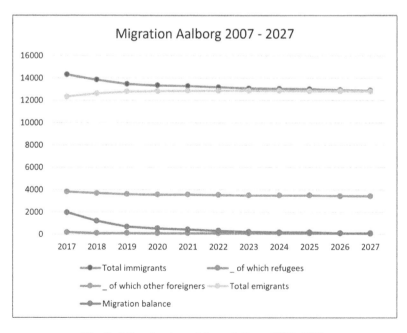

Fig. 3. Migration to and from Aalborg 2007–2027.

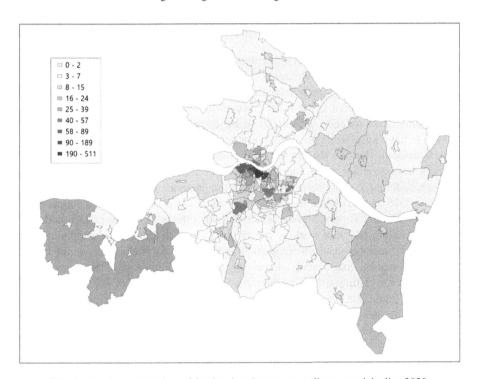

Fig. 4. Spatial distribution of foreign immigrants to Aalborg municipality 2020.

4   Discussion

As illustrated in the previous paragraphs, we have tried to enhance our former population projection model described in [10]. The current initiative was partly a result of the lack of precision concerning external migration and the refugee crisis in 2015–2016. About two thirds of the movement of people takes place within a given municipality, leaving one third for external immigration, which is a significant number of people. Therefore, the subdivision of external immigrants into immigrants from other municipalities, from other countries, and through the refugee system was introduced.

The results from Aalborg municipality shows interesting results when the school administration plans the allocation of pupils into schools, so there will be a balanced distribution between native Danish and foreign pupils on each school to omit predicates like 'foreign schools' or even worse 'ghetto schools'. By having such results available some years ahead, the necessary efforts to learn smaller foreign children Danish language before they start at school can be developed. Furthermore, the projections on new foreign immigrants at age between 6 and 18 can be used to prepare for providing well planned teaching to new foreign pupils, and thus facilitating a good start in their new Danish schools. The labour market can also benefit from knowledge in advance about the number of foreign immigrants from year to year, of specific age intervals, and in specific areas. Early knowledge about the local language is very important for an effective integration.

The developed model is a first attempt to involve a detailed analysis and implementation of the origins of immigrants. The immigration from other municipalities is modelled explicitly from each municipality to the target municipality, while the immigration from foreign countries are estimated without considering their different demographic characteristics. This could be beneficial knowledge for the local administration to have knowledge about this in at least a 3–5 years' time span.

It is evident, that we do not know the number of refugees and immigrants to Denmark in the coming years, and accordingly we have developed different scenarios based on different assumptions about the future number of refugees. The refugees peaked in 2015, but has fallen dramatically in the last two years, due to the agreement between the EU and Turkey, and the police control at the border between Denmark and Germany. There is a lack of working capacity in Denmark, and beyond people coming from other EU member states, there is good opportunities for people outside the EU, if they have the needed qualifications. Especially people with higher education have good opportunities for getting a working permission. Thus, the effect of different flows of refugees and immigrants can be assessed by the use of scenarios, which shows possible futures. For the administration in the municipalities, it is important to know the age distribution of the immigrants as well as to know in which part of the municipality they settle.

5   Conclusion

As mentioned several times throughout the paper, immigration and movements of refugee is a major challenge today – and will be it in the future. Wars and catastrophes has always been part of human history – and will also be it in the future. Wishes for better quality of life for yourself and your family is fundamental for all people and has been that throughout history. Europe is currently a rich, mainly peaceful and attractive continent, and therefore a dream for many people in Asia, Africa and the Middle East.

Europe has a declining population and needs immigration to keep productive people in balance with the unproductive children and elderly people. What is needed is a planned and well organised immigration. The current paper has demonstrated how use of detailed simulation and decision-support systems can support a positive integration of immigrants through knowledge about the future immigration of foreigners – at least in the shorter 3–5 years' time span. This, is a first attempt to do this kind of population projections, but we are currently developing the software to be more precise on the characteristics of the foreign immigrants – mainly regarding nationality and original language.

Acknowledgement. This research is carried out in cooperation with Thomas Jensen and Mads Laursen from COWI and Uffe Kousgaard from RouteWare, for inspiring and valuable discussions during the development process.

References

1. Lee, E.S.: A theory of migration. Demography **3**, 47–57 (1966)
2. Flahaux, M.-L., de Haas, H.: African migration: trends, patterns, drivers. Comp. Migr. Stud. **4**, 1–25 (2016)
3. Missirian, A., Schlemker, W.: Asylum applications respond to temperature fluctuations. Science **358**, 1610–1614 (2017)
4. Statisitcs Denmark: Immigrants in Denmark 2017. Statistics Denmark, November 2017 (2017). (in Danish)
5. Nielsen, H.: CPR – The Danish National Population Register. Ministry of Interior (1991). (in Danish)
6. Lind, M.: Developing a system of public addresses - as a "language" for location dependent information. In: URISA Proceedings (2001)
7. Smith, S., Tayman, J., Swanson, D.: State and Local Population Projections – Methodology and Analysis. Springer, Heidelberg (2001). https://doi.org/10.1007/0-306-47372-0
8. Isserman, A.M.: The right people, the right rates – making population estimates and forecasts with an interregional cohort-component model. J. Am. Plan. Assoc. **59**, 45–64 (1993)
9. Wilson, T., Rees, P.: Recent developments in population projection methodology: a review. Popul. Space Place **11**, 337–360 (2005)
10. Hansen, H.S.: Small-area population projections - a key element in knowledge based e-Governance. In: Andersen, K.N., Francesconi, E., Grönlund, Å., van Engers, T.M. (eds.) EGOVIS 2010. LNCS, vol. 6267, pp. 32–46. Springer, Heidelberg (2010). https://doi.org/10.1007/978-3-642-15172-9_4

Author Index

Printed in the United States
By Bookmasters